SCANNING
How to Train it and Develop Game Awareness

See More | Think Quicker | Play Better

Soccer eyeQ Methodology

Written by
Kevin McGreskin

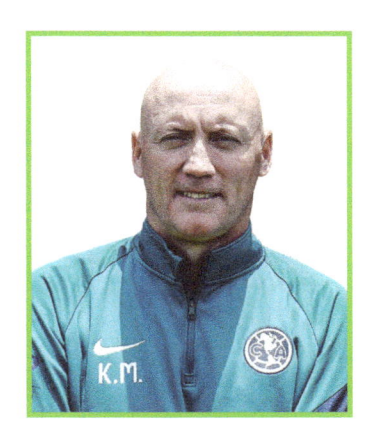

Published by
SOCCER TUTOR.COM

SCANNING
How to Train it and Develop Game Awareness

See More | Think Quicker | Play Better

Soccer eyeQ Methodology

First Published September 2021 by SoccerTutor.com

info@soccertutor.com | www.SoccerTutor.com

UK: 0208 1234 007 | **US:** (305) 767 4443 | **ROTW:** +44 208 1234 007

ISBN: 978-1-910491-50-8

Copyright: SoccerTutor.com Limited © 2021. All Rights Reserved.

All rights reserved. No part of this publication may be reproduced, stored in a retrieval system, or transmitted in any form or by any means, electronic, mechanical, photocopy, recording or otherwise, without prior written permission of the copyright owner. Nor can it be circulated in any form of binding or cover other than that in which it is published and without similar condition including this condition being imposed on a subsequent purchaser.

Author
Kevin McGreskin

Editor
Alex Fitzgerald - SoccerTutor.com

Diagrams Design by SoccerTutor.com

All the diagrams in this book have been created using SoccerTutor.com Tactics Manager Software available from www.SoccerTutor.com

Cover Design - Alex Macrides, Think Out Of The Box Ltd.
Email: design@thinkootb.com Tel: +44 (0) 208 144 3550

Note: While every effort has been made to ensure the technical accuracy of the content of this book, neither the author nor publishers can accept any responsibility for any injury or loss sustained as a result of the use of this material.

CONTENTS

Kevin McGreskin: Coach Profile 07
Kevin McGreskin: Coach Educator 08
Coaching References 09
What is Scanning? 10
Introduction 11
What is Soccer eyeQ? 15
Soccer eyeQ: Coloured Visual Cues to Force Players to Scan the Pitch 16
Soccer eyeQ Practices: Options for Available Visual Cues 17
Soccer eyeQ: Adding the Soccer eyeQ Method to Any Practice 18
Importance of Neck Swivelling for Game Awareness 20
When and How was Soccer eyeQ Developed? 21
How does Soccer eyeQ Develop and Improve Players? 23
Interview: Jackie McNamara 24
Dundee Utd Soccer eyeQ Scanning Practice Example 27
How can the Soccer eyeQ Methodology be Implemented? 28
Interview: Nigel Best 29
How does Soccer eyeQ Help Coaches, Players and Teams at All Levels? ... 33
Interview: Geir Jordet, PhD 35
Xavi's "Off the Scale" Scanning: Match Example 39
Scanning to Defend Effectively: Man City's Laporte Example 40
The Importance of Scanning with Arsene Wenger 41
De Bruyne, Lampard & Ronaldo: "Masters of Scanning" 42
Interview: Torbjörn Vestberg, PhD 43

SECTION 1: The Soccer eyeQ Methodology 47

Soccer eyeQ Decision Making Model 48

Decision Making and its Importance in Football 49
The 3 Fundamental Components of the Decision Making Model 51
The Basic Decision Making Model 1.0 and its Limitations 52
New Decision Making Model 2.0: A Cycle of Interactive Elements 54
Referencing: Signals, Situations, and Scenarios 55
Framing: Tactical, Technical, and Tendencies 57
Localizing: Prospecting, Perspective, and Priming 59
Decision Making Models - A Conclusion 62

A Model for Game Awareness in Football 64

Game Awareness and Situation Awareness 65
A Simplified Model for Game Awareness in Football 67

Contents

Level 1: Scanning of the Playing Area 67
Level 2: Reading the Game Situation 69
Level 3: Predicting How Play Will Develop 70

Level 1 - Observation: Scanning of the Playing Area 72
Observation (Level 1): Scanning of the Playing Area 73
Key Aspects of Scanning (Level 1) 74
When to Scan and When Not to Scan 75
5 Key Moments a Player Should Engage in Scanning 76
Scanning Study 1: Comparing How Often Premier League Players Look Around Before
Receiving Against their Forward Pass Completion Statistics (Geir Jordet, PhD) 78
Geir Jordet, PhD: Key Factors of Decision Making and Highest Performing Players 79
Scanning Study 2: Comparing Scan Frequency in Games vs Specific Training Practices 80
Observation - Summary 81

Level 2 - Realization: Reading The Game Situation 83
Realization (Level 2): Reading the Game Situation 84
Adaptive Positioning and Identifying Key Reference Points 85
Key Aspects of Reading the Game Situation (Level 2) 86
Incorrect and Correct Reading the Game Situation (Attack) 87
Incorrect and Correct Reading the Game Situation (Defence) 88
Realization - Summary 90

Level 3 - Anticipation: Predicting How Play Will Develop 92
Anticipation (Level 3): Predicting How Play Will Develop 93
Key Aspects of Predicting How Play Will Develop (Level 3) 95
Incorrect and Correct Predicting How Play Will Develop 96
Anticipation - Summary 97

Game Awareness Model: Observation, Realization, and Anticipation 100
Soccer eyeQ Game Awareness Model: Observation, Realization, and Anticipation 101
Soccer eyeQ Game Awareness Model: The 6-Step Performance Cycle (A to F) 103

SECTION 2: Soccer eyeQ Training Practices 105
Practice Diagram Key 106
Practice Format 106

Level 1 - Observation: Scanning of the Playing Area 107
Why We Should Encourage Scanning in Training Sessions 108
Soccer eyeQ Observation: The Advantage of Scanning 109
Observation Practices: Scanning of the Playing Area 111
Soccer eyeQ Practices: Options for Available Visual Cues 114
Practice Example: Pass to Opposite Colour in a Basic Awareness Practice 115
Progression 1: Pass to Opposite Colour with Visual Cues (Outside Team Flashers) 117
Progression 2: Coloured Balls + Visual Cues (Outside Colour-Coded Flashers) 120
Progression 3: Colour-Coded Flashers and Team Flashers + Switching Roles 122

Contents

Drill Example: Basic "Ajax Square" Passing Drill - Pass and Follow 124
Progression 1: "Ajax Square" with Visual Cues to Spot and Call Out 125
Progression 2: Spotting + Reversing Direction of Play 126
Progression 3: Spotting, Reverse Direction, and Diagonal Passing 127
Observation Practices - Summary 128

Level 2 - Realization: Reading The Game Situation 129
Realization Practices: Reading the Game Situation 130
Practice Example 1: Vision and Awareness Sequence Passing Practice 132
Progression 1: Vision and Awareness Sequence Passing with Visual Cues 134
Progression 2: Sequence Passing with Visual Cues and Positional Play 137
Soccer eyeQ: Adding Tennis Balls to Practices for Extra Scanning 140
Progression 3: Third Man Support by Adding Throwing of Tennis Balls 141
Progression 4: Footballs, Throwing Tennis Balls, and Positional Play 143
Progression 5: Positioning, Support, and Maintain Space from Opponents 145
Progression 6: Maintain Space from Opponents + Outside Visual Cues 147
Practice Example 2: Pass to Opposite Colour with Team Flashers 150
Progression 1: Team Flashers + Avoid Being Tagged by the Jokers 151
Progression 2: Third Man Support Play with Tennis Ball Throwing 153
Realization Practices - Summary 155

Level 3 - Anticipation: Predicting How Play Will Develop 157
Anticipation Practices: Predicting How Play Will Develop 158
Practice Example 1: Opposed 6v3 (+4) Vision and Awareness Practice 160
Progression 1: Opposed 6v3 (+4) Practice with Scanning and Positioning 163
Progression 2: Increased Scanning and Positioning + Tennis Ball Throwing 165
Progression 3: Scan, Position, Third Man Support, and Player Rotation 168
Practice Example 2: Awareness Game (6v3) with 4 Cone Gates 171
Progression 1: Visual Cues and Colour-Coded Cone Gates 173
Progression 2: Scan, Position, and Support Play + Throwing Tennis Balls 175
Practice Example 3: 6 (+2) v 3 Pass to Floating Players Game 177
Progression 1: Visual Cues to Promote Scanning and Positioning 179
Progression 2: Scan, Position, and Support Play + Throwing Tennis Balls 181
Anticipation Practices - Summary 183

SECTION 3: Adding the Soccer eyeQ Method to Existing Practices 184
Practice Diagram Key 185
Practice Diagram Key 185
Soccer eyeQ: Coaches Can Add Game Awareness Skills to Any Practice 186
Rondo Example: Liverpool Rondo with "Magic Player" 187
Rondo Example: Adding the Soccer eyeQ Method - Progression 188
Passing Drill Example 1: Passing "Y" Drill 189
Passing Drill Example 1: Adding the Soccer eyeQ Method - Progression 1 190

Contents

Passing Drill Example 1: Adding the Soccer eyeQ Method - Progression 2 191
Passing Drill Example 2: Short and Long Passing Circuit 192
Passing Drill Example 2: Adding the Soccer eyeQ Method - Progression 193
Passing Drill Example 3: Dynamic Passing Double Square 194
Passing Drill Example 3: Adding the Soccer eyeQ Method - Progression 195

Possession Game Example 1: Pocket Box Possession Game 196
Possession Game Example 1: Adding the Soccer eyeQ Method - Progression 1 197
Possession Game Example 1: Adding the Soccer eyeQ Method - Progression 2 198
Possession Game Example 2: End to End 3 Zone Possession Game 199
Possession Game Example 2: Adding the Soccer eyeQ Method - Progression 1 200
Possession Game Example 2: Adding the Soccer eyeQ Method - Progression 2 201
Possession Game Example 3: 6v4 +6 Outside Support Players 203
Possession Game Example 3: Adding the Soccer eyeQ Method - Progression 1 204
Possession Game Example 3: Adding the Soccer eyeQ Method - Progression 2 205

Small Sided Game Example 1: Scan to Play Forward Bounce Game 206
Small Sided Game Example 1: Adding the Soccer eyeQ Method - Progression 1 207
Small Sided Game Example 1: Adding the Soccer eyeQ Method - Progression 2 209
Small Sided Game Example 2: Play to Advanced Wide Players Game 210
Small Sided Game Example 2: Adding the Soccer eyeQ Method - Progression 211

Adding the Soccer eyeQ Method to Existing Practices - Summary 213

KEVIN MCGRESKIN: Coach Profile

Kevin McGreskin

- UEFA 'A' Coaching Licence
- First Team Coach at Club América Femenil
- Technical Director
- Consultant Performance Coach

kevin@soccereyeq.com

Coaching Qualifications:

- UEFA 'A' Licence
- Oceania Football Confederation (OFC) Coaching Instructor
- FA Youth Award Modules
- FA Psychology for Soccer
- Life Kinetik Team Coach

Coaching Roles:

- Club América Femenil (Mexico) First Team Coach (2021 - Present)
- Forfar Farmington Women Head Coach (2020 - 2021)
- Soccer eyeQ Founder (2008 - Present)
- Cook Islands FA National Technical Director (2019 - 2020)
- Burlington SC Technical Director (2016 - 2019)
- Bahamas FA National Director (2015 - 2016)
- Dundee United First Team Coach (2013 - 2014)
- Partick Thistle First Team Coach (2011 - 2013)

Consultant Performance Coach Roles:

- Dinamo Zagreb (Croatia)
- FK Molde (Norway)
- SC Heerenveen (Netherlands)
- Wigan Athletic (England)
- San Jose Earthquakes (USA)

KEVIN MCGRESKIN: Coach Educator

Kevin McGreskin
- Coach Educator
- Coaching Instructor
- Coach Education Programs Designer
- Coach Mentor

kevin@soccereyeq.com

Coaching Instructor for:
- UEFA Pro/A/B Licence
- CONCACAF
- Oceania Football Confederation (OFC)
- Irish FA – UEFA Pro/A/B Licence Courses
- Croatian FA – UEFA Pro/A Licence Courses
- Welsh FA – UEFA A/B Licence Courses
- Scottish FA and Danish FA CPD Events
- NSCAA (now USC) Featured Clinician
- FA Level 1 and Level 2 Tutor

Designer of Coach Education Programs:
- Design and delivery of national coach education programs, including D Licence and Grassroots Certificates.
- Implemented player and coach pathways from Grassroots to Elite level.
- Technical Director of 2 National Associations (Bahamas and Cook Islands) - responsible for all technical matters, including coaching national teams, implementing elite player pathways for national team programs, and coach education.

Coach Mentor:
- Experienced coach mentor with knowledge of implementing personalised development action plans for club and national team coaches to meet their long-term development goals as well as meet the short, medium, and long-term requirements of the association.

COACHING REFERENCES

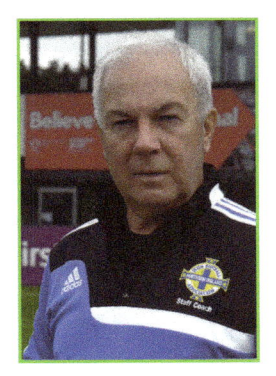

Nigel Best
Head of Coach Education, Irish FA

"Kevin has worked with the Irish FA since 2009 as a presenter and Staff Coach on our UEFA Coach Education Programme, where he delivers both practical pitch sessions and lectures. The sessions are extremely well structured and provide great detail. He has an excellent coaching style which creates an effective learning environment. This is further illustrated through his fluent, coherent teaching style when delivering lectures."

Jason deVos
Canada Soccer Technical Director and former Canada National Team Player

"Kevin's on-field practical sessions focus on the dynamic variables, and they are some of the best sessions I've ever seen or participated in, and he puts paid to the myth that training perception and decision-making skills cannot be done."

Steve Robinson
Former Head Coach at Motherwell FC and former Northern Ireland National Team Player

"I absolutely love Kevin's sessions and my players really enjoy the exercises. Constant awareness of what's going on around you and the ability to know what you're going to do with the ball before you receive are a necessity in the modern game. I'd happily recommend Kevin to any club or coach who wants to develop their players."

Jackie McNamara
Former Manager of Dundee United and Partick Thistle

"I have worked closely with Kevin, first at Partick Thistle and then Dundee United, where he worked with the first team squad but would also do regular coaching sessions with the professional youth team. He is an excellent coach and his sessions are always detailed, effective, and enjoyable and he demands the highest standards from all those he works with."

What is Scanning?

WHAT IS SCANNING?

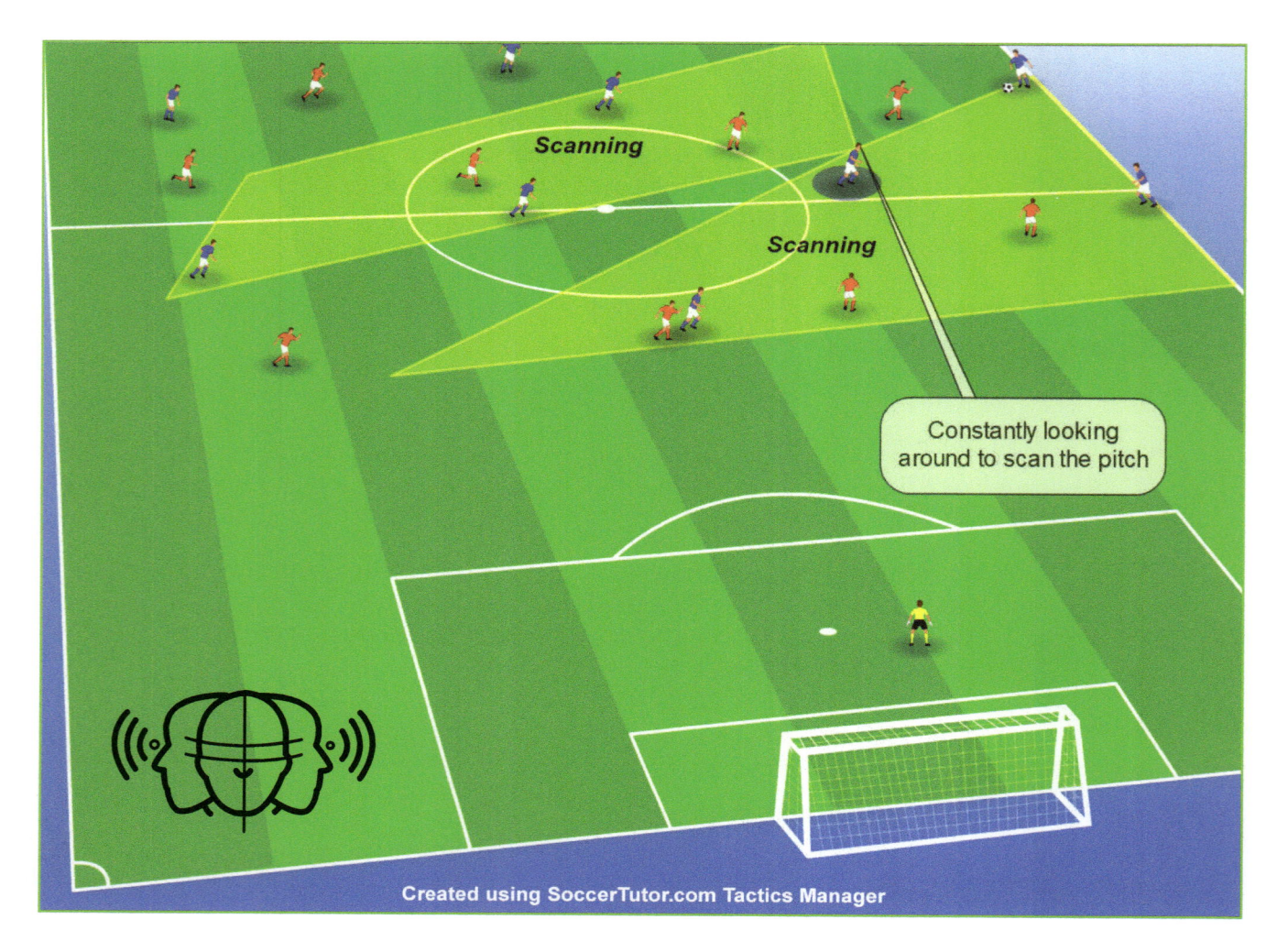

Constantly looking around to scan the pitch

SCANNING = Taking your eyes off the ball and looking around the pitch to access information.

LOCATE = Scanning is done to locate teammates, opponents, and space, so the players can have a full "picture" of what is around them.

PANORAMIC POSITIONING = To scan in the most effective way, players also open up their body shape to see as much of the playing area as possible.

CREATING HABITS = Looking around all the time is an essential skill and habit.

Without this essential skill (scanning), it is highly unlikely that a player will consistently make good decisions. It will lead to poor positioning and inefficient game actions.

Scanning is so fundamental to overall performance, yet is too often overlooked.

We are often guilty of assuming players are looking around all the time, but do they really do it often enough or well enough?

With this book, the aim is to improve and develop this key aspect of the game.

Soccer eyeQ with SoccerTutor.com — SCANNING - How to Train it

INTRODUCTION

SCANNING of the playing area is done **to locate the ball, teammates, opponents, and space**. This is the foundation of this book and **enables players to make the best decisions in the game** by reading the game situation and predicting how the play is likely to develop.

GAME AWARENESS is the difference maker between players at the various levels of the game.

A **study of players in the English Premier League showed that those who scanned the most completed almost twice as many of their passes** as those who scanned the least.

Think about that for a moment. We are talking about the English Premier League. These are all very good players. Yet, one seemingly simple behaviour, moving their head to look around, impacts significantly on their effectiveness.

The problem is **we take looking around for granted, as we assume everyone just does it, so we don't really coach it**. I believe we need to think differently. Scanning isn't everything of course, but it is an essential foundation for good awareness and effective decision-making. And it plays it's part in separating the best from the rest.

What I will share with you in this book is a methodology that **helps players develop this essential habit of scanning by using simple constraints that force the player to look around far more frequently than they need to in "normal" sessions**.

The ideas I will show you can easily be implemented into all of your training sessions to increase scanning and improve game awareness. Whilst some of the things I do in my coaching are very different, you will find some of the practices in this book are similar to ones you are already using. This is very much on purpose, as I like to show that you don't need to drastically change what you are already doing to get results. Almost everything I do is based around sessions that are commonly used by coaches all over the world; **I just add layers into the session that put an extra emphasis on scanning, forcing the players to look around more often and be more aware** of everything that is going on around them.

By immersing your players in these "awareness-gym sessions," you will help them to develop and enhance their abilities to scan and take in information quickly during the game. This will **give the players the tools they need to make better decisions and really unlock their potential**, which will improve individual player development and overall team performance.

Since 2009, I have worked with the **Irish FA** to present on their **UEFA Licence Courses about scanning**, game awareness, and developing cognitive performance. **Nigel Best**, the **Head of Coach Education at the IFA**, wanted to add something about this to their curriculum and these annual trips to Belfast quickly became one of the highlights of my year. The presentations on the courses are a mix of theory and practical and it's always the pitch sessions where it all comes to life – the coaches always like putting their boots on and everyone enjoys the challenge of something different.

Introduction

The Irish FA and I also worked together in 2010 to produce 2 DVDs/Videos showing some basic practices, which they issue as a resource on their courses. I enjoy the opportunity to share these ideas on the courses and it has been great to see that many of those coaches have embraced the ideas and integrated them into how they work with players.

The concept of scanning has become an increasingly hot topic in coaching circles in the past few years, as a growing body of research shows just how crucial it is.

Leading the line with these studies is **Geir Jordet PhD**, a **Professor at the Norwegian School of Sport Sciences**, who I have been lucky enough to have known for over ten years. I first reached out to Geir after reading his paper about using visualisation to improve perception and I still vividly remember our first meeting in 2010, a chat over coffee in Camden (London), where we passionately discussed our shared interest in scanning – it was exciting to finally talk with someone who was as obsessed about this as me! It was his study of midfielders in the English Premier League in 2013, linking scanning with pass completion rates, which was the breakthrough in raising awareness of this aspect of performance to a wider audience and his ongoing research clearly illustrates the **importance of scanning and shows how the elite performers do it more often, and more effectively, than the rest**. Geir's research over the years has been fantastic and his work continues to inspire me in my coaching and reinforces my belief that this essential behaviour must be actively developed in our players.

There has also been research by **Torbjorn Vestberg**, of the Karolinska Institute in Sweden, indicating that the **top players in football have better executive function than the rest of us**. Executive functions are the cognitive processes responsible for controlling the flow and processing of information, as well as selecting and monitoring goal-directed action, and aspects such as focus, cognitive flexibility, and inhibition.

Torbjorn has assessed the executive functions of players at all levels of the game, two of the most famous being **Xavi** and **Iniesta**, and he has consistently found that there is a significant difference between footballers and the general population. Not only that, he has also observed that players score differently from each other depending on the level they play – International players score higher than Premier League players, and Premier League players score higher than Championship players. Torbjorn's findings indicate that **good executive function is a key ingredient for reaching the top level of the game and he advocates the use of practices that overload our players in creative ways, to stimulate these functions, just as the Soccer eyeQ practices** you will find in this book do.

The practices I will show you are a fantastic way to **develop the habit of scanning, and challenge the cognitive abilities, of players at all levels of the game**. Coaches often think this is something you would only do with younger players, during their development, but this kind of training has also been proven to work with first team professionals.

I was fortunate to work with **Jackie McNamara** and **Simon Donnelly** at **Partick Thistle**, and then **Dundee United**, in Scotland. When Jackie got the manager's job at Partick Thistle in 2011, he asked me to come in to coach and we integrated the practices into the daily training sessions with the team, as well as using some of the ideas in the warm-ups on match days.

Introduction

The important thing was that Jackie was open-minded, he was always willing to embrace new ideas and he didn't mind doing things that were different if it helped improve the players. In fact, whilst Thomas Gronnemark may be grabbing headlines now because of his work with Liverpool, Jackie brought in a throw-in coach to work with our full backs, Stephen O'Donnell, and Aaron Taylor-Sinclair, back in 2012. So, when you saw us doing our awareness sessions, to some people in the game it might have seemed strange that first-team players were wearing bright green and yellow gloves and throwing tennis balls around in training. But it was working, and Jackie believed it was having the right effect in training and games – you can read more of his thoughts about this in his interview later in this section.

Coaches often ask how often they should be doing sessions like these with their players. My simple answer is everyday! It doesn't need to take up the whole session; you can do it as part of the **warm-up, or as an activation exercise, or the main body of the session itself** – that will be up to you. There is a famous quote, where Durant paraphrases the thoughts of **Aristotle**, which says, "We are what we repeatedly do. Excellence, then, is not an act but a habit." Therefore, I'm a big believer in the everyday effect if you want to get better at something; a little bit everyday is much better than once a week, once a month, or once a year.

Finally, I would like to emphasise that I do not claim that this is the only way to train scanning and awareness; it is a way. I have some good friends who are very successful with their own ideas, and I am sure there are many more coaches being creative with their approach to coaching this. The important thing is to find the way that suits you and helps the players you are working with to develop these essential habits. Ultimately, **players develop as the environment demands development** so, if we want to help our players succeed, we must be willing to challenge them in new ways and design sessions that force them to **see more**, **think quicker**, and **play better**.

"Using the Soccer eyeQ method of holding up colours forces players to look all the time before they receive a pass, because we have given them a reason to look.

They didn't have to look before, as the next player was in a fixed position and never moved, so they didn't have to check anything, but now they have to look to see which coloured cone is held up."

Kevin McGreskin

Founder of Soccer eyeQ & First Team Coach at Club América Femenil (Mexico)

WHAT IS SOCCER EYEQ?

What is the Soccer eyeQ Training Methodology?

It is a football coaching methodology with an extra emphasis on developing the habit of constantly scanning the playing area

- ▶ Sessions = Strong focus on **developing scanning** (looking around).
- ▶ Not necessarily "awareness specific" - The **practices still include all other football aspects** e.g. Combinations, movements, etc.
- ▶ The **technical, tactical, and physical components are all still present** in all of the practices.
- ▶ **Scanning is added as an extra layer** as normal sessions don't address it well enough (meaning players don't develop the habit).

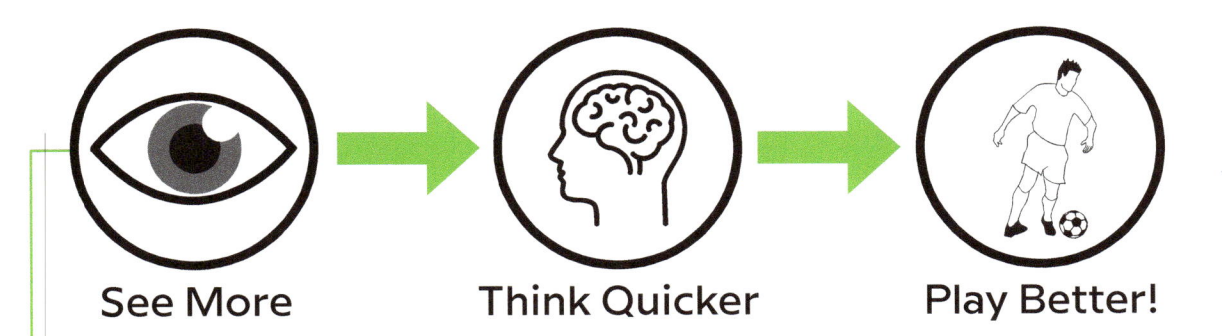

See More → **Think Quicker** → **Play Better!**

What is the Soccer eyeQ Philosophy?

- ▶ **Players make better decisions** when they know what is going on around them.
- ▶ Soccer eyeQ game awareness model helps **players add scanning to their game, so they have a full view of the pitch** (ball, teammates, opponents, and space).
- ▶ This **enables the players to develop this key aspect of football** and provides a greater opportunity to be the very best they can be.
- ▶ Looking around more = **Better decisions!**
- ▶ Players will be **faster and more effective** in training and in matches.

SOCCER EYEQ: Coloured Visual Cues to Force Players to Scan the Pitch

Ryan Gauld (Scotland International) and **Ryan Dow** using the Soccer eyeQ gloves during a Dundee United first team training session at Dundee United's Training Ground, in Scotland 2013.

Why use visual cues e.g. Gloves in training sessions?

Holding up colours forces the players to scan the playing area and to then identify the correct colour, which helps to create an essential habit.

- **Players normally only focus on the ball in training. Having coloured cones/gloves to look for forces the players to scan away from the ball during the practices.**

- The cones/gloves aren't important, just that the players are scanning! Calling out the correct colour a player is holding up simply confirms that the player did look and knew where that player was.

- Players holding up colours for others to spot are often on the move, so players have to constantly look to be aware of where they are.

- This takes a lot of scanning and a lot of awareness - the players learn the habit of continually doing this when they are off-the-ball.

- Even in drill type exercises (less player movements), it still forces players to have a quick look and reinforces the habit of scanning as part of their receiving skills.

- The coloured signals also force the signalling players to concentrate and understand the flow of play, so they hold up the visual cue at the correct time.

SOCCER EYEQ PRACTICES:
Options for Available Visual Cues

1. GLOVES - Players wear 2 gloves of different colours and hold one of them up as a visual cue (method used most with Soccer eyeQ practices)

2. WRISTBANDS

Alternative to using gloves with the players wearing 2 different colour wristbands

3. CONES

The players carry 2 cones of different colours and raise one as a visual cue

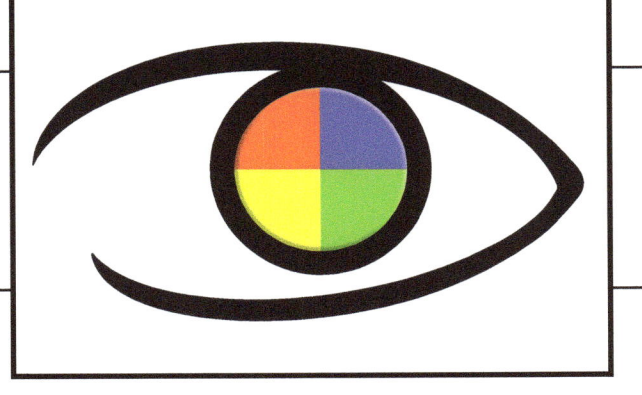

4. BIBS

Alternative to using cones with players carrying 2 different colour bibs

5. HANDS

Players hold up one hand or two hands - The players shout out "One" or "Two" to spot the visual cue

SOCCER EYEQ: Adding the Soccer eyeQ Method to Any Practice

Example: Pep Guardiola's "Juego de Posición" 4v4 (+3) Game

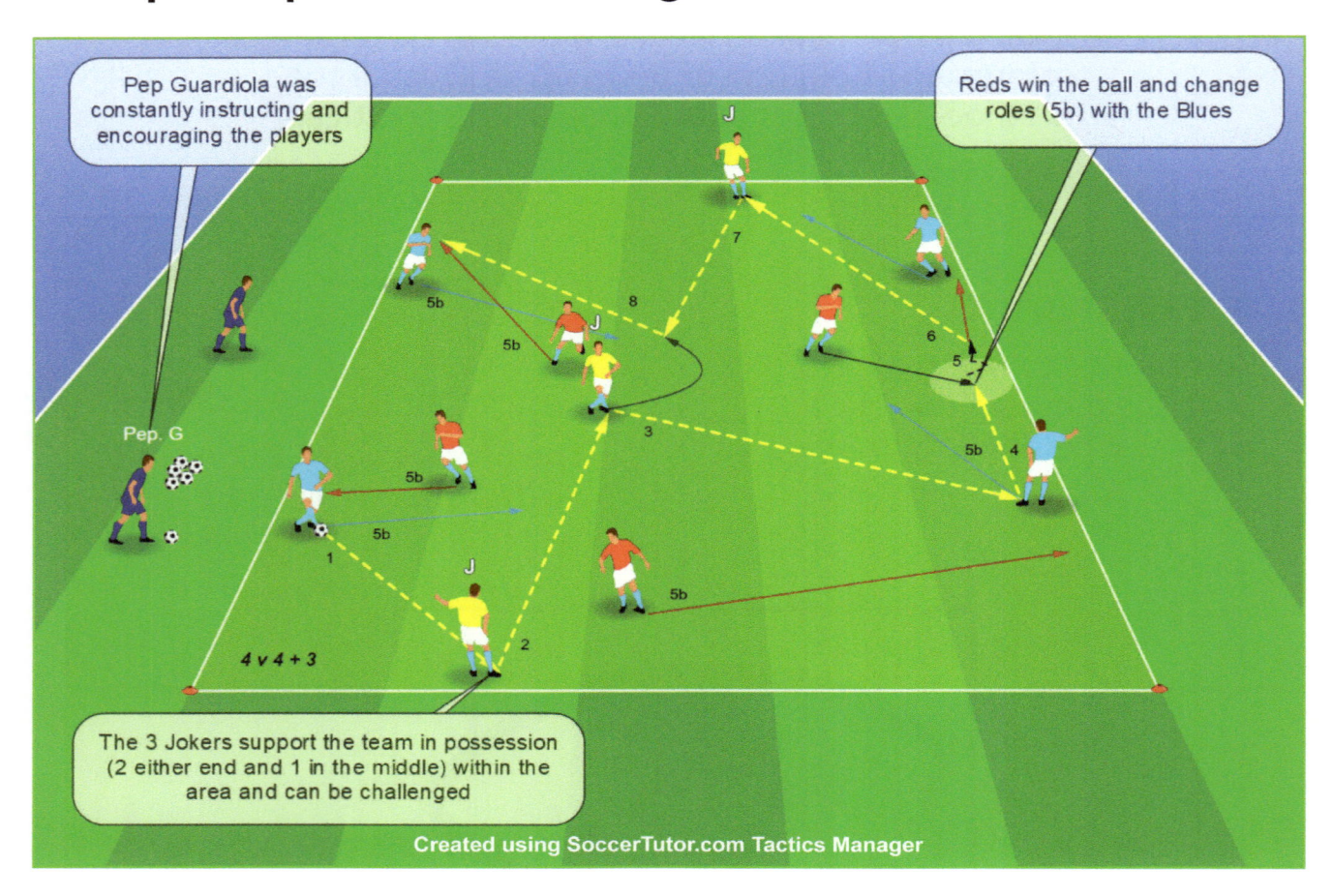

Pep Guardiola was constantly instructing and encouraging the players

Reds win the ball and change roles (5b) with the Blues

The 3 Jokers support the team in possession (2 either end and 1 in the middle) within the area and can be challenged

Practice Description

- In a 10 x 15 yard area, we have 2 teams of 4 players (blue and red) + 3 yellow jokers who play with the team in possession.

- All 4 blue players are positioned on the long sides (2 on each side) and all the red players start inside the area. There is 1 yellow joker at each end and 1 joker inside.

- The practice starts with the Coach and the blue team try to maintain possession with help from the 3 yellow jokers.

- The red team work together (pressing) to close off the angles and try to win the ball.

- If the reds are able to win the ball, the teams switch roles.

- The blues all move inside and work together to try and win the ball back immediately (counter-press).

- The reds move to the outsides and try to maintain possession with help from the 3 jokers.

SOURCE: Pep Guardiola's Manchester City training session at Etihad Campus Training Ground, Manchester - from the book: "Pep Guardiola - 85 Passing, Rondos, Possession Games & Technical Circuits Direct from Pep's Training Sessions," by Terzis Athanasios

Soccer eyeQ: Adding Soccer eyeQ Method to Any Practice

Adding the Soccer eyeQ Method

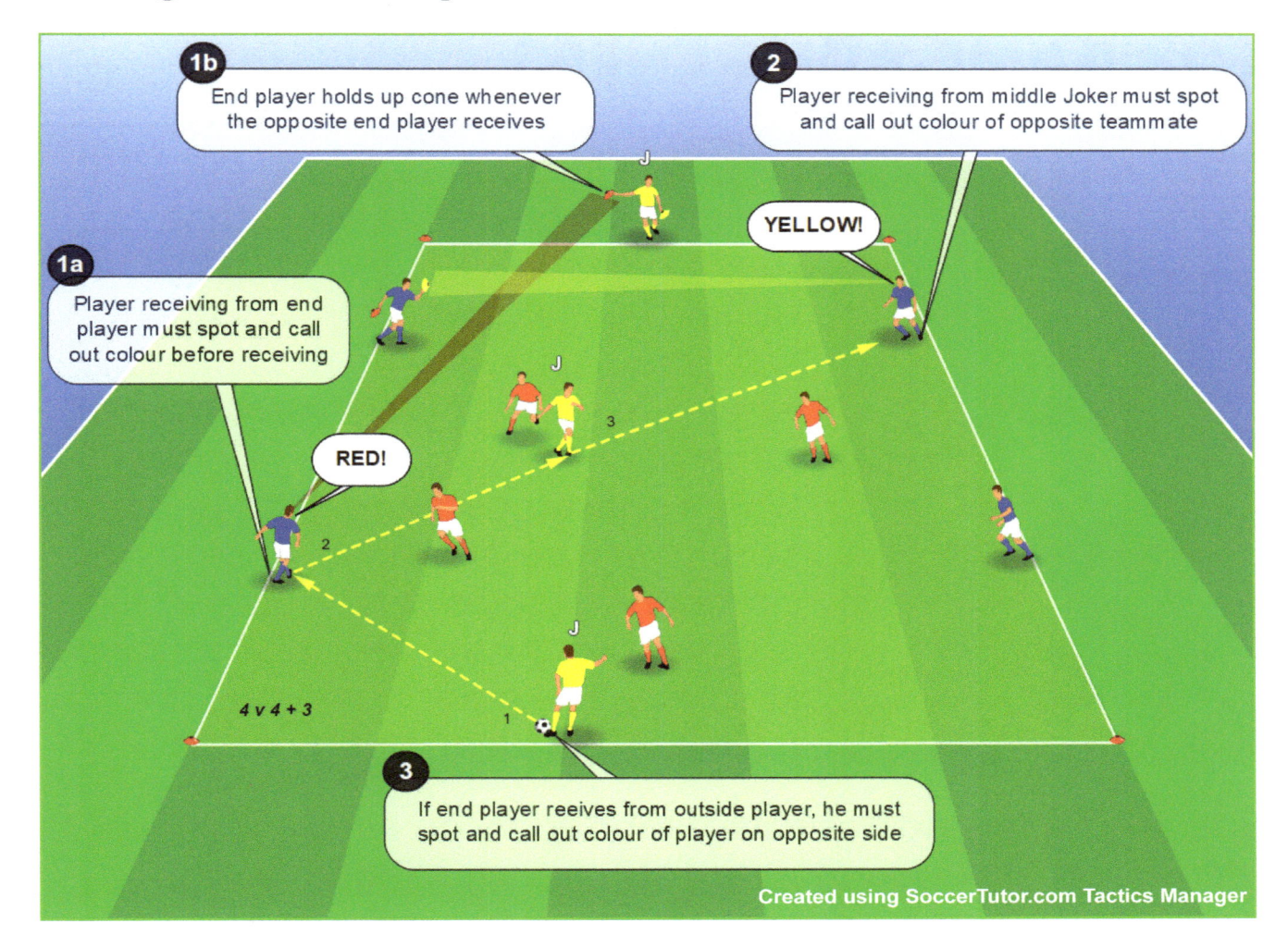

1a Player receiving from end player must spot and call out colour before receiving

1b End player holds up cone whenever the opposite end player receives

2 Player receiving from middle Joker must spot and call out colour of opposite teammate

3 If end player reeives from outside player, he must spot and call out colour of player on opposite side

4 v 4 + 3

Created using SoccerTutor.com Tactics Manager

What have we added? (2 Progressions)
- Visual cues are flashed when specific players receive. Players receiving from specific players must spot and call out the colour of the visual cue before receiving.

Why have we added it?
- Force scanning as the ball is travelling to the trigger player (or as he's taking his controlling touch) to locate the player who will be flashing the visual cue.
- Force scanning as the ball is travelling to you, so you can spot and call out the colour of the visual cue before taking a first touch.

How does it improve game awareness?
- Players have to look away from the ball to know the positioning of key players around the playing area.

- Players adopt better body positioning, particularly when receiving from a neutral end player, as it makes it easier to scan forward and see the opposite end player.
- Players cannot solely focus on the ball during the practice, as they must spot the visual cues at the correct time. They must still focus on their opponents too so must learn to divide their attention well.

What benefit will the players get?
- They develop the habit of scanning away from the ball at key moments.
- Learn to divide their attention.
- Take in quick snapshots of the positioning of teammates and opponents throughout.
- After training this, the players are far more confident and competent in matches.

IMPORTANCE OF NECK SWIVELLING FOR GAME AWARENESS

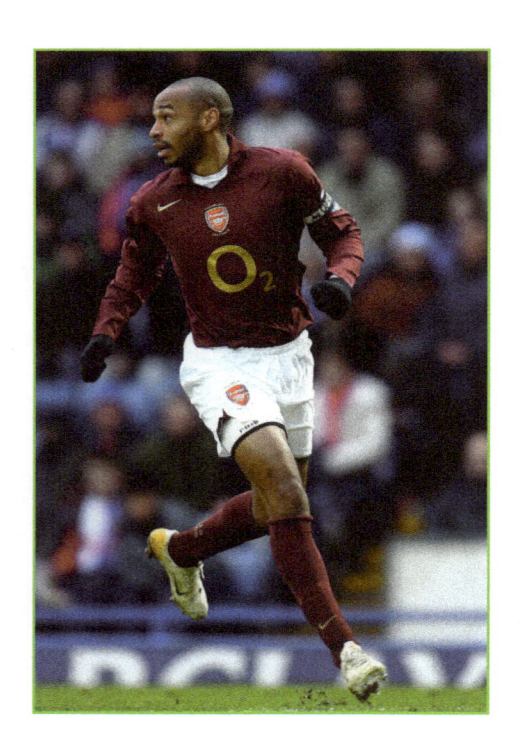

"The best footballers, too, think with their eyes. The difference is that they have to work in four dimensions rather than two, which is why the neck is so vital. A player who has spent his whole life swivelling his head, building perceptual judgement; a player for whom constant scanning has become second nature, has an advantage that cannot be exaggerated. Football, like art, is about the appreciation of space and time. The great players do not have it by accident, but by design.

Spanish players do not have a monopoly on head-swivelling. Many footballers from other nations, including England, have supreme situational awareness. My point, really, is that this message needs to be constantly emphasised in youth football. Coaches should talk less about the importance of a good right peg (foot), or ability to head the ball. They should talk less about dribbling and shooting. Instead, they should talk about the neck. They should make it a condition of every training session that players swivel their heads before taking possession of any pass."

Matthew Syed,
The Greatest: The Quest for Sporting Perfection
(John Murray: 23 Feb. 2017).

WHEN AND HOW WAS SOCCER EYEQ DEVELOPED?

Players' Focus on the Ball Too Much

I have been doing these types of practices for over 20 years and it all started because I wanted to find a way to help players to not solely focus on the ball during training and games. I had **noticed that my players tended to be ball-focused most of the time** and their eyes would follow the ball wherever it went. They would **focus intently on the ball, control it, and only then would they look up** to see what their options were. This meant they **didn't really have a picture of what was going on around them and, therefore, they couldn't make a good decision of what to do next with the ball when the got it**, so I knew I had to find a way to help the players look around more when they were off-the-ball and before they received the ball.

The Lack of Training Available

Of course, I know I am not the first coach to realise the importance of this but back then I didn't know of anyone who knew how to train this – **it seemed the only thing that was ever done was telling the players to check their shoulders or to have a look** (and I admit that's all I did at the time too).

However, just telling the players to do it didn't sit well with me as, from what I saw, sometimes they did it but, more often than not, usually they didn't scan at all. **I wanted to find a way that forced the players to do it, as often as possible, and I wanted to find a way to make it part of the session** so the players would do it themselves without me constantly telling them to do so.

These were also the days before the internet was like it is now, so there wasn't the same kind of resources available or the knowledge sharing that we have today, so I felt I was pretty much on my own trying to figure this out.

The Moment Soccer eyeQ Was Born

Then one day I was doing a square passing drill and I was telling the players (once again) to have a look at the player they were going to pass to next before they got the ball. I noticed they would do it once or twice after I reminded them, but they would then quickly revert back to their habit of only watching the ball. **I thought, right I'm going to force you to look, and I just decided to stick a couple of coloured cones in all the players' hands, so the player had to look and call out the colour of the cone held up**.

Almost straight away there was a difference and **the players started looking (almost) all the time before they received the pass – all because I had given them a reason to look**. They didn't have to look before, as the next player was in a fixed position and never moved, so they didn't have to check anything, but now they had to look to see which coloured cone was held up.

The hardest thing in the rest of that exercise was actually getting the player who was meant to be holding up a cone to do it at the right time, as they would be entranced by the ball as usual and wouldn't think that step ahead to hold up a cone for their teammate to spot.

When and How was Soccer eyeQ Developed?

That was how the idea of Soccer eyeQ was born, it was my light bulb moment. I then went home and figured out other drills I could add. Since then, I have also developed ways to incorporate the method into more dynamic practices, as opposed to just static drills, and into opposed practices too.

The Development

It has been far from an exact science, and, over the years, there was plenty of trial and error along the way. There have been numerous practices that I have tried, thinking they were a stroke of genius as I sketched them out on paper, that I found simply didn't work how I wanted them to when I was out on the field with the players.

Nowadays, I don't try to have a million different practices that I try to use. Instead, I rely on a core set that I use regularly, each of which has a number of variations and progressions to suit what I want out of the session on any particular day. These are my preferred sessions, but I don't claim that these practices are the only ones that should be used - **every coach has different thoughts, and I continue to enjoy looking at the practices I see other coaches using and finding ways to incorporate the Soccer eyeQ ideas into those.**

Stuart Armstrong (Scotland international) and **Sean Dillon** using the Soccer eyeQ gloves during a Dundee United first team training session at Dundee United's Training Ground, in Scotland 2013.

HOW DOES SOCCER EYEQ DEVELOP AND IMPROVE PLAYERS?

Soccer eyeQ has been used to help in the development of youth players and has also been implemented successfully at senior first-team level.

I have had great feedback from coaches all over the world who have introduced the Soccer eyeQ ideas into their training sessions, particularly those working with young players who have not only seen the benefits, but they have also expressed how much fun the players can have whilst doing it.

Over the years I have worked with players from all different levels of the game, whether as an individual or in team training, and I have really seen the players benefit from this kind of work.

Once the players are scanning regularly, they seem to play with far more composure because they are scanning more and know what's going on around them.

The players also seem to keep their concentration throughout the game better because they have been training their in-game concentration skills.

This means that they tend to switch off and get caught out less, and they generally look sharper with the ball because they already have a picture of what's around them before they even receive it. Therefore, they make better and quicker decisions.

Are they perfect all of the time? Of course not! But this is another small piece of what is required to help them play better and, over time, you see an improvement in their competitive performances.

The main thing to understand is that we are **ADDING** something to their game.

I am not saying that a player will become world class just because they are brilliant at scanning, as they still need the other tools that go along with it. But, **once the players add good quality scanning to their game, they are able to use their technical and physical attributes much more effectively**.

We saw this at the professional level too, when I worked with **Jackie McNamara** at both **Partick Thistle** and **Dundee United**, where we successfully incorporated this kind of training into our daily sessions. There were good players at both clubs and, **for some, simply improving their scanning helped them elevate their game to a new level**. They were already able to pass and control the ball, they had a good understanding of the game, and now they had a tool that **helped them make better decisions and execute their game actions more quickly**.

I interviewed Jackie McNamara and you can read it in full on the following page...

Interview: Jackie McNamara

INTERVIEW: Jackie McNamara

Jackie McNamara

- **Manager at Partick Thistle and Dundee United**
- **Captained Celtic**
- **Played for Scotland at the World Cup**

How important is scanning and awareness?

I think it's crucial. When I first looked at it, the perception was that it was all just about midfielders scanning, and it seemed to be the one area that they scan. But, if you actually look and dissect every game, you see centre backs switching off, and you see full backs getting caught on the wrong side because they haven't got a full picture. So scanning is imperative for every position. Goalkeepers as well, nowadays, because they get more and more involved with the ball at their feet - they get it from one side, and they've got to scan to see where they're going to put the ball next. The game has changed quite a lot in that aspect in terms of being possession based, and with goalkeepers more involved.

What are your thoughts on the Soccer eyeQ practices and how they develop scanning and awareness?

I think they are great and really challenging. As I said, when I first looked at it and Kevin used a few examples (Lampard and Scholes) they were always taking a picture in. But it's so important in every position on the pitch and then I could actually see the training working. I took part in it myself and thought wow, this is quite hard after a few instructions, but the idea of it was great and it really switches your brain on. It's very easy to look foolish with it if you're not switched on, when you get two commands or two actions to think about and then you put a third or a fourth in and then it's really challenging.

But there is a reason for it all and if you're looking around and taking things in, and keeping switched on, you know what you've got to do and then you can concentrate on something else too, whether it be to put your hand up or your colour, or shout something out.

And also, that side of it actually helps players with their voice, especially younger players, to communicate and not be embarrassed to shout something or talk. Because

Interview: Jackie McNamara

it's something you're always trying to put across as a manager, for players to use their voices and help each other, talk to each other. So the communication side of it was definitely a lot better as well. It's not like the normal stuff people do where you don't need to see things when you're doing little passing exercises or drills, as you have to stay switched on throughout, constantly concentrate, and know what's going on around you.

That's what it is, taking things in and then being in the right position to defend, the right position to intercept or just have a good awareness of what's around you. And it's something, as a player, I was okay at. I was not bad at sensing danger and being in the right position if I was playing at left back or right back, or as a defensive midfielder. I wasn't bad but I always knew I could be better. When you're playing against teams like Barcelona, you're basically defending for 90 minutes, waiting for through passes and darting runs and you're trying to give yourself a chance, and if you switch off for one second, it's in the back of your net. And these practices are good for switching the brain on and making you concentrate because concentration is extremely important in the game.

Why was it important to integrate the practices into your daily training sessions at the clubs?

Because I knew it was important and they would improve the players - I could see the improvement during the practices. You could see the way they would receive the ball and how they would have their touch set-up. This is because they were thinking about the next thing rather than just having their head down at their feet.

Training was always geared towards the Saturday for me, it's always geared towards the game. Everything that we worked on, we always put an edge on it, whether it be a challenge for the crossbar or shooting. When doing the awareness drills, everything was geared to take into the games on Saturday.

It's very hard to recreate the 90 minutes of a match, or what's going to happen in that 90 minutes. But this gives us a chance to do that because it's unpredictable. And that's what football is. It's problem solving. When it comes up to you, how do you deal with it? What picture have you got? What's the best way to score a goal? What's your best way to see something and defend? It's problem solving all the time.

It was something I liked to do in the warm-ups going into games as well, so they get their head up and have a picture too, instead of only working on their touch in a normal passing drill or something.

So, it was all about getting the players to do everything quicker and seeing and having a picture, having something in their head that they're going to do, and we could actually see it working. It wasn't overnight, but it was gradual, and the team got better and better with doing it.

How do you think the players responded to the sessions?

They responded differently, you had the ones that enjoyed it right away and you had the other ones, obviously, that were like, "what's this all about?" So, if it's the green and the yellow gloves, and they're all doing little extra things, or the tennis balls come out and some of them are thinking "what are we doing this for? Why are we passing tennis balls about?" And I think it's because a lot of players don't like change, and if it's something they're not good at as well they don't want to be found out, and they don't like to be embarrassed in front of their peers. But, as a manager, I would just say we're doing this and we're doing this for a reason – it's good fun, and everything else, but more importantly, it's going to improve you and make you better. We managed it all, the players got into it, and it really helped.

Which players in particular benefited from the sessions?

Well, I think all of them. All of them had a benefit. Off the top of my head, at Partick Thistle I'd have said Paul Paton was a good successful example. We moved him from right back into central midfield and he became an international player. He's one. I thought it really helped him with how he received the ball and moved it on quickly - he was fantastic for us at switching the ball. The way we played there, we had full backs that got forward, right, and left side, and Paul would have his head up and get his first touch out, then hit the diagonal across to Stephen O'Donnell on the right or Taylor-Sinclair on the other side.

Another great example was Stuart Bannigan, likewise at Partick Thistle. It was fantastic for him in the midfield area. But I think in general, all of the players benefitted a lot. The defenders too, to actually see danger or take a look around and see where opponents were. And it was no surprise that we started moving the ball quickly and doing things that teams couldn't live with us that season.

And then we took it to Dundee United and, likewise, a lot of players kicked on with it, and I thought it improved a lot of them all over the park. And our movement and our freedom, playing with that intuition, when they started to see things quicker and do things quicker.

We scored a lot of goals in that period as well and played fast exciting football. People said it was counter attacking, but it wasn't counter attacking, it was just because it was done that quickly, with movement and vision and third-man running. It would kill teams who were too slow to react, and we scored some great goals. I think the actual benefits of it were extremely good.

Interview: Jackie McNamara

DUNDEE UTD SOCCER EYEQ SCANNING PRACTICE EXAMPLE

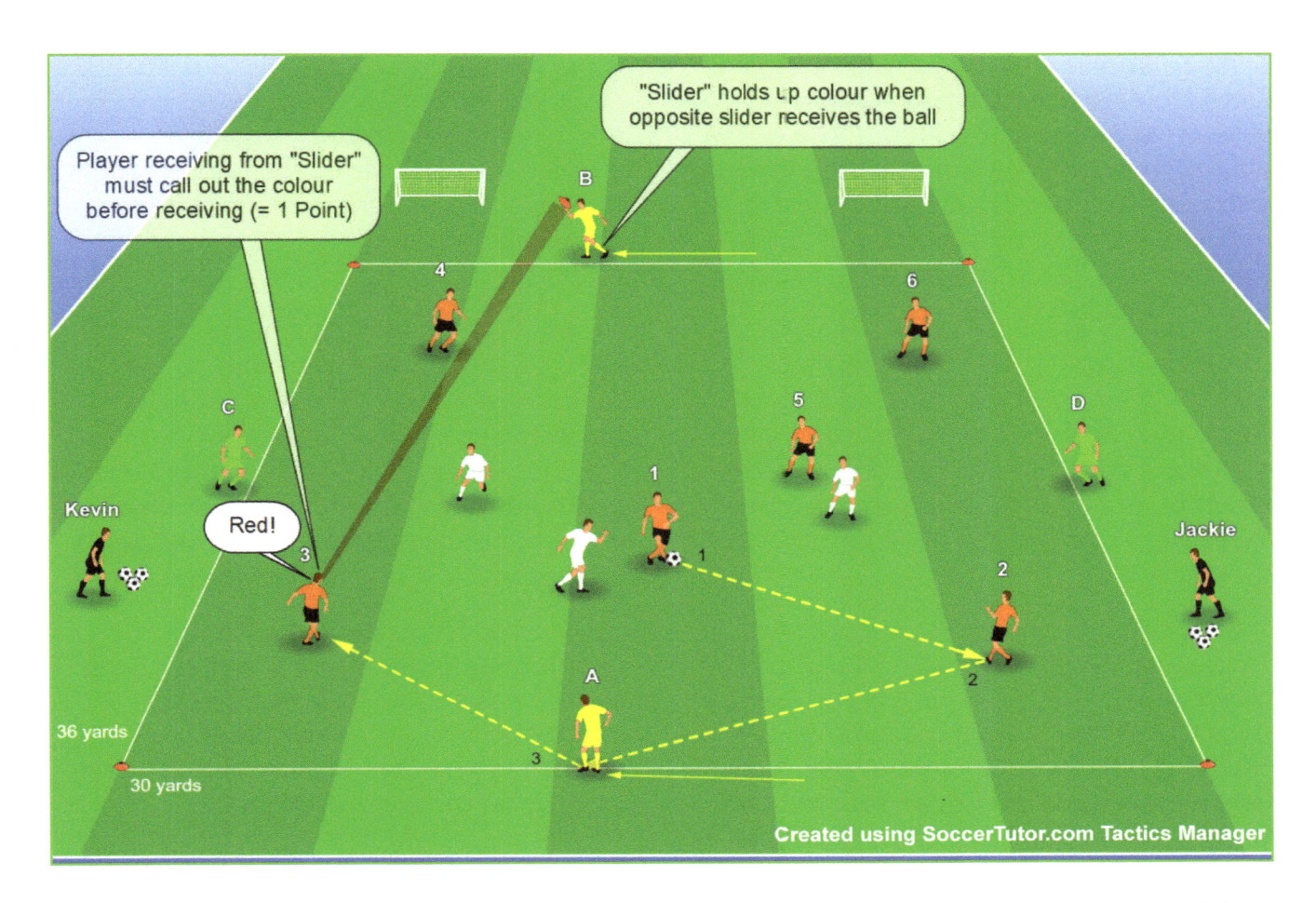

Diagram labels:
- "Slider" holds up colour when opposite slider receives the ball
- Player receiving from "Slider" must call out the colour before receiving (= 1 Point)
- Red!
- Kevin / Jackie
- 36 yards / 30 yards
- Created using SoccerTutor.com Tactics Manager

The diagram above shows one example of a practice we used to use with Jackie McNamara at Partick Thistle and Dundee United - for the full description, practice analysis, coaching points + progressions **please see Page 163**.

In the normal form of the game, the orange team score by receiving from a "Slider" (outside player). The only limitation is that they must complete at least 1 pass inside the area before passing to a slider. The whites try to win the ball and then score in either mini goal.

Our game awareness progression shown here aims to improve body shape and develop scanning in an opposed practice.

To progress and force the player receiving from the slider to engage in scanning and promote better body shape, we modify the scoring method.

Now, when the ball is played to a slider, the opposite slider holds up a visual cue.

To score, the orange player receiving from the slider must spot and call out the colour the opposite slider is holding up (after the pass and before his first touch).

For example (in diagram), when the ball is played to Slider A, Slider B holds up a visual cue (red or yellow) for the orange Player 3 to spot and call out e.g. "Red!"

Soccer eyeQ with SoccerTutor.com — 27 — SCANNING - How to Train it

HOW CAN THE SOCCER EYEQ METHODOLOGY BE IMPLEMENTED?

It can be **implemented easily into almost every training practice and session**. As you will see in the book, the great thing is that I use practices most coaches will be familiar with and are probably already using. In addition, I have used examples of many popular practices and added the Soccer eyeQ method to them.

This is on purpose, as I like to show coaches they don't have to change how they coach or throw away their favourite sessions – you can simply **add layers into what you are already doing to challenge the players further** and add in this concept of scanning.

I have been presenting these concepts on the Irish FA UEFA Pro/A/B Licence courses since 2009, so we have shown the ideas to coaches working at all levels of the game. I know that **some of the ideas have been used from grassroots level all the way to the English Premier League**.

Of course, that's not to say all of them do everything exactly as I have shown them. Like most coaches, they take the practices, or parts of the ideas that they like, and make them their own to incorporate into the work they do with their players.

If we want our players to maximise their potential, and our teams to play to the best level they can, then we must help them improve their awareness on the pitch. Therefore, we must find **innovative ways to adapt our sessions and challenge our players to develop this essential habit of scanning**.

I interviewed Nigel Best, the Coach Education Manager at the Irish FA, about how coaches should look more at this game awareness aspect within the training sessions they deliver. You can read the full interview on the following page…

Club América Femenil using the Soccer eyeQ gloves during a first team training session at The Instalaciones de Club de Fútbol América Training Ground, in Mexico City (2021).

INTERVIEW: Nigel Best

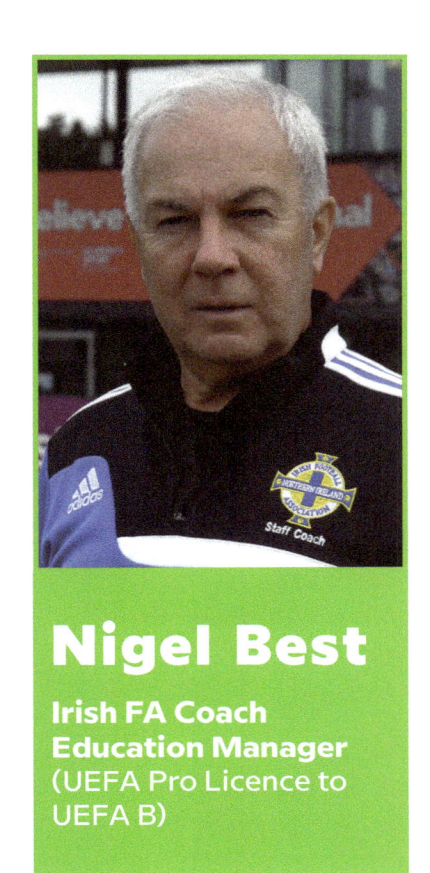

Nigel Best

Irish FA Coach Education Manager
(UEFA Pro Licence to UEFA B)

How important is scanning and awareness?

It has become increasingly clear to me that the game at the higher level is changing. This is not in terms of the distances players run but in the speed of their movements, with short, high intensity runs to break the opponent's defensive line when attacking or initiating a high press as a defensive tactic. For me, the implications of this are that players must think more quickly and have greater awareness of the picture on the pitch around them.

For example, there is now a widely adopted tactic of the goalkeeper playing out from the back in combination with his centre backs, full backs and central midfield players. Given the high risk, if caught in possession or a pass is intercepted, these players must have an enhanced awareness of the situation (picture) around them, and the ability to be quick and correct with their decisions.

Players are being closed down as soon as the ball arrives at their feet, so they don't have time to get it under control and look up - the opponent is already on them. When you watch Manchester City and they decide to impose a high press, they are all over the opposition. And the speed that they run at is highly impressive - these guys are highly mobile.

As I said, players aren't really running larger distances now at the top level, it's the speed at which they cover the ground over short distances, and that ties in with the tactic of the high press or quick counter attacking football. And both of these tactics are only effective if players have a better appreciation of what's around them. They must know where their teammates and opponents are positioned.

Taking the example of playing out from the back, imagine the goalkeeper plays out to the centre back, the centre back is watching the ball come to him with head his down and watches himself take a touch. He is closed down and it's a disastrous area of the pitch to lose possession. Alternatively, you could lose possession

Interview: Nigel Best

with the defensive midfielder coming to receive the pass from the goalkeeper (or from the centre back) facing his own goal. I think it was Fernandinho for Man City in a major Champions League game, came and took a pass from the keeper and went to play it out to the left centre back and the opposition read it, intercepted, and scored.

And even in other areas of the pitch, the players have to look and make sense of it all because football is organised chaos. It seems to be structured as you have team formations, you have supposed patterns of play that you can work to, and defensive lines that you hold up. But it's chaotic by nature as there's always somebody there destroying. It can be the opposition, or it could be one of your own teammates who doesn't come up with the line, or he drops behind the line, or whatever, and it becomes chaotic. If it was all nice and easily structured, all games would be boring, and everybody would be drawing. But it's not. So, that's why there has to be an ability for players to understand well that there is chaos and I have got to make some sort of sense out of the chaos.

How do I do it? Well, you need to get the picture. If I haven't got a picture, I can't create any structure in my thinking out of what is a very quick chaotic movement, because players are moving at extremely high speeds. And the ball is now moving even quicker. So, the players need to take quick pictures, they need to scan to make sense of it all.

Do you think this should be actively trained and developed in players?

When I'm watching high level games, I'm seeing players like **Bruno Fernandes** at Manchester United and the commentators are saying, "How is he seeing that pass?" They're saying it as if he's playing passes blind. He is not playing blind passes. He has scanned and observed the pitch and knows where people are before he has got the ball. And then plays the ball using the most effective passing option. Implying that he is playing a pass blind reflects a lack of knowledge because top players like Bruno Fernandes scan. Kevin often shows the clip of **Frank Lampard** at Chelsea as an example of the number of times he scans out of possession. Bruno's got that constantly, so he knows what's going on around him and he has more than one pass option in his head - he will nearly always pick the most effective one. And quite often the ball goes forward to challenge the opposition, it's a challenging pass. Therefore, what we should be doing as coaches is creating sessions to encourage our players to play in this most effective way, a way in which they already know what their opportunities are for the next pass before receiving.

The more I watch the high speed modern game, the more I am of the view that the old-style coaching style does not develop what we need at the higher levels, and we must have this alternative way of provoking players and stimulating players. So, that is why I think there is a need for a challenging type of coaching based around the Soccer eyeQ game awareness training methods. Incorporating the scanning aspect is critical because the game is so fast now.

And I would actually suggest that a lot of what Kevin is doing should be strongly recommended to development coaches, as I think it's particularly important for young players to get an understanding of the importance of being aware and being able to make decisions based on that awareness, and they can build that into their game from the youngest of ages. Coaches are comfortable with the

Interview: Nigel Best

technical side - they can do sessions on control, and they can do sessions on passing. What they are not good at, though, is developing awareness and decision making effectively. They think it is enough to say, "I told him to look around" and "I see him moving his head," but there's no evidence of what they're looking at. That's what I see happening, coaches tell a player to scan, they look around, and the coach assumes they picked up the detail. But they're not picking up effective detail to use constructively in the situation they find themselves in immediately. That's the difference. So, I have a strong view that we are not developing players as well as we could.

Why was it important for you to include this on the Irish FA Coach Education Program?

The game has changed dramatically, and you have got to look at it in its entirety, which means the way you train players has to change. So, this kind of training has value and its on the course because it's relevant to what the modern player needs to be able to do on the pitch.

The game's not only evolved tactically, the technical side has also pushed the conditioning side and the intensity is also going up - it's now about how can we speed our players up. The outcome of that then, combined to tactics, is the training sessions that the coach puts on must reflect both, which means we must increase the speed at which players make good effective decisions.

The next question is how do we do that? We have to train our players to scan better. They not only have to look more, but they have to change their body positioning, so their body is at an angle that allows their head to revolve in different directions. This then allows them to take in information effectively and do the next action quickly and efficiently.

I was becoming concerned with what I was seeing with coaches, dominating sessions, telling players where and when to move, how many touches they were allowed, and who pass to, which was often in a dictated rotation. Players did not need to look and were not required to make a decision. Some coaches may have encouraged players to play with their head up to look around them before receiving the ball by shouting instructions like "head up, take a look" but my concern was, how did the coach know what the player was taking in? He may be rotating his head, but not absorbing information. So, how could a coach reassure himself that the player was scanning effectively?

So, that's why it's important to teach this type of training to coaches on the coach education program. However, I don't know many associations that will go beyond the typical type of sessions and show something different. So, coaches aren't seeing anything like the Soccer eyeQ sessions anywhere else, and they aren't being challenged about how to make their players better at receiving information by scanning, and then improving their decision making at speed. Unless they get to see this type of session, they don't know any other way.

We have been showing coaches this method since 2009. We've taught it on the Pro Licence, the A Licence, and the B Licence courses. We've presented it at the right age groups, and we've done CPD (Continuing Professional Development) for those who have never seen it before. So, we've consistently presented it to coaches but after that it's up to them. We can't insist they do it of course, but we make sure they are given the opportunity

Interview: Nigel Best

to observe and take all the ideas on board. It's each coach's decision as to what to do with all the information but they have a big opportunity watching and participating in your sessions, to see that this is maybe a method that they can use, or they could adapt, take bits of yours and reformulate it into a way they feel more comfortable with and make it their own.

I think the coaches who have innovative minds, who are willing to challenge their own thinking and look for things that are different and effective, the ones that challenge themselves in the sessions that they deliver, those are the ones that should be in the key positions at clubs and academies. The sessions have been helpful for our coach education program because of the challenge to the coach, and it's why I bring you back every year to be part of the team that develops coaches (on courses at various levels). We need to challenge our coaches to think about the way they coach, they need to think about their sessions, and they need to think about the way the modern game is and make sure their coaching sessions reflect that.

What are your thoughts on the Soccer eyeQ practices and how they develop scanning & awareness?

I think the sessions challenge the players to develop effective scanning, which will support their decision making, and also help the coach become aware of whether the players are absorbing information when looking around.

Because the speed of the game is now intensified, I believe it's critically important to have practices that encourage players to become aware of what's around them in advance of receiving the ball, and in advance of making their next movement in support of a pass. For example, in your sessions, when there's a few tennis balls coming in, that player has to receive the ball and throw it to the teammate, and call the colour from another player, before getting the football and passing that to a different player. You need to scan early to know where those key players are. The player receiving the pass, who has to throw the tennis ball, has to know where people are around him and those players around him have to move into good receiving positions whether they're getting the football or the tennis ball. So, the sessions that you're doing are not just simply focused on the player receiving and to whom he's going to pass. They also deal with a potential third pass and the third man running to get into position for the next pass that could come your way. Therefore, the players need to think off the ball all the time.

The coach sees clear evidence of improved awareness from the practices; from the player calling the colour, or who he throws the tennis ball to, or the movement of the supporting players to be in the view of the player receiving the football so that they're providing an option. The coach can use this evidence to evaluate and assess whether players are scanning effectively, know where their teammates and opponents are and can use that information to make quick and correct decisions in terms of their movement or how they should receive and pass the ball. So, the coach can now make effective decisions on a player at a developmental stage or at the highest level e.g. If that player should be playing as Nº6 on a Saturday. Because if the Nº6 doesn't look around (scan), doesn't get his body shape right, and doesn't know where the players are, he will struggle when the ball is played to him.

That is why I am always keen to advocate for coaches to look at what you do.

HOW DOES SOCCER EYEQ HELP COACHES, PLAYERS AND TEAMS AT ALL LEVELS?

There is an increasing body of research showing just how important scanning is, and it consistently shows that the best players do it more than the rest. Of course, I am not claiming that Soccer eyeQ is the only way to train this – it is *a* way of training scanning.

Any coach can take the concepts I outline in this book and incorporate them in their own way. They can be taken into the sessions that you do to help your players develop this essential skill.

If players and teams want to perform to their maximum potential, as consistently as possible, then this is something that they have to be good at. Therefore, scanning is an aspect of performance that has to be explicitly addressed in how we train and develop players.

How does Soccer eyeQ make players/teams better and what aspects will the player improve?

The training practices/exercises strongly promote scanning, both off-the-ball and when receiving, and the development of this essential habit is crucial if players want to be able to maximise the effectiveness of their competitive performances. **Having a picture of what is going on around you and knowing what your options are is a crucial aspect of the decision-making process** and, to have a picture, you must scan.

Another benefit of the Soccer eyeQ practices is that the **players are actively engaged more continuously throughout**, so they are training and developing their in-game concentration skills to a far greater degree. Of course, there is the scanning element that they will be asked to do and this itself requires a lot of concentration to do consistently well at the right times. However, even the seemingly simple job of just raising a hand (visual cue) at the correct time requires the players to pay attention to what is happening just that little bit more than normal.

Furthermore, when we introduce the extra task of the tennis balls (see practices later in the book), this further challenges the players concentration and how quickly they can switch on to position themselves correctly to receive.

The **best players in the world not only scan more, they can also take in more information from shorter looks**. Therefore, when we advance things to the opposed practices, and have these extra tasks added, the players must learn to be able to take as much information as possible about teammates, opponents, and space from the briefest of glimpses.

In these practices, we are not only reinforcing the habit of scanning but the extra tasks act as an overload, which means the players cannot take too long to only assess opponents because they also have extra jobs. They also cannot only focus on spotting visual cues, as they have opponents applying pressure and trying to win the ball. This means the players must be continually assessing to understand how much time and space they have, sometimes from the quickest of looks, in order to be as effective as possible on the ball.

How Does Soccer eyeQ Help Coaches, Players and Teams at All Levels?

How will the team improve as a whole?

If all the players are better at maintaining their concentration and are engaged in scanning, then there will be a greater level of awareness throughout the whole team.

This means they will be far more effective at identifying, reading, and utilising the non-verbal communication that is crucial in team performance.

What is the potential impact?

It strongly impacts performance because teams will have better collective decision-making and be able to move the ball around quicker when they want to, and the opposition will find this incredibly difficult to deal with.

Geir Jordet, PhD is a researcher and teacher of Psychology and Elite Football Performance and has been a pioneer in the field of research in this area. He is considered by many to be the Godfather of scanning and has worked with some of the top players, teams, and associations in the world.

I have been fortunate to have known Geir for many years and I interviewed him for this book to discuss his work and show how important scanning is for players at all levels.

You can read the full interview with Geir on the following page...

Kevin McGreskin overseeing a **Club América Femenil** first team training session with Soccer eyeQ gloves at The Instalaciones de Club de Fútbol América Training Ground, in Mexico City (2021).

INTERVIEW: Geir Jordet, PhD

Geir Jordet, PhD

- **Professor at Norwegian School of Sport Sciences**
- **Researcher and Teacher of Psychology and Elite Football Performance**

What has your research been about?

The research has been about visual perception in football, and how that is linked to decision making and performance. Because you can't really see inside the brain to see what football players are perceiving, the way I study visual perception is I take a type of proxy, which is scanning behaviours, or visual exploratory behaviours as I used to call them, and this is basically when players look away from the ball in the period leading up to them receiving it. And that activity of looking away from the ball is a very simple indication of perception that had the big benefit of it being measurable, so you can quantify it, code it, and analyse it.

That has been a big research focus, without saying in any way that it explains it all. This is just one indication, it's one observable behaviour that says something. I never say that it says everything, but it says something. And then you have to interpret it, you have to contextualise it, you have to see how it fits in with different players, different situations, and so forth, and so forth.

In essence, we have looked at scanning in many different types of populations, different age groups, different levels, different positions, and different specific contexts. We try to see what characterises players in these situations with respect to scanning. And above all, we tried to see if there's a connection between scanning and performance.

What have been your findings?

Throughout all of these studies, we have found solid positive links between scanning and performance. And sometimes these relationships are quite high and solid. In one study that has been cited a few times **I studied 118 Premier League players**. When we focused on the midfielders, we found that the **players who scan a small amount only completed 39% of their forward passes, but those who scan a lot completed 77% of their forward passes**, which is almost twice as many forward passes. This is a massive difference, nearly 40% higher accuracy, it's huge!

Since this was done in 2013, I've always thought that has to be a connection here, a relationship, but then I don't know for sure statistically, when you factor in all these types of situations, the contexts - it could be that other factors are responsible for this effect. So, I've always presented this as something I believed, but I fell short of saying that I know. And then three and a half years ago, we set out to do what we felt would be the big conclusive study on this so we can get this answer once and for all. So, I **teamed up with Arsenal and we had three cameras at the Emirates throughout the 2017-18 season**. We had a team of about 20 students code and analyse all this footage and we ended up with about **10,000 individual ball possessions, with 27 different players across 21 games**. Then we used Arsenal's own data analysts and they put all their computer power and their statistical model into this data. When we controlled for everything, for different types of players, different types of situations, the context, the pass difficulty, and all these things, **we found that, very clearly, scanning has a robust and positive effect on performance**. And that of course supports what we believed all this time but it's nice to be more conclusive.

Have you found differences depending on the playing level?

Yes, we consistently find differences when we compare different playing levels. The players at the higher levels tend to be higher frequency scanners than players at a lower level.

The very latest study we did was looking at the European Championships for U17 and U19 level and we compared them. We compared basically like we did with the others (the relationship between scanning and performance), and we basically found that the U19s scored higher on scanning than the U17s.

We did the same in the Ajax football academy a few years ago, looking at players and different age groups. We found the same there. The players who have advanced and progressed to a higher age group through a top European Academy are more frequent in their scanning than the players in the lower age groups.

We did the same when I looked at Premier League players the first time.

It's always the same, same, same, we find out the better players scan more.

Who are the top players to scan and perform at the highest levels?

Over the years our studies have revealed the usual suspects, which are some of the Barcelona players from the golden generation. **Xavi (Hernandez)** is still the number one ever that we measured. So, he's high up there. **Iniesta's** up there and **Messi** is up there too. And then **Pirlo**, when he was playing, was up there. And then you have the ones that I have identified from the Premier League studies we've done; **Frank Lampard** and **Steven Gerrard** are all kind of in the same area. **Xavi** though is a little bit above that again. And then, when you look at the current top players, **De Bruyne** is up there, **Gündoğan** is up there. **Odegaard** and **Frenkie de Jong** too, both of them.

All of the players we've identified here so far are midfielders. So, lately, I've been fascinated with forwards because they typically score much lower on scanning than others. In fact, the results show they have half the frequency of central midfielders. But then you look at **Mbappe**, he is up there with **Lampard**, **Gerrard**, and **Iniesta**. There's something special about this kid. And my compatriot **Haaland** is the same. He's not quite at Mbappe's level, but he's just behind. And so, you have players who kind of defy the constraints of the role that they have, and just find new ways to solve this forward role. And that, to me, is just incredibly exciting.

And you see it also with these players that they're not just goal scorers, they're the players who tend to look for teammates, they tend to see if they can pass to a teammate in a better position. And then, as they are super quick, they see if that's not the case, and go for a shot.

It's very complex when you get to this level, but to analyse scanning as a part of it kind of gives us a little bit of an insight. Actually, I feel like it's a code book, to say a little bit more about these very intangible processes that we typically can't say so much about.

Can you train scanning?

There is a tendency to think that whatever you're born with is what you have. But the scanning that we speak about is a behaviour, and it's a habit that you can shape and develop. It's something that even you and I in our older age could improve. If we really focused on it for a week of our own football training, we would get better at it, too. Scanning is extremely trainable.

And we've done studies on this, and we've shown that **you can double your scanning frequency in a matter of a weeks, even for top level players**. And then, for kids, you know, it's even more trainable. Again, no one is saying that scanning is everything, but it is a pretty important foundation.

The training worked well for Paul Paton at Partick Thistle who moved from right back to central midfield and then played at a higher level...

Yeah, and that's it. I think there are many stories like that, and I have many of them myself where if you give players this key, it kind of opens up a world to them that they wouldn't otherwise access. And that key will then unlock other processes that will set a momentum, which will then help them develop other things as well. Because I also have many similar stories and I think there's something to it, that this gives players access to tools, and ways, and paths to develop in a way they otherwise wouldn't have, and then you can accomplish some things. So, I would want to give all my players these types of tools and then they have to figure out what to do with them, of course.

Is this something that coaches should actively coach?

Yeah, yeah, absolutely. So, I absolutely think that this needs to be a part of a coach's toolbox, that this should be something that coaches are aware of that they analyse, that they instruct on, and give feedback on. And that they make sure that their players work on this, and get better at this, because this is it. **If you teach players to receive the ball, you should also teach them to scan before they receive.**

Now, again, this is not everything, of course, but it's an integrated part of everything. And then you know, as a coach, there are many ways that you can work on this. You can work on this more in isolation (individual training), or you can work on this as an integrated part of the whole (team training). And I think you should do both.

Interview: Geir Jordet, PhD

What do you think of the Soccer eyeQ practices?

All these types of practices will work in the proper direction. If they're set-up so that they properly consider what we know about scanning, I think they add value. And I think that coaches should be creative when it comes to setting up different ways to stimulate players scanning and perception.

I believe in these types of practices, and it satisfies the criteria needed. To solve the practices well, you need to pick up some information and to pick up that information you need to scan.

I think these are good examples of practices that will have the desired benefit. And I think kids above all should do more of these types of practices where you're rehearsing the necessity of scanning before you get the ball and even when you have the ball. Then when you know you're more mature as a player and you're at a more advanced stage where the focus is much more to win the games you play, you can get into more advanced game models and playing styles, and all that stuff. But with practices like these (Soccer eyeQ), you're rehearsing a tactical-technical repertoire that's linked with your perception. That will make it easier for you to then adapt to the more advanced types of football. So I like it.

Finally, tell me about Be Your Best...

I'd been looking for ways to see if something can be done structurally to assist in the training of some of these skills. I believe in football training because I believe training the skills on the pitch is always going to be the foundation. That's always the most important way to get players to acquire and rehearse these habits and integrate them with the rest of the game and everything. But I have always felt that there's room for so much more than that. Because of physical limitations, there's only so much football training you can do per day before it becomes an injury hazard. But that doesn't mean that you can't train mentally, cognitively, and perceptually. Maybe you can train that for another hour per day, but there was no way to do that.

So, we created this space where you can put on VR Goggles and suddenly you are playing for Real Madrid in the Champions League Final. You're actually out there on the pitch and you know that you're going to get the ball in 5 to 10 seconds. And you better prepare, you better scan, you better pick up what's going on around you because, when you get the ball and you're playing Juventus, there's going to be a guy on you within half a second. So, if you don't do something with the ball quickly, you're going to get killed.

We have thousands of these situations that we have replicated from real games. And we had experienced football coaches rate the different decisions that you can make, because you get the ball, and you have to do something with it. So, it's an interactive game and we use all of our research to analyse and give feedback on the details of your scanning. So, it's the timing of your scanning, the last scan that you do right before you get the ball, and what you see. And once you're mastering it, you can turn the speed up and now you're playing Champions League level x 1.3. And that's going to be fast Kevin. That's ridiculously fast.

So, you can take 10 minutes of this training per day, and you have a very focused (intense) perceptual and scanning training that is a very good supplement to regular training.

Xavi's "Off the Scale" Scanning: Match Example

XAVI'S "OFF THE SCALE" SCANNING:
MATCH EXAMPLE

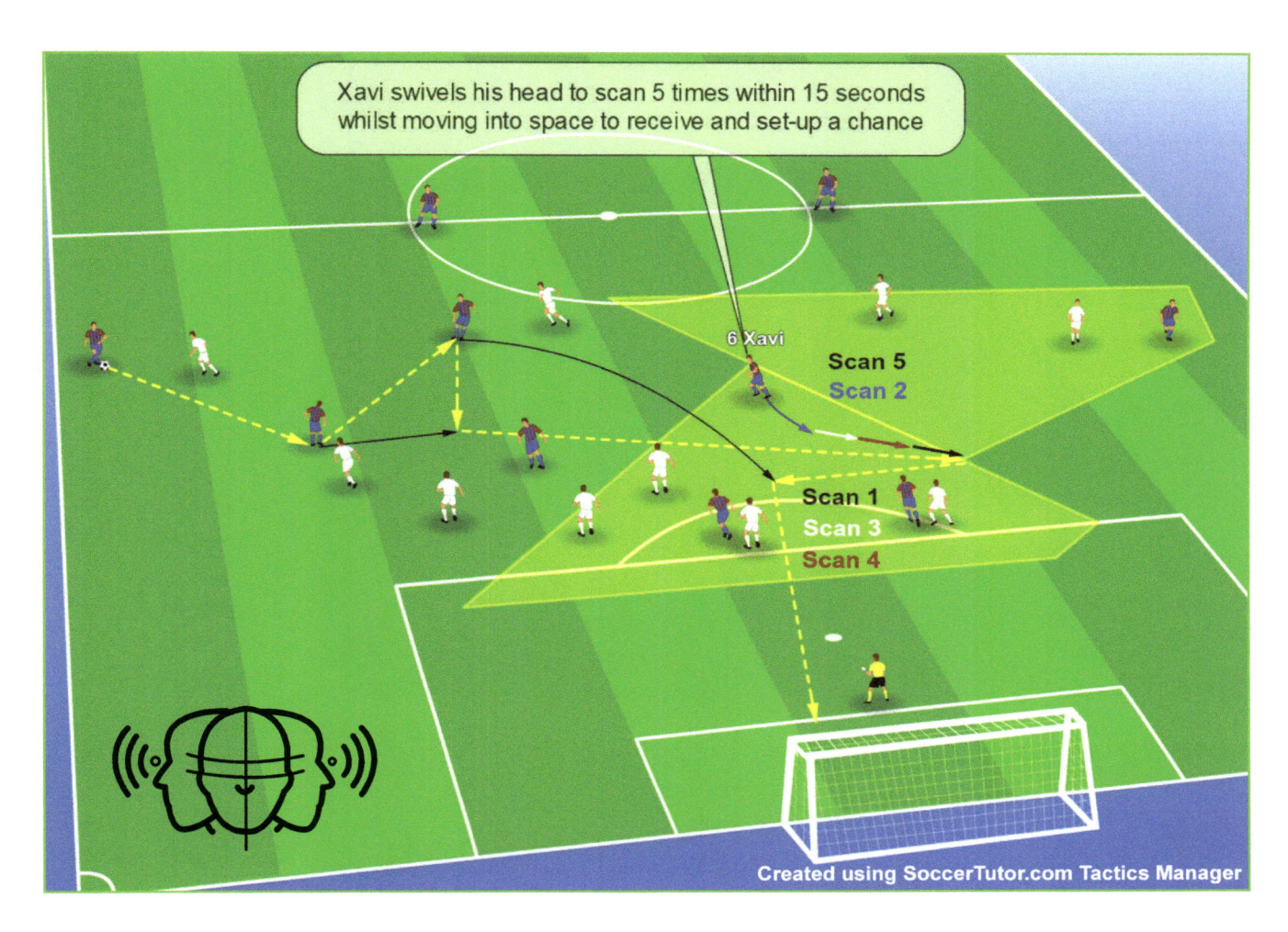

> Xavi swivels his head to scan 5 times within 15 seconds whilst moving into space to receive and set-up a chance

Geir Jordet PhD (read the full interview on **previous pages**) is the leading expert on scanning. He studied and recorded a large group of players, analysing how many times they scan before receiving a pass.

Steven Gerrard and **Frank Lampard** were deemed to be "outstanding" at scanning with 0.61 and 0.62 scans per second respectively.

However, **Xavi was "off the scale"** with an incredible **0.83 scans per second**.

For more detailed information on Geir's studies into scanning, **see pages 78-80**.

Xavi is constantly scanning, and this is what he said on the subject:

"Think quickly, look for spaces. That's what I do: look for spaces. All day. I'm always looking. All day, all day."

The diagram above shows an example of **Xavi** scanning during a La Liga game. Before receiving the ball and creating an opportunity, he performs 5 scans of the area around him within 15 seconds.

This enables **Xavi** to exploit potential spaces to receive and see the best passing option available to create a chance.

SOURCE: Keepitonthedeck. "Xavi - Scanning Surroundings Examples." YouTube, uploaded by Keepitonthedeck, 6 Nov 2018, www.youtube.com/watch?v=oMez1ZpJxDQ

SCANNING TO DEFEND EFFECTIVELY: MAN CITY'S LAPORTE EXAMPLE

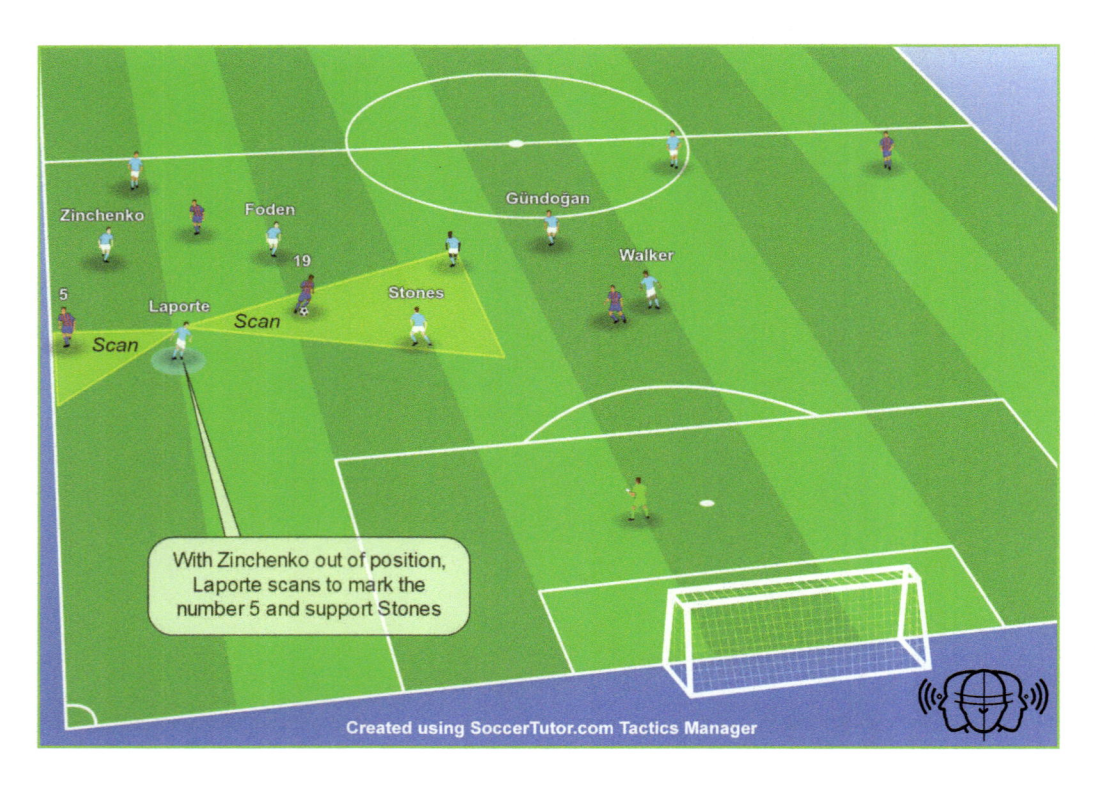

Diagram 1: Zinchenko, Foden, Gündoğan, Walker, Laporte, Stones (No. 19, No. 5) — Laporte scans left and right.

With Zinchenko out of position, Laporte scans to mark the number 5 and support Stones

Diagram 2:

1. Laporte continues to scan (turning head) and maintains the perfect position to mark No.5 and support CB Stones

2. Laporte's scanning and position enables him to tackle No.19, and then launch a quick counter-attack

It is important to note that scanning should be constantly done all over the pitch, in every different position, and by goalkeepers, defenders, midfielders, and forwards.

In this example, we show how Man City's centre back **Laporte** uses scanning to help defend.

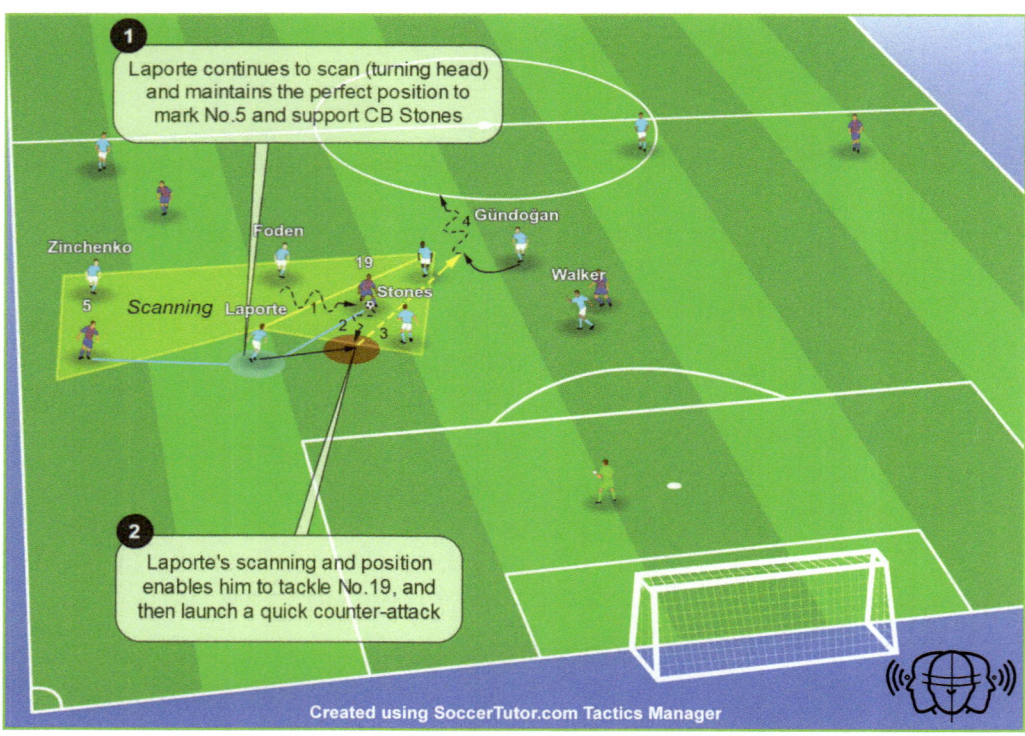

Laporte is in an unnatural wide position as the LB **Zinchenko** is out of position.

Laporte swivels his neck many times to scan left and right so he has a full picture of what is going on around him.

This enables him to cover Nº5, support Stones and then time a very good tackle on Nº19.

SOURCE: Sławek Morawski. [@m1ndfootball]. (2021, August 1). The concept of defensive support [Tweet]. Twitter. https://twitter.com/m1ndfootball/status/1421919868107042824

THE IMPORTANCE OF SCANNING WITH ARSENE WENGER

Speaking at the 2018 Paris Sport Innovation Summit, Arsene Wenger spoke about the importance of scanning, which was reported by Training Ground Guru (see source below). Here are some highlights with references to Geir Jordet's studies (see previous pages for more details into scanning in football:

"Great players isolate from the ball; their head is like a radar."

"As a player, whenever I get the ball, I have to analyse, then decide and finally execute. Perception plays a huge role in this. I worked with a University in Norway [referring to Geir Jordet] to identify how I could improve perception."

"Basically, I came to the conclusion that it is about getting as much information as possible before I get the ball. I call that scanning. I try to see what happens to a player in the 10 seconds before he gets the ball, how many times he takes information and the quality of information he takes. It depends on the position."

"What is interesting is that very good players scan six to eight times in the 10 seconds before getting the ball and normal ones three to four times. That is a major step for improvement."

"However, more important - you have to analyse the quality of perception and decision making. My challenge is to get my players to know which the best choice is and make the optimal decision every time they get the ball."

"The player has to scan and decide. When he has decided, he has to make the best possible solution. This means a compromise between risk and the progress of the ball."

SOURCE: Training Ground Guru 2019 - Simon Austin, Arsene Wenger: Top players have radars in their heads, accessed 6 August 2021, <https://trainingground.guru/articles/arsene-wenger-top-players-have-radars-in-their-heads>.

DE BRUYNE, LAMPARD & RONALDO: "MASTERS OF SCANNING"

Geir Jordet PhD did an interview with Sky Sports about scanning and specifically the top players at it (see source below). Here are some highlights:

Geir tells a story of listening to commentary in a game when **Kevin De Bruyne** assisted a goal for Belgium against Denmark, and not many people were able to see the available pass. There was therefore some conjecture as to how De Bruyne could have noticed the positioning of his teammate Thorgan Hazard. Their conclusion was that he "must have eyes in the back of his head."

Geir told Sky Sports, "I love that example so much. It was a fantastic pass in the end, but they were saying that he had picked the pass without looking. I knew they were wrong even when I was watching it live because I had seen him scan in the build-up to the goal."

"What I have come across a lot is that many of the players who are considered to be really good at scanning share the same story. They were told about it or discovered that it was important at a really early age and when you start early you have an advantage on others."

"Clearly, this was something that **Frank Lampard** was exposed to at a young age but then it became habit. Like all skills, it becomes automatic after a while, and you just do it. That is the case with many of these players. Some of them do this and they are not thinking about it." [Lampard's father spoke about instructing his son to ALWAYS get a picture before receiving.]

"The first player who really showed me how it is done was **Cristiano Ronaldo**. I was watching him live in a Champions League game in Copenhagen some years ago and it struck me so hard that his timing was like a clock, like a metronome that keeps the rhythm.

"If you start this at a young age you will definitely have an edge. I have done training studies where we see that even with adults at a high level, it is quite easy to get a pretty good impact quickly. But you need to work more on it for it to benefit your performance."

SOURCE: SkySports.com 2021 - Adam Bate, Kevin De Bruyne is a master at scanning: Geir Jordet on the science behind the importance of vision and perception in football, accessed 6 August 2021, <https://www.skysports.com/football/news/11096/12341305/kevin-de-bruyne-is-a-master-at-scanning-geir-jordet-on-the-science-behind-the-importance-of-vision-and-perception-in-football>.

INTERVIEW: Torbjörn Vestberg, PhD

Torbjörn Vestberg, PhD

- Licensed Psychologist at PRIMA
- Consultant and Researcher
- Focus: Brain's Executive Functions in Sports
- Works with Elite Football Teams

Can you tell me what your research is about?

My research area is looking at executive functions and its importance for success. So that is actually what my study is about. And why I'm studying in football? You can see it's very good because it's more or less a controlled environment. You have a certain area, and you have a specific goal. Everyone all over the world is agreed what success is, and you know when you are successful, and you know when you fail. And because of that, it's a very good area to understand how the human brain works when you are in a pressurised situation. So, to get a better understanding about the human brain and how it works in the information processing, football is very good.

Here in Sweden, I tested the executive functions of players in men's and women's teams and followed them for three years. We found these players have much higher executive function than the normal population. I also tested players from the best football teams in the world. I tested players from 15 different national teams and the best players in the world, but I cannot tell you more than that because then I go outside confidentiality. The only players I can tell you about are **Xavi** and **Iniesta** because they made a TV program in Japan and they were, at that time, the best midfielders in the world. It is very interesting to analyse the executive function of the best players in the world, especially when it comes to flexibility and creativity - they are at least three standard deviations above the normal population.

So, I don't actually study football, I study the human brain when you are in a limited situation and under pressure and what part of success the executive function has there. So that is what I do.

What is executive function?

Executive function is what handles the information processing. A human being receives a lot of information, and how to handle this information is the purpose of the executive functions.

Interview: Torbjörn Vestberg, PhD

You have different sorts of executive functions. The lower part, the core functions, is about how you can stay in focus and then how flexible we are and how fast we can change between different sorts of targets.

Inhibition is another and this is when you are doing something, but your brain says no, this will not work, you must stop and change what you do. And then you have the working memory and that is like the RAM in a computer, it helps you with the information you have online. So, how much information, and for how long you can hold it online, and what you are going to do with this information.

And then you have higher executive function, where you put these things together to find a creative solution. And to be successful or not depends on how these different parts of the brain collaborate.

What role does executive function play in football performance?

It is interesting because we have actually seen in the second study I did with the elite junior players (from 12 to 19 years old) there was a significant difference in the executive functions. The most successful players had a very good working memory and there was a significant correlation between how successful they were in scoring goals and this executive function.

But when you are a top professional, this is not enough and you must have more, and other things are important too. The first is the inhibition and, for defenders, it's very important as the most successful defenders are very good at stopping and changing their decisions. Most of us make a decision and then go for it but in football, response inhibition is extremely important. For a midfielder or playmaker this is important too, as you must stop and get a new idea if something happens which means your first decision will not be successful. You can decide to pass one way but then a defender comes, and you must change. A striker can be average at this as the inhibition is less important, but he must have very high levels of creativity, be able to take in a lot of information, and be very fast at decision making.

And that is the other thing you need as a top professional, the creativity, which is even more important. When you are a young player, it's OK to just be fast with your working memory and only make one decision because the other players don't think as fast. But later, players at the high level think fast and the opponent does something you have not trained for, so your brain needs the creativity to make a lot of possibilities and sometimes you must find a new solution. And this is not completely experience because, if it's only experience, you cannot do anything new. You have the experience, and you can use it, but sometimes a player does something really unexpected. You must find new ideas and put new things together. You need to have the old experience but from that you can start to do new things. When you look at someone like **Iniesta**, he is much higher than everyone else and only 1 in a 1000 people can think of the number of possibilities he can in a given situation.

So, to be successful in the top of football, you have to be in the right place at the right time and make the right decision. And also change the decision if you need to. This all works by the executive functions. You supervise your behaviour, you change your behaviour. And it's about flexibility. It's about working memory. It's about inhibition. And it's also about creativity to find a new solution.

Interview: Torbjörn Vestberg, PhD

Have you found there's a difference between players?

Yes. In the first study we did in 2012, we compared elite players in the English Premier League with semi-elite players from League One (two divisions below), and we found that the higher level players have better executive function.

We also have a study published last summer and it shows the differences between international players and non-international players from the same club teams in Sweden and the English Premier League. The results showed that there was a significant difference (increase) in the executive function of the international players. And these players are playing in the same Premier League team, and had the same coach and training there, but there is a significant difference. The flexibility and creativity are significantly better for the international players, in general, than for their teammates in the same Premier League team. It would seem that although these players most often play at the same level, to go to the next level and become an international player, you need higher executive function.

Are you born with these abilities, or can you develop them?

I think you must think in both ways here. Yes, you are born with it in one way but of course you should train, you must train, you must practice, because you must develop what you have. And no one can actually say today where the limit is.

Should coaches look to challenge and develop these aspects in their players?

Of course. As a coach, it's your job to develop the players in every area, and you should try to develop their executive function. As you don't know where the limit is, I think it's important for the coach to start to think about inhibition, flexibility, working memory and creativity, and how to develop that.

But today, we actually don't know how much you can develop. What we know so far through studies is that it's possible to develop via physical or cognitive training. If, for example, you are average, you can maybe come up one standard deviation with this training, and maybe you can reach even higher.

The difficulty here is that you are trying to develop players for the unknown and a lot of coaches work to help them only with the known. I know a lot of coaches that work always with technique, and it's interesting that they don't even talk about executive function because they think it's all about technique. But you can be the most wonderful player with technique, and the ball can actually be a part of your body, but if you don't, in that millisecond, understand where to stand, before anyone else understands where the ball will go, it doesn't help you.

So, you should start to think about how to develop inhibition, how to develop flexibility, and how to force the player's brain to start to be under pressure in this because you must have these important factors.

And even if you're not so good at them, you can learn ideas and build compensating strategies. And that is a very important issue here. Actually, I think that is the key thing here. It's not the strongest person that will be the most successful and it's not the fastest person that will be the most successful, it's the one that can adjust and build good compensating strategies.

Interview: Torbjörn Vestberg, PhD

What are your thoughts on the Soccer eyeQ practices?

When I saw the practices, I thought yes, they would challenge the players, because they really challenged me to understand. And I don't mean anything bad when I say this, not at all, it is good, because you really have to force your brain into new areas to improve. If it's too easy for you, there's no challenge, so you must make the challenge for the brain and a good coach knows how to take it step by step to learn these things.

And what I could recognise in these methods was that it looks like it challenges inhibition, flexibility, working memory, and creativity. And it challenged these factors all at the same time. So, it is really challenging for the brain, and I can see from this idea and theory what you are trying to accomplish, that it was really good.

And I like when you do these practices, you do it as football. There's a lot of ideas for how to develop the brain, especially when it comes to the working memory, and you have these gadgets. And what we have seen is that, yes, you developed the working memory on that gadget, on that app, but it does not transfer to how you play the game. That is the problem.

When you start to practice, what actually happens is you build new pathways in the brain. It's in the same way as you build muscle, when you take weights, and you build more muscle fibres and get stronger. It's actually the same way when you are working the brain, you build new pathways, you build a network, and you develop the network to be stronger and quicker for what you are training.

So, when you do that, it's important that everything is as much like football as possible, because you put it into the memory and when you're in that millisecond moment in a game, in a situation where you must handle a new way, you go back into the brain and into the memory. And if you practiced these things not in football, it would be difficult to find it, as you would go to the wrong storage. So, I think, because we have not found this, how to make this transfer effect, you should do it as close to real football as possible. So, this [Soccer eyeQ practices) is actually very good.

SECTION 1

The Soccer eyeQ Methodology

Soccer eyeQ Decision Making Model

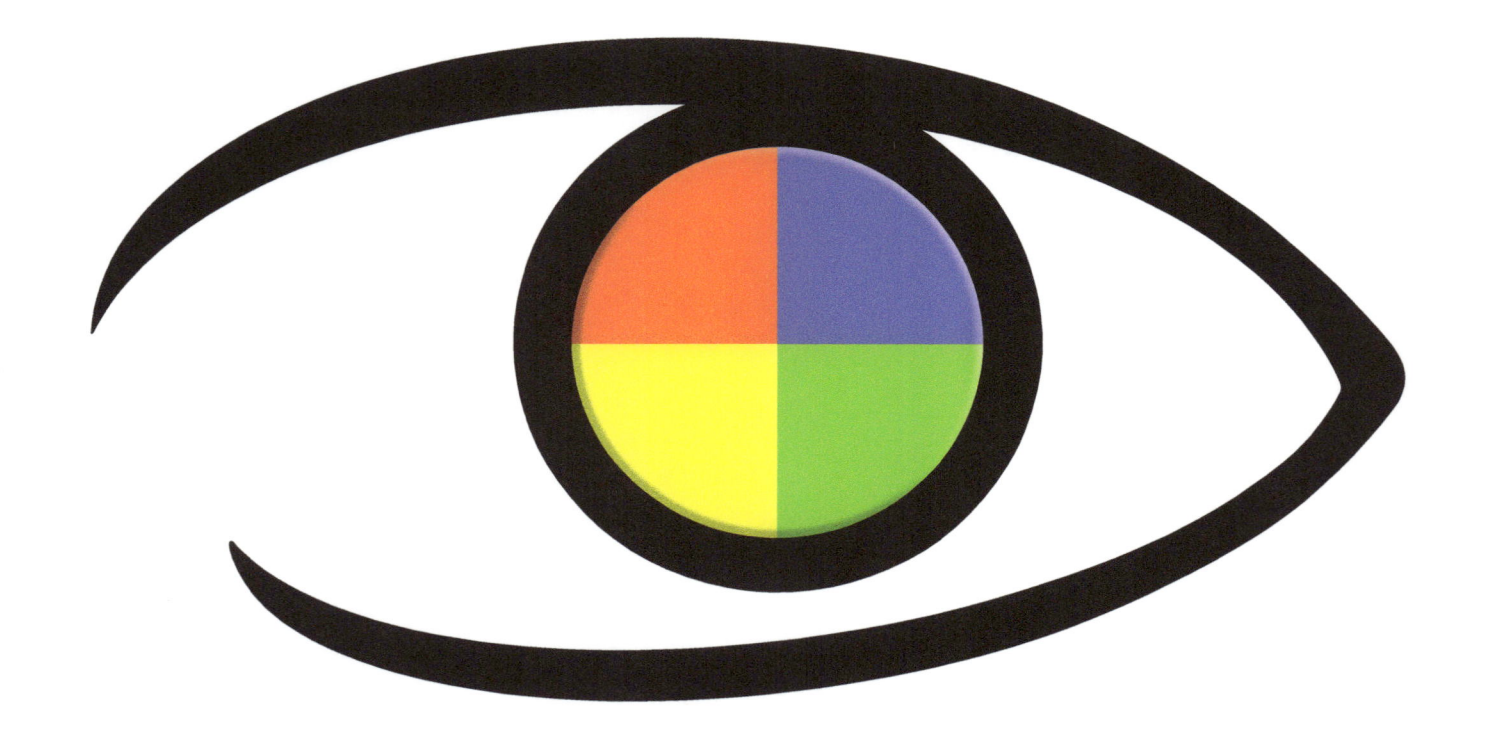

DECISION MAKING AND ITS IMPORTANCE IN FOOTBALL

Good decision-making is crucial to the performance of the player, and the team, and it is one of the skills consistently ranked at the top by coaches when asked what attributes they want their players to have. I would like you to take a moment to consider how important you believe decision-making is and mark your rating on the scale below.

During my coaching clinics and presentations, I ask this very question and I almost always get told it's a 10 – it is a "must have." In fact, I am "almost always" told it is a 10 as there is usually a coach or two who will (partly joking) even give it an 11. And, if I'm being honest, I am not really going to disagree with them!

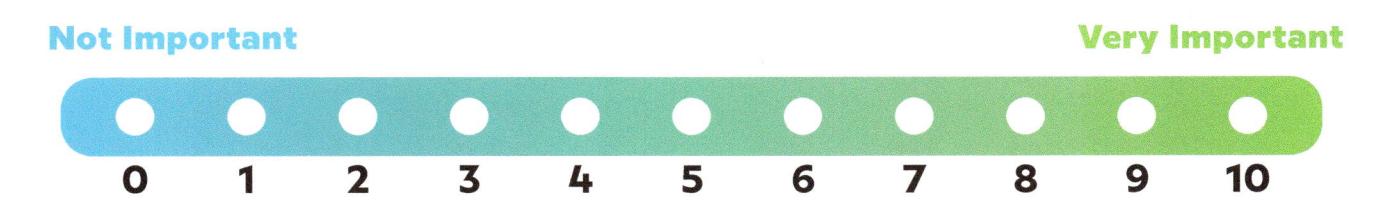

Not Important ———————————————————— **Very Important**

0   1   2   3   4   5   6   7   8   9   10

The Importance of Decision Making in Football

A colleague of mine (Watt Nicoll) talks about decision-making during his presentations on the UEFA Pro and A Licence courses for the Irish FA. Watt has worked with teams and coaches at the very highest levels of the game, and he is one of the most dynamic, engaging, enthusiastic, and insightful presenters I have ever seen. I enjoy his sessions every year and I always come away feeling invigorated, knowing that I have, yet again, learnt something new.

In one of his presentations, Watt asks the coaches to come up with a list of 10 things they believe are "must haves" in players. He then asks the group to identify these "must haves" as either mental or physical. In almost all of these sessions at least 80% of these "must haves" are identified as mental, with the vast majority directly linked to decision making.

Think about it this way, players will make far more decisions than passes, dribbles, or shots over the course of a game. Decision-making does, of course, guide the execution of those actions with the ball. However, decision-making also directs a player's on-the-ball AND off-the ball game actions.

This means decision-making also steers actions such as when to press, when to drop back defensively, and when to support the attack by making overlaps or third man runs, etc.

In fact, playing the game involves a continuous series of decisions on how to manage the space in relation to the ball, your teammates, your opponents, and what to do with the ball when you get it.

Good decision-making is crucial to elite level performance. So, with all that said, maybe some of those coaches are right and maybe decision-making is an 11 after all!

How do Players Make Decisions?

There are numerous models on decision-making which have been well-researched and publicised, and they offer varying degrees of complexity and a number of stages.

Gary Klein's (cognitive psychologist) recognition primed decision model and John Boyd's (strategist) OODA Loop are two such models out there.

Klein's research into naturalistic decision-making is fascinating and his book, *Sources of Power*, is well worth a read. His recognition primed decision model, which was based on initial research on firefighters, and is a useful model of how people make quick decisions in time-pressured, dynamic situations, with imperfect information and changing goals. There are a number of variations, which offer flexibility for specific circumstances, but the primary model has 4 main stages:

1. **EXPERIENCE SITUATION**
2. **IS SITUATION TYPICAL?**
3. **RECOGNITION**
4. **IMPLEMENT ACTION**

The basis is that if they have encountered a similar situation before, they can access that information to produce a fast decision. Therefore, the more experienced you are, and in a football context the more you train & play, the quicker and better your decision making will be.

John Boyd's OODA Loop contains four independent yet connected loops:

1. **OBSERVE**
2. **ORIENT**
3. **DECIDE**
4. **ACT**

These 4 loops encourage good decision making where people think critically, anticipate threats, and neutralise them. A football coach named Larry Paul has put together some fantastic presentations on Boyd's work, which are freely available and offer a great insight into the model and some excellent detail on its application.

More recently, Dr Leonard Zaichkowsky and Daniel Peterson proposed a model specific to sports in their book *The Playmaker's Decisions*. Len and Dan developed the Athlete Decision Model, which has two dimensions and six components:

1. **TRAITS**
   a. Attention
   b. Cognition
   c. Emotion
2. **CONSTRAINTS**
   a. Rules
   b. Time
   c. Tactics

I think their work is excellent and both *The Playmaker's Decisions* and their first book *The Playmaker's Advantage* are must-reads for any coaches interested in this aspect of performance.

If we truly believe decision-making is that important, then we should try to be as knowledgeable about it as possible. I strongly recommend all coaches have a look at these resources and investigate the concept of decision-making.

On the following pages, I am going to show the model that I use for decision-making in football and explain the rationale behind it. It only has three main components and is a multi-dimensional cycle, as opposed to the simple linear or unidirectional models that are commonly associated with decision-making.

Let's start by having a look at the three main components on the next page...

THE 3 FUNDAMENTAL COMPONENTS OF THE DECISION MAKING MODEL

Decision-making is an incredibly complex process and, as I mentioned previously, different models have varying degrees of complexity and number of stages or components. For the purposes of applied football coaching, I like to use a simplified decision-making model that I have refined into three fundamental components:

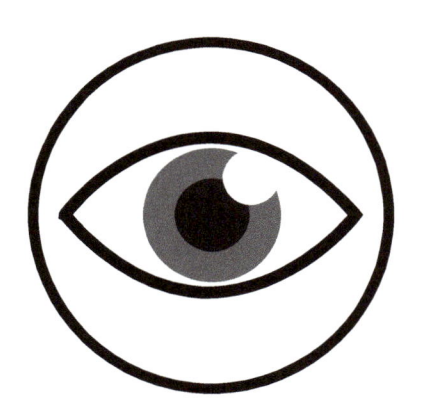

1. SEE

This is the use of the eyes to take in information from the game picture. In some models, it is sometimes referred to as the "input" or "perception" stage. Whilst players may make use of their other senses, it is the visual system that dominates and the vast majority of game decisions are based on visual triggers – in football, the eyes do indeed lead the body.

2. THINK

Based on the information and opportunities available, the player will make a decision on an action to carry out. Whilst the focus is often on what the player does with the ball, it is important to remember that most players do not have the ball for around 97% of the game!

Therefore, informed decision-making should direct both on-the-ball (such as, to pass or dribble) and off-the-ball actions (such as, to move or hold position).

3. PLAY

This is the game-action phase of the model, normally considered as the "output" of the process, and is the execution of the technique, or movement, which the player has chosen to perform. This is the outcome that we all see, and how the player's performance is normally judged, but it is a product of the entire process. Therefore, as coaches, we must ask if we have helped the players develop their "See" and "Think" skills, not just their technical abilities.

THE BASIC DECISION MAKING MODEL 1.0 AND ITS LIMITATIONS

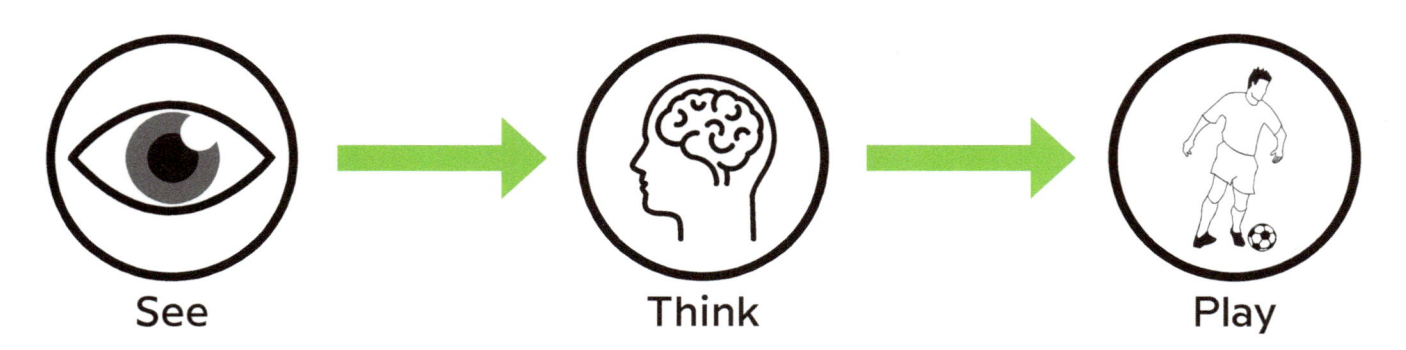

See → **Think** → **Play**

Now that I have identified the three components (see, think, and play), let's see how they fit into decision-making. To avoid any direct comparison to the work of any specific researcher or author, I will simply call the model's 1.0 and 2.0.

Decision Model 1.0 is the most basic version of a decision model and how it is commonly illustrated. It runs sequentially left to right, with each component simply acting to feed forward to the next. Information comes in (see), is passed on to be processed (think), and the whole thing is completed with the execution of the selected game-action (play).

This type of model functions strictly linearly, with a clear start and end. While it offers logical structure, it is not the best way of thinking about decision-making in football. The game is not a series of "start and stop" events, it is a continuous flow of action in an environment that is dynamic, which often seems chaotic.

Nevertheless, the model does fit in with what most coaches will be telling their players, which is to have a look and know what you're going to do before you get the ball. Despite what the coaches are telling them however, it is not how most players actually play.

THE AVERAGE PLAYER'S LIMITED DECISION MAKING PROCESS

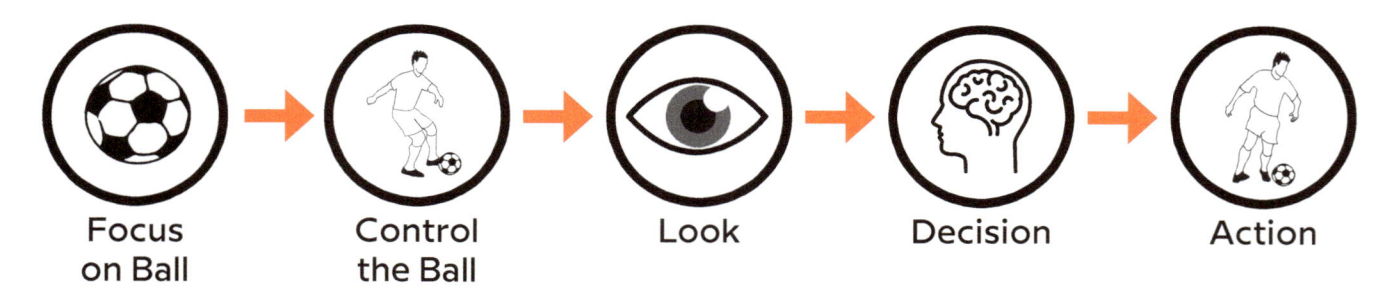

Focus on Ball → **Control the Ball** → **Look** → **Decision** → **Action**

Here, I have adapted the model slightly to show a more accurate reflection of the average player's decision-making process:

The average player often waits to receive the ball before getting into the decision cycle. If you watch the average player, they focus intently only on the ball, **THEN** they control it, **THEN** they have a look, **THEN** they decide what to do, **THEN** they execute the game action. This is clearly not what we want but it is how most players play, most of the time.

Soccer eyeQ Decision Making Model

These players have failed to engage in the proactive strategies required to continually refresh their knowledge of the game picture or optimise their body position. It is this aspect of performance that is so fundamentally lacking in a lot of players, which results in severely depleted game awareness and has a huge impact on the quality of their decision-making.

As a result, the **player is not prepared (physically or mentally) to be as efficient and effective as possible with the ball, as they aren't aware of the most up-to-date (and best) information** and, usually, they have not been able to optimise their body position in order to be as efficient with the ball as possible.

Furthermore, **once they have executed their game-action, they tend to think their job is done**. This is the critical moment where too many players switch off, albeit briefly, and fail to follow-on with the next phase (see) as quickly as they should. Instead of moving and scanning, they have a habit of focussing on the ball and watching to see not only the outcome of the game action they have just performed, but also spend time watching the player who now has the ball.

These players fail to be consistently effective for a number of reasons, including:

- **Failure to see opportunities** – windows of opportunity can be open for the briefest of moments before they slam shut again. If you don't look, you won't see them.

- **Tempo of their play is too slow** – they only look after they get the ball, so they need time to do the next action. It may only be fractions of a second but, at the highest levels, it is these fractions that make all the difference.

- **Allow the opposition to react and defend effectively** – the slow tempo, which is usually coupled with a lack of incisive actions that hurt the opposition, result in more attacks being ineffective and more turnovers of possession.

- **Poor support in both attack and defence** – the players' fail to optimise their off-the-ball positioning and, as a result, they fail to join in the attacking play and are regularly caught out of position defensively.

As I have mentioned, I think the linear start and stop type model is unsatisfactory when you consider the nature and demands of the game. I also feel the one-dimensional nature of this linear and sequential decision-making model fails to give a real sense of how the abilities and limitations in one component affect performance in the others.

KEY POINT: The elements of decision-making in football (see, think, play) work in a loop and are all connected, plus all affect each other - it is certainly not a model where you move from one level to the next.

Let's now have a look at a model that I think is closer to what decision-making performance in the game should be like (**please see the next page**).

Soccer eyeQ Decision Making Model

NEW DECISION MAKING MODEL 2.0:
A Cycle of Interactive Elements

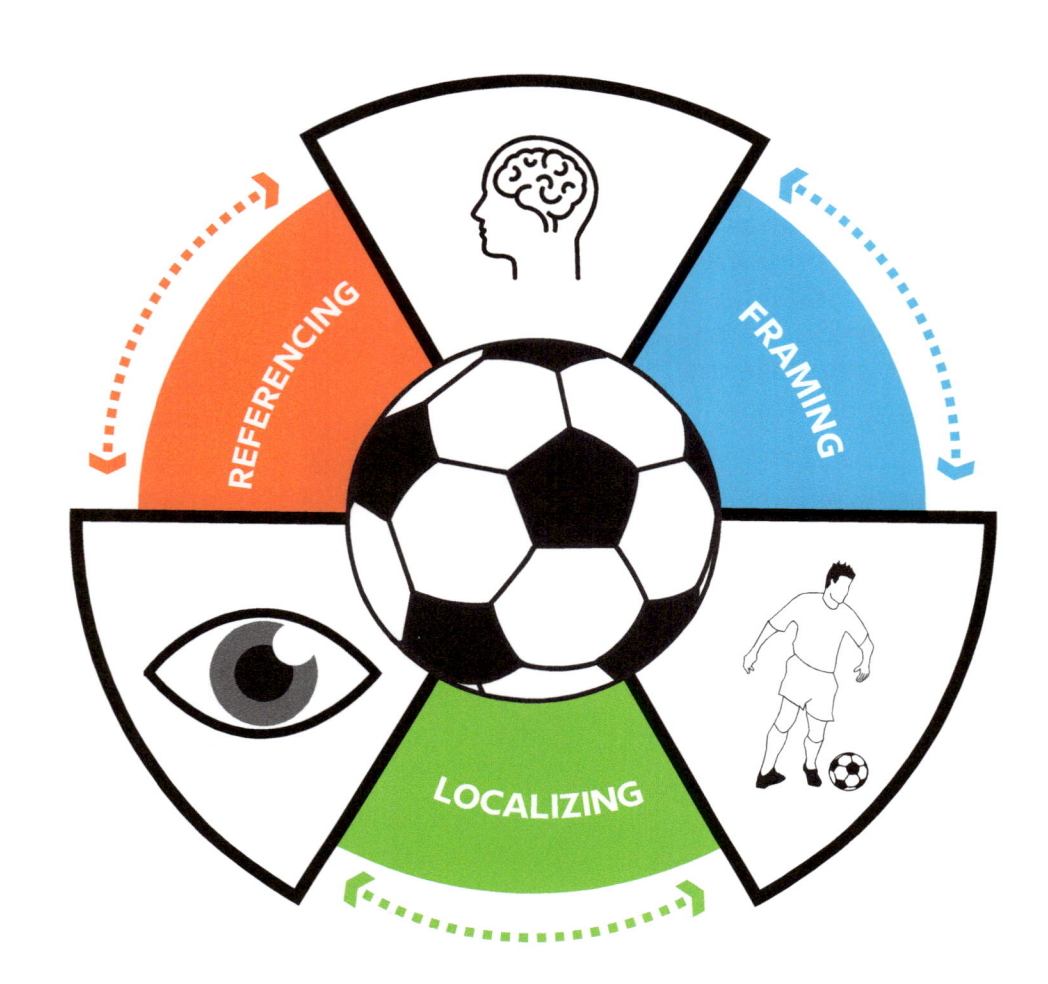

[Diagram: A circular model with a soccer ball at the center, surrounded by three segments labeled REFERENCING (orange, with brain icon), FRAMING (blue, with player icon), and LOCALIZING (green, with eye icon), connected by curved arrows indicating a cycle.]

Instead of sequences or linear processes, I prefer to consider decision-making as much more of a cycle of interactive elements.

Decision Model 2.0 is a multidimensional model in which **see**, **think**, and **play** are all active influencers upon each other through processes I call **referencing**, **framing**, and **localizing**.

More detail will follow but here is the simplified logic in short:

- What we see (picture) influences how we think AND what we think influences how we see (interpretation).

- How we think influences what we play (action) AND how we play (action options) influences what we think.

- How we play (action capabilities) influences what we see AND how we see influences what we play (action).

As I mentioned, this is a simplified version of the logic and there is a lot more to the decision-making process than this, but the main point is that the components do not work in isolation from each other.

Instead, decision-making is a holistic (complete) process that is a product of who the player is, and what their capabilities are, interacting with the game environment.

Soccer eyeQ with SoccerTutor.com   54   SCANNING - How to Train it

Soccer eyeQ Decision Making Model

REFERENCING:
Signals, Situations, and Scenarios

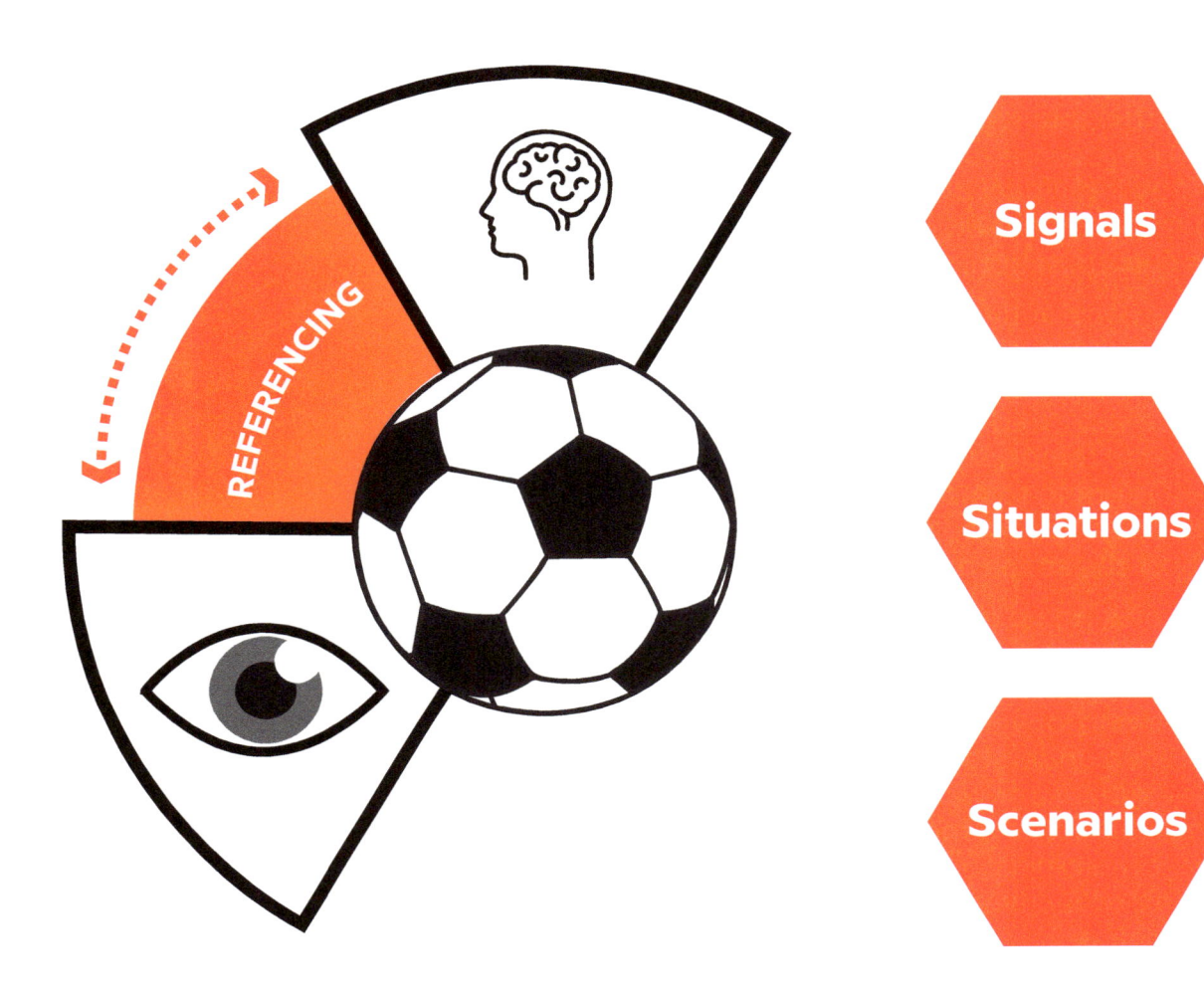

Signals

Situations

Scenarios

REFERENCING = The brain compares and contrasts the game picture against a bank of memories from your accumulated training and playing experience.

During the game, there are 23 dynamic variables (player, teammates, opponents, ball) constantly on the move in a large playing area, with an infinite number of permutations, where no two situations are ever exactly the same. Within all this chaos, how can a player possibly make sense of what he sees and anticipate what may happen next?

When you look around in the game, the brain immediately tries to make sense of what you see through a process I call **referencing.** In the blink of an eye, the brain compares and contrasts the game picture against a bank of memories from your accumulated training and playing experiences.

Whilst this is actually an incredibly complex process, with numerous theories on how it is done, we will quickly look at three key strategies that are used to achieve this:

1. **Signals**
2. **Situations**
3. **Scenarios**

Soccer eyeQ with SoccerTutor.com   55   SCANNING - How to Train it

Signals
Non-verbal cues of teammates and opponents

It has been shown that **elite players are able to detect subtle body cues, which indicate a player's intentions, and use these to anticipate what they are likely to do next**. The recognition of these signals given off by individual players, and acting upon them, is commonly referred to as advance cue utilisation.

Players are constantly trying to read their opponents so they can counteract them by closing off any opportunities before they can be exploited. The players will be trying to read things, such as where an opponent is going to move with the ball, or who they are going to pass to, so they can shut off the space or intercept the ball.

However, picking up on these signals is not just restricted to the reading of an opponent's intentions. Players also read these essential nonverbal cues offered by teammates to understand what they are either going to do, or want to do next, such as the timing of a movement or pass. These become crucial for the team to inform their collective decision-making and positioning.

Situations
A memory bank of similar situations that act as a template for decision-making

Players interpret the overall game picture through the positional relationships of the ball, their, teammates, and their opponents on the pitch. Research has shown that **elite players do not just see individual players in isolation, and instead see groups of players together**.

During play, players build an internal map of where their teammates and opponents are, and detect patterns that are familiar to situations they have seen before. While no two situations are ever the same, there are many very similar ones and these work as recurring templates for decision-making. This internal mapping and pattern recognition enables the player to quickly identify the opportunities and threats of the game situation.

Scenarios
Pre-planned reference points that trigger specific tactical plans

The brain is not just passively waiting to interpret patterns and then trying to match them to previously experienced situations. Instead of waiting to see the game picture and then choosing a solution that fits the situation, the **players are actively looking for the cues for specific scenarios based on the team's strategic and tactical plans**.

This is why many coaches run "patterns of play" type practices, which are designed to build a bank of scenarios that the players can use as a reference. They work as interactive positional maps encoded with explicit cues that trigger certain actions or movements.

These game plans and patterns will guide the players active scanning to search for the predetermined triggers to see if the pattern of play is on or not.

These scenarios establish the critical nonverbal communication required to develop shared expectancies, and offer globalized team solutions. And as soon as the players recognise one of these predefined scenarios, they will automatically (in theory) execute the coordinated game-actions required.

Soccer eyeQ Decision Making Model

FRAMING:
Tactical, Technical, and Tendencies

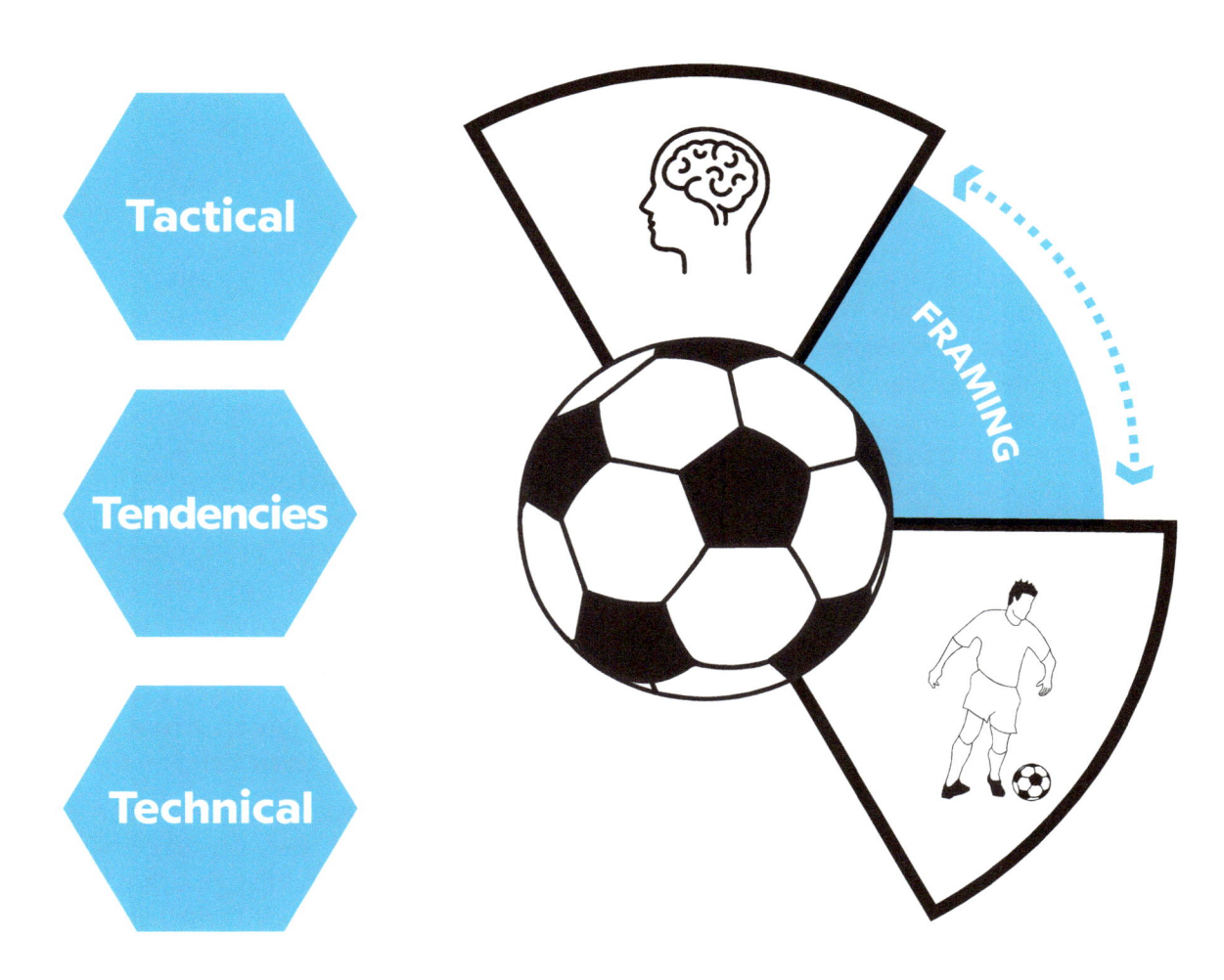

- Tactical
- Tendencies
- Technical

FRAMING = The context that constrains the decisions and actions the player will make.

The execution phase is usually portrayed as a passive element, one which is only thought of as the outcome of the decision-making process.

However, in the **Decision Model 2.0** it is considered that, whilst players process the "see" information to make a decision on what action they will carry out, the range of actions they will realistically consider during the "think" stage is limited by a process I call **framing**.

As before, I keep things simple by focussing on the three key areas:

1. **Tactical**
2. **Tendencies**
3. **Technical**

Soccer eyeQ with SoccerTutor.com

57

SCANNING - How to Train it

Tactical
The game model of the team

The coach's direction to the players and the **game plan of the team will constrain the game-actions the players are likely to consider in any situation** – these are the **"tactical frames"** the player will operate within.

The tactical plan outlines the players roles & responsibilities.

Some coaches may be insistent on what players should do in certain situations, such as who to pass to or where to move when the team are in possession, or about a key player or area to close down quickly when the opposition have the ball. Although the player may be capable of doing other things, these instructions will constrain the players' initial considerations of game-actions in those particular situations.

The specifics of a player's roles and responsibilities will usually vary depending on the area of play (e.g. Defensive, middle or attacking third) and, of course the team's tactical plan may depend on the state of play i.e. Winning or losing and the amount of time left in the game.

Technical
Performance capabilities of a player

Each player will likely **only consider those game-actions that are within the range of their own individual capabilities** – these are the **"technical frames"** the player will operate within.

Through their accumulated training and playing experience, players will constantly be assessing their performance capabilities (passing, dribbling, shooting, running speed, etc) and this knowledge will constrain the action-responses each player considers in any game situation.

For example, if a player is capable of passing the ball a maximum of 40 yards, they are unlikely to even consider anything that is beyond that range.

As a player becomes more advanced, this technical component will also increasingly refer to a player's understanding of the strengths and weaknesses of their teammates and opponents.

Tendencies
The default action of a player in given situations

The game picture may offer the player a number of opportunities for action and different players will favour certain solutions when confronted with the same or very similar situation. Whilst these solutions may be influenced by the technical/tactical frame, they are not necessarily determined or constrained by them. Instead, they are simply **a player's preferred game-action, almost their default choice, in any given situation – these are what I call their tendencies**.

For example, a player may find themselves in a situation where they could choose to pass or dribble and, whilst the player may be technically capable of being successful with either solution, they may have a tendency toward the passing solution – whereas another player may be more inclined to dribble and want to take on an opponent 1v1.

Similarly, a player may have a tendency to cut inside or outside with the ball or make a particular type of off-the-ball run in certain attacking situations.

As a player progresses, and gains more experience, they will begin to understand the tendencies of other players (teammates/opponents) and will take that knowledge into consideration when deciding on their own game-action in a situation.

Soccer eyeQ Decision Making Model

LOCALIZING:
Prospecting, Perspective, and Priming

Prospecting **Perspective** **Priming**

LOCALIZING

LOCALIZING = How the players access information, how they perceive it, and how they respond to it as an individual.

It is obvious that what a player perceives impacts on his choice of game-action, but a player's actions, and action-capabilities also affect how the player perceives the situation.

For me, **"see" and "play" are almost intrinsically linked** and influence each other in the **Decision Model 2.0** through a process I call **localizing**.

As before, I keep things simple by focussing on the three key areas:

1. **Prospecting**
2. **Perspective**
3. **Priming**

Soccer eyeQ with SoccerTutor.com   SCANNING - How to Train it

Prospecting
How players look for information about the game picture

How the players make themselves aware of what is going on around them is one of the most important aspects of performance in the game. The players must continually optimise their positioning, and engage in scanning, to enable them to be aware of as much of the key information as possible – this is what I call prospecting.

Fundamentally, what the player is aware of limits what he is capable of perceiving. Therefore, the more key information a player can make available to themselves, the more opportunities for action they will potentially have.

Scanning is, essentially, the simple art of looking around. In some situations the players may be able to observe the information they need with quick eye movements. However, scanning in football usually requires a significant movement of the head, particularly when the players are readying themselves to receive the ball. Research by Geir Jordet PhD has shown that **players who engage in more frequent visual exploration (they look around more) successfully complete more passes**. Of course, what the players look at and the sense they make of it is important but, fundamentally, the more the players look around the better chance they have of being effective.

Frequent engagement in **scanning helps the player to optimise what is sometimes referred to as spatial updating (a mental map of where the other players are)**, which allows them to continuously manage their off-the-ball relationships with the ball, their teammates, and the opponents. These relationships should be constantly fine-tuned until the player is directly involved with the ball (defence or attack).

Then they can be at their most effective because they have the most up-to-date, high value information available and have positioned themselves to take maximum advantage of the situation.

Whenever possible, **players should also have one last look after the pass is played and the ball is travelling towards them**. Obviously, there will be certain situations where this may not be possible, such as short quick passes or when under intense pressure from an opponent. However, **watch the top players in action**. They do it. And **they do it a lot**. It almost seems as if it is **ingrained as part of their receiving skills**.

Positioning is crucial when it comes to the players knowing and understanding what is going on around them. The **players can effectively open-up or cut-off the opportunities they are aware of, as well as how they can exploit them, by adjusting both their position** on the pitch and their body shape.

Good body shape will correctly orientate the player's useful field of view to the most important information, as well as enable quicker and easier scanning toward other key reference points the player wants to see, all of which increases their awareness. A player's body shape when receiving, particularly the positioning of their feet, will also impact on how efficiently they can perform their next game action – this can affect not only the execution but how they perceive any affordances (opportunities for action) in the first place.

The position on the pitch affects the relative degree of affordance available, as it can subtly change how and even if a player can receive the ball, as well as influence what they can do with it next. Just a yard or two can provide more space to exploit, make a pass slightly easier or more difficult, or even bring an extra teammate into passing range.

The position (location) will also affect a player's body shape as it determines the degree of "openness" required to his key reference points – where he is getting the ball from and where he wants to go with it next.

As I mentioned before, the game involves both on-the-ball and off-the-ball actions. With off-the-ball movement accounting for about 97% of a player's overall game actions, prospecting should account for almost all of this 97%.

Perspective
How a player perceives the game situation dependant on their own action capabilities

The term **"Affordances"** describes the **opportunities for action available to a player in any game situation**.

We may assume the same affordances are available to everyone, but they are not. Not every player perceives a game situation in the same way. It is not a globalized picture shared by all and is very much localised to the individual's perspective.

This is because each player has a particular way of seeing the game that is very much dependant on their own ability levels.

Where technical (from framing) referred to the actions a player would consider, perspective refers to how **each player will only detect and see affordances that are within their range of action-capabilities** – a player is unlikely to even notice opportunities that are beyond their scope.

This means that a player's technical proficiency actually limits the affordances that they are capable of detecting in the first place. Therefore, **the greater repertoire of technical ability a player has, the more opportunities they have the potential to see**.

Priming
The situation triggers an automatic response from the player

Players will sometimes (particularly when under intense pressure) carry out a game-action that feels like an instinctive response to the situation they see. This is because the player has experienced something similar before and, with little or no time to think, the situation itself has primed the body to execute a game-action that has been successfully used in similar circumstances.

Whenever the players find themselves in moments like these, the situation (what is happening) acts as a vivid visual trigger to execute the specific game-action. However, that's not to say the action is executed in exactly the same way (as this is almost impossible) and will instead be adapted to suit the circumstances of the moment.

Instead of thinking through a list of all possible solutions, the **player sees things directly through this picture-action filter (of what has worked before) and they intuitively perform the necessary correct game-action**.

Of course, some players may improvise a solution in high-pressured situations. However, the action they execute is usually still based on a technique or skill that they already have a degree of competence in and is simply a variation of that technique.

Whether the solution has been improvised or performed automatically, it could be argued that there is still a decision being made. However, in these instances, it would be done at such a sub-conscious level that the player may not even feel like they actually made a decision in that moment.

DECISION MAKING MODELS
- A CONCLUSION

I believe it is the quality of decision-making that will largely determine what level a player will reach in the game - the more correct decisions he can make on the pitch, the higher the level he will play. However, it is not the aim of this book to go into the detailed complexities of the decision-making process. I have offered a brief glimpse into the concept of decision-making and barely scratched the surface of what is an incredibly important aspect of football performance.

I have identified three main components of a decision model and **Decision Model 2.0** shows how they affect and influence each other. There are many well-researched models with more stages, but I use three components as it simplifies decision-making in the context of coaching. I have also shown how the components look in a traditional linear format, whilst highlighting a couple of areas where I feel that model doesn't properly reflect dynamic decision-making in the game.

Of course, depending on the exact model you refer to, even those in a format similar to the 1.0 model will have feedback loops from one part of the model to another. However, I feel these loops don't illustrate the whole nature of the process and how the components influence each other in everything we do.

I have discussed some of the strategies players use to make their decisions and execute game-actions, but this is not a full list and I have only touched on a few ideas – there are many more theories on the exact strategies employed in decision-making, with plenty of debate on the validity and subtle differences of those theories. There are many overlaps among the different areas I have discussed. This is because decision-making is a holistic (complete) process, and it is not as easy as simply saying you make a decision based on what you see, and you execute an action based on what you decide. It is also not as simple as saying players only use one strategy to make a decision. **Time, space, position of the ball, teammates, opponents, position on pitch, state of play, confidence, and even emotions can all play a part in how a player makes a decision in a particular moment**.

However, I would like to make it clear that Decision Model 2.0 is not the definitive model or superior to anyone else's model, it simply illustrates how I see decision-making in the game. I strongly recommend that coaches also look at other resources too.

Finally, the one essential factor for good decision-making in any situation is awareness. Taking all the other factors into consideration, it is a player's awareness (or lack of) that will determine how effective a decision they can make in the moment. Awareness is the ultimate limiting factor in the decision-making capabilities of the player. Too few players maximise the benefit of the 97% of the game spent off the ball. They fail to engage in active prospecting (a combination of active scanning and body position). This can have a direct consequence on how effective they are with their 2-3% on the ball, as it means they miss good opportunities that they are more than capable of exploiting. This lack of awareness also means they cannot optimise their off-the-ball body position, in relation to the ball, teammates, or opponents, which means they are poorly prepared to offer the most effective support in any attacking or defending situation.

Awareness is the key to good decision-making in all moments of the game, so we will now have a look at a model for that.

Soccer eyeQ Decision Making Model

"Taking the right decision in the right moment. That is the most difficult thing in football."

Pep Guardiola

A Model for Game Awareness in Football

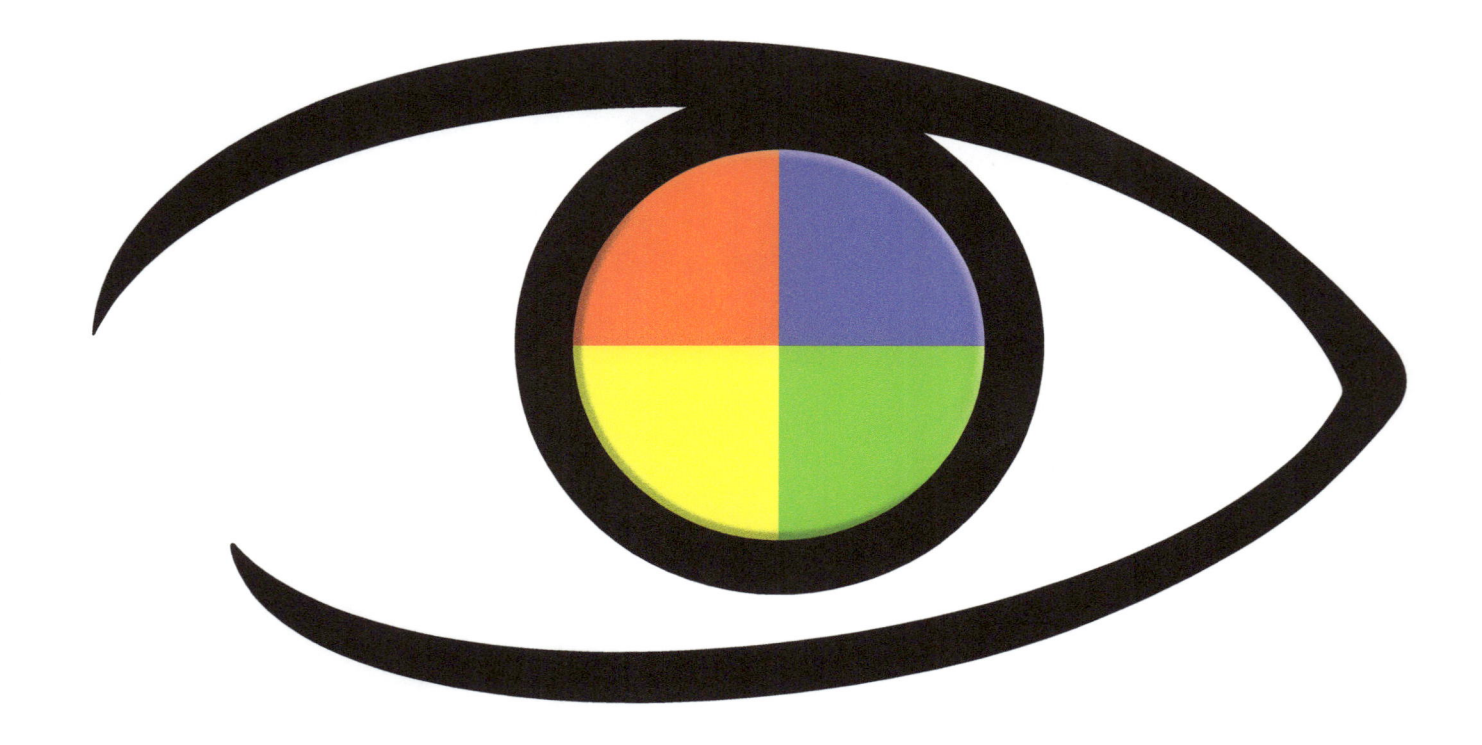

Soccer eyeQ with SoccerTutor.com

SCANNING - How to Train it

GAME AWARENESS AND SITUATION AWARENESS

The majority of football coaches understand that game awareness is an essential component of high-level performance, but it continues to be a somewhat vague concept that is often portrayed as some sort of mystical ability – and you either have it or you don't.

What does "Game Awareness" mean?

Most coaches will at least agree that it involves some degree of being aware of what is going on around you on the football pitch. However, **there seems to be no clear consensus of what it is, what it is not, and how it is achieved**. This has left game awareness as an ill-defined concept, left to our own individual interpretation, with little insight into how to help our players develop and improve it as a skill.

What is "Situation Awareness" and how can it help us with game awareness?

As there is a shortage of research into game awareness and no clear definition, it is **necessary to look beyond football (and sport) to find theories and models that could be applied to the game to help us better understand** what it is.

Fortunately, there has been a lot of research into a something called **"Situation Awareness"**. Although the concept has its roots in aviation, studies have shown that situation awareness is a crucial component of the decision-making process in a wide variety of contexts. In simple terms, situation awareness is about the perception and understanding of what is going on around you and forms an essential part of the decision-making process. Therefore, it is logical to consider game awareness as a form of situation awareness when playing football.

One of the leading authorities in this field is **Dr Mica Endsley, the former Chief Scientist of the US Air Force**. She was a pioneer in modelling the concept and defines **Situation Awareness** as:

"The perception of the elements in the environment within a volume of time and space, the comprehension of their meaning, and the projection of their status in the near future."

Linking with this definition, Endsley designed her renowned three-stage model of **"Situation Awareness"**:

- **Level 1:** Perception of elements in the current situation
- **Level 2:** Understanding of the current situation
- **Level 3:** Projection of the future status

Endsley's work offers a clear insight into what situation awareness is and gives us a well-defined reference point when trying to describe or explain game awareness in football. However, Endsley's model was developed primarily with pilots and air traffic controllers in mind and, whilst it has a much broader application, the majority of the work in this area has been done with operators who read information from static display units positioned to be as easily accessible as possible. Furthermore, any display units positioned outside their field of view are usually secured in a fixed position, so the operator knows exactly where to look as and when needed.

Now, let's look at the contrast between those environments and what a player experiences during a game. For this comparison, we can consider the ball, teammates, and opponents as the "display units" that are the source of information for the player. Instead of being static and easily accessible, the display units are almost always on the move. The relative importance of each of the display units fluctuates during the flow of the game, which means the player has to prioritise depending on the current game situation. The most important display unit(s) in any given situation will rarely stay directly in front of the player, so they will have to adjust their positioning to optimise their viewpoint.

As the player deals with the current game situation, and focuses on the important display for that particular moment, the other displays do not stay in fixed positions. The player never knows exactly where to look (to locate an opponent or teammate behind him) to update his picture as the situation evolves and changes. Therefore, the movement and positioning of the player is a critical aspect of operational game awareness.

All this being said, and whilst Endsley's model may be principally cognitive, I do understand that there is an implied expectation that operators would carry out any physical actions required to access relevant information that is important to the situation.

However, football is played in a 360 degree environment where all the elements are constantly on the move, and a player's body position, in terms of both orientation (body shape) and location (position on the pitch), in relation to the ball/teammates/opponents has a significant impact on what the player sees, how the player reads the game, and the understanding of what they see.

Therefore, it is the degree and the variability of the physical actions required to access relevant information during the flow of the game that means this physical component of positioning has to be explicit within the model for game awareness in football.

A SIMPLIFIED MODEL FOR GAME AWARENESS IN FOOTBALL

Now that we have seen that we can look at game awareness through the lens of the concept of situation awareness (**see previous 2 pages**) and incorporating a physical component, we can now apply a simple three-level model for understanding and developing game awareness, specifically in football.

First, let's have a look at a simplified definition of game awareness:

"Scanning of the playing area, reading the game situation, and predicting how the play is likely to develop."

From this simplified definition, we have the three levels of our model:

LEVEL 1: Scanning of the Playing Area

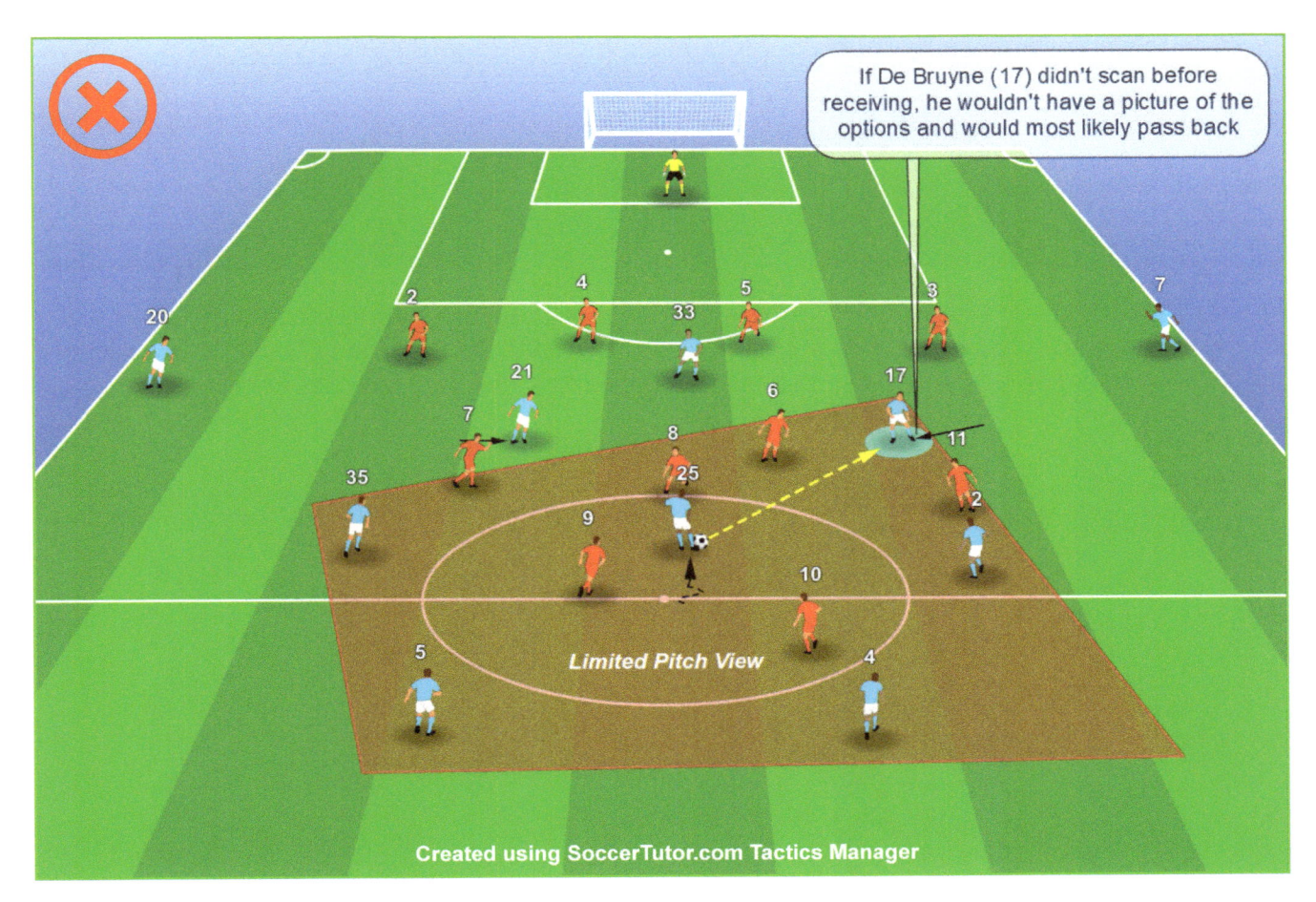

If De Bruyne (17) didn't scan before receiving, he wouldn't have a picture of the options and would most likely pass back

Limited Pitch View

Created using SoccerTutor.com Tactics Manager

Level 1 = Observation is scanning of the playing area, which is done to locate the ball, teammates, and opponents.

In this example, we show what happens if **De Bruyne (17)** didn't scan - he would be unable to see the options ahead of him.

SOURCE: Tactical example of Pep Guardiola's Manchester City team during the 2018/2019 season - from the book: "Pep Guardiola Attacking Tactics - Tactical Analysis and Sessions from Manchester City's 4-3-3," by Terzis Athanasios

A Model for Game Awareness in Football

Scanned Pitch View

De Bruyne (17) has scanned the area before receiving, to see the positioning of opponents and teammates ahead of him

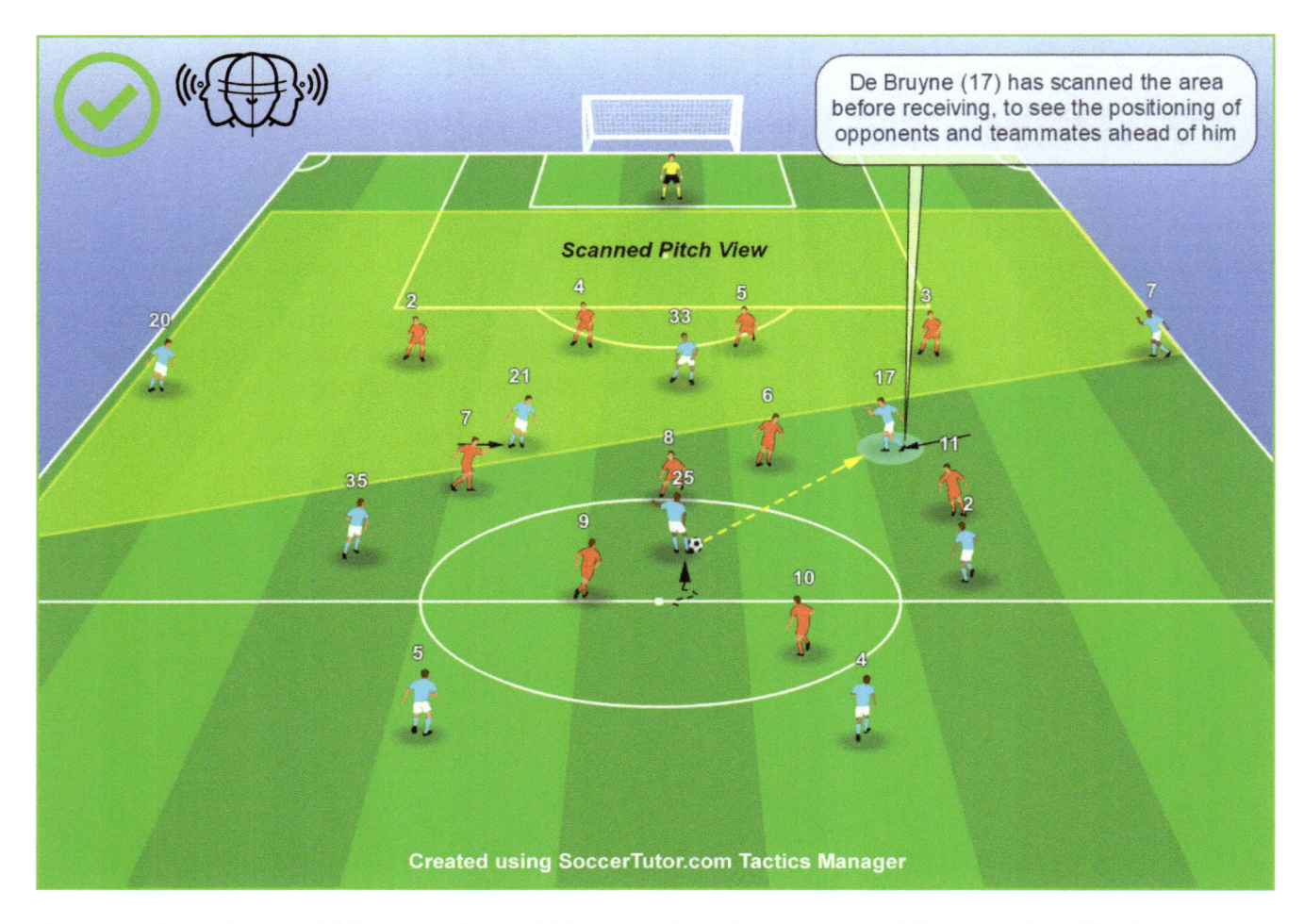

As mentioned, Level 1 is scanning of the playing area, and it is done to locate the ball, teammates, opponents, and space.

In this example, Manchester City's central midfielder **De Bruyne (17)** scans the pitch ahead of him before receiving.

SOURCE: Tactical example of Pep Guardiola's Manchester City team during the 2018/2019 season - from the book: "Pep Guardiola Attacking Tactics - Tactical Analysis and Sessions from Manchester City's 4-3-3," by Terzis Athanasios

A Model for Game Awareness in Football

LEVEL 2: Reading the Game Situation

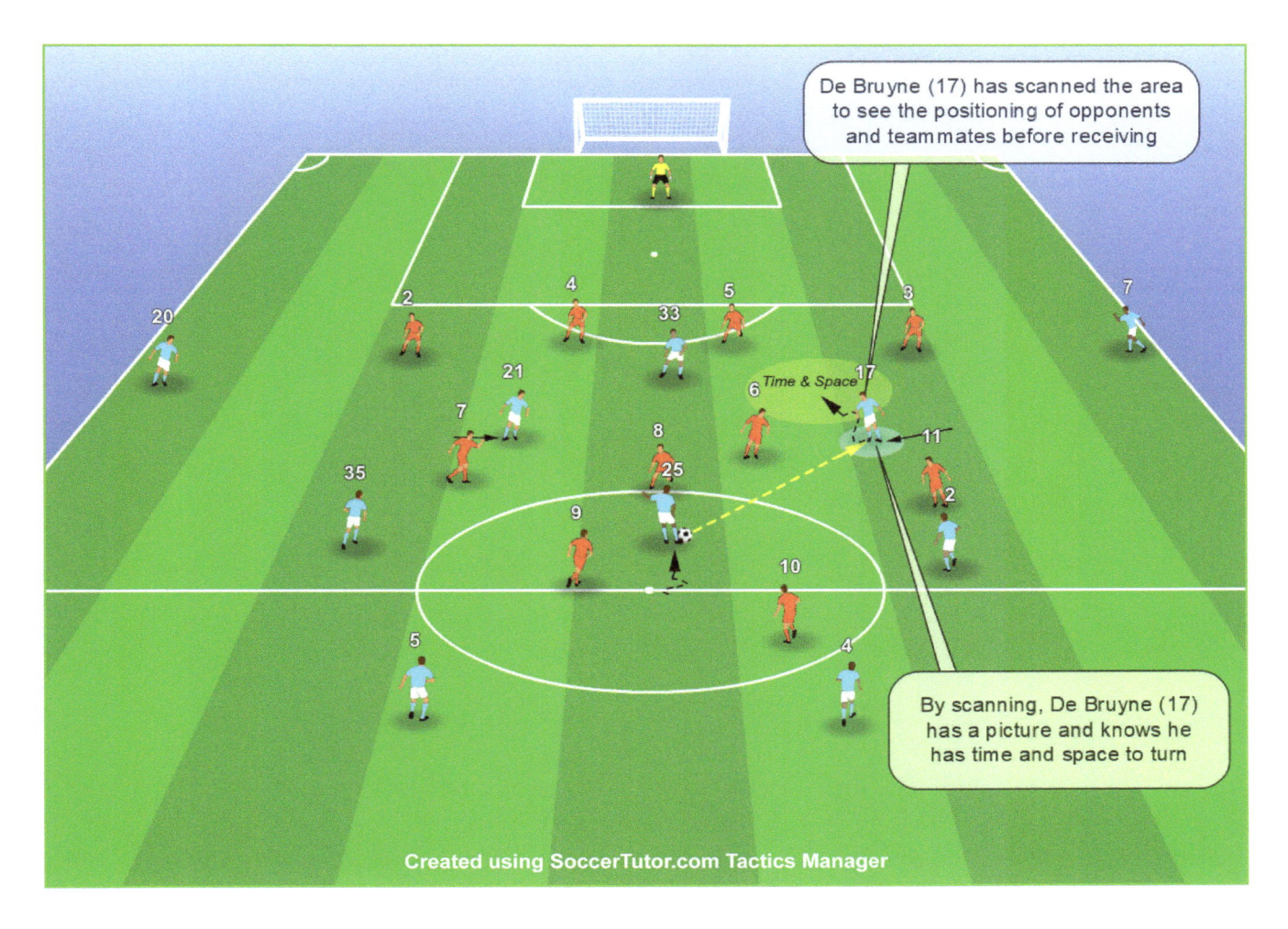

[Diagram: Tactical example showing De Bruyne (17) receiving the ball on the right side. Annotations read: "De Bruyne (17) has scanned the area to see the positioning of opponents and teammates before receiving" and "By scanning, De Bruyne (17) has a picture and knows he has time and space to turn". An area near player 17 is marked "Time & Space". Created using SoccerTutor.com Tactics Manager.]

Level 2 = Realization is reading the game situation, which is where the players understand the context of the information and the current state of play.

As shown in the diagram on the previous page, **De Bruyne (17)** has scanned - moved his head to look around at the positions of his teammates and the opponents ahead of him. When scanning, he takes in a picture of the game (Level 1).

For Level 2 (Realization), the player must then understand the significance of where the ball, teammates, and opponents are positioned. This then enables him to make the best decision.

The key is to recognise patterns and understand the tactical perspective, to see a picture of what is happening.

In this example, **De Bruyne (17)** knows that the opposing defenders are a significant distance away from him and that he has 3 or 4 teammates who could support a potential attack.

He therefore exploits the time and space he has to turn and dribble the ball towards the goal.

SOURCE: Tactical example of Pep Guardiola's Manchester City team during the 2018/2019 season - from the book: "Pep Guardiola Attacking Tactics - Tactical Analysis and Sessions from Manchester City's 4-3-3," by Terzis Athanasios

A Model for Game Awareness in Football

LEVEL 3: Predicting How Play Will Develop

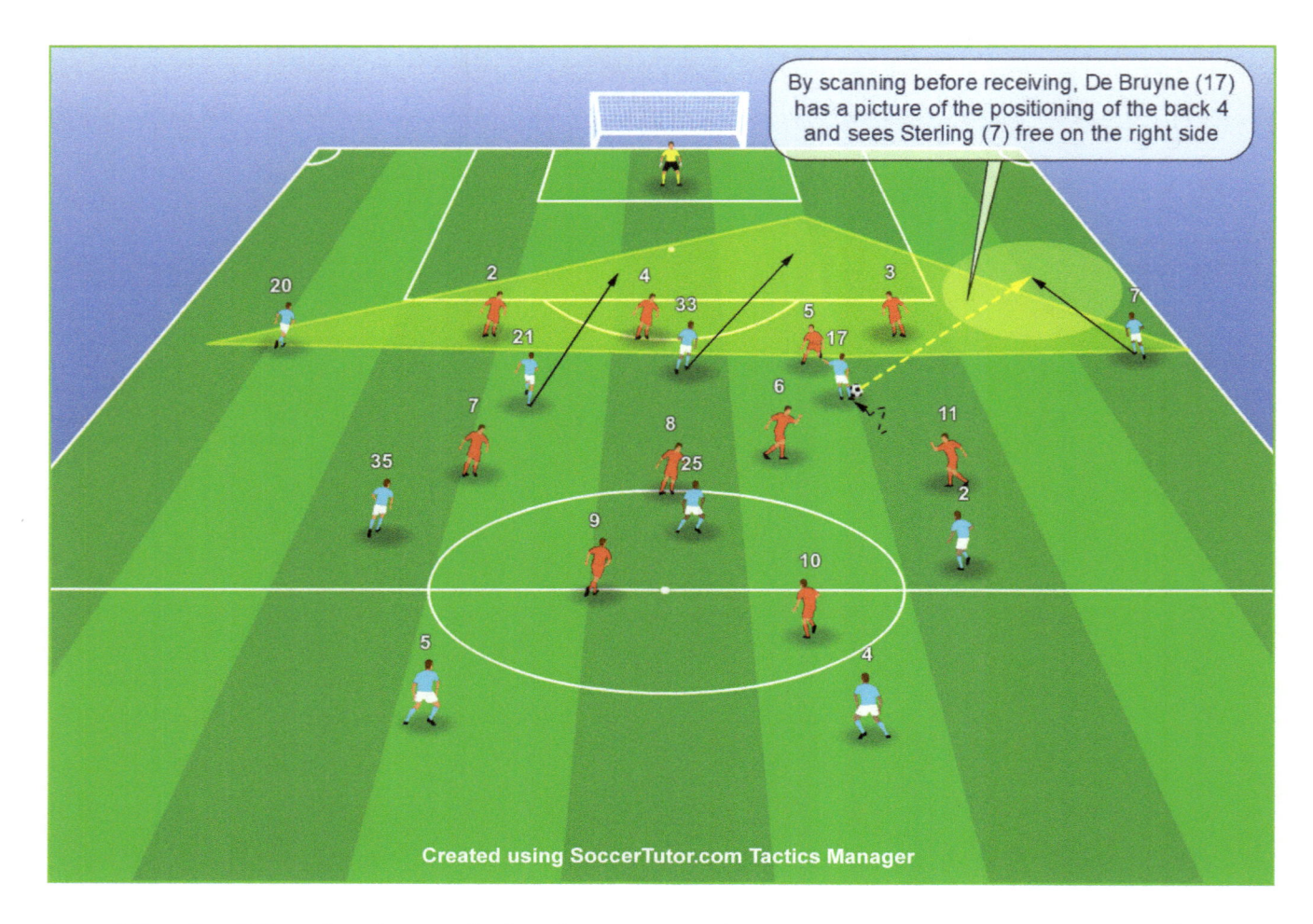

> By scanning before receiving, De Bruyne (17) has a picture of the positioning of the back 4 and sees Sterling (7) free on the right side

Created using SoccerTutor.com Tactics Manager

Level 3 = Anticipation is predicting how the play is likely to develop, which is where players use the current information to foresee opportunities/threats in advance.

Anticipation builds on the first 2 levels, so players not only understand what is happening but also know what may happen next. They must quickly recognise signals and situations to see how play will develop.

In this example, **De Bruyne (17)** was able to see and recognise that the opposing back four is narrow within the width of the box, the left back (3) is moving inside, and the centre back (5) is moving quickly forward to close him down.

He is also able to see his teammate (right forward **Sterling - 7**) free in space out wide and knows he is likely to make a forward run into the space.

Therefore, with all the information **De Bruyne (17)** has taken in and, after assessing the tactical situation, he is able to conclude that the best decision is to pass to **Sterling (7)** in behind the defensive line. From this point, Manchester City have a good opportunity to create a goal scoring chance.

In the next section, I have a look at each of these 3 levels individually and see how positioning is incorporated into each one.

SOURCE: Tactical example of Pep Guardiola's Manchester City team during the 2018/2019 season - from the book: "Pep Guardiola Attacking Tactics - Tactical Analysis and Sessions from Manchester City's 4-3-3," by Terzis Athanasios

"Why does a player have to chase the ball? Because he started running too late. You have to pay attention, use your brain and find the right position."

Johan Cruyff

LEVEL 1 - OBSERVATION: Scanning of the Playing Area

Game Awareness

Observation

Level 1

OBSERVATION (LEVEL 1):
Scanning of the Playing Area

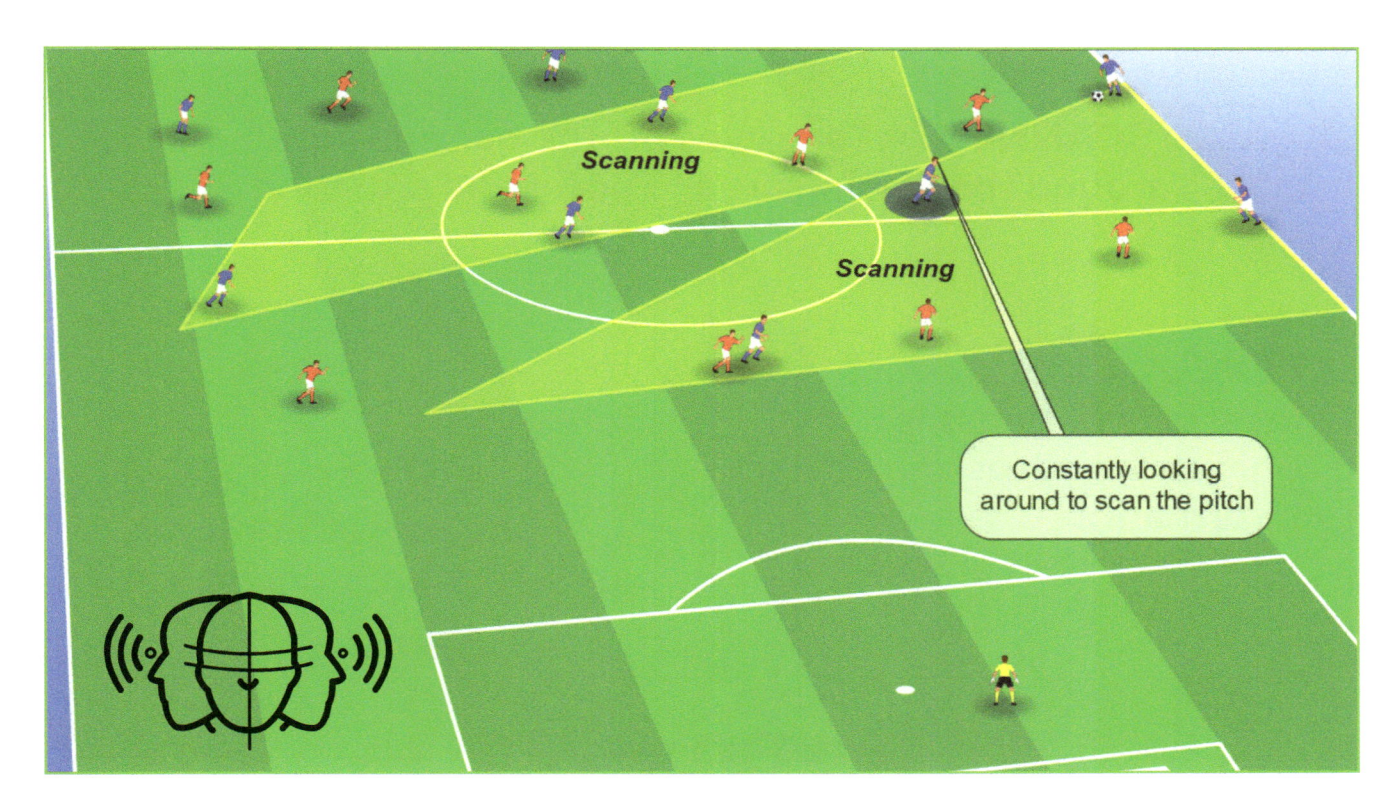

Constantly looking around to scan the pitch

Scanning of the playing area is taking your eyes off the ball to look around the pitch to access information - locate teammates, opponents, and space. In the diagram example, the highlighted player constantly swivels his head to scan and locate the ball, teammates, opponents, and space (to gets a full picture).

In Dr Mica Endsley's Model **(see page 65)**, Level 1 (Perception of the elements in the environment) is considered the lowest level of situation awareness and it is only about accessing information – there is no interpretation of data at this stage.

Similarly, **this level of game awareness is about the player engaging in scanning to locate the ball, teammates, opponents, and space**. It is not about understanding what teammates or opponents are doing or what their intentions are. It is not about recognising patterns and seeing the opportunities or threats. This level is only about **players taking their eyes off the ball and looking around the playing area to access information** (first stage).

It seems so simple but **without this essential skill (scanning) it is highly unlikely that a player will make consistently good decisions**. As a result, they will be poorly positioned off-the-ball and execute inefficient game actions with the ball. This level is so fundamental to overall performance, yet its simplicity makes it too easy to overlook.

The problem is that, because it is not something we consciously think about, we just assume that everyone looks around and that players do it all the time. Maybe players do look around, but do they really do it often or well enough?

KEY ASPECTS OF SCANNING (LEVEL 1)

SCANNING = Take eyes off the ball and look around the playing area to access information

LEVEL 1 = This lowest level of awareness is only about accessing information

LOCATE = Locate the ball, teammates, opponents, and space

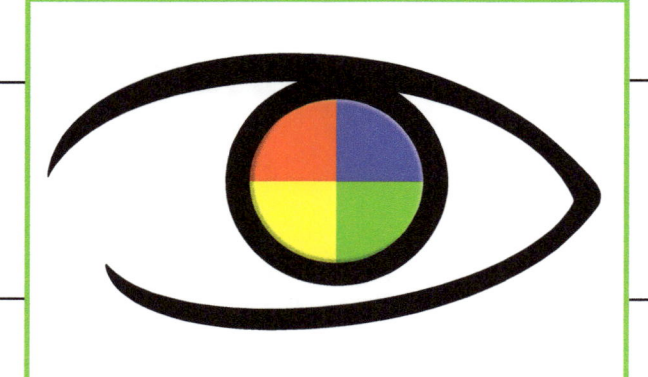

CREATING HABITS = Force the players to look around all the time to improve an essential skill

PANORAMIC POSITIONING = Open up (body shape) to see as much as possible

WHEN TO SCAN AND WHEN NOT TO SCAN

Kevin McGreskin
- Quote from:
Soccer eyeQ Vol.1 Video

When are you meant to look over your shoulder?

"After that pass is played because the important thing is what you're doing in the first fraction of a second when that ball is coming to you. When that ball has been passed, you've got to judge the flight of the ball.

So, you're trying to pick up the information in the ball in that first fraction of a second. So you know if it's coming to the left a little bit? Is it coming to the right a little bit? Or is it coming straight at me? So you can adjust your feet while you're scanning to get in line with the ball."

When are the moments when a player shouldn't scan?

Scanning is a fundamental skill required to optimise performance and the majority of players should scan far more frequently.

However, it's important to understand that it is not just about swivelling your neck at random moments during the game – it's equally important to understand when to scan and when not to scan.

We will identify 5 key moments when a player should scan but, first, let's consider when a player should not look away from the ball:

- A player **should not scan as a pass is being played** (as contact is being made).
- Instead, the player **should be focussing on the ball at that moment**.

- When the pass is played and for the first few fractions of a second afterwards, the player needs the information the ball will offer about the direction and the pace of the pass.

- Once the player has this information, he can then scan as he will know how to adjust his feet and body in order to receive the ball effectively - and he can do this whilst looking away and before he looks back at the ball.

Now that we understand when a player should not look away, let's take a look at 5 key moments when a player should engage in scanning - please see the next page...

Game Awareness Level 1 - Observation: Scanning of the Playing Area

5 KEY MOMENTS A PLAYER SHOULD ENGAGE IN SCANNING

1 As the Ball is Travelling when Receiving a Pass
(As late as possible, as early as needed)

When a player is receiving a pass, he should only scan after assessing the ball. Ideally, he should scan as late as possible, so he has the most up to date information about the game picture, in order to decide on his game action.

However, the player will scan as early as he needs to depending on the opposition pressure that is around him – remember this is the last scan so he should already have made an assessment of his surroundings by pre-scanning (preparation for receiving the pass). Of course, the player may also be able to scan more than once as the ball is on the way and you see some of the top players managing to make two or three quick scans during this key moment.

2 As the Ball is Travelling After Passing the Ball
(As early as possible, as late as needed)

When a player has passed the ball, he should scan as early as possible to assess what's going on around him. This is so he knows where to move, or how to position himself effectively (as quickly as possible). Players who do not do this tend to get caught ball-watching and lose vital fractions of a second where they could gain an advantage against their opponents.

Most of the time, players will have to assess the ball in the first few fractions of a second as it's travelling. However, top players can largely do this by the "feel" of the strike without needing to make a long observation of the ball.

Players may have to leave this scan a little later if they play a poor pass, and therefore have to look at the ball for longer to assess the outcome (consequences).

3 As the Ball is Travelling Between 2 Players
(Teammates or Opponents)

After the ball has been passed and is travelling between two players, nothing else is going to happen to the ball until it has reached the receiving player. Therefore, this is the perfect time to scan.

Obviously, the distance between the two players (and how close the player is to the play) will determine how much time the player will have to scan:

- A **long distance** may mean that the player receiving can make **two or three scans** (to the same or different locations)
- A **short distance** may mean the player can only fit in **one quick scan** just outside the range of his peripheral vision, or possibly no scan at all.

Game Awareness Level 1 - Observation: Scanning of the Playing Area

4. In Between Touches when a Player (Teammate or Opponent) is Moving with the Ball

When a teammate or opponent is moving with the ball, unopposed or with little pressure, the player should scan in between touches, especially when the teammate/opponent is running with the ball and takes touches that move the ball significantly out of their feet.

To clarify, running with the ball is not the same as dribbling, which is used for close control and to beat opponents, and there is almost no opportunity for a player to scan between fast or deceptive dribbling touches.

5. As a Player (Teammate or Opponent) Takes a Controlling Touch

When a player takes a controlling touch, there may be a moment (however short) that provides a player with a quick opportunity to scan.

It should be clear that this is a controlling touch, where the teammate/opponent is maintaining possession of the ball, and NOT a first-time pass, so the receiving player will be using at least two touches.

This moment is a challenging one for players but one they will become better at identifying with experience, as they become better at recognising the signals (postural cues) and reading the intentions of the receiving player.

Game Awareness Level 1 - Observation: Scanning of the Playing Area

SCANNING STUDY 1:
Comparing How Often Premier League Players Look Around Before Receiving Against their Forward Pass Completion Statistics (Geir Jordet, PhD)

High VEB Frequency Players

77% Forward Pass Success

Low VEB Frequency Players

39% Forward Pass Success

VEB = Visual Exploratory Behaviour (Looking Around/Scanning)

Studies have revealed that, even at the top level of the game, there is a **considerable difference in how often players look around and it has a significant impact on their performance**. Have a look at the pass completion rate statistics above and think about which players you would like in your team. I think most coaches would prefer to have the players that complete twice as many passes (High VEB Frequency Players).

This data is taken from Geir Jordet's research into visual exploratory behaviour (VEB) amongst players in the English Premier League. This study investigated how often the players looked around before receiving the ball. The findings revealed that those players with high VEB frequency completed 77% of their forward passes, whereas those with low VEB only completed 39%.

This study only looked at how often players looked away from the ball at other areas of the pitch but did not examine what they looked at or their understanding of what they saw. So, this research investigated what we are talking about as level 1 awareness – scanning.

Some coaches will say players acquire this skill naturally and pick it up playing the game. But if that's the case, why was there such a difference amongst the EPL players in the study? These players have accumulated a vast amount of training and playing experience and are performing at the highest level. Maybe players can develop it "naturally," but will they develop it sufficiently?

Geir's findings clearly show **not all players develop this ability to the same degree and that the best performers do it more than the rest – the players that scanned the most completed almost twice as many forward passes as those who scanned the least**.

SOURCE: Football Network World. "Learning from the Game to Design Drills that Develop Scanning Skills." YouTube, uploaded by Football Network World, 11 Aug 2020, https://www.youtube.com/watch?v=zvHezOqrz_U

Game Awareness Level 1 - Observation: Scanning of the Playing Area

Geir Jordet, PhD: Key Factors of Decision Making and Highest Performing Players

Reference: Jordet, G. (2018) Learn to Anticipate. In Lyttleton, B. (Author) Edge: Leadership Secrets from Football's Top Thinkers. Harper Collins Publishers.

Geir Jordet, PhD breaks down the key factors of decision-making in football into three segments:

- **Visual Perception** – the ability to take in and interpret information
- **Visual Exploratory Behaviour (VEB)** – the ability to actively search and scan for information
- **Anticipation** – the ability to see what is about to happen

Geir is the world expert on scanning and recorded 250 players to analyse their actions before receiving. Players with **over 0.5 scans per second are considered "high scanners."**

Frank Lampard had the highest VEB in the Premier League during the period of Geir Jordet's research.

Increased Visual Exploratory Behaviour (VEB) results in more information. This allows the player to improve their ability to process this information effectively.

Things change within seconds in football and information that was relevant before can quickly become very different. Therefore, those players who constantly update their information and their "picture" can act before others, and gain a big advantage.

Taking about Lampard, Tony Carr (Director of Youth Development West Ham United Academy) said "In his first game for West Ham, his dad (Frank Lampard Sr) would sit in the stands and shout at his son all the time. He'd say the same thing every time: **'Pictures! Pictures!' He just wanted Frank to have a picture in his head before he got the ball. That was all. 'Pictures!'**"

Lampard sat up. "That's true, he was yelling at me and I did what he said."

This showed Geir Jordet that Frank Lampard had indeed not been "born" with a high scanning frequency - he was constantly encouraged to 'take pictures' from a very young age.

0.83 scans per second	**Xavi**
0.75 scans per second	**Fabregas**
0.62 scans per second	**Lampard**

0.61 scans per second	**Gerrard**
↑ **0.5** scans per second	**Messi / Iniesta / Pirlo / Ibrahimovic**

Game Awareness Level 1 - Observation: Scanning of the Playing Area

SCANNING STUDY 2:
Comparing Scan Frequency in Games vs Specific Training Practices (Geir Jordet, PhD)

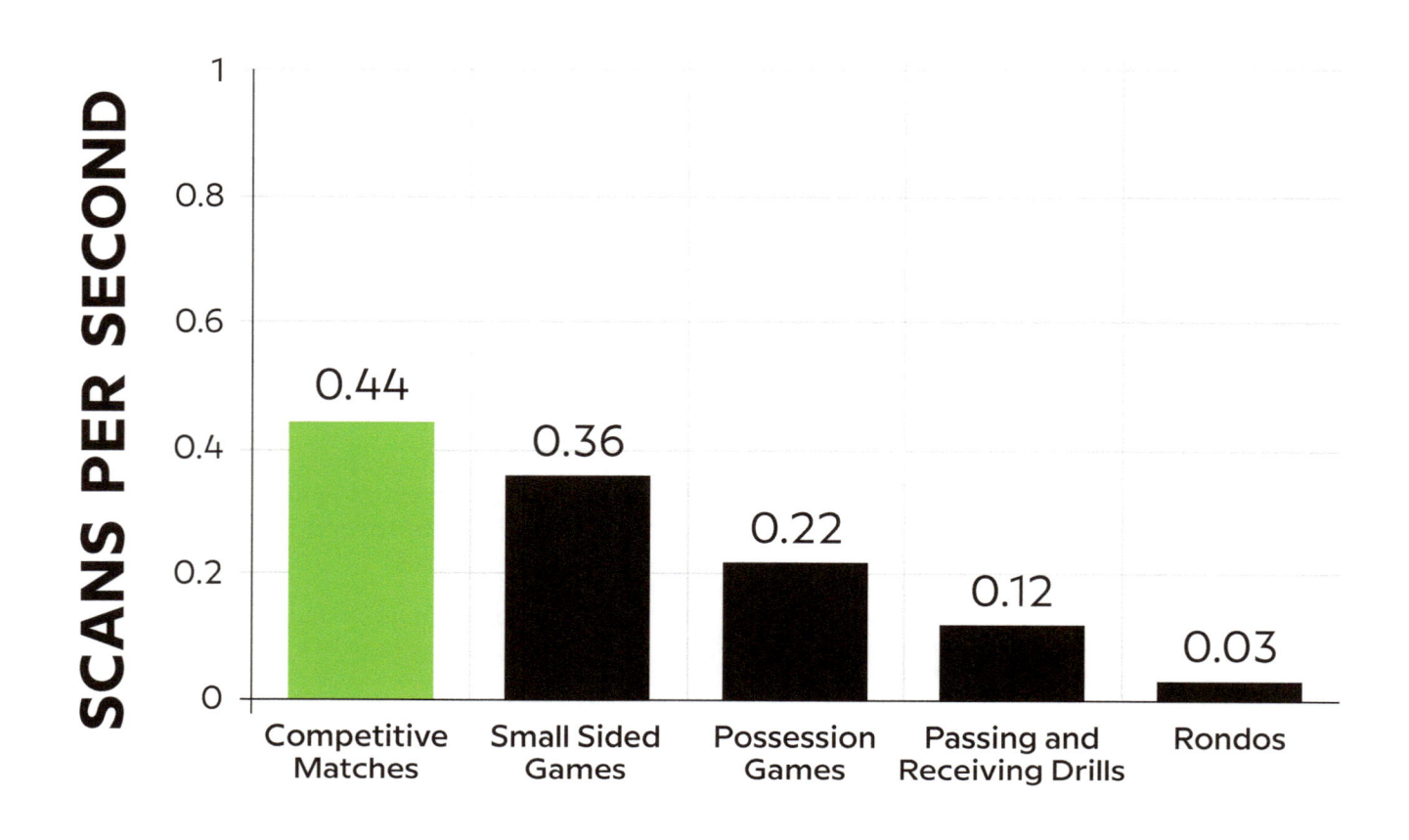

SCANS PER SECOND

Competitive Matches	Small Sided Games	Possession Games	Passing and Receiving Drills	Rondos
0.44	0.36	0.22	0.12	0.03

N = 6 Top Dutch league players (1418 registrations)
(De Vries, Frencken, Hujigen, & Jordet, in review in scientific journal)

This study was with players at FC Groningen (top league in the Netherlands - Eredivisie). It looked at scanning frequency in matches compared with practices in training.

The researchers found that all the practice formats used in training which were analysed produced much less scanning than in competitive matches (based on scans per second).

This clearly shows that **some of the practices we use to train our players do not develop all of the essential habits they need to perform at the top level** in the game.

However, this is not to say they are bad practices, or they shouldn't be used. It simply raises our awareness of the limitations of these different practice formats and maybe challenges us to think how we can adapt them to raise scanning frequency to the level required in a match.

OBSERVATION - SUMMARY

If we want our players to build functional game awareness, it is essential they have the solid foundations here at Level 1 (scanning). The art of scanning cannot be overlooked and must be developed as an intrinsic part of playing. If we leave it to chance, in the hope players will somehow pick it up along the way, then they may end up with deficiencies in their game that can significantly impact their effectiveness on the pitch. As Geir Jordet's study revealed, the more you look around, the more passes you complete. When we are training Observation, it is primarily about helping the players feel comfortable taking their eyes off the ball and **creating the simple habit of looking around on a continuous and consistent basis**.

There are 5 key moments a player should engage in scanning, if possible:

1. As the ball is travelling when receiving a pass (as late as possible, as early as needed)
2. As the ball is travelling after passing the ball (as early as possible, as late as needed)
3. As the ball is travelling between 2 players (teammates or opponents)
4. In between touches when a player (teammate/opponent) is moving with the ball
5. As a teammate/opponent takes a controlling touch

In addition to scanning, we also have the physical component of the model to consider. At this level, we look at what I call **panoramic positioning and we will consider 2 key moments** for the player:

1. Positioning when they are off-the-ball
2. Positioning when they are receiving a pass

When players are off-the-ball, they close off too much of the pitch. Moving just a couple of yards or adjusting their body shape would allow them to see so much more. At this stage, we are simply looking at the players' ability to maximise their field of view by positioning themselves (location and body shape) to see as much of the pitch as possible, as often as possible.

Likewise, when players are receiving a pass, too many restrict their field of view by standing square on to the passer. Once again, this limits how much of the pitch they can see. So, at this stage, we are only looking at the players' ability to consistently adopt an open body shape when receiving a pass relative to where the ball is coming from.

Game Awareness Level 1 - Observation: Scanning of the Playing Area

"Think quickly, look for spaces. That's what I do: look for spaces. All day. I'm always looking. All day, all day."

Xavi

Soccer eyeQ with SoccerTutor.com

SCANNING - How to Train it

LEVEL 2 - REALIZATION:
Reading the Game Situation

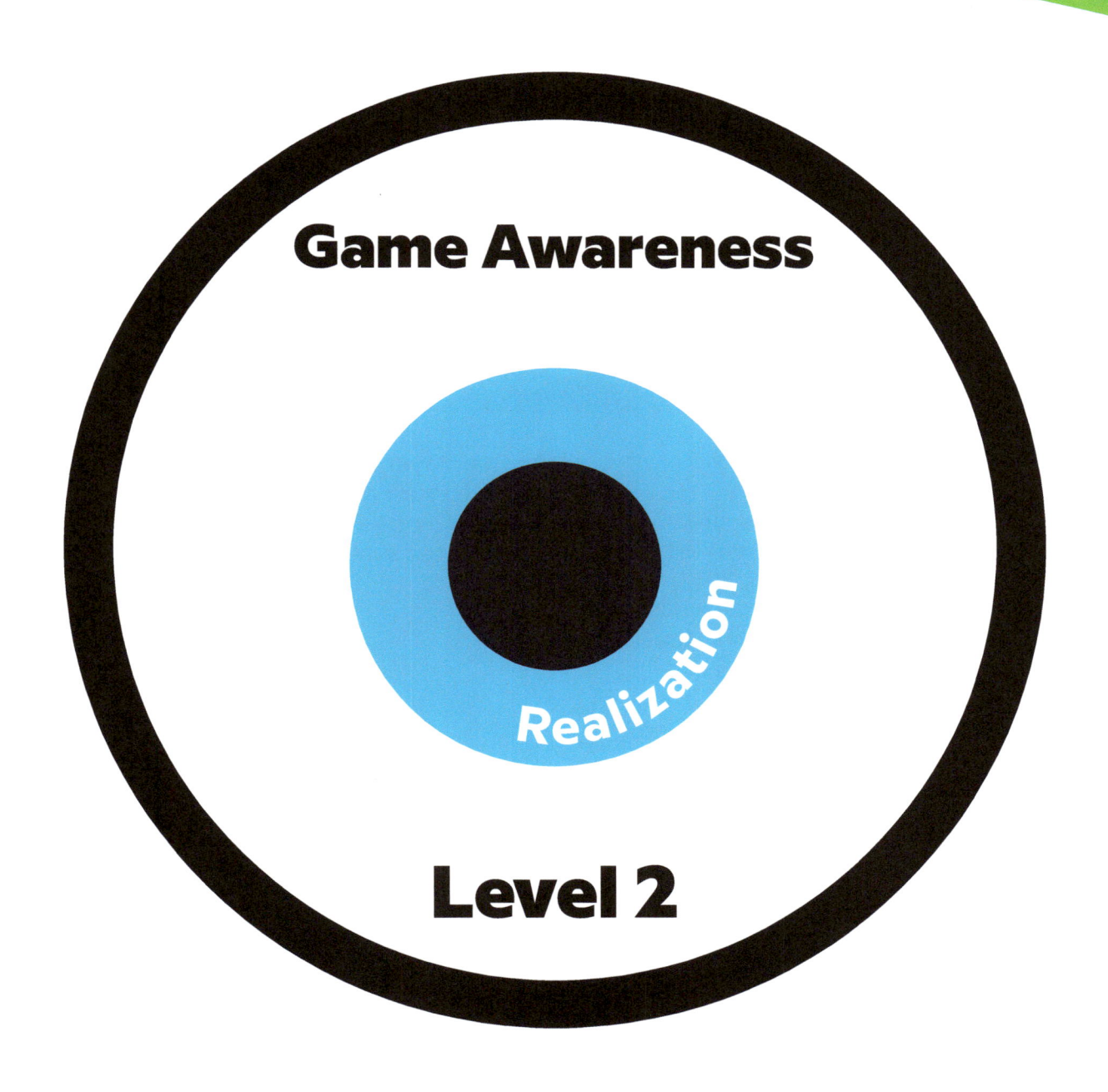

Game Awareness

Realization

Level 2

Game Awareness Level 2 - Realization: Reading the Game Situation

REALIZATION (LEVEL 2):
Reading the Game Situation

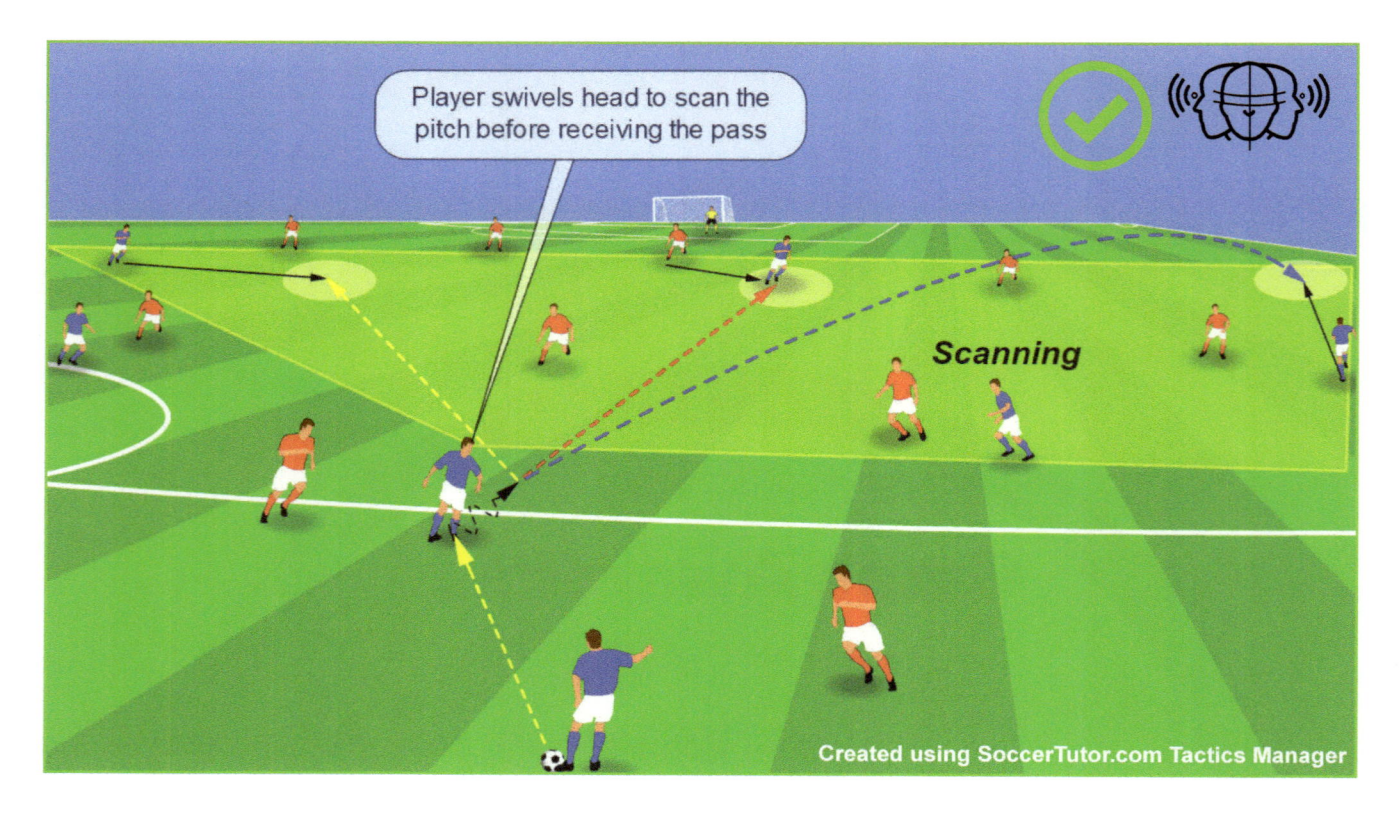

Player swivels head to scan the pitch before receiving the pass

Scanning

What is REALIZATION?

Level 1 and Observation in the game awareness model is about scanning to locate the ball, teammates, and opponents. **Level 2 and Realization is about the players understanding the current game situation** through the significance of where the ball, teammates, and opponents are in the playing area.

At this second level of game awareness, **players now put meaning to what they see**. They recognise patterns and understand what their teammates or opponents are doing from a tactical perspective and achieve a picture of what is going on.

The diagram above shows the highlighted player using the information gathered from scanning to read the game situation and get a picture of potential options.

As the player receives, he knows he has space to turn and move forward - he can also see 3 potential passing options with 3 teammates available in space.

Soccer eyeQ with SoccerTutor.com — SCANNING - How to Train it

ADAPTIVE POSITIONING AND IDENTIFYING KEY REFERENCE POINTS

Players cannot be bystanders watching the play as it happens around them...

If a player is consistently caught out of position, we would say that player lacked game awareness.

Therefore, in addition to understanding what is happening, we also have the physical component of the model to consider, and, for Realization, we look at what I call **Adaptive Positioning**.

At this level of awareness, the players must:

- Prioritise key reference points in the current situation
- Position themselves to optimise their viewpoint of key reference points
- Position themselves to interact effectively with key reference points
- Adjust position as the ball, teammates and opponents move
- Reprioritise reference points as the ball position and/or possession changes

Where panoramic positioning (part of level 1 - active scanning) was about opening up to see as much as possible, **adaptive positioning is now about the players' ability to use what they see to be in a specific position in relation to specific teammates and opponents**.

In order to do this effectively, the players must first use their understanding of the game situation to **prioritise which of the ball, their teammates, or their opponents are the most important for them at that specific moment in time**. Once the players have identified their key reference points, they must actively manage their spatial relationships and optimise their positioning relative to these. They do this by **changing their body shape and adjusting their position (location) on the pitch appropriately** for the game situation.

Of course, due to the nature of the game, these key reference points will be on the move, or could change from moment to moment (especially if there is a quick change in ball position or possession), so the **players must have the ability to adjust and adapt to suit the changing circumstances**, so they are in the most effective position possible at any given moment.

To be clear, the positioning element in the game awareness model only deals with the movement the players use during the ongoing process of managing their spatial relationships with the ball, their teammates, and their opponents. It does not include attacking or defending game actions such as overlaps or recovery runs, which would be included in the "play" part of the decision model.

KEY ASPECTS OF READING THE GAME SITUATION (LEVEL 2)

READING THE GAME SITUATION = Understand the significance of where the ball, teammates, and opponents are positioned

LEVEL 2 = Recognise patterns and understand the tactical perspective (see a picture of what is happening)

READ = Prioritise between the ball, teammates, and opponents

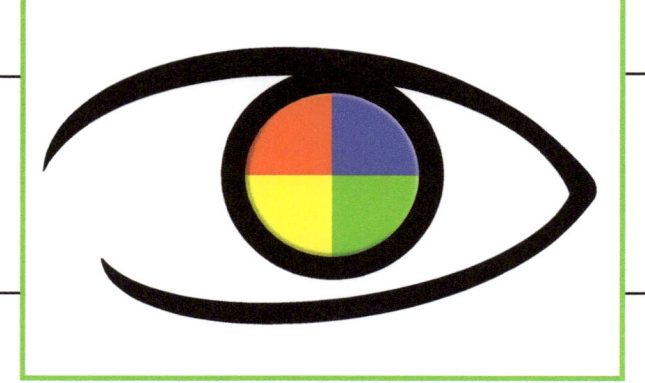

CREATING HABITS = Manage space and adjust to suit the changing circumstances, to be in the most effective position possible at any given moment

ADAPTIVE POSITIONING = Use what you see to be in the best position in relation to teammates and opponents

Game Awareness Level 2 - Realization: Reading the Game Situation

INCORRECT AND CORRECT READING THE GAME SITUATION (ATTACK)

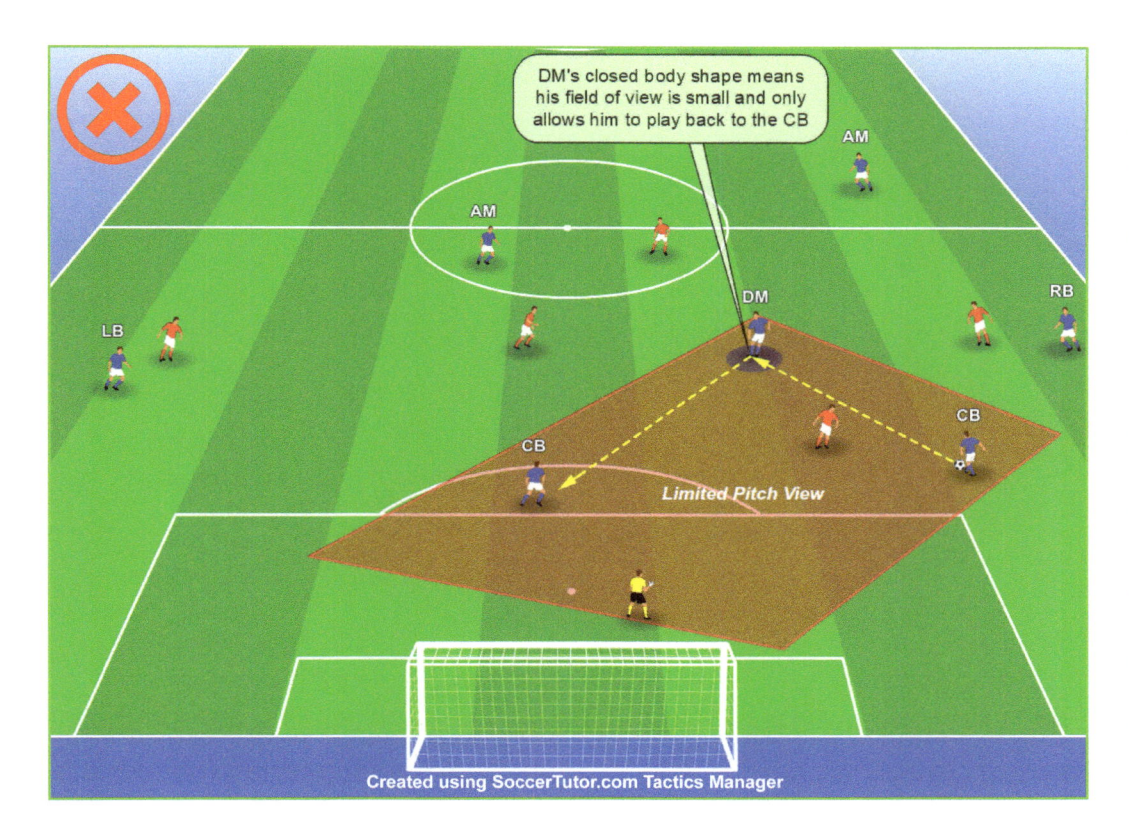

DM's closed body shape means his field of view is small and only allows him to play back to the CB

Limited Pitch View

DM's open body shape allows him a wider view of potential options so he can play forward

Scanned Pitch View

Lets' consider the positioning of the defensive midfielder **(DM)** in these two diagrams.

In diagram 1, we can see the player's body shape is oriented in such a way that only really allows him to play the ball back towards the centre back.

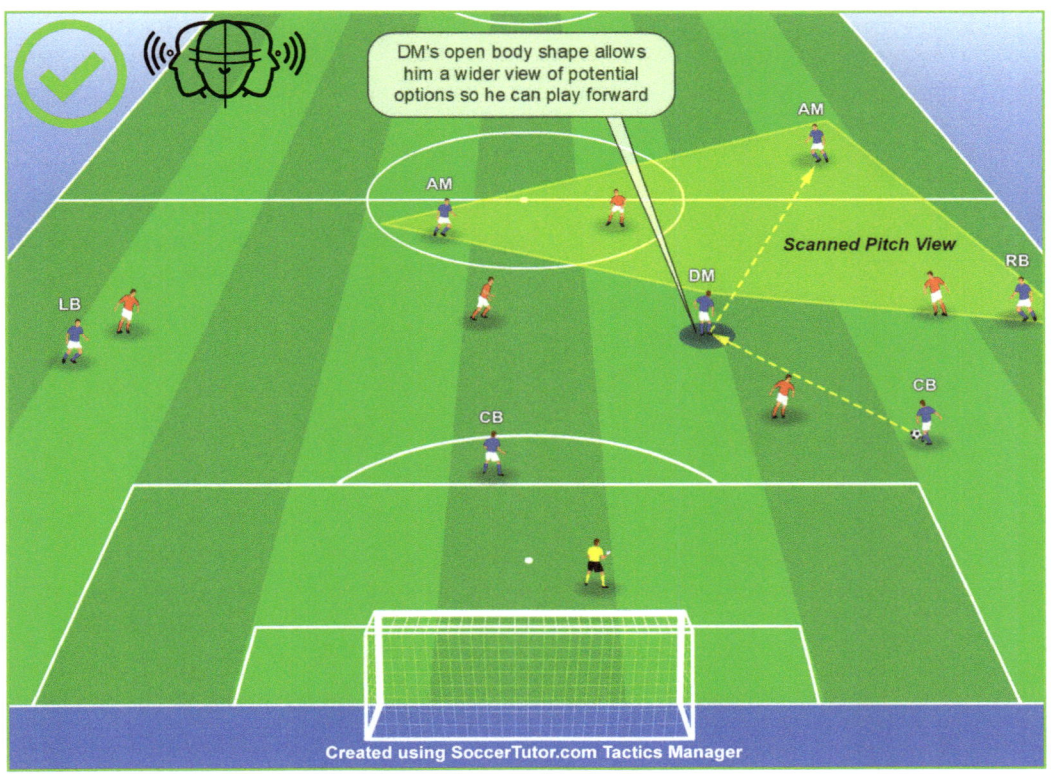

In diagram 2, the **DM** is positioned in a way that allows him a much wider view of the pitch (see highlighted area). He sees he has space to turn and can then play the ball forward and through the opposition's midfield line, which is the most effective play in this situation.

Soccer eyeQ with SoccerTutor.com — SCANNING - How to Train it

Game Awareness Level 2 - Realization: Reading the Game Situation

INCORRECT AND CORRECT READING THE GAME SITUATION (DEFENCE)

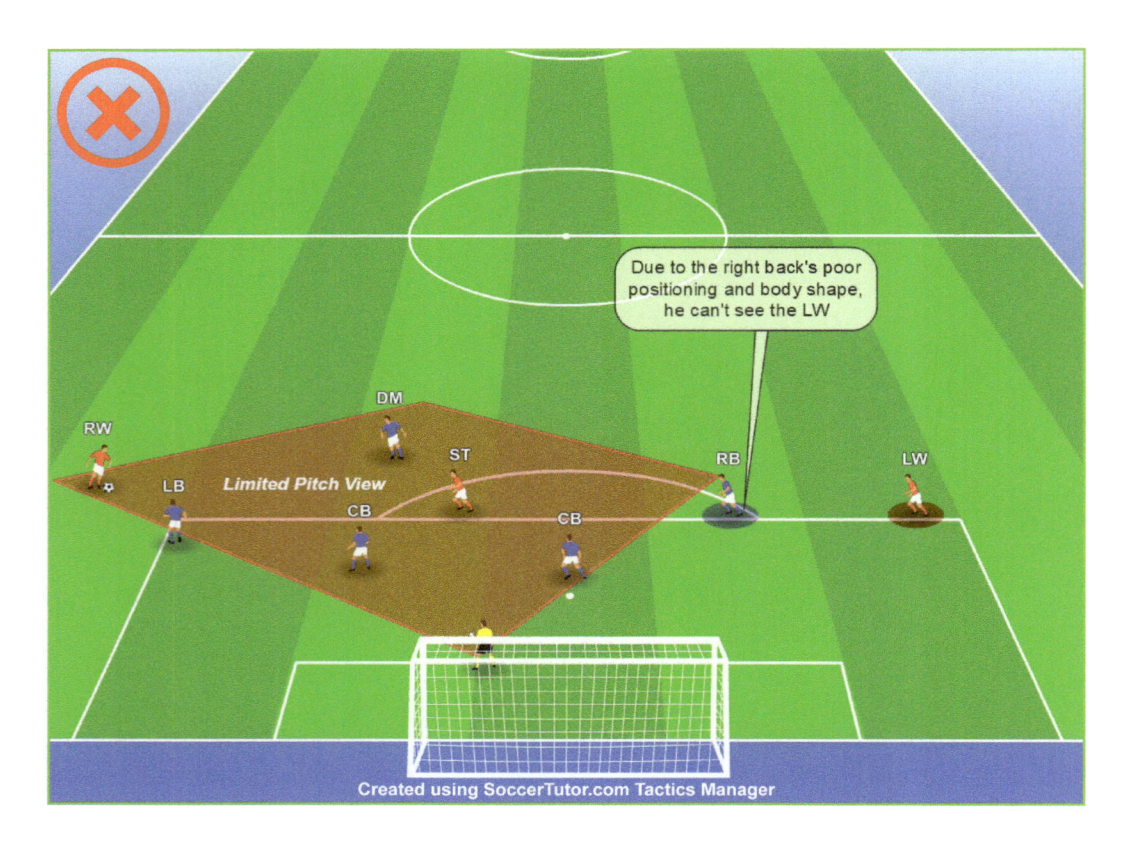

Due to the right back's poor positioning and body shape, he can't see the LW

Positioned deeper and with open body shape, the RB can see the ball, his teammates and the LW

We now look at a defensive example.

In diagram 1, we can see that the blue right back **(RB)** is vulnerable to the blind-side run of the opposing red left forward **(LW)**.

This is due to poor positioning and the incorrect body shape.

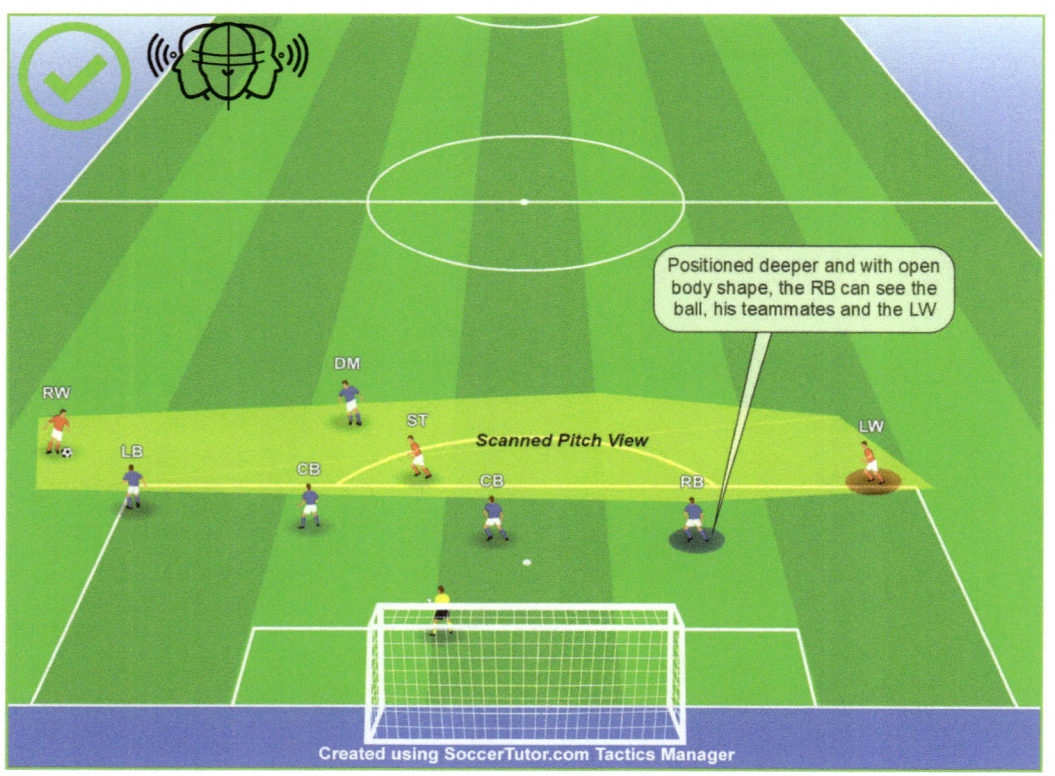

In diagram 2, the right back is deeper and has an open body shape. This allows him to keep track of the ball, his teammates, and the position of the red **LW**.

With this much more effective positioning, the opponent is less likely to gain an advantage on the blind-side.

Soccer eyeQ with SoccerTutor.com
SCANNING - How to Train it

Game Awareness Level 2 - Realization: Reading the Game Situation

"Which parts of my body hurt after games? My arms because I was really thrusting myself around.

"And my head from constantly looking for what is around me."

Ashley Cole
England, Arsenal, Chelsea, Roma, LA Galaxy, and Derby County

REALIZATION - SUMMARY

Hopefully you can see how important positioning is when looking at a player's awareness and understanding of the game.

Understanding the situation is almost meaningless from a practical perspective if the players cannot position themselves appropriately in that moment.

Adaptive positioning gives the player operational context of the situation, and it shows utility of their understanding - how to use what you see on the pitch (tactical understanding). This enables the player to be much more effective in the game.

Of course, it may not always be possible to position yourself perfectly, but good awareness will at least allow the players to position themselves sufficiently well enough to achieve the best outcome they can. If they realise an option is too difficult, they can adapt their choice of game action accordingly.

However, poor positioning is not usually just about what is happening in that moment of the game – it is often the cumulative effect of a lack of awareness and inadequate adaptive positioning in the seconds building up to that moment.

Let's remind ourselves of the key factors of adaptive positioning:

- Prioritise key reference points in the current situation
- Position themselves to optimise their viewpoint of key reference points
- Position themselves to interact effectively with key reference points
- Adjust position as the ball, teammates and opponents move
- Reprioritise reference points as the ball position and/or possession changes

KEY POINT: Adaptive positioning is a constant and ongoing process – the players must be continuously adjusting their body shape and location on the pitch in relation to their changing reference points.

Game Awareness Level 2 - Realization: Reading the Game Situation

"If you want to increase the speed of your game, you have to develop quicker minds rather than quicker feet.

Improvement translates as taking things in more quickly, analysing them more quickly, acting more quickly.

At RB Leipzig, we work on increasing the memory space and the processing pace."

Ralf Rangnick
Former Manager of RB Leipzig, Schalke 04, 1899 Hoffenheim, + many more...

LEVEL 3 - ANTICIPATION: Predicting How Play Will Develop

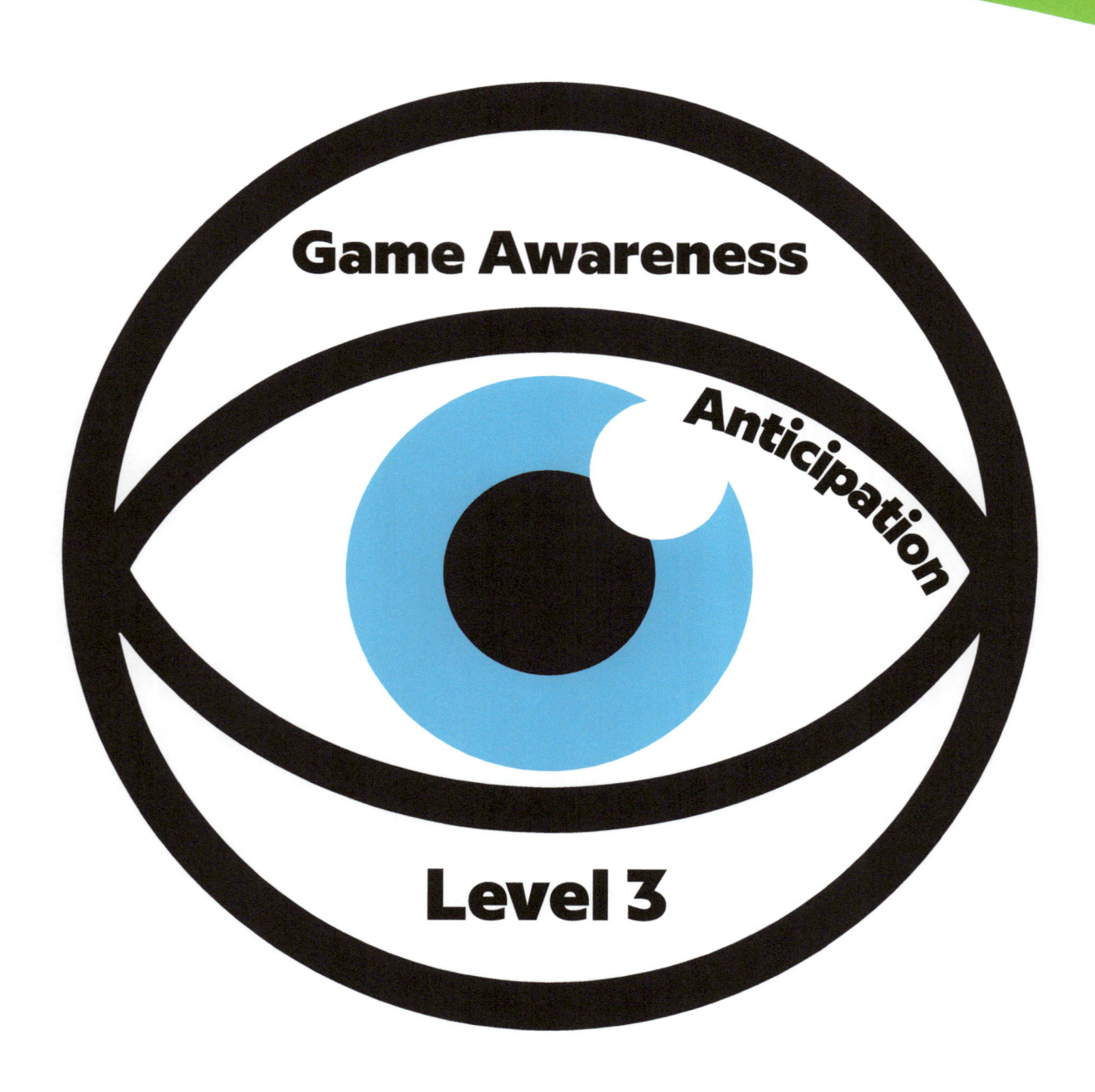

Game Awareness

Anticipation

Level 3

ANTICIPATION (LEVEL 3):
Predicting How Play Will Develop

What is Anticipation?

In Dr Mica Endsley's Model **(see page 65)**, it states that "the ability to project the future action of the elements in the environment – at least in the very near term – forms the third and highest level of Situation Awareness. This is achieved through knowledge of the status and dynamics of the elements and comprehension of the situation (both Level 1 and Level 2 of Situation Awareness)."

Due to the inter-related nature of the levels in the model, the accuracy of these predictions can be highly dependent upon the quality of Level 1 (Observation) and Level 2 (Realization) of Situation Awareness achieved by the operator. Anticipation builds on the previous two levels, and this is where the players not only understand what teammates and opponents are doing but also know what they may do next.

At this **third and final level of game awareness, the players are able to quickly recognise signals, situations, and scenarios, and predict how play is likely to develop**. Good anticipation skills enable the player to sense opportunities or threats in advance and ready themselves to exploit or nullify them as required.

Prospective Positioning

As with the previous two levels, we have the physical component of the model to consider and with Anticipation we now have prospective positioning, which is where the player will:

- Identify (in advance) where to be positioned based on predicting how play is likely to develop

- Modify spatial relationship with one or more current key reference points (ball, teammates and/or opponents) and be set for movement to a new position

- Be primed for the next game action and ready to exploit opportunities or neutralise possible threats

Adaptive positioning was about being in a specific place in relation to the key reference points, but **prospective positioning involves the players readying themselves for what they are expecting the next game moment to be**. This will usually require the player to modify one or more of their current specific relationships, so they are ready to move into a new position. This could be just a step or two, or a simple adjustment of body shape, which means they are in a good starting position to respond to the play they are anticipating.

Defensive Game Actions

For example, if the players anticipate the opposition are going to switch the play, they will then relax the distances they have with their current teammates/opponents, moving slightly in the direction of the anticipated switch, so they are ready to quickly shift across and defend effectively as soon as the switch of play happens.

We could go through many examples but whenever the opposition have the ball, the players will find themselves in situations where they have to adjust their position in relation to new reference points (teammates/opponents), or ready themselves for defensive game actions such as intercepting, pressing or tackling. This is all based on their prediction of how they think the play is likely to develop.

Game Awareness Level 3 - Anticipation: Predicting How Play Will Develop

Attacking Game Actions

From an attacking perspective, players need to anticipate where they should move to support the play, be available to receive the ball, and know what they will do with it when they receive it.

Most players support the player with the ball, but too often with the sole purpose of being a passing option for that player – their aim at that moment is only to get the ball instead of it being what they will do with the ball. One of the main causes of this is the failure to maintain sufficiently engaged in scanning – the player may have done it up to a point to support the player with the ball, but at some stage they have become ball-focused and lost awareness of the bigger picture.

This is why it is so important to train and reinforce the behaviour of scanning in opposed practices. **If we allow the players to get away with being largely ball-focused in the sessions we put on, then we shouldn't really be surprised if that is how they play**, particularly when under opposition pressure.

Forcing players to engage in scanning in opposed practices, even in the tightest of spaces, means they will feel far more comfortable doing it consistently during competition and it is more likely to be their default behaviour in the game.

Identifying in advance where and when to support the player who has the ball can be considered as basic anticipation. Players with higher levels of anticipation skills are able to think at least one step ahead of this – they can identify where and when to support the player who is supporting the player with the ball. These players have the ability to not only take up good positions to help their team maintain effective ball possession but can also execute effective third man runs, which the opposition will find very difficult to defend against.

How to Coach the Highest Levels of Anticipation

The best players not only understand more from what they see, and anticipate better, they do it more quickly. They can do this in a snapshot, as they do not have to look at things for as long as other players do, in order to understand the game picture. We may only be talking fractions of seconds here, but it is those fractions that make the difference. This means that it is also **important to help our players develop the ability to take maximum information from the briefest of glimpses of what is going on around them**. Players will learn to be effective from quicker snapshots only if we force them to survive with quicker snapshots. Therefore, part of the design of the training sessions at this level is intended for the players to have an increasingly smaller window of time to look at teammates/opponents but very importantly, still demands they be effective with the ball whilst under opposition pressure.

However, the exact nature of how a player will anticipate during performance can be position specific, team specific, or game specific. In fact, it is normally a combination of all three and these will influence how a player should position and scan, and what information they should be looking for. This means the player must have adaptable skills when it comes to game awareness and the ability to scan.

KEY POINT: As a final point on Level 3 (Anticipation), I want to reiterate that although I have mentioned some game actions here (intercepting, pressing, third man runs, etc), prospective positioning only includes the movements that pre-set a player for a game action and does not include the game action itself – these come under the "play" component of the decision model and are not part of the model for game awareness.

KEY ASPECTS OF PREDICTING HOW PLAY WILL DEVELOP (LEVEL 3)

PREDICTING HOW PLAY WILL DEVELOP = Identify in advance where to be positioned in relation to how the play is likely to develop, and be ready to exploit opportunities

LEVEL 3 = Builds on first 2 levels, so players not only understand what is happening but also know what may happen next

PREDICT = Quickly recognise signals and situations to see how play will develop

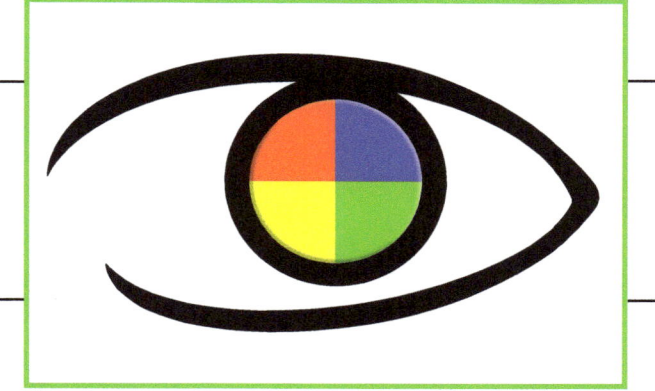

CREATING HABITS = Good anticipation skills to sense opportunities/threats in advance and ready themselves to exploit/nullify them as required

PROSPECTIVE POSITIONING = Players readying themselves for what they are expecting the next game moment to be

Game Awareness Level 3 - Anticipation: Predicting How Play Will Develop

INCORRECT AND CORRECT PREDICTING HOW PLAY WILL DEVELOP

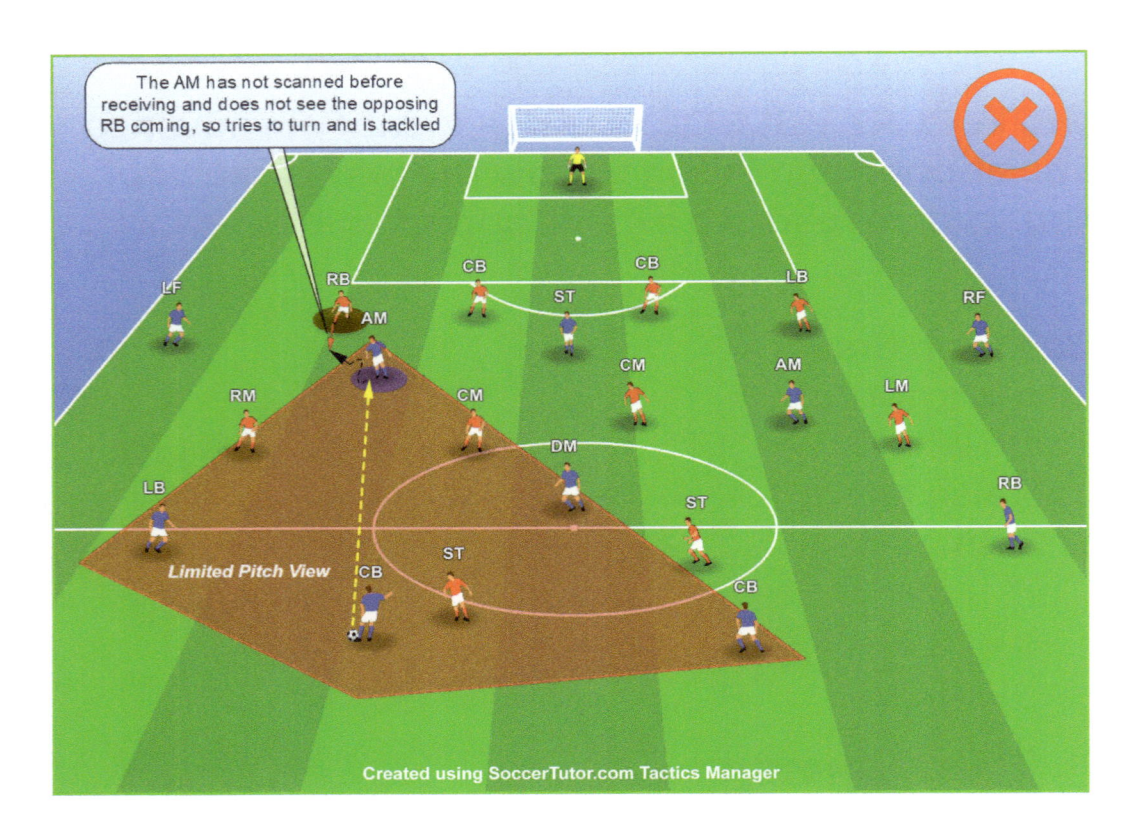

The AM has not scanned before receiving and does not see the opposing RB coming, so tries to turn and is tackled

Limited Pitch View

This shows what can happen when a player doesn't scan before receiving. His limited "map" is shown in the red highlighted area.

As the attacking midfielder (**AM**) doesn't see the positions of his teammates or the oncoming red right back (**RB**), he is easily tackled when he tries to turn.

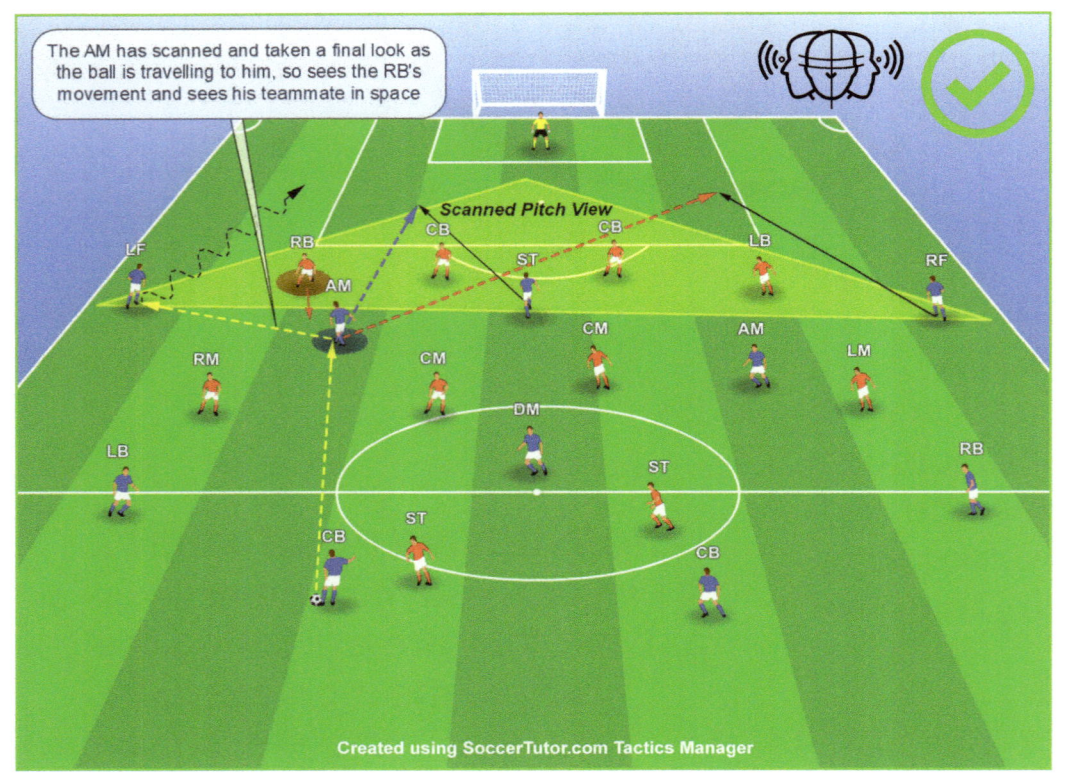

The AM has scanned and taken a final look as the ball is travelling to him, so sees the RB's movement and sees his teammate in space

Scanned Pitch View

The green highlighted area shows the extra information the **AM** was able to get a picture of because he scanned (positions of opponents and teammates + red **RB's** movement).

This time the AM knows he should not turn and instead takes the best decision to play an early pass to a teammate.

Soccer eyeQ with SoccerTutor.com   96   SCANNING - How to Train it

ANTICIPATION - SUMMARY

Although players will use a degree of anticipation in unopposed situations, this level of the model of game awareness is really dealing with **anticipation that occurs in a pressured environment with opposition**.

It is about **being able to see through the blur of the complex dynamics of the game, where the ball, teammates, opponents, and space are almost constant variables, and make sense of it all in a split-second**. That is what separates the great players from the good ones.

Whilst I have described the game awareness model as three levels (Observation, Realization, and Anticipation), they should not be considered as levels that are independent of each other.

How good a player is at scanning (Observation) will impact on how they read the game and their understanding of the game situation (Realization).

The ability to understand what is happening now (Realization) will obviously affect how a player is able to predict what will happen next (Anticipation).

However, well-developed anticipation skills will increasingly be used to guide a player's scanning (Observation) and will direct his attention to where he will find the most important information for the game situation.

This means that as a player becomes more experienced, understands the tactics of both his own team and the opposition, as well as knows the tendencies of teammates and opposing players, he is more likely to know where to look to find his most meaningful reference points - both for the here and now and for how he thinks the play is likely to develop.

This is why many coaches develop explicit game models using practices that work on shape and develop patterns of play, as well as compiling detailed analysis of the opposition at both a collective and individual level. This practice and planning provides the player with a useful guide of where to look, and what to look for, to inform his in-game decision-making.

Whilst understanding all of these will help guide the players attention, it is important that the players have well-developed scanning skills as these reference points could change from week to week, depending upon the opposition, or in a more

Game Awareness Level 3 - Anticipation: Predicting How Play Will Develop

significant way if the player plays for a different team (moves club or is involved in international football).

Changes like these will (more than likely) have a significant impact on how a player should position themselves to scan and what key information they should be looking for – meaning how they anticipate and what they will need to anticipate will change to some degree.

So, players must be good at scanning both left and right, they must be good at scanning both horizontally and vertically, and they must be good at picking the right moments to scan **(please see "When To Scan And When Not To Scan" on pages 75-77)**.

Just as good anticipation skills will guide a player in what they look for, poor scanning (and positioning) will impact on how effective a player is in detecting and identifying the important cues to predict how the play is likely to develop (anticipate) during the course of a game.

This will also have a significant impact on the player's ability to engage in effective prospective positioning – if they are unable to predict how the play is likely to develop, how can they possibly carry out the actions required to position appropriately for the possible upcoming situation?

If they can't do this effectively, the player will more often than not find himself a yard or two out of position, and consistently lagging behind his opponents and teammates.

Therefore, **because the elements of anticipation can be so variable, I think it's crucial that we develop a player's all-round scanning abilities under pressure**. If we help our players to be **capable of scanning 360 degrees** then they will be able to adapt to any position specific, team specific, or game specific demands.

As a result, they will be much better at the Anticipation level of this model of game awareness (Level 3) and will be a much more effective player wherever they play.

Game Awareness Level 3 - Anticipation: Predicting How Play Will Develop

"Intelligent players anticipate. Unintelligent players react. Always. If you think faster, you are faster on the field. If you react, you are always too late."

Peter Bosz

Head Coach of Olympique Lyonnais (Lyon), former Head Coach of Bayer Leverkusen, Borussia Dortmund, and Ajax

GAME AWARENESS MODEL:
Observation, Realization, and Anticipation

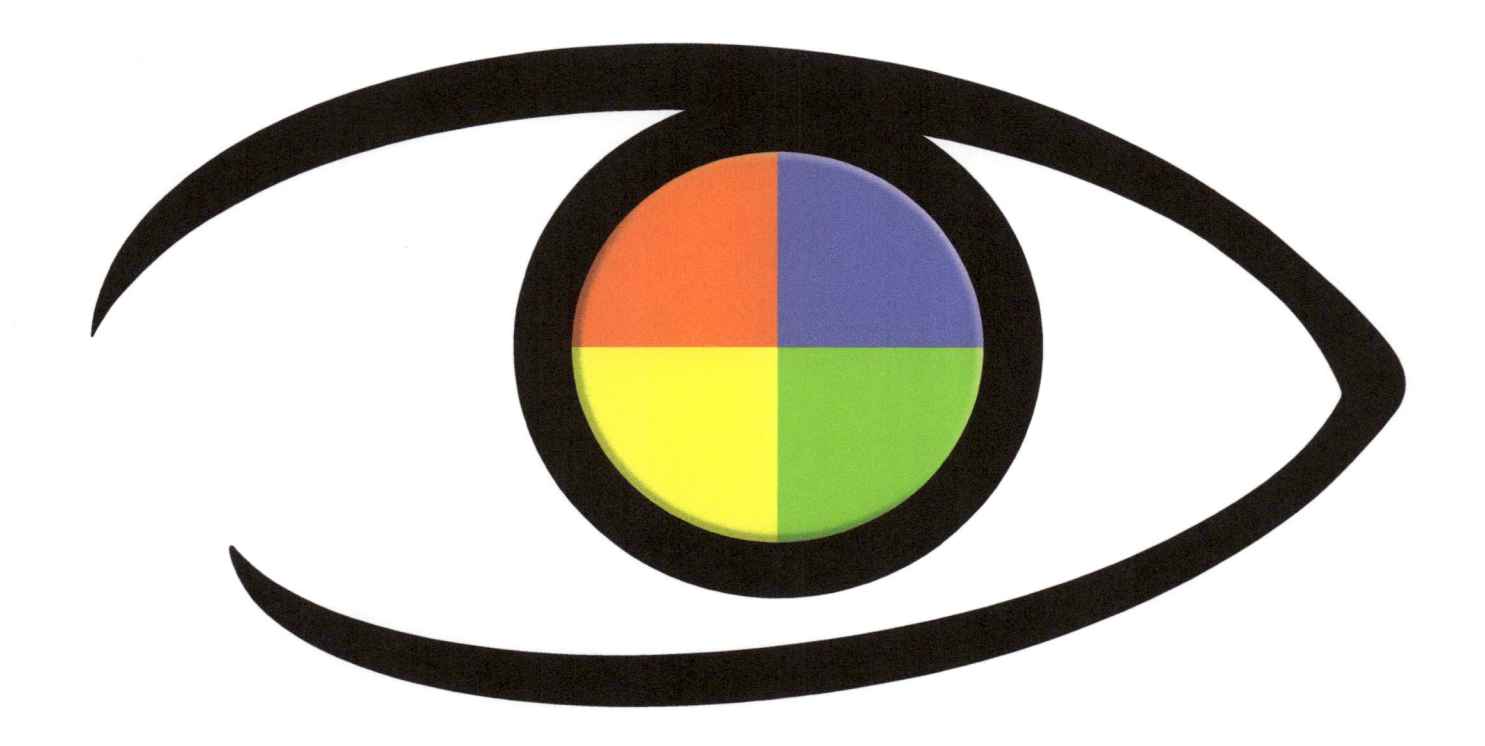

SOCCER EYEQ GAME AWARENESS MODEL:
Observation, Realization, and Anticipation

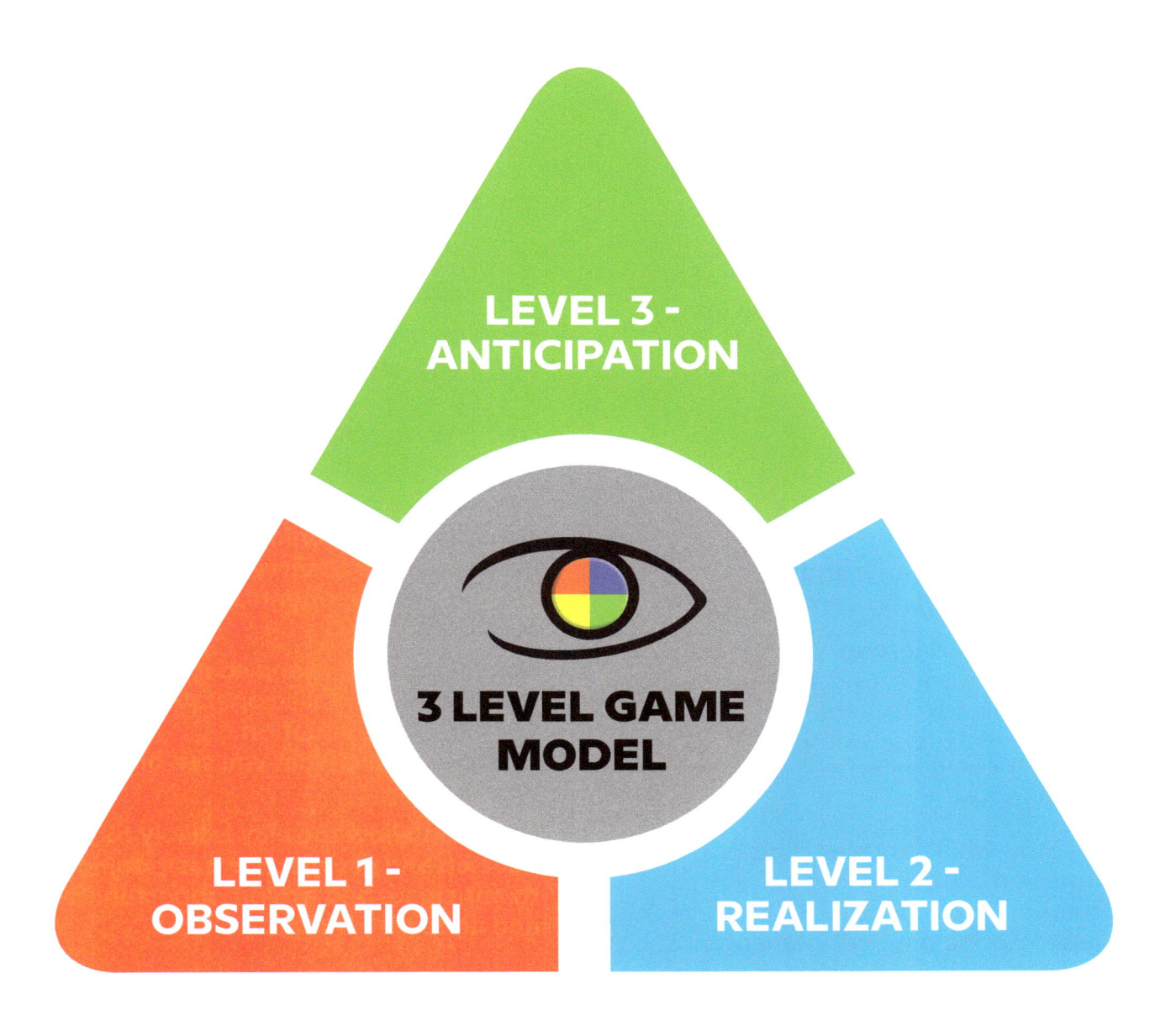

LEVEL 3 - ANTICIPATION

3 LEVEL GAME MODEL

LEVEL 1 - OBSERVATION

LEVEL 2 - REALIZATION

The Soccer eyeQ Game Awareness Model is made up of the 3 levels we outlined in the 3 previous sections:

- **Game Awareness Level 1 (Observation)** - Scanning of the Playing Area
- **Game Awareness Level 2 (Realization)** - Reading the Game Situation
- **Game Awareness Level 3 (Anticipation)** - Predicting How Play Will Develop

Game Awareness Model: Observation, Realization, and Anticipation

As already mentioned, Dr Mica Endsley's work offers us an understanding of the theory and application of Situation Awareness. Whilst the research initially focussed on pilots and air traffic controllers, Endsley has also investigated the Situation Awareness of infantry soldiers in the army, and this offers an insight into the needs and demands of an operator who is imbedded in the environment (much like a player is in a football game).

There is a lot of fascinating work that is being done and it continues to show that the concept of Situation Awareness applies whether you are flying a plane, driving a car, or playing sports.

I would strongly recommend that all coaches read the research into this area, in order to get a more detailed understanding of the concept and make your own considerations of how it can be applied to our game and how you can develop it in the players you work with.

As you have seen throughout the last few sections of the book, Endsley's model has been an invaluable tool for me in my work in this area and provides the basis for the model I use for defining and developing game awareness.

Once again, whilst Endsley does not exclude physical actions (to acquire information) from her model, I believe that it is essential the physical element must be explicit within our model for game awareness in football.

This means that, as with Endsley's model, we have a three-level model for game awareness but now each level has an integrated element of positioning.

Our three levels of game awareness are:

- **Level 1 (Observation)**
- **Level 2 (Realization)**
- **Level 3 (Anticipation)**

At each level we have our element of positioning:

- **Observation** – Panoramic Positioning
- **Realization** – Adaptive Positioning
- **Anticipation** – Prospective Positioning

Now that we have discussed the model in a little more detail, and shown how we incorporate positioning at each level, let's look again at our definition of game awareness.

The simplified definition I gave earlier was:

- **Scanning of the Playing Area**
- **Reading the Game Situation**
- **Predicting How Play Will Develop**

The more comprehensive definition I offer now is:

- **Scanning of the playing area and panoramic positioning** to maximise viewpoint and observe ball/teammates/opponents in the playing area
- **Reading the game and adaptive positioning** to realise operational context of the situation (understanding what you see on the pitch)
- **Predicting how the play is likely to develop and prospective positioning** to anticipate and exploit opportunities and neutralise threats

In the next part of the book - **Section 2 (Soccer eyeQ Training Practices)**, we look at how to train and develop game awareness in alignment with our 3 Level Game Model.

Game Awareness Model: Observation, Realization, and Anticipation

SOCCER EYEQ GAME AWARENESS MODEL:
The 6-Step Performance Cycle (A to F)

A = Active scanning - Have a look!

Does the player scan and look around the playing area, away from the ball, on a consistent basis?

B = Body Position - Adopt and Adapt!

Does the player optimise their body shape and their location (position on the pitch) to maximise their field of view and their opportunities for action?

C = Confirm - Check Again!

Does the player scan and look around the playing area, away from the ball, on a consistent basis?

D = Decision - Think Quickly!

Does the player optimise their body shape and their location (position on the pitch) to maximise their field of view and their opportunities for action?

E = Execution - Make the Play!

How effective is the execution of the player's action? This is evaluated independently from the decision.

F = Follow-on - Next Action!

How quickly does the player re-engage with the game, re-establish awareness and minimise the time delay between one game action and the next?

Soccer eyeQ with SoccerTutor.com — SCANNING - How to Train it

Game Awareness Model: Observation, Realization, and Anticipation

"Most players I came across were quicker and stronger than me.

Decision making is what controls our physical actions.

Some players have a mental top speed of 80, while others are capable of reaching 200.

I always tried to reach 200."

Xavi

SECTION 2

Soccer eyeQ Training Practices

SECTION 2: Soccer eyeQ Training Practices

PRACTICE DIAGRAM KEY

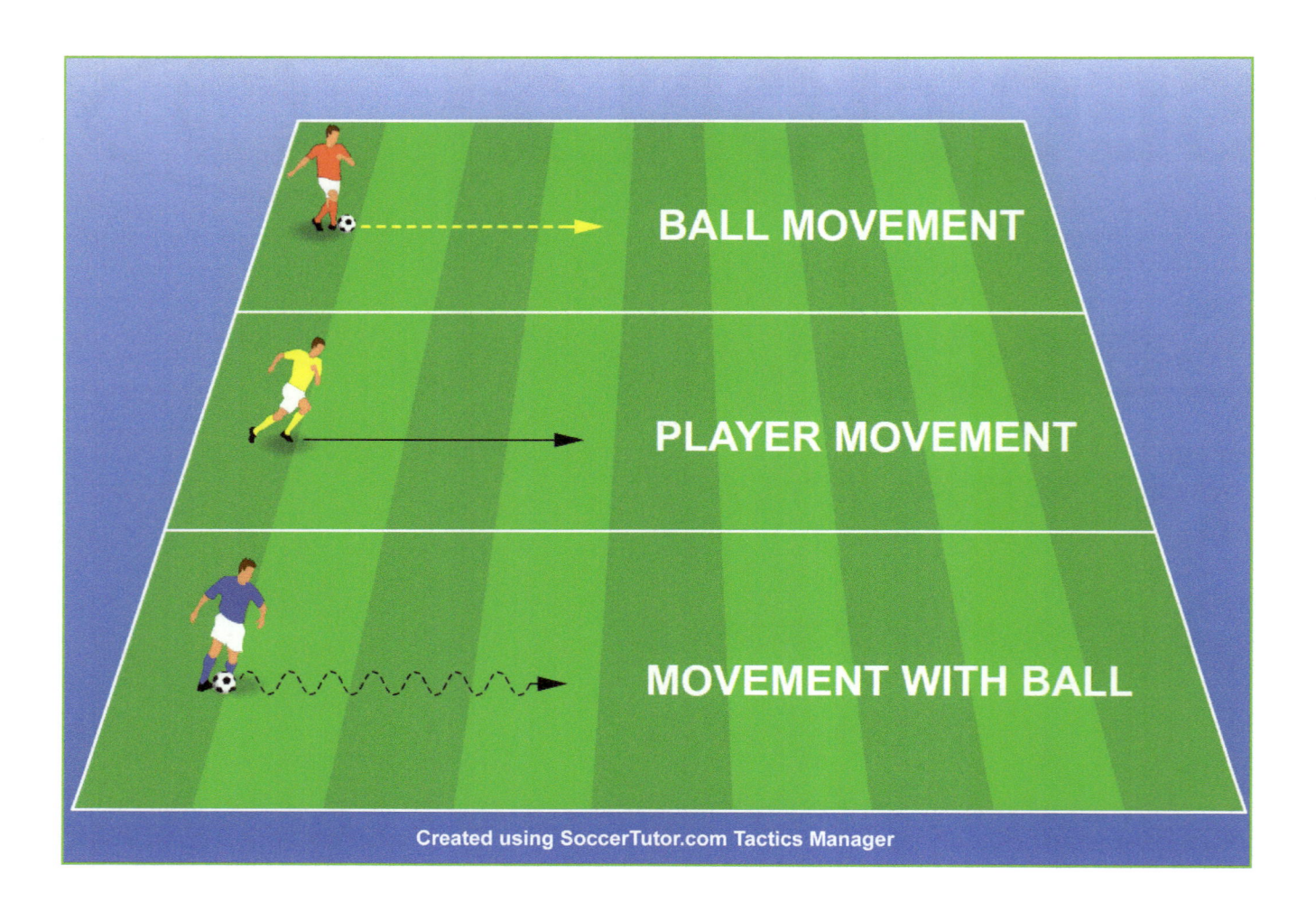

- BALL MOVEMENT
- PLAYER MOVEMENT
- MOVEMENT WITH BALL

Created using SoccerTutor.com Tactics Manager

PRACTICE FORMAT

- The practices in this book are created by Kevin McGreskin using the Soccer eyeQ game awareness training methodology.

- They are practice examples to show the method of training players to use scanning and improve their game awareness.

- The method can be input into almost any training practice that you want to use.

- Each practice includes the practice topic/name, clear diagrams and detailed description including the practice objective, practice analysis for the coach, and coaching points.

LEVEL 1 - OBSERVATION: Scanning of the Playing Area

Game Awareness

Observation

Level 1

WHY WE SHOULD ENCOURAGE SCANNING IN TRAINING SESSIONS

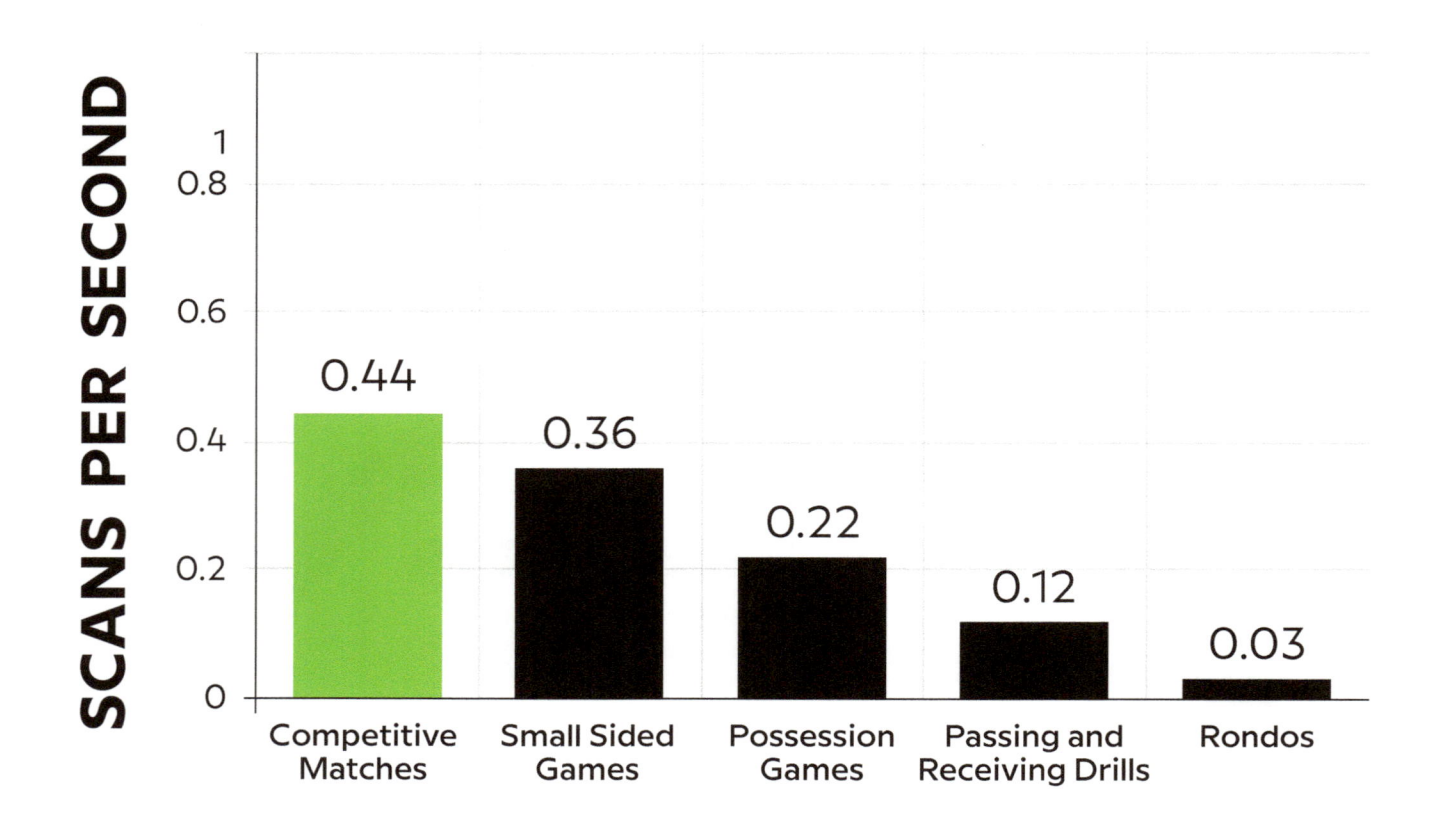

SCANS PER SECOND

Competitive Matches	Small Sided Games	Possession Games	Passing and Receiving Drills	Rondos
0.44	0.36	0.22	0.12	0.03

N = 6 Top Dutch league players (1418 registrations)
(De Vries, Frencken, Hujigen, & Jordet, in review in scientific journal)

The statistics above are from Geir Jordet's Study comparing scan frequency in competitive matches compared to specific training practices - for full details please see page 80.

This data clearly shows that players do not scan anywhere near as much in training practices as they do in games (some types more than others).

Therefore, our aim is to adapt our practices to include scanning and game awareness elements so that our players improve and develop this essential skill.

The practices in this section and later sections were all created with this aim and have been used to achieve the exact results that I was aiming for.

You can of course use the same practices, but you can also add these elements to any of your existing practices or future practices you use.

Game Awareness Level 1 - Observation: Scanning of the Playing Area

SOCCER EYEQ OBSERVATION:
The Advantage of Scanning

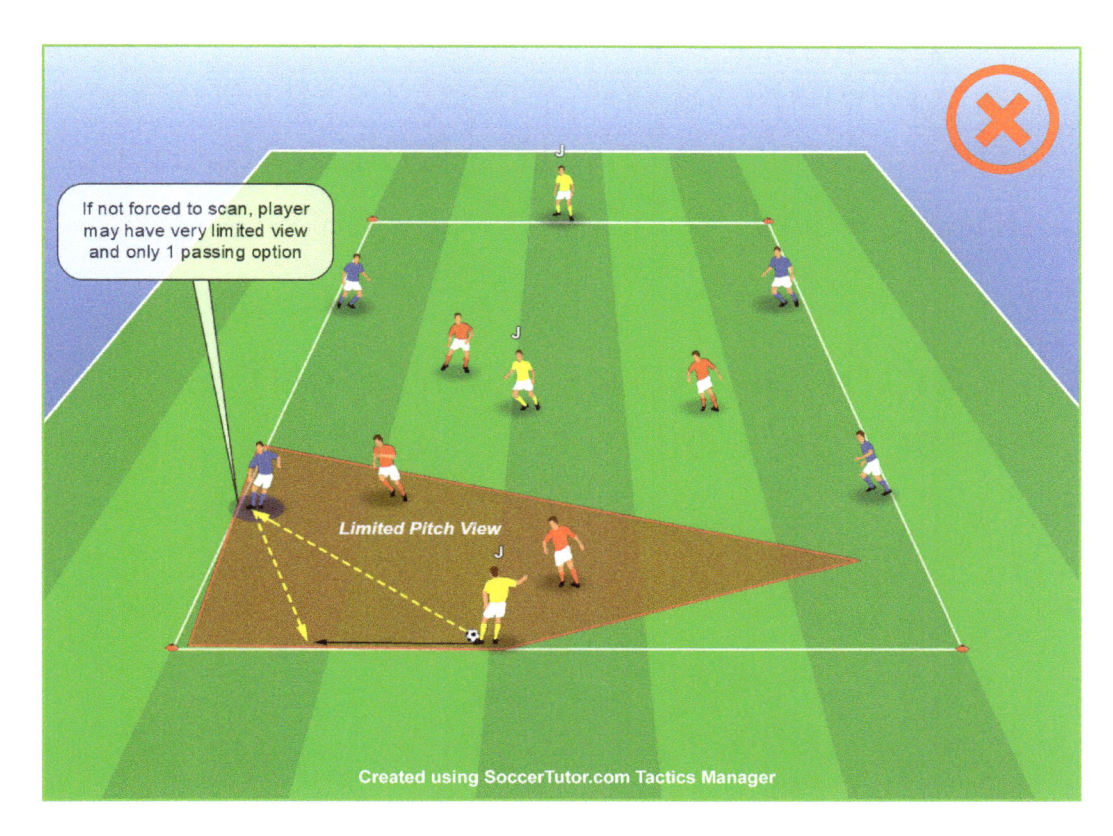

If not forced to scan, player may have very limited view and only 1 passing option

Limited Pitch View

As the player is forced to look around and scan before receiving (to spot red cone), he has a full view of all players

RED!

Scanned Pitch View

For the full description of these two variations, see pages 18-19.

This diagram shows you what can happen if players aren't forced to scan in a possession game.

The player has a limited view of all the player positions and is forced to simply play the ball back.

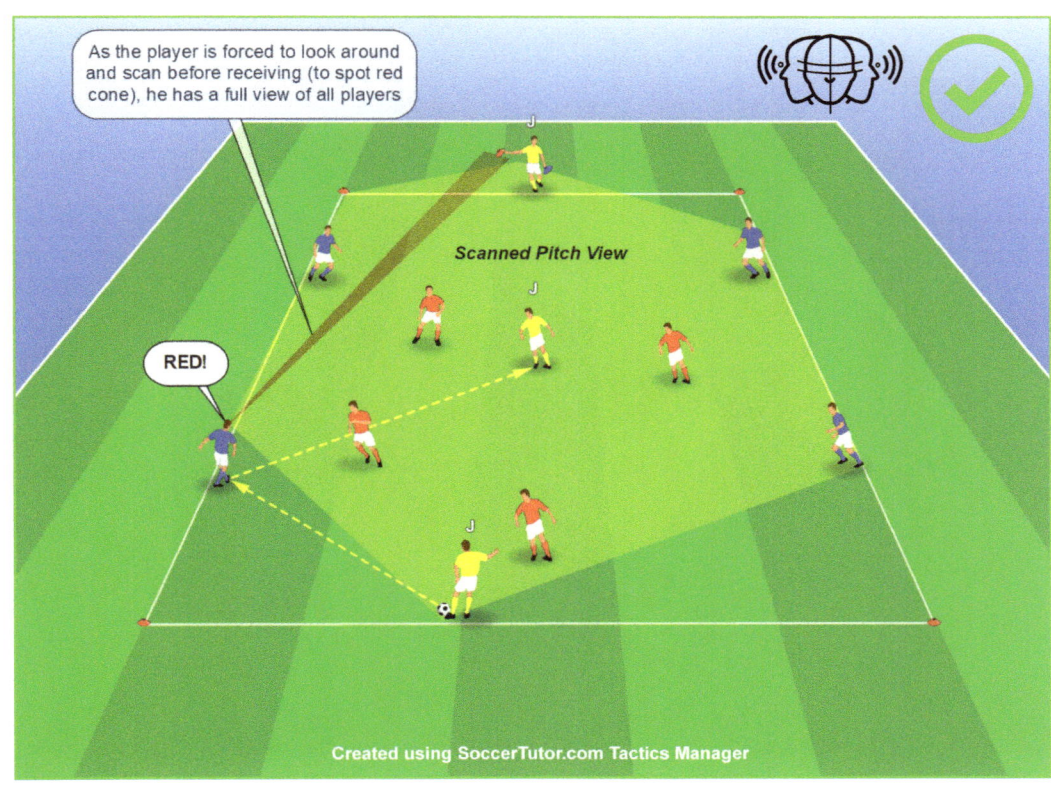

In this example, the player is forced to scan and spot the colour of the cone before receiving a pass from the Joker.

Therefore, he has a full picture of all player positions and is able to see the Joker in the middle, who he passes to.

Soccer eyeQ with SoccerTutor.com

SCANNING - How to Train it

Game Awareness Level 1 - Observation: Scanning of the Playing Area

"The difference between players is the ability to take in information.

In the Premier League the good players take in around 4 to 6 pieces of information in the 10 seconds prior to receiving the ball, and the very good players take in 8 to 10 pieces of information.

It is therefore important to develop exercises that help increase this ability to gather information."

Arsene Wenger

OBSERVATION PRACTICES:
Scanning of the Playing Area

High VEB Frequency Players

77% Forward Pass Success

Low VEB Frequency Players

39% Forward Pass Success

VEB = Visual Exploratory Behaviour (Looking Around/Scanning)

The statistics above are from Geir Jordet's Study comparing how often Premier League players look around before receiving against their forward pass completion statistics - for full details please see page 78.

Let me start by asking a simple question:

Would you rather have a player in your team who retains possession and creates opportunities for your team almost 8 times out of 10...

Or the player that gives the ball away over 6 times out of ten?

The answer of course is obvious. Level 1 Observation is the foundation that game awareness and, therefore, good decision making is built on.

This level of awareness is simply about the ability to give yourself the opportunity to take in information in the first place.

Without this essential skill it is highly unlikely that a player will consistently make good decisions and, as a result, they will execute inefficient game actions.

This level is so fundamental to overall performance, yet it is its simplicity that make it so easy to overlook.

The important thing to understand is that, at Level 1, there is no meaning attributed to the information that the players see at this stage – the context is irrelevant here. Context only comes in Level 2.

The Importance of Level 1 Observation as the Foundation

Some coaches will argue that it is where the players look and the meaning they take from what they see that makes the difference, and this is very true. However, **if you do not have the ability to make the information available to yourself in the first place (by scanning), then you have no information to take any meaning from**.

Therefore, **Level 1 Observation is all about developing the habit of looking around on a more continual and consistent basis**.

Yes, that's right. Looking around. It seems so incredibly simple, doesn't it?

Yet, I believe that it is this simplicity that betrays us coaches in developing this essential attribute - it is too easy to believe that everybody just does it, and that we all do it the same. However, research has shown that not everyone does it with the same efficiency or frequency, some players look around far more often than others.

Geir Jordet's Study of Premier League Players

Indeed, findings by the Norwegian researcher Geir Jordet have indicated that this seemingly simple act has a strong correlation with how successful a player is. Simply put, the players who look around the most are the most successful.

In a study of English Premier League players, Jordet found a significant difference amongst the players in how frequently they looked around – clearly demonstrating that players certainly do not all do it the same. Remarkably, when comparing the midfielders with the highest and lowest visual exploratory rate (how often they scan), he found that the **players who looked around the most successfully completed almost twice as many of their passes**. And worryingly, those that looked around the least gave the ball away over 6 times out of 10!

Remember, these are Premier League players we are talking about here. These guys are playing at one of the highest levels in the world, yet a simple deficiency in their game seems to have a significantly negative impact on their performance. Let me be clear, I am not saying they are bad players - the level they are playing at is a clear indication of how good they are - I am just asking, could we help them be even better?

In most games, you will also see plenty of moments where there is a lack of looking around by players when they are defending.

How often have you seen the far side defender beaten to a cross by an attacker making a blind side run?

Although these are frequently put down to poor body shape, it is actually the result of the player being blissfully unaware of what is going on around him.

The cause?... The player has usually become fixated on the ball and has not looked around at the appropriate moments. It is this lack of looking that is the problem, not the body shape. Of course, good body shape certainly makes it easier to look and see, particularly as it helps the player make better use of their peripheral vision, but players may not always get the chance to adjust their body shape (for example, when facing a fast counter attack). However, they can always move their head to look!

How often have you seen a player pass the ball back into the area he received it from, instead of turning into the available space behind him? Again, this is usually because the player has become fixated on the ball and not looked around.

Game Awareness Level 1 - Observation: Scanning of the Playing Area

How to Improve the Coaching of Scanning

There are many coaches who understand the importance of looking around and acknowledge that it is something we must coach. However, the most common methodology seems to be the use of throwaway comments such as telling the players to remember to "have a look" or "check their shoulders." Almost no training is done to help players develop scanning as a habit, both on and off the ball – it **should be an automatic behaviour that forms part of their receiving skills and part of what they do as they move around** the field of play.

A few years back, one of the national associations I was doing some work with was running a program for their elite youth players from all around the country. I delivered a presentation to the staff coaches and did a session with each squad of players. Later in the week, the Performance Director and I were watching one of the coaches doing a session with his group of players and I commented that the players were ball watching most of the time and were hardly ever looking around. The Performance Director agreed and went to have a quiet chat with the coach to reiterate how important he felt this was, and that that's why he had got me over to work with the players and staff. The coach said, "but I tell them to have a look." Quick as a flash the Performance Director said, "well, if it's that easy, let's just tell them to score goals!"

This seemingly simple act of looking around is far too important to leave to chance. It is the **foundation of game awareness, which is at the core of good decision making**. Looking around is a trainable skill and it is, therefore, essential that we help our players to develop this fundamental ability.

Here, at Level 1, the players will become comfortable with taking their eyes off the ball and scanning other areas of the playing area. Once again, it doesn't matter necessarily what areas they look at, or what they see, it is the **habit of looking around and the ability to regularly get their eyes away from the ball and onto other potentially information rich areas** that is important here.

We will now have a look at a practice with a number of simple progressions which help the players develop this first level of Game Awareness. If we want players to develop habits it must be an intrinsic part of the practice.

This is a basic practice that many coaches will already be familiar with. I will then progress by layering in constraints that force the player to look around – and it becomes very obvious when they don't, to both the coach AND the player!

At the youngest ages, where much research says there is limited understanding in tactical or team play, much of what they see around them may have less value in the terms of meaning or context. However, we can still help the players learn and develop the habit of taking their eyes off the ball and scanning around the playing area.

Game Awareness Level 1 - Observation: Scanning of the Playing Area

SOCCER EYEQ PRACTICES:
Options for Available Visual Cues

1. GLOVES - Players wear 2 gloves of different colours and hold one of them up as a visual cue (method used most with Soccer eyeQ practices)

2. WRISTBANDS
Alternative to using gloves with the players wearing 2 different colour wristbands

3. CONES
The players carry 2 cones of different colours and raise one as a visual cue

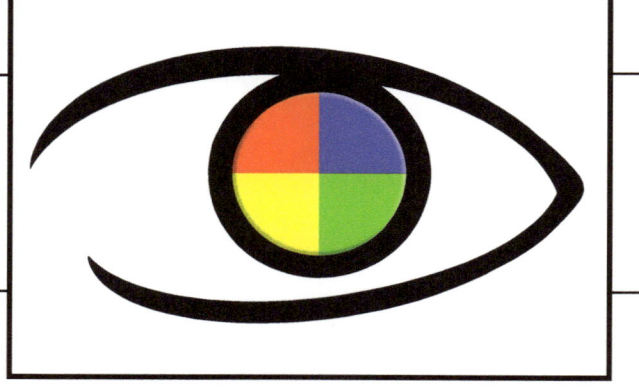

4. BIBS
Alternative to using cones with players carrying 2 different colour bibs

5. HANDS
Players hold up one hand or two hands - The players shout out "One" or "Two" to spot the visual cue

Soccer eyeQ with SoccerTutor.com

SCANNING - How to Train it

Game Awareness Level 1 - Observation: Scanning of the Playing Area

PRACTICE EXAMPLE: Pass to Opposite Colour in a Basic Awareness Practice

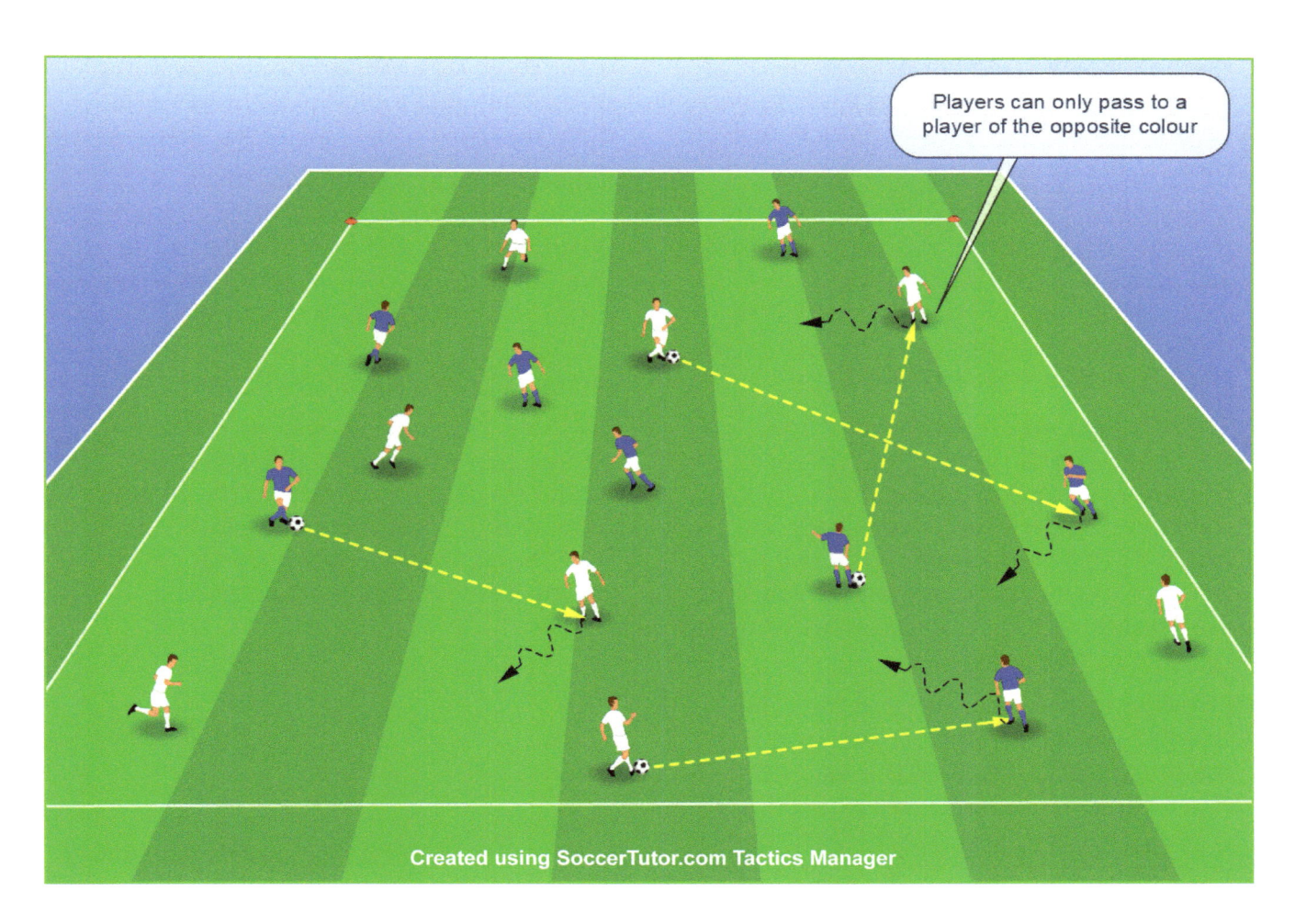

Players can only pass to a player of the opposite colour

Practice Description

- In a 20 x 30 up to 40 x 60 yard area (depending on the age, level, and number of players), we split the players into 2 teams (6-8 players per team).
- Play with 3-4 balls and increase the number of balls to increase the tempo.
- Players pass the balls around the playing area but can only pass to a player in the opposite colour.

Practice Analysis for Coach

- This is a commonly used practice that will be familiar to most coaches. Here we have a cooperative passing exercise and a basic constraint of passing only to an opposite colour, which limits the choices and forces the players to look for specific passing options.
- When we use a practice like this, one of the main aims is to **get the players to identify where their passing options are before they get the ball**.
- **However, you will notice how many players look at the ball most of the time and only look around after they receive the pass...**
- This is a major problem in football and has a significant impact upon performance.

Soccer eyeQ with SoccerTutor.com

SCANNING - How to Train it

Game Awareness Level 1 - Observation: Scanning of the Playing Area

- Only looking after receiving means that **players don't know what the picture is, so they can't make a decision before they get the ball**.

- Next, watch how the players receive the ball. You will likely find that most of the players do not prepare themselves properly and their body position will most likely be poor.

- Many players will stand square on to the ball when receiving a pass and they will be closed off to the field of play, with some players even receiving the ball while facing the touchline with their back to 80% of the playing area.

- Therefore, even at this early stage, we can try to reinforce the concept of **panoramic positioning**. We can try to encourage the players to have as much of the field of play as possible in front of them, which will **maximise their viewpoint** and have an **open body shape** relative to the passer.

- Looking before you receive the ball doesn't just enable good decision making, it is also one of the essential ingredients that facilitates good body shape/position. You should position your body in relation to where the ball is coming from and where you intend on going next with it.

- If you don't look, how can you really know where you are going next with the ball?

- And, if you don't know where you are going next, how can you position your body effectively?

- Also, pay attention to the quality of passing. See how many passes seem to be played with no real thought behind them and are just kicked in the general direction of the receiver. The problem is probably that the passer has no real information to work with for how to play the pass.

- **Good body positioning** doesn't just help what the receiver will do next, it **"tells" the passer where the receiver wants the ball**.

- If you don't "tell" the passer where you want the ball, how can he do anything other than just kick it in your general direction?

- While our main focus will be on developing the simple habit of looking around in the next few progressions of this practice, we will also look at these other aspects of performance.

- **HOW DO WE PROGRESS?**
We now look at how we can make a simple progression to this practice which forces the players to look away from the ball, scan more frequently, AND helps them to learn purposeful orientation of their body position.

Game Awareness Level 1 - Observation: Scanning of the Playing Area

PROGRESSION 1: Pass to Opposite Colour with Visual Cues (Outside Team Flashers)

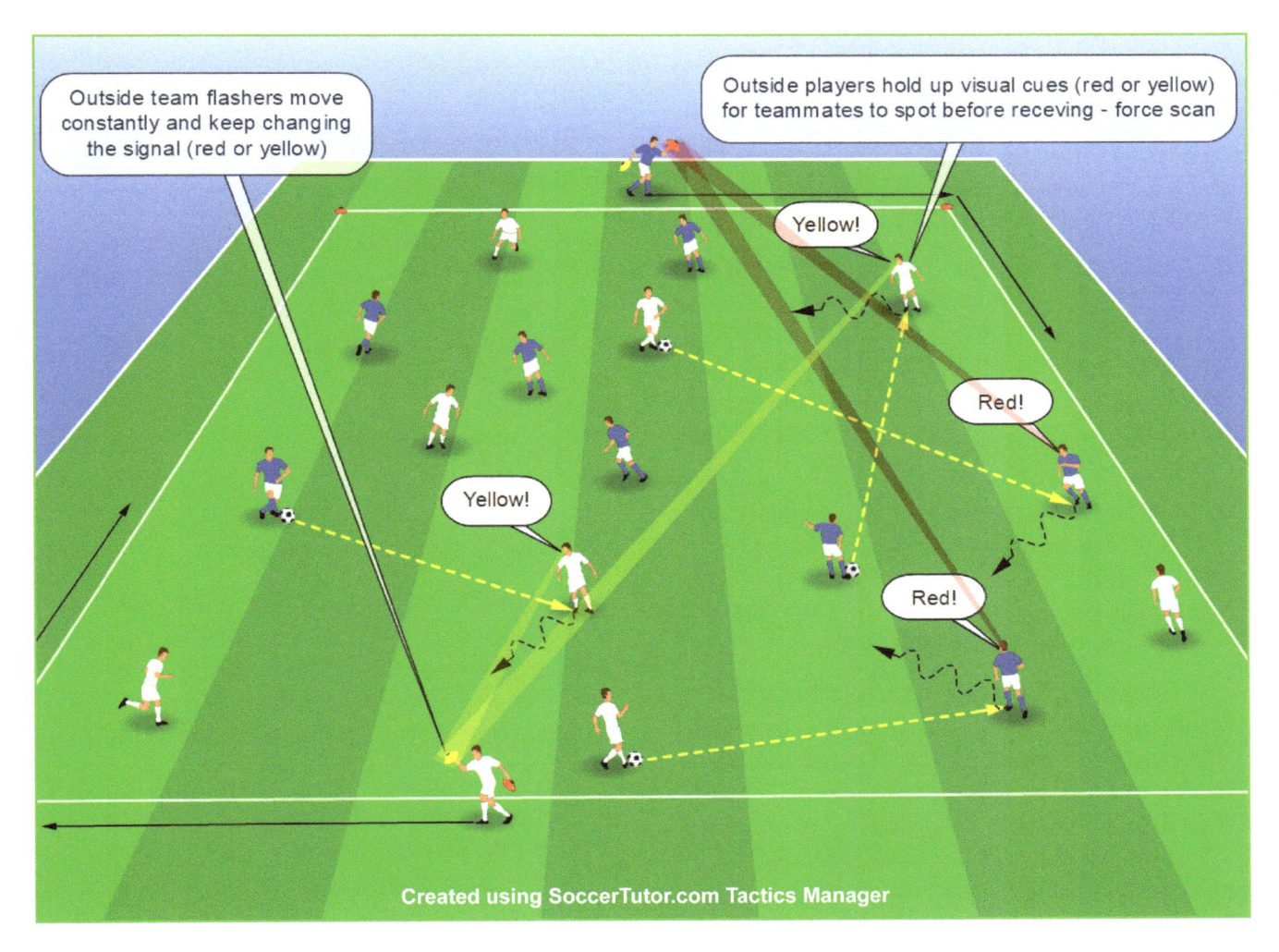

Outside team flashers move constantly and keep changing the signal (red or yellow)

Outside players hold up visual cues (red or yellow) for teammates to spot before receving - force scan

Objective: To develop scanning and good body positioning/shape.

Practice Description

- To progress from the previous practice, we have added team cone flashers (white and blue) on the outsides of the area to force the players to look for something specific.

- These outside players are constantly on the move and holding up a visual cue.

- Players continue to pass to a player in the opposite colour and do not pass to the outside cone flashers.

- All players must spot and call out the colour held up by their teammate outside the area before receiving any pass e.g. Blue players spot and call out colour held by the outside blue player.

- **KEY POINT:** Players must spot and call out the colour **AFTER** the ball has been passed to them and **BEFORE** they have taken their first touch.

SCANNING - How to Train it

Game Awareness Level 1 - Observation: Scanning of the Playing Area

Practice Analysis for Coach

- The simple introduction of the team flashers on the outside now forces the players to direct their attention purposefully and look for something specific before receiving a pass.

- The player receiving the pass now also has two reference points, enabling them to adjust their body position – open to the player who is passing the ball to him **AND** his team flasher on the outside.

- It is essential that the team flashers are constantly on the move and holding up a visual cue. The movement around the playing area forces the players to continually check the position of the team flasher, adjust, and readjust their body position as required.

- Importantly, I ask the players to spot and call out the colour of the visual cue at a very specific moment – **AFTER** the ball has been passed to them and **BEFORE** they have taken their first touch.

- The regular **changing of the visual cue from one colour to the next (at random intervals) challenges the players to have that last look as late as possible**. This is because the "picture" may have changed – the visual cue could have been red before the pass but it may have changed to yellow just as the pass was played!

- The great thing about this set-up is that **you will very quickly notice which players are prone to ball watching** during the practice – they will be the ones frantically moving their heads around, searching for their teammate only when the ball is on its way to them. This is too late!

- One of the **key questions** to ask the players during this exercise is, **"when should you know where your teammate is on the outside?"**

- Usually, the first answer is "when I'm receiving the pass" – meaning when the ball is on its way to them. It is important to help the players understand that this is when they should have their **FINAL LOOK** to spot the colour, and this should not be the first time they look for where their teammate is.

- Some players will then say, "just before the pass is played," which is better but still not where we want them to be. If a player only looks just before the pass is played during the game, it will be difficult for him to consistently make the most effective decision – he simply doesn't have a good enough picture in his head to act upon. Of course, he may retain possession, which is great, but does he cause problems for the opposition and create opportunities for his team?

- Eventually we will get to the best answer......... **ALL THE TIME!**

- And that's exactly what we want, we want the players to be as continuously aware as possible of the other players around them. This is not something that just happens though, the players have to work at it.

- I ask the players to engage in a simple scanning pattern as they are moving about inside the playing area. Can they constantly be thinking **"where are the footballs, where's my teammate (flasher), where are the footballs, where is my teammate (flasher)?"** And importantly, physically look. This is the start of teaching them the principle of **SCANNING**, which is so important for developing their awareness skills.

- You will notice that some players will start to "cheat" by only taking an early look before the pass is played, and they will not look after the pass and before their first touch. Once again, taking their eyes off the ball can be a very uncomfortable experience for them.

Game Awareness Level 1 - Observation: Scanning of the Playing Area

- **The important thing is not to discourage these early looks – praise them!** Congratulate the players on looking early, so they can know where their teammate is, and simply reinforce that you also want the final look to be after the pass is played and before the first touch.

- **NEXT THING: What happens once the player has played his pass to an opposite colour?**

- Watch the players closely. Notice how many players start ball-watching as soon as they have played their pass. Some players will ball-watch until they are about to receive another pass, and only then do they remember to scan for their team flasher again.

- After releasing the ball, players should immediately re-engage in scanning to know the position of their team flasher. This is a simple example of **FOLLOW-ON** - **the sooner the player scans the sooner he can sort his body position and be fully ready to receive the next pass**.

- **KEY POINT:** We have now introduced the concept of **SCANNING** and established a basic scanning pattern between two points of reference.

- Achieving this is a great start for the players but the game frequently demands awareness of more than two points of reference.

- **HOW DO WE PROGRESS?** In the practice progression on the next page, we look at how we can challenge the players to build this scanning pattern to an increasing number of points of reference.

Coaching Points

A. Active Scanning – Know where your team flasher is before you receive the ball.

B. Body Position – Open to player you are receiving the ball from and to your team flasher on the outside. Maximise your viewpoint as much as possible.

C. Confirm – Check again! Look after the pass and before your first touch to spot and call out the colour held up by the outside team flasher.

D. Decision - There are decision making elements e.g. When/where to pass in traffic but because this practice is unopposed it is not considered as part of the game decision making process.

E. Execution – Pass to the appropriate side of the player (to his "back foot" or "open" side).

F. Follow-on – As soon as the player has played his pass to an opposite colour, he should immediately re-engage in scanning to know where his team flasher is.

Soccer eyeQ with SoccerTutor.com — SCANNING - How to Train it

Game Awareness Level 1 - Observation: Scanning of the Playing Area

PROGRESSION 2: Coloured Balls + Visual Cues (Outside Colour-Coded Flashers)

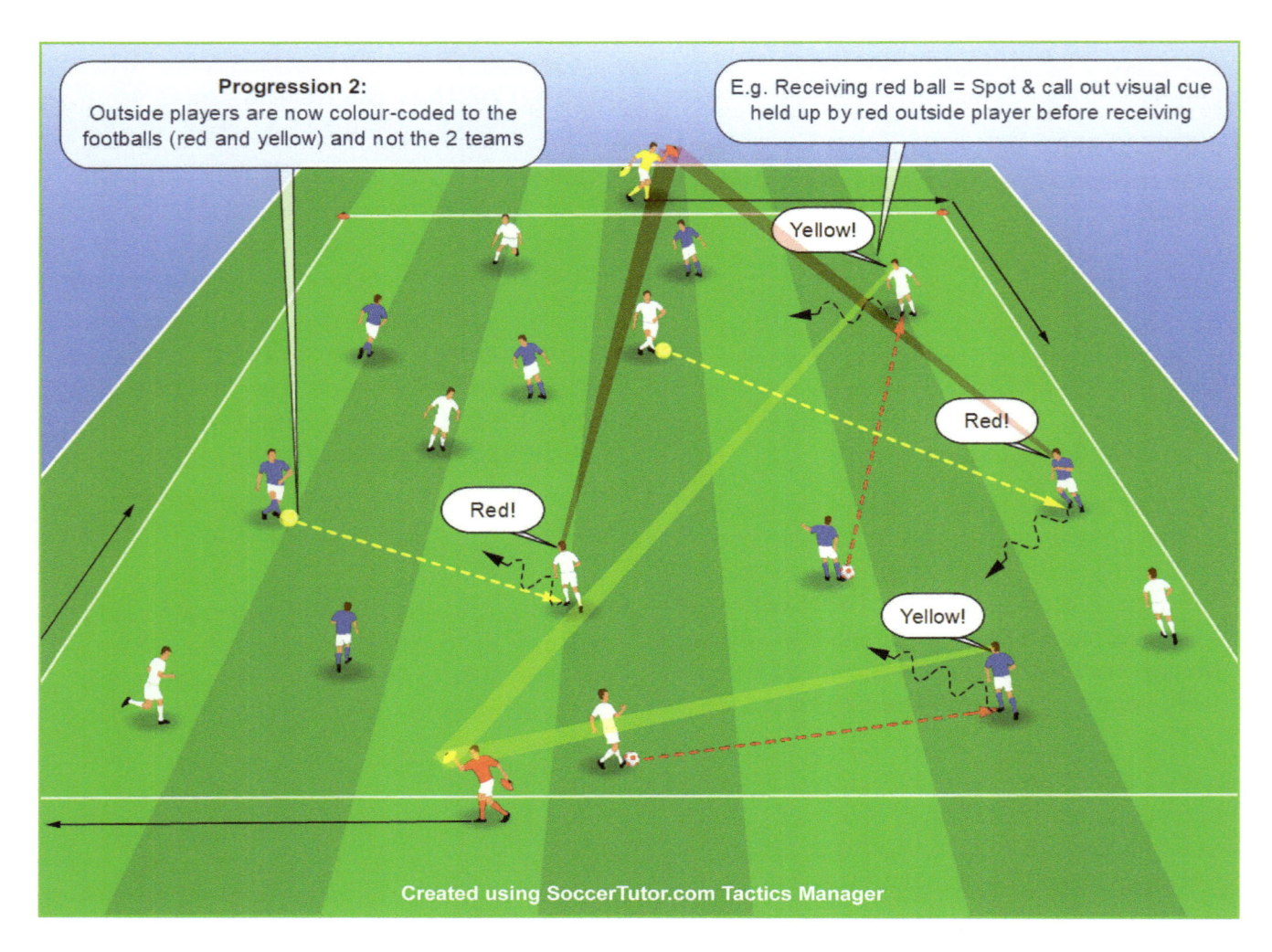

Progression 2: Outside players are now colour-coded to the footballs (red and yellow) and not the 2 teams

E.g. Receiving red ball = Spot & call out visual cue held up by red outside player before receiving

Practice Description

- To progress the practice further, we use coloured footballs (red and yellow) and the flashers on the outside are now colour-coded to the balls (not the team). The red ball = red flasher and the yellow ball = yellow flasher. These players are constantly on the move and holding up a visual cue (cone or glove).

- Players continue to pass to a player in the opposite colour and they do not pass to the outside flashers. Players receiving a pass must spot and call out the visual cue held up by the flasher colour-coded to the ball they are receiving e.g. When receiving the red ball, they call out the visual cue held up by the red flasher and vice versa with the yellow ball and flasher.

Practice Analysis for Coach

- **What is the different challenge for the players now?** The players now have 2 players to think about on the outside of the playing area, not just one team flasher. While they could previously concentrate on the position of just one player, they now have a red player and a yellow player to consider (depending on the ball colour).

Game Awareness Level 1 - Observation: Scanning of the Playing Area

- During the practice, the players do not necessarily know which colour ball they will receive next. The **players should constantly be aware of where both outside flashers (red and yellow) are positioned** so they are as ready as possible for whichever ball is passed to them. If they are searching for the red flasher as they are about to be passed the red ball, it is already too late!

- The set-up of this progression forces players to build the scanning pattern further. We are **now asking the players to actively scan between 3 points of reference**, as opposed to the previous two. I ask the players to constantly be thinking **"where is the red flasher, where is the yellow flasher, where are the footballs?"** And, once again, they must physically look.

- During the flow of the practice, the player will be in an area and situation where he is very likely to receive a particular ball. At this point, the player should focus more on that ball and the flasher of that colour.

- Example: If a player is likely to receive a yellow ball, he should **open his body shape** to see the yellow ball and yellow flasher, and **alternate quick looks between the yellow ball/flasher**.

- Only by doing all of this is the player ready to receive the pass and, if he is passed the ball, he is in a good position to **CONFIRM (have one last look at the visual cue the flasher is holding up) after the pass is played and before his first touch**.

- In the context of the game, it means the player is in the best position and has the most up-to-date information available to make the best decision and execute the next game action.

- Once again, **watch what the players do once they have played the pass to an opposite colour**.

- Do they immediately re-engage in scanning to know where both colour-coded flashers are, or do they ball-watch?

- There is also another important moment to consider when thinking about awareness, I ask the players **"what are the two options available to the player with the ball?"** Well, he could pass you the ball or he may not pass you the ball – he could decide to continue to dribble instead, or even pass to someone else. If he doesn't pass you the ball, what do you very quickly have to do? Who is it you have lost track of? Recover your scanning pattern and re-orientate yourself with **BOTH** flashers on the outside!

- This is another simple example of **FOLLOW-ON, where the sooner the player scans, the sooner he is fully ready to receive the next pass**.

Coaching Points

A. Active Scanning – Know where the flashers are before you receive the ball.

B. Body Position – Open up your body shape to best see the player you are receiving from and the correct flasher on the outside (maximise viewpoint).

C. Confirm - Check again! Look after the pass is played and before your first touch. Spot and call out the colour held up.

D. Decision - There are decision making elements but because this practice is unopposed, it is not considered as part of the game decision making process.

E. Execution – Pass to the appropriate side of the player (to his "back foot" or "open" side).

F. Follow-on – As soon as a player passed, he should re-engage in scanning to know where both flashers are.

Game Awareness Level 1 - Observation: Scanning of the Playing Area

PROGRESSION 3: Colour-Coded Flashers and Team Flashers + Switching Roles

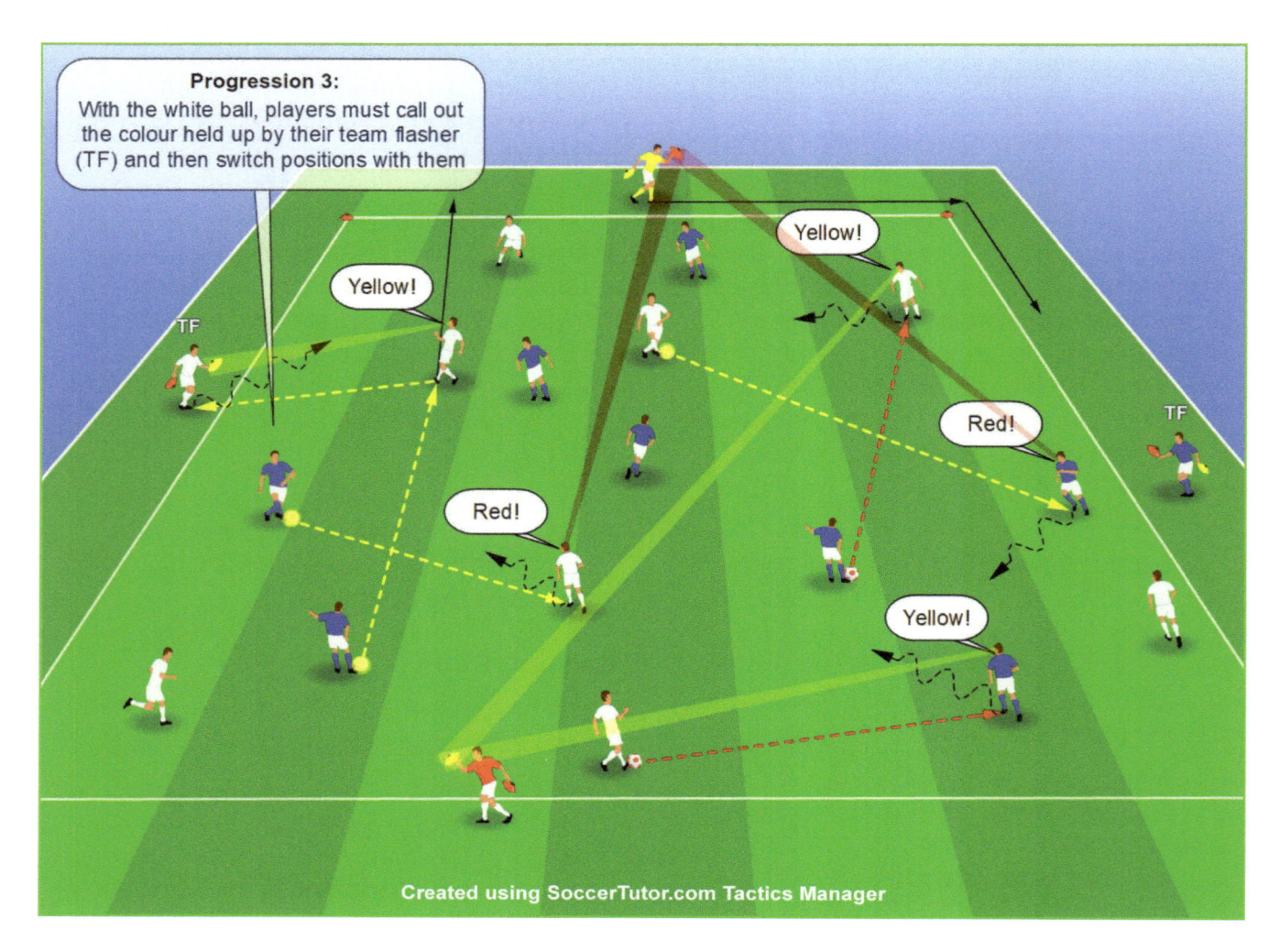

Progression 3:
With the white ball, players must call out the colour held up by their team flasher (TF) and then switch positions with them

Objective: To develop scanning and good body shape/positioning.

Practice Description

- To further progress the practice, we add a white ball and reintroduce the team flashers on the outsides of the area.
- **KEY CHANGE:** Players must spot and call out the colour held up by their team flasher before receiving the **White Ball**.
- They then pass to the team flasher and move outside to switch roles - the team flasher dribbles the ball into the area to pass to an opposite colour player.
- Players continue to spot the colour-coded flashers when they receive the red or yellow balls e.g. Spot and call out visual cue held up by the yellow outside flasher when receiving the yellow ball.
- They do not pass to the colour-coded flashers and continue by passing to a player in the opposite colour.
- Players must spot and call out the colour of the visual cue **AFTER** the ball has been passed to them and **BEFORE** they have taken their first touch.

Game Awareness Level 1 - Observation: Scanning of the Playing Area

Practice Analysis for Coach

- We have now integrated everything together, so we have team flashers plus colour-coded flashers and balls.

- To add to the challenge, I also ask the players to switch roles with their team flasher when they get the white ball. Initially, with this interchange, you may find players will follow their pass out and replace the team flasher in the exact position they were standing in. Instead, **encourage the players to drop out of the area on a different side (as shown in the diagram)**. This ensures the position of the team flasher is always changing and forces the players to continually scan to find him.

- **What is the different challenge for the players now?**

- There are now **3 points of reference (red flasher, yellow flasher, and team flasher) on the outside to think about, plus the different colour balls inside the area**. This means they must build their scanning pattern further in order to be continuously aware of where these players are.

- Players also now face a challenge of when to pass to the flasher and when not to. This may seem simple enough, but don't be surprised when you see players not passing to the team flasher when they should and passing to the colour-coded flashers by mistake! Some players will also pass out to the team flasher and then forget to move outside of the area (switch roles).

- This practice becomes a very physically active and **mentally demanding exercise for the players, as they must continually engage in scanning and optimise their body position** to see the flasher and as much of the field of play as possible (maximising their viewpoint).

- Hopefully, you can see how we have progressed a basic practice to help the players develop their Level 1 Game Awareness by forcing them to scan the playing area.

Coaching Points

A. Active Scanning – Know where the colour-coded flasher is before you receive the ball.

B. Body Position – Open body shape to the player you are receiving the ball from and to the correct flasher on the outside. Maximise your viewpoint as much as possible.

C. Confirm – Check again! Look after the pass and before your first touch to spot and call out the colour held up by the correct flasher.

D. Decision - There are decision making elements e.g. When/where to pass in traffic but because this practice is unopposed it is not considered as part of the game decision making process.

E. Execution – First touch to set-up the pass to the correct flasher (only if receiving the white ball) or dribble into space. Pass to the appropriate side of the player (to his "back foot" or "open" side).

F. Follow-on – As soon as the player has played his pass to an opposite colour, he should re-engage in scanning to know where all the flashers are.

Game Awareness Level 1 - Observation: Scanning of the Playing Area

DRILL EXAMPLE: Basic "Ajax Square" Passing Drill - Pass and Follow

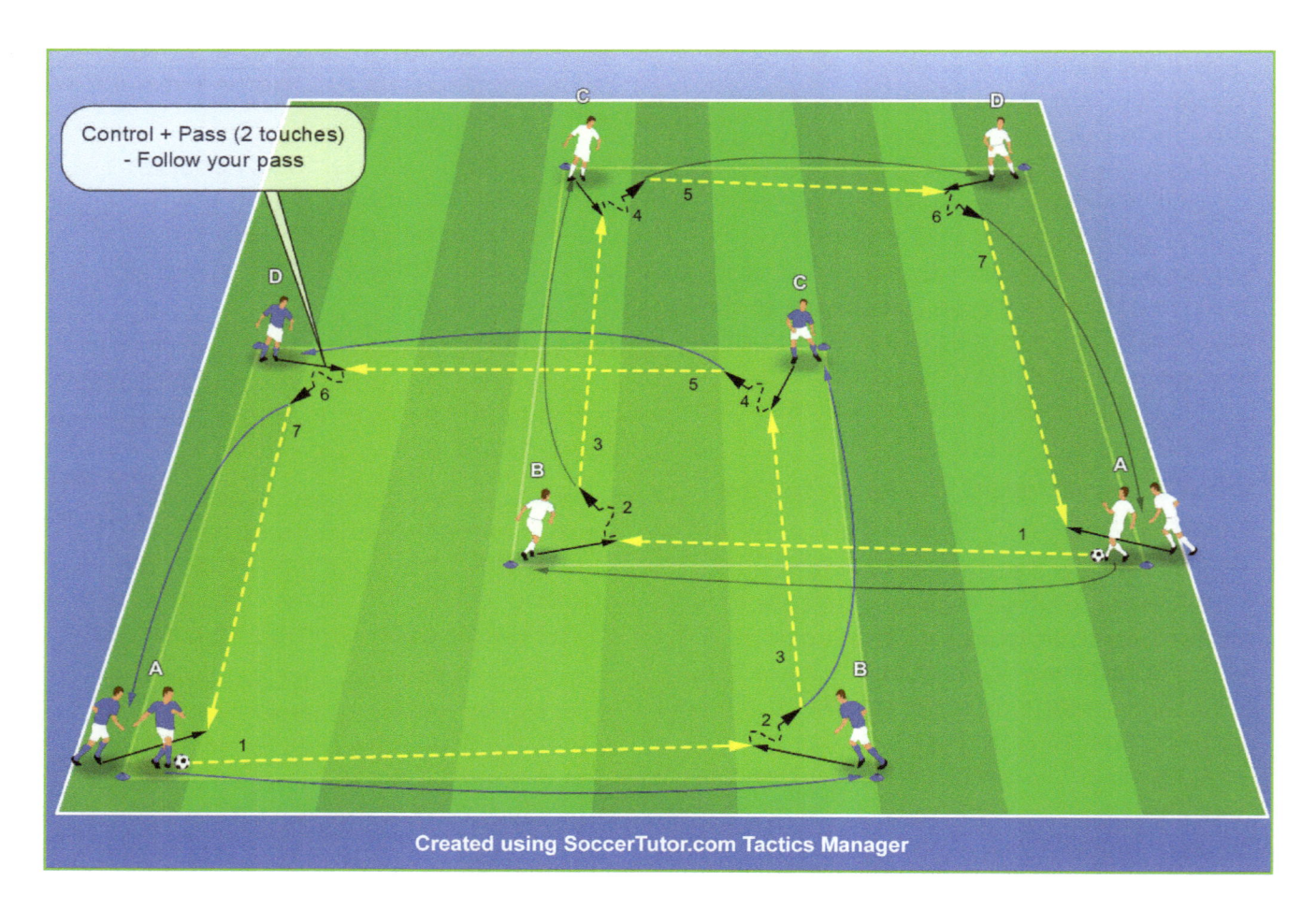

Control + Pass (2 touches) - Follow your pass

- Now we look at how you can incorporate some of these ideas into a drill type practice...
- This example is a square passing practice, commonly referred to as an **Ajax Square**, where the players pass the ball around the outside of the square and follow their pass.
- I like to interlock two squares together, which introduces some traffic along two sides of each square.
- The important thing when using a drill is still to demand high standards in everything, otherwise the players will end up simply going through the motions.

- In this practice, I emphasise various technical coaching points such as quality of pass (line/pace) and movement off the cone (timing/speed).
- I also emphasise how I want the players to control the ball when they receive it. Some coaches may ask the players to get the ball out of their feet, but I prefer what I call a **tight touch** – this is a touch that keeps the ball at their feet, but not under them. It keeps the ball just far enough away to punch through it with a pass without any unnecessary steps, and close enough should they need to change direction.

Soccer eyeQ with SoccerTutor.com

SCANNING - How to Train it

Game Awareness Level 1 - Observation: Scanning of the Playing Area

PROGRESSION 1: "Ajax Square" with Visual Cues to Spot and Call Out

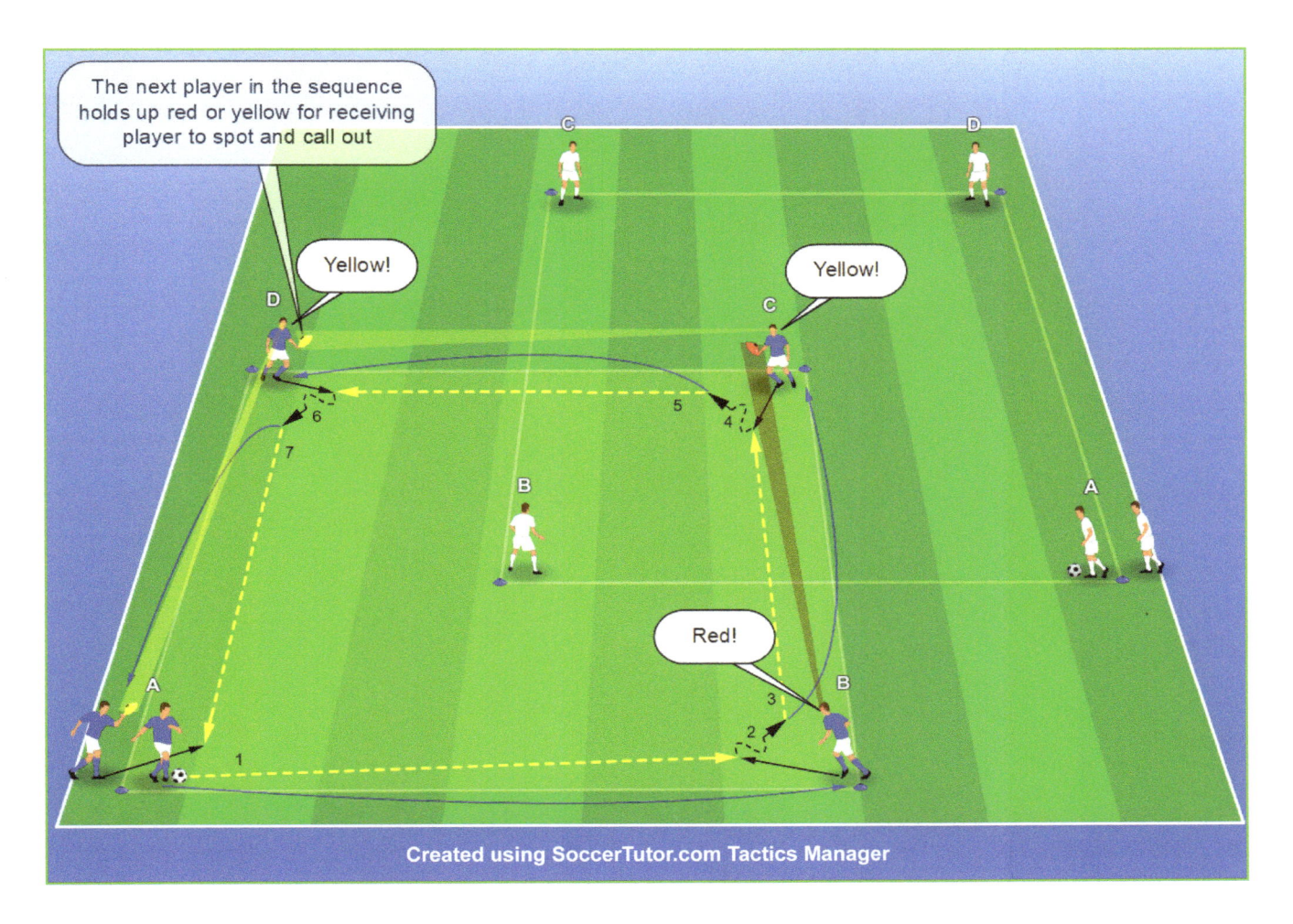

Practice Description

- We now add visual cues. The players need to spot and call out the correct colour before receiving a pass. The next player around the square must hold up a visual cue for the player receiving the pass to spot.

Practice Analysis for Coach

- Looking ahead is something most players don't do in this type of drill as they already know where the next player is going. Why look? They don't have to, even though we want them to. **Adding the visual cues forces them to physically look at where they are going next**.

- It also **forces the players to concentrate more continuously throughout the drill (off the ball)**. Players can switch off in between their involvement with the ball. Now, they have an off-the-ball job to do (holding up a visual cue at the correct time) – many players are caught out by this simple task to start with!

- At this stage, the ball is only going around in one direction so it's important for the coach to take the opportunity to change the direction of the drill. We want the players to not only have the ability to work off both feet but also have the ability, and feel comfortable, to scan in both directions.

Game Awareness Level 1 - Observation: Scanning of the Playing Area

PROGRESSION 2: Spotting + Reversing Direction of Play

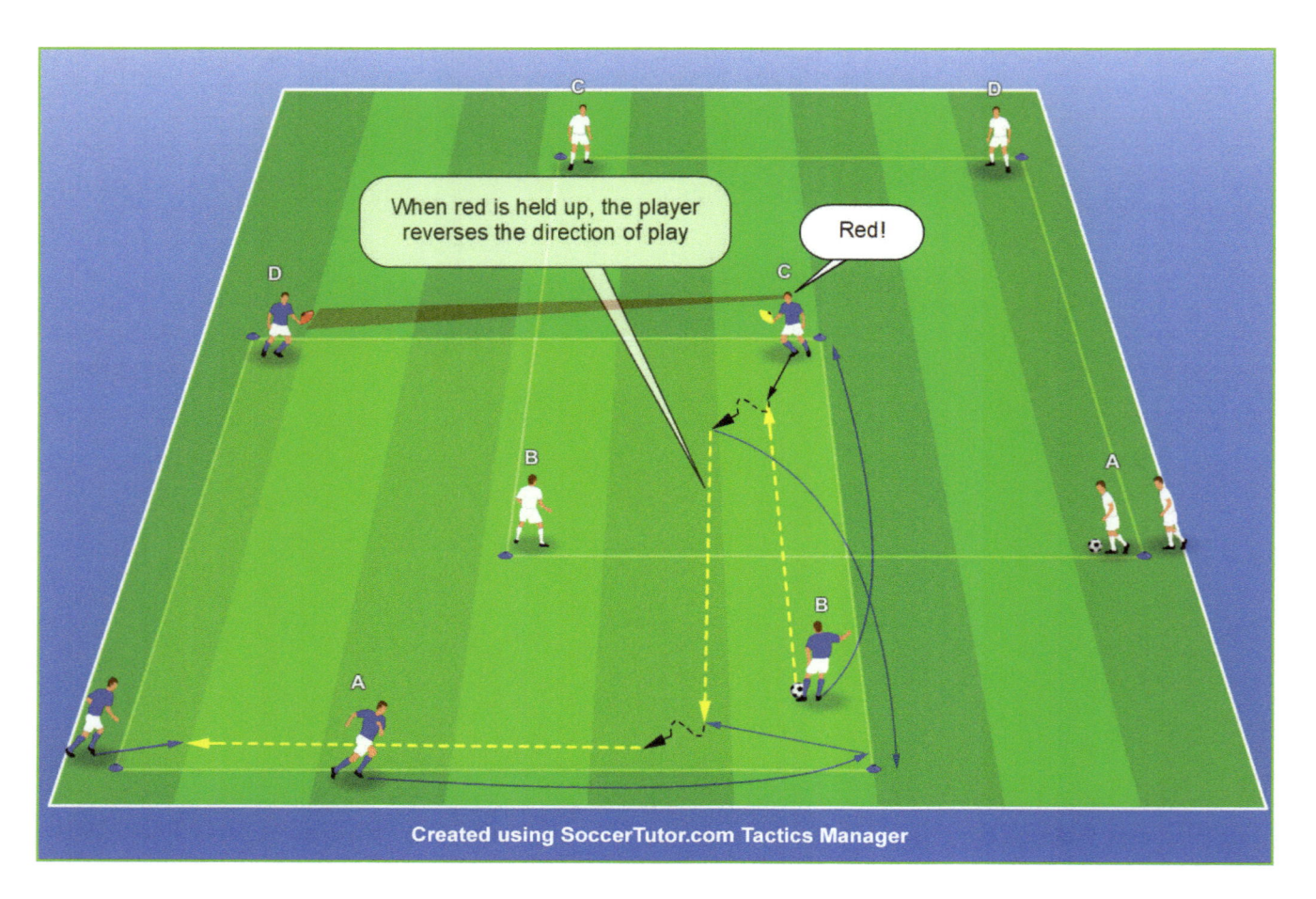

When red is held up, the player reverses the direction of play

Red!

Practice Description

- To further challenge the players, we add an extra variable when spotting the visual cue held up by the next player.

- This creates 2 different outcomes:
  1. **Yellow** = Continue in same direction
  2. **Red** = Reverse the direction of play

- The diagram shows what happens when the visual cue is red - the direction of play is reversed e.g. Anti-clockwise to clockwise (from Player C back to B).

- We now have more players actively involved both on and off the ball at any given time.

Practice Analysis for Coach

- You will find that the **concentration levels of the players will be really challenged**. The players will become disorientated on where they are meant to look and when they are meant to be holding up a visual cue.

- You will also find that players may neglect the technical standards you are asking for (timing of movement, quality of pass, quality of touch) – this is understandable due to the mental challenges they now face with these progressions. However, after allowing them some time to get used to the progression, it is important to demand high quality with the ball.

Game Awareness Level 1 - Observation: Scanning of the Playing Area

PROGRESSION 3: Spotting, Reverse Direction, and Diagonal Passing

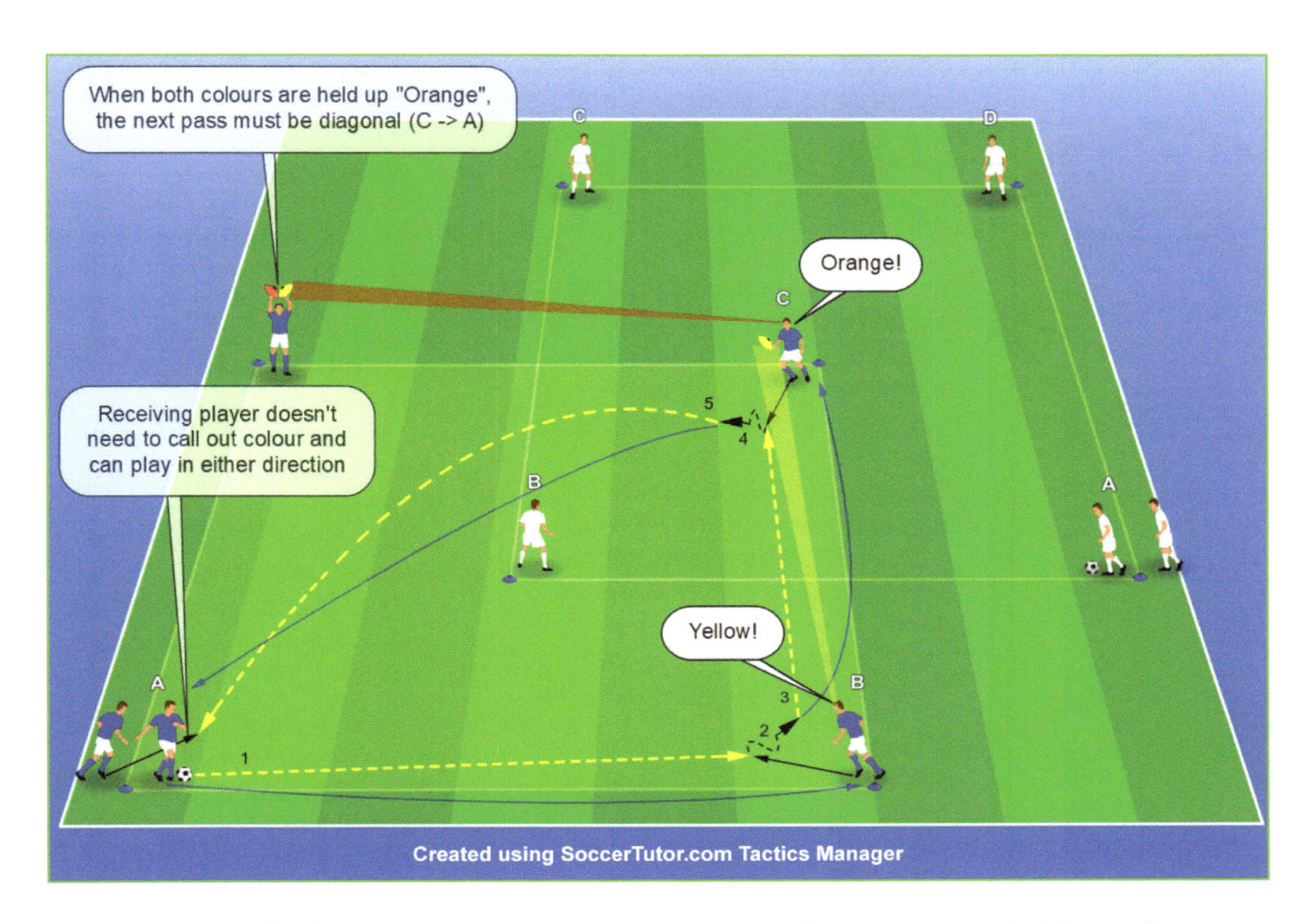

When both colours are held up "Orange", the next pass must be diagonal (C -> A)

Receiving player doesn't need to call out colour and can play in either direction

Orange!

Yellow!

Practice Description

- To further challenge the players, we now give them the option of holding up both visual cues at the same time.
- This creates 3 different outcomes:
  1. **Yellow** = Continue in same direction
  2. **Red** = Reverse the direction of play
  3. **Both (Orange)** = Diagonal pass
- The diagram shows what happens when the visual cue is orange (both colours held up).
- The receiving player must play the next pass diagonally across the square.

- In the diagram example, Player C spots both cones held up, so receives and plays a diagonal pass across the square to the start position.
- When the ball is switched diagonally, the passer still follows his pass.
- The receiving player does not have to spot a visual cue and can choose which direction to go next with the ball.

Practice Analysis for Coach

- See previous page (Progression 2).

SCANNING - How to Train it

OBSERVATION PRACTICES - SUMMARY

I have shown how we can purposefully develop scanning in a dynamic exercise and how we can incorporate it into a passing drill.

I prefer the dynamic practices as they develop behaviours that are closer to what the player will need in the game. However, I also sometimes use drills and I know many coaches that use them regularly. Therefore, **whilst a drill may have its limitations, I think it is useful to show how we can layer these ideas into one so those coaches who use drills regularly can consider adding these ideas** into what they do.

However, whilst we can introduce the concept of Level 1 Observation into a drill, the set-up does mean that the scanning element is significantly more limited than in a dynamic exercise. A dynamic exercise offers a 360 degree environment and the player will have to engage in scanning in order to locate his teammates, whereas he already knows where his teammate is positioned due to the set-up of a drill.

Also, whilst we can add meaning to the colours, so the player has to execute a specific game-action, this is not decision-making. The colour simply tells the players what to do.

I know some people will argue that, by using the colours, we are not developing "contextual cues" here. However, as I have mentioned previously, **at Level 1 we are simply trying to help players feel more comfortable taking their eye off the ball to develop the habit of looking around far more frequently** than they currently do. Furthermore, whilst calling out a colour is not contextual, the fact the players were able to engage in scanning (take their eye off the ball) and locate a key player (the one holding up the visual cue) is significant in the context of the game.

Some coaches get too focused on the use of coloured cones or gloves and fail to notice we are getting the players to scan for other players – calling out the colour is just confirmation that they have seen them.

With these constraints added, the sessions are also **far more engaging for the players and the levels of concentration required to perform consistently well are quite intense**. Instead of the switch on/off nature the sessions previously had, they have now been developed into practices that demand continuous focus from the players. Believe it or not, just holding up a visual cue at the correct time can be mentally challenging!

LEVEL 2 - REALIZATION:
Reading the Game Situation

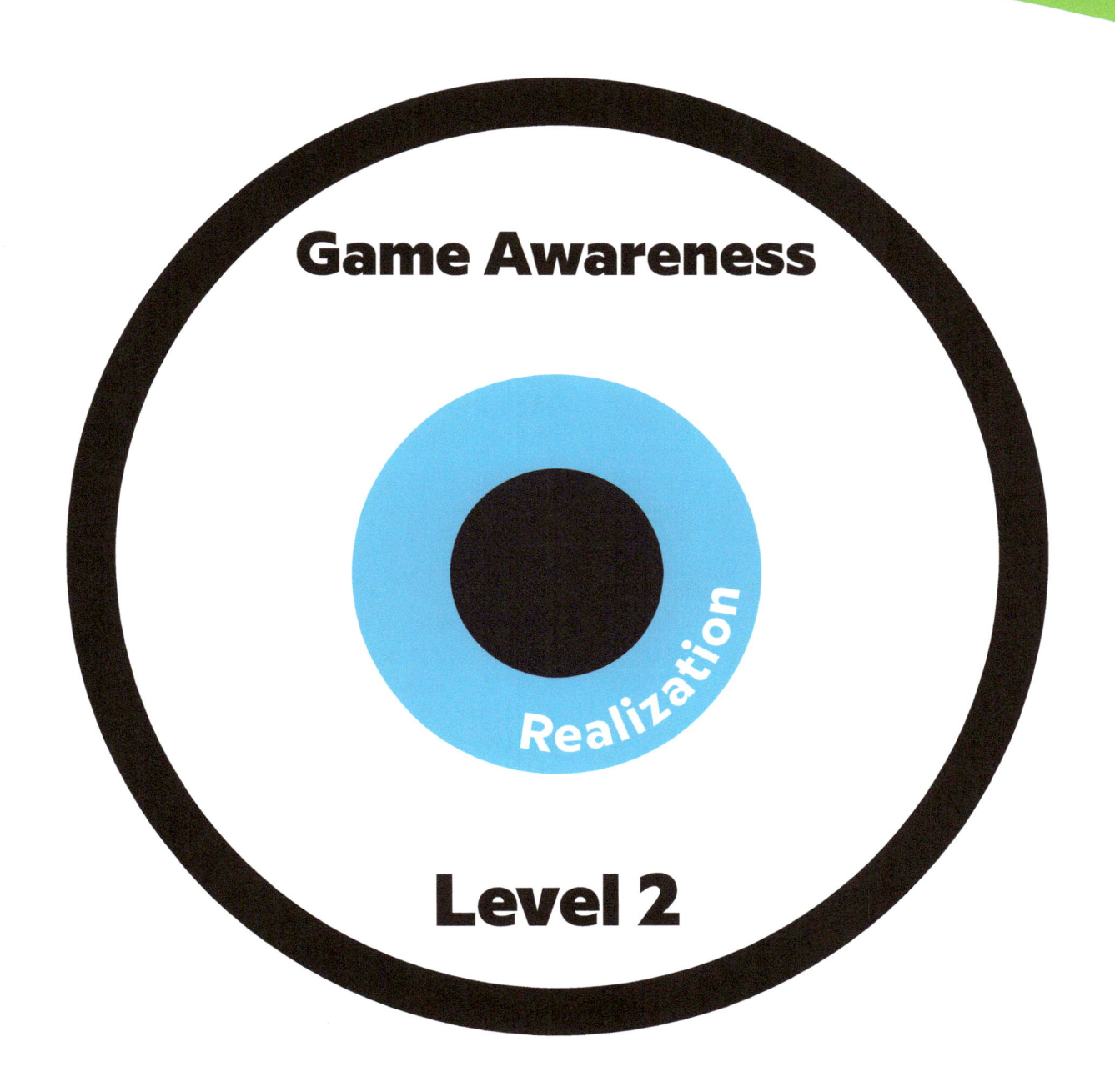

Game Awareness

Realization

Level 2

REALIZATION PRACTICES:
Reading the Game Situation

KEY POINT: You will not be able to progress through all the stages of these practices in one session!

What we are going to look at here would be built up over a number of sessions and could take some players and teams months to perform consistently well.

Realization is the next element of the model, and this stage builds upon the foundational Observation skills that have been developed (see previous section), with the **players now attaching meaning to the information that they are taking in**.

As I discussed in the first part of this book, adaptive positioning is a fundamental element of awareness during the game. The ability of the player to optimise their body position (orientation and location) in relation to the ball, teammates, and opponents is crucial.

As Level 1 Observation practices primarily focussed on positioning in relation to the passer and a teammate (team flasher), there was little significance attached to their position in relation to any of the other players in the area.

In **Level 2 Realization, the players now have to position themselves in relation to multiple players around them** and, due to the dynamic nature of the practice, will have to continually adapt this positioning to be in the best place possible at any given moment.

At this stage, I will continue to use unopposed practices as I like to show that Realization can still be developed, to a degree, in unopposed practices if you create the right environment.

It can obviously be developed in opposed practices too. However, in a traditional unopposed practice, it can be too easy for players to move around without paying attention to where they are in relation to the other players around them or position themselves appropriately – they don't need to care, as no significance has been attached to any of the positional relationships.

This means that, for the players to develop an understanding of adaptive positioning, we must **provide an environment that forces them to continuously assess where other players are and understand where they should be positioned in relation to them** – and demand that they be there.

Knowing where you should be and actually being there are two very different things, so beware the players that can tell you the correct answer but don't do it on the pitch!

Let's now look at how we can develop a practical exercise using constraints and overloads that demand the players perform the necessary habits and behaviours essential for effective Realization.

Game Awareness Level 2 - Realization: Reading the Game Situation

"The ball is coming but, while the ball is coming, I'm looking. Ball is coming, right, but I'm looking there - are they moving, are they not moving? While the ball is coming, I'm picturing what I'm about to execute, right.

You look, picture, boom. Because I always say that the best camera you can have is your brain, right.

Turn, boom, picture again. When the ball comes it's not the same picture anymore.

Can you quickly analyse what's happening and see a path at that particular moment?"

Thierry Henry

Game Awareness Level 2 - Realization: Reading the Game Situation

PRACTICE EXAMPLE 1: Vision and Awareness Sequence Passing Practice

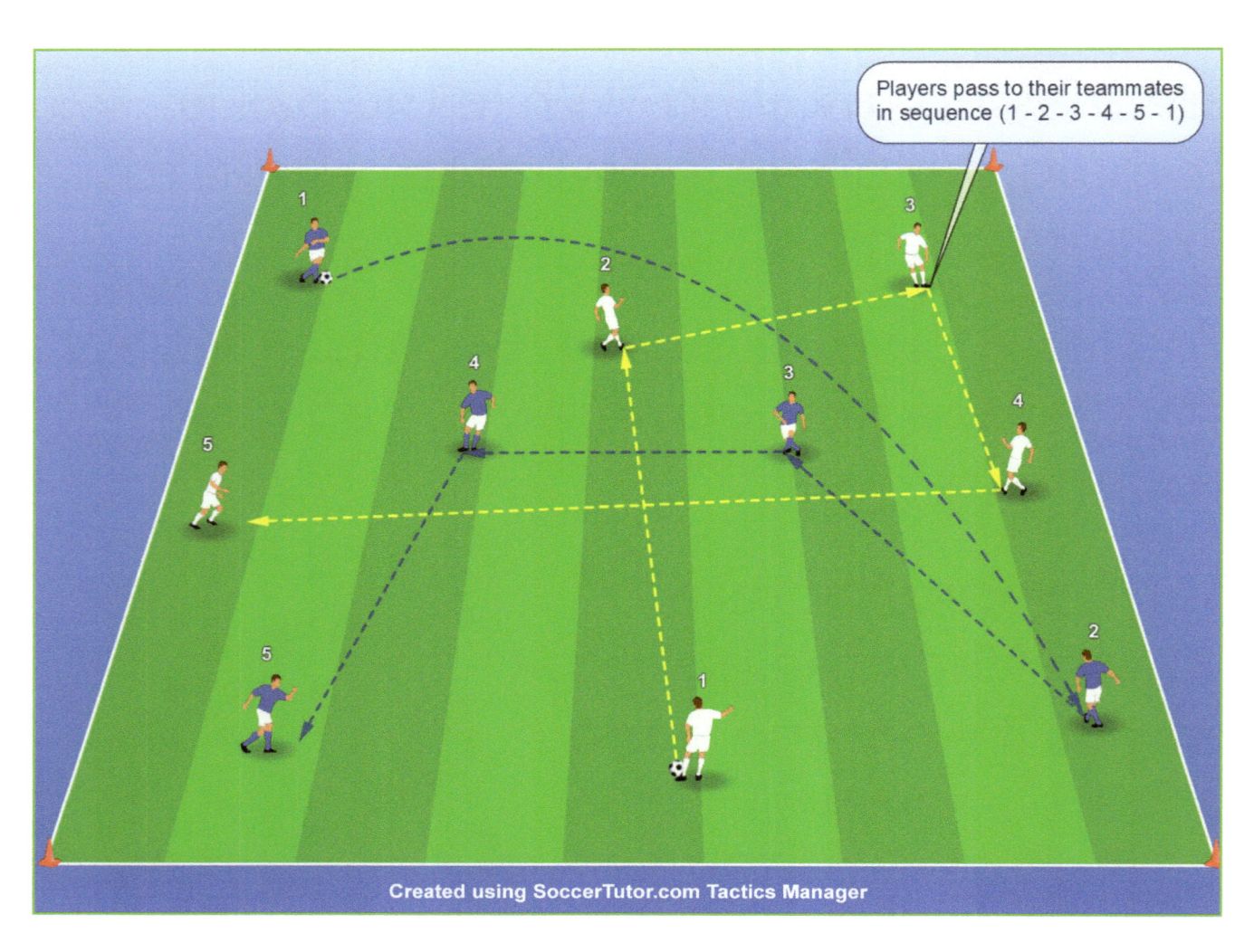

Players pass to their teammates in sequence (1 - 2 - 3 - 4 - 5 - 1)

Practice Description

- In a 24 x 24 up to 42 x 42 yard area (depending on the age, level, and number of players), we split the players into 2 teams of 5-7 with 1 ball per team.
- Number every player on both teams and start with the players moving around the area, passing the ball in sequence.

Practice Analysis for Coach

- This starts as a basic practice that most coaches will be familiar with, and we can use our **3 fundamental conditions (scanning, body shape and passing)** as the key coaching points.
- The main purpose of sequence passing is to **encourage the players to look and know where they will be passing the ball next** before they have the ball.
- If you ask the players what they should know before they get the ball, they will give you the correct answer – they must know where the player they have to pass to is positioned.
- The set-up should make it easy as you only have to pass to one specific player **BUT** just observe how many players receive the pass, control the ball, and **then** look around for their teammate –

Soccer eyeQ with SoccerTutor.com

SCANNING - How to Train it

Game Awareness Level 2 - Realization: Reading the Game Situation

this is the wrong order, and they won't know where their teammate is.

- You will also see the players whose heads are furiously swivelling back and forth, frantically searching for their teammate as the ball is on its way to him – this is still too late!

- This **panic-scanning shows a player did no pre-scanning off-the-ball and before the pass to know where his teammate is**. The last look as the ball is on its way should only be for final confirmation of the picture.

- Evaluate the players' performance through their behaviours on the pitch, and not the answers they give to your questions!

- However, because the practice rarely breaks down, and the ball continues to be passed in sequence and gets to its next destination, it is easy for coaches to miss the fact that the players are not being as aware as they should be.

- Therefore, it is clear we cannot just ask the players to look for their teammate – we must force them to.

- Remember, if we want the players to adapt their behaviours, we must put them into an environment that proves to their body that these changes must be made.

- **HOW DO WE PROGRESS?**
  We will introduce one of our overloads to force the players to adapt and carry out the behaviour we want – please see the progression on the next page where we use visual cues for players to spot.

Coaching Points

A. Active Scanning – Know where your teammate is before you receive the ball.

B. Body Position – Open to player you are receiving a pass from and the player you are passing it to next.

C. Confirm - In this original practice setup, scanning is often limited and players rarely make the last scan as the ball is on its way (because they don't HAVE to).

D. Decision - There are basic decision making elements in all practices but because this practice is unopposed, it is not considered as part of the game decision making process.

E. Execution – Pass the ball into the space just in front of the player's open body shape and towards their back foot.

F. Follow-on - After playing the pass, the player should quickly scan for the player he receives the pass from to provide support. However, in this original practice setup, players will rarely do this.

Game Awareness Level 2 - Realization: Reading the Game Situation

PROGRESSION 1: Vision and Awareness Sequence Passing with Visual Cues

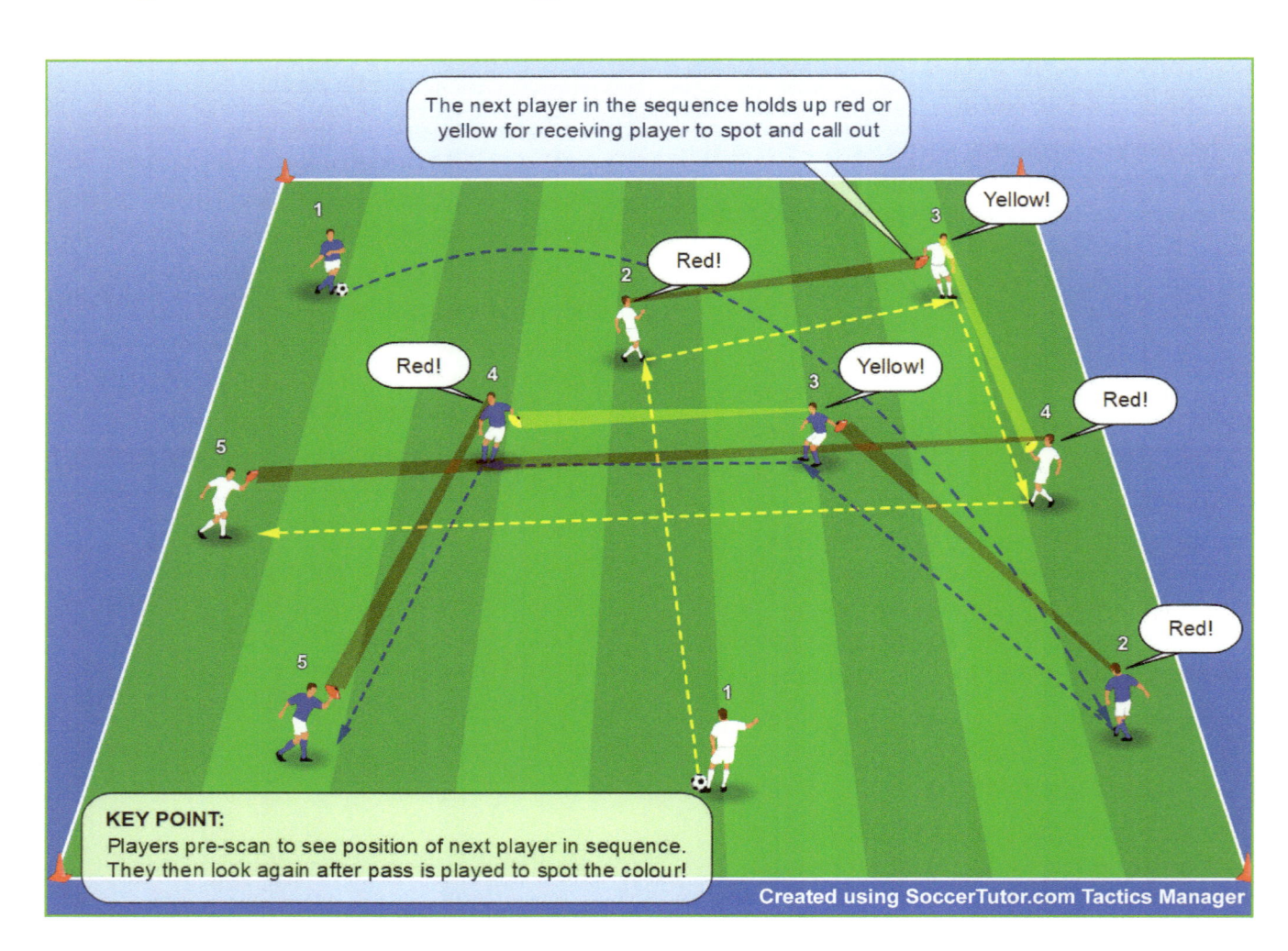

The next player in the sequence holds up red or yellow for receiving player to spot and call out

KEY POINT:
Players pre-scan to see position of next player in sequence. They then look again after pass is played to spot the colour!

Objective: To develop specific awareness of a teammate within sequence passing.

Practice Description

- To progress the practice and force the players to look, we ask the next player in the sequence to hold up a visual cue for the player receiving the ball.

- **Diagram Example:** As Player 1 is passing the ball to Player 2, Player 3 holds up a visual cue for Player 2 to spot and call out before his first touch. Then, when Player 2 passes to Player 3, Player 4 holds up a visual cue for Player 3 to spot and call out before his first touch.

Practice Analysis for Coach

- This simple constraint (visual cue to spot) **forces the player to know where his teammate is before receiving the ball** - he has to spot and call out the colour before taking his first touch.

- Calling out the visual cue is critical for 2 reasons. Most importantly, the **player needs to look at the visual cue**, and this is essential behaviour we are trying to continue to reinforce and develop. It **also helps the coach to confirm that the player has indeed looked**, and not just made a quick movement of the head.

Game Awareness Level 2 - Realization: Reading the Game Situation

- To start with, you may spend time coaching players to hold up a visual cue. Some players switch off and don't hold up the cue in time for their teammate, which is a clear sign that they have lost focus. In normal practices, the players only have to switch on as they are about to become directly involved in the play and switch off again once the ball has gone (until it comes to them again).

- As coaches, we demand that our players maintain concentration during the game, yet we consistently fail to optimise our training environments to increase the development of this skill.

- Some players will avoid making this mistake by constantly holding up a hand whilst they are moving around off-the-ball, and this is OK to get the practice moving. However, some players will cheat and only look before the pass is played and not when the ball is on its way to them – the plus point being that at least they are now engaging in off-the-ball scanning!

- Once again, this **pre-scanning is a good habit, and should be positively encouraged, but you must challenge the players to make that last look after the pass and before the first touch**. This **"check again"** is important in the game **as the picture may suddenly have changed** - in this practice their teammate may just have switched hands on them!

- As the players get used to the practice, it is important to progress and **demand detail in the timing of exactly when the players hold up the visual cue**.

- Being precise with this will force the players off-the-ball to concentrate more continuously throughout the practice and not just when they are about to receive the ball. It will force the player receiving the pass to have the last look as the ball is on its way.

- For example (see diagram), I would ask Player 4 to hold up the visual cue just as Player 2 is striking the ball to pass it to Player 3. Player 3 should pre-scan to know where Player 4 is, so he knows where to direct his last look. He must also look after the pass is played to spot and identify the visual cue, as it is not held up until the pass is made.

- **Player 4 has to stay alert as he can't just think about switching on when Player 3 gets the ball. He must switch on at least one pass earlier because he has an action to perform as Player 2 is passing the ball.**

- Now that we are forcing the player to look at their teammate, we can really reinforce **good body shape** – the player should be **"open" to the player he is receiving the ball from and who he is passing it to next**.

- This obviously makes it easier to play the next pass in the shortest time possible and also makes it much easier to have that last quick look (to spot the visual cue) as the ball is on its way to them.

- **If the player's body shape is correct, then the last look can be made with minimum head movement**, which means there is more time available to take in information and have your eyes back on the ball – giving the player more time to readjust, if necessary, and act effectively to the situation.

- **KEY POINT: The players are now proactively working on scanning, body shape, the check again, and the execution of the pass.**

- However, where the players are on the pitch in relation to each other still has no real meaning or thought behind it – the players will tend to run around somewhat aimlessly, as they have no landmarks to position themselves or guide their movement...

Game Awareness Level 2 - Realization: Reading the Game Situation

- **HOW DO WE PROGRESS?**
  In the next progression we have a look at how we can adapt the environment to develop awareness of positional relationships between the players.

Coaching Points

A. Active Scanning – Know where your teammate is before you receive the ball.

B. Body Position – Open to the player you are receiving from and the player you are passing it to next.

C. Confirm – Check again! Look after the pass and before your first touch to spot and call out the colour held up by a teammate.

D. Decision - There are basic decision making elements in all practices but because this practice is unopposed, it is not considered as part of the game decision making process.

E. Execution – Pass the ball into the space just in front of the player's open body shape and towards their back foot.

F. Follow-on - After playing the pass, the player should quickly scan for the player he receives the pass from to provide support. However, in this first progression players are not yet pushed enough to do this. The addition of the columns and rows in the next progression makes this follow-on scan more important (and gives a purpose for it), although players might still not do it as quickly as they should.

Game Awareness Level 2 - Realization: Reading the Game Situation

PROGRESSION 2: Sequence Passing with Visual Cues and Positional Play

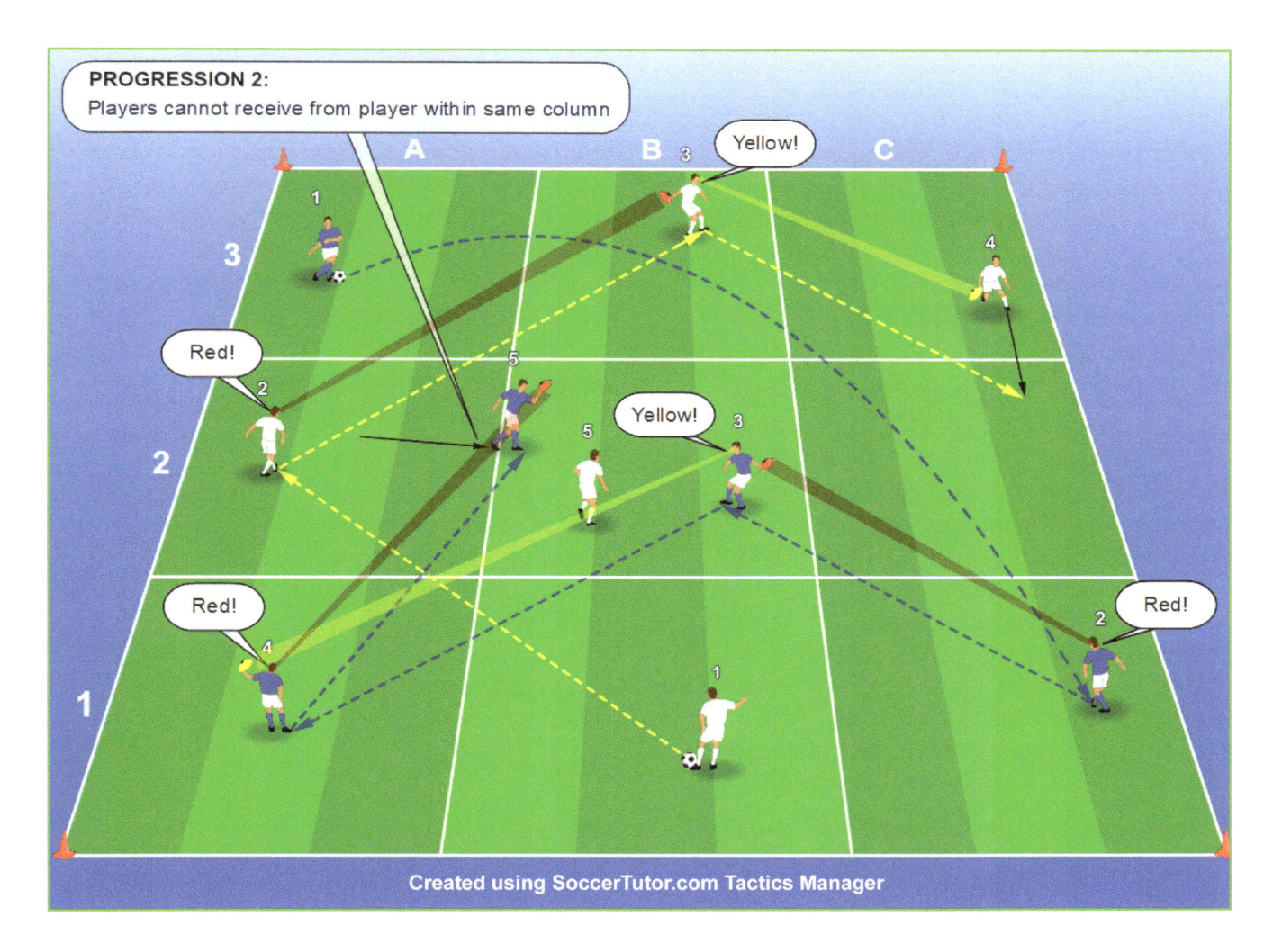

PROGRESSION 2:
Players cannot receive from player within same column

Objective: To develop awareness of positional relationships with teammates in a sequence passing practice.

Practice Description

- To progress the previous practice, we have divided the grid into 3 vertical columns (A/B/C) and 3 horizontal rows (1/2/3). We add the condition that the players cannot be in the same column or row as the player passing them the ball.

- This forces the players to be aware of their positional relationships with their teammates.

- **Diagram Example:** Blue Player 1 passes to Player 2, 2 to 3 and 3 to 4 in sequence. These passes are OK as the ball has moved into a different columns and rows each time.

- However, Player 5 needs to move out of Column A, as Player 4 is in the same column. He moves into Column B to be able to receive a pass from Player 4.

- As in the previous practice, the players continue to spot and call out the colour held up by the next teammate in the sequence e.g. Player 4 calls out Player 5's visual cue.

Soccer eyeQ with SocccerTutor.com — SCANNING - How to Train it

Game Awareness Level 2 - Realization: Reading the Game Situation

Practice Analysis for Coach

- You will notice a lot of players not concentrating sufficiently and failing to be aware of where they are - they will frequently find themselves in the same column or row as their teammate. This lack of positional awareness demonstrates they are not continuously assessing their relationship with the key players around them. **Players should be constantly adjusting and optimising their positioning, even if it's just a yard or two, based on the movement of the other players around them**.

- The introduction of the columns and rows gives the players' positioning a significance that was not necessarily there before. They have to **pay attention to the movement and positioning of the player that passes them the ball**, as this now directly impacts where they should and should not be to receive the next pass. They not only have to change column or row in order to receive the ball but that they may also have to adjust their body shape to be "open" to the player they are receiving from and the player they are passing to.

- Whilst maintaining good positional relationships is the key outcome of this practice, you will find that, even after extensive practice, the **players may still occasionally end up in the same column or row**. For these situations, we can use **3 Alternative Solutions**:

  1. The player to receive the pass can quickly move into a different column or row – although, this is where they should already be!
  2. The player with the ball can shift into a different column or row.
  3. The player with the ball can pass it into a different column or row and into space for the receiver to run onto.

- Options 1 and 2 will be dependent on which player is closest to the border of a different column or row, and Option 3 is used when either of the first 2 options will take too long – and we may only be talking about fractions of seconds of "waiting" time.

- I coach the players these solutions because the game does not always run perfectly, and players don't always manage to get into the position they should be. It is usually those who adapt quickest to the situation that come out on top. However, for training purposes it is important to ensure the players do not use these solutions as an excuse to not pay attention or to be lazy – **being in the right position at the right time should always remain the priority**.

- So far, we have managed to force the players to improve scanning, body shape, and the check again – all in order to know where the teammate who is passing the ball to them is. This is so they can be in an appropriate supporting position and know the whereabouts of the teammate they are passing to before receiving the ball.

- In sequence passing, the players generally need to be aware of only 2 players – who they get the ball from and who they pass it to. This is a great starting point but there are more than 2 teammates in the game, so now it's time to put the players in an environment that helps them increase the number of players they are continuously aware of.

- **HOW DO WE PROGRESS?**

  Whilst we may want the players to be aware of more players, we need to give them a meaningful reason to pay attention to these other players. So, in the next progression, we move on to looking at how we can use an overload to force the players into an environment where they must be aware of more players.

Game Awareness Level 2 - Realization: Reading the Game Situation

Coaching Points

A. Active Scanning – Know where the teammate who is passing you the ball is so you can take an appropriate supporting position and know where the teammate you are passing to is before you receive the ball.

B. Body Position – Open to the player you are receiving from and the player you are passing to next (in the correct area of the pitch).

C. Confirm – Check again! Look after the pass and before your first touch to spot and call out the correct colour.

D. Decision - There are basic decision making elements in all practices but because this practice is unopposed, it is not considered as part of the game decision making process.

E. Execution – Pass the ball into the space just in front of the player's open body shape and towards their back foot.

F. Follow-on – After passing the football, quickly re-engage in scanning so you can position yourself to support the player you receive from.

SOCCER EYEQ: Adding Tennis Balls to Practices for Extra Scanning

Why use Tennis Balls in training sessions?

The tennis balls increase the amount of scanning required during the session and also force the off-the-ball to players engage and concentrate more continuously.

- **KEY POINT 1:** The players must use "Accurate Passing Throws" aimed directly at their teammates. There should be no sloppiness or aimless throwing.

- **KEY POINT 2:** You will not be able to progress through all the stages of these practices in one session! What we are going to look at here would be built up over a number of sessions and could take some players and teams weeks or months to perform consistently well.

- The tennis balls are a secondary targeting task that force the players to scan for further players. The tennis balls element is added to an opposed practice, with the full Soccer eyeQ constraints in place, and the player needs to know where the flasher is to spot the colour, where opponents are applying pressure, where teammates are to maintain possession of the football, AND where a free teammate is to throw the tennis ball to.

- They add another layer of players that the player must be aware of because they are forced to interact with them through the throwing (accurate passing) of a tennis ball.

- In some practices, the tennis balls are used as part of the scoring mechanism, and this forces the players to look for specific teammates to pass to as the most effective passing option (but they can maintain possession through any teammate).

- In other practices, the players MUST pass the football to a player with a tennis ball. The players are again forced to scan for specific teammates, as they have strictly limited passing options available.

- This constraint also forces the off-the-ball players to engage more continuously throughout the practice. They must position themselves to provide support for the football AND also for those players with a tennis ball.

- Making these runs to support are similar to third-man runs in the game, where a player makes an advanced run to provide attacking support for the player who will be receiving the football.

- To see how the tennis balls are added and used in the Soccer eyeQ methodology practices, please see the following practices, starting with **"PROGRESSION 3: Third Man Support by Adding Throwing of Tennis Balls"** on the next page...

Game Awareness Level 2 - Realization: Reading the Game Situation

PROGRESSION 3: Third Man Support by Adding Throwing of Tennis Balls

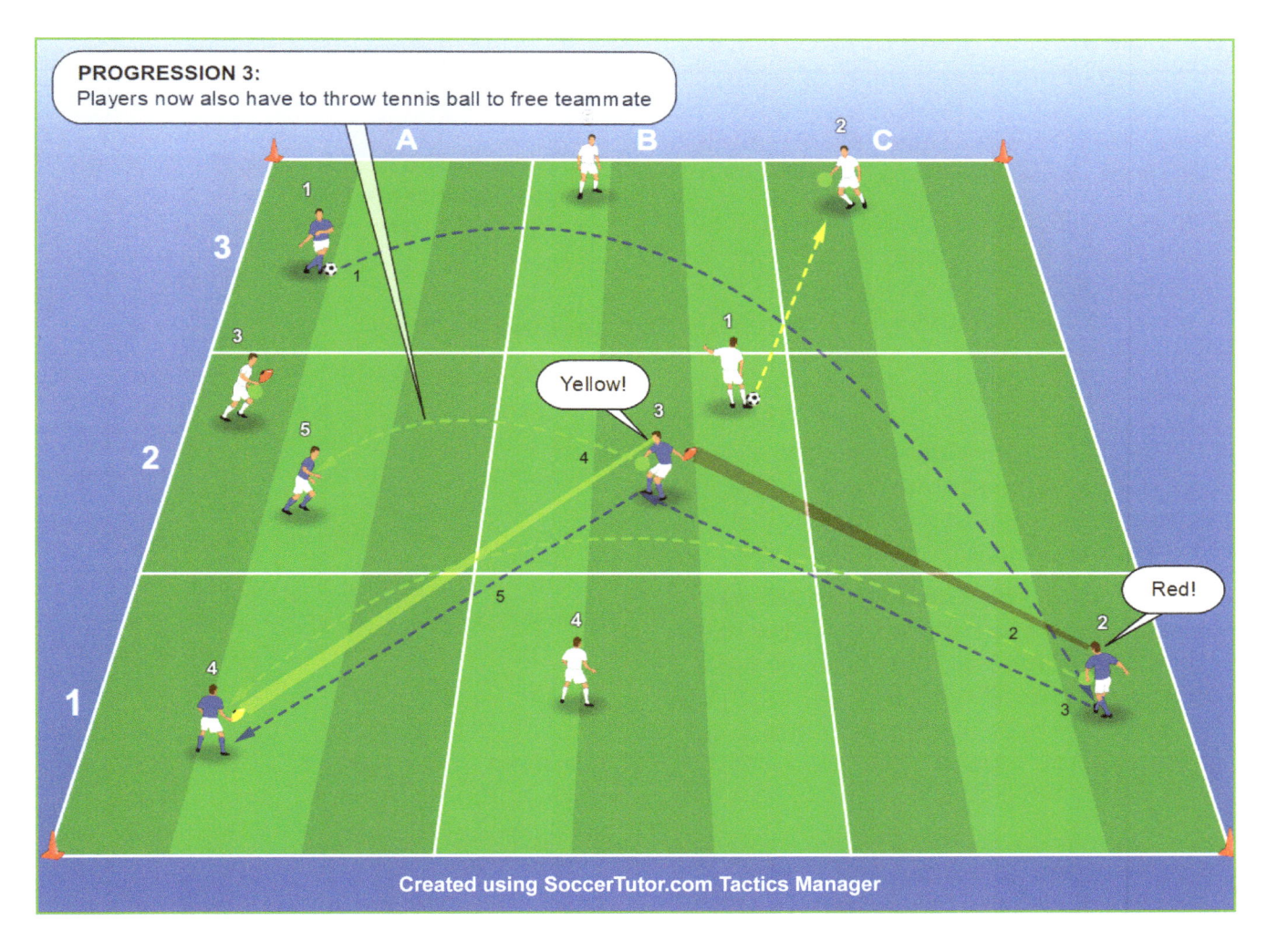

PROGRESSION 3:
Players now also have to throw tennis ball to free teammate

Practice Description

- To progress further, and to force the players to be aware of more teammates, we add 2 tennis balls for each team.

- Player 1 starts with a football and there are also 2 tennis balls in play (one with Player 2 and another with Player 3).

- The football still gets passed in the same exact sequence (1-2-3-4-5-1) and all previous rules from the previous practice apply. However, now tennis balls are also thrown by the players.

- The players only throw the tennis ball when they are receiving the football.

- The tennis balls jump a number and follow the sequence 2-4-1-3-5-2. The spotting and columns/rows conditions are not applied to the tennis balls.

- **How does it work?** When Player 2 is receiving the football from Player 1, he spots and calls out the colour held up by Player 3 **AND** throws the tennis ball to Player 4 all before his first touch.

- As Player 2 passes the football to Player 3, Player 3 must spot and call out the colour held up by Player 4 **AND** throw the tennis ball to Player 5.

SCANNING - How to Train it

Game Awareness Level 2 - Realization: Reading the Game Situation

Practice Analysis for Coach

- In sequence passing, players generally need to be aware of only 2 players – who they get the football from and who they pass it to. **By introducing the tennis balls, we are now going to force players to have a general awareness of 4 players** - who they get the football from, who they pass it to, who they get the tennis ball from, and finally who they throw to.

- For example, Player 3 gets the football from Player 2 and passes it to Player 4, and also gets the tennis ball from Player 1 and throws it to Player 5. Previously, Player 3 only had to be aware of Player 2 and Player 4, but now also has to be aware of Player 1 and Player 5. This now gives him **4 points of reference to be aware of throughout the practice**, although not necessarily all with the same focus of attention at all times.

- **After passing the football, the players have to catch the tennis ball. After they catch the tennis ball, they have to hold up a visual cue**. Then they have to divide their attention between receiving the football, spotting the visual cue and the player they have to throw the tennis ball to.

- It is important to **demand accuracy when throwing the tennis ball**. To start with, you may find that some players will throw the tennis ball aimlessly and expect the receiving player to work hard to catch it, but it is important to emphasise that we want the players to throw the tennis ball directly to their teammate for an easy catch.

- **What about the players off the ball, what challenges do they face now?** Earlier we discussed the benefits of asking the players to hold up a visual cue as it forces them to engage one pass earlier than in normal sequence passing. By adding the tennis balls, they are now engaged yet another pass earlier!

- The **players are thinking 2 passes ahead of receiving the football**. For example, Player 5 previously had to be ready to hold up a visual cue when Player 3 was passing to Player 4, but now Player 5 has to be ready when Player 2 is passing to Player 3, so he can catch the tennis ball from Player 3. This means that Player 5 has to move **off-the-ball to support the player who is receiving the football (to receive a tennis ball)**, which is the concept of the third-man run in the game.

Coaching Points

A. Active Scanning – Know where the teammate who is passing you the ball is so you can take an appropriate supporting position. Also know where the teammates you are passing the football to AND the tennis ball to are before you receive the football.

B. Body Position – Open to player you are receiving the football from and the player you are passing it to next (in the correct area of the pitch).

C. Confirm - Check again! Look after the pass and before your first touch to spot and call out the colour held up by your teammate.

D. Decision - There are basic decision making elements in all practices but because this practice is unopposed, it is not considered as part of the game decision making process.

E. Execution – Throw the tennis ball to your teammate so he can catch it. Pass the football into the space just in front of your teammate's open body shape, and towards their back foot.

F. Follow-on – After passing the football, quickly re-engage in scanning so you can position yourself to support the player you receive the tennis ball from.

Game Awareness Level 2 - Realization: Reading the Game Situation

PROGRESSION 4: Footballs, Throwing Tennis Balls, and Positional Play

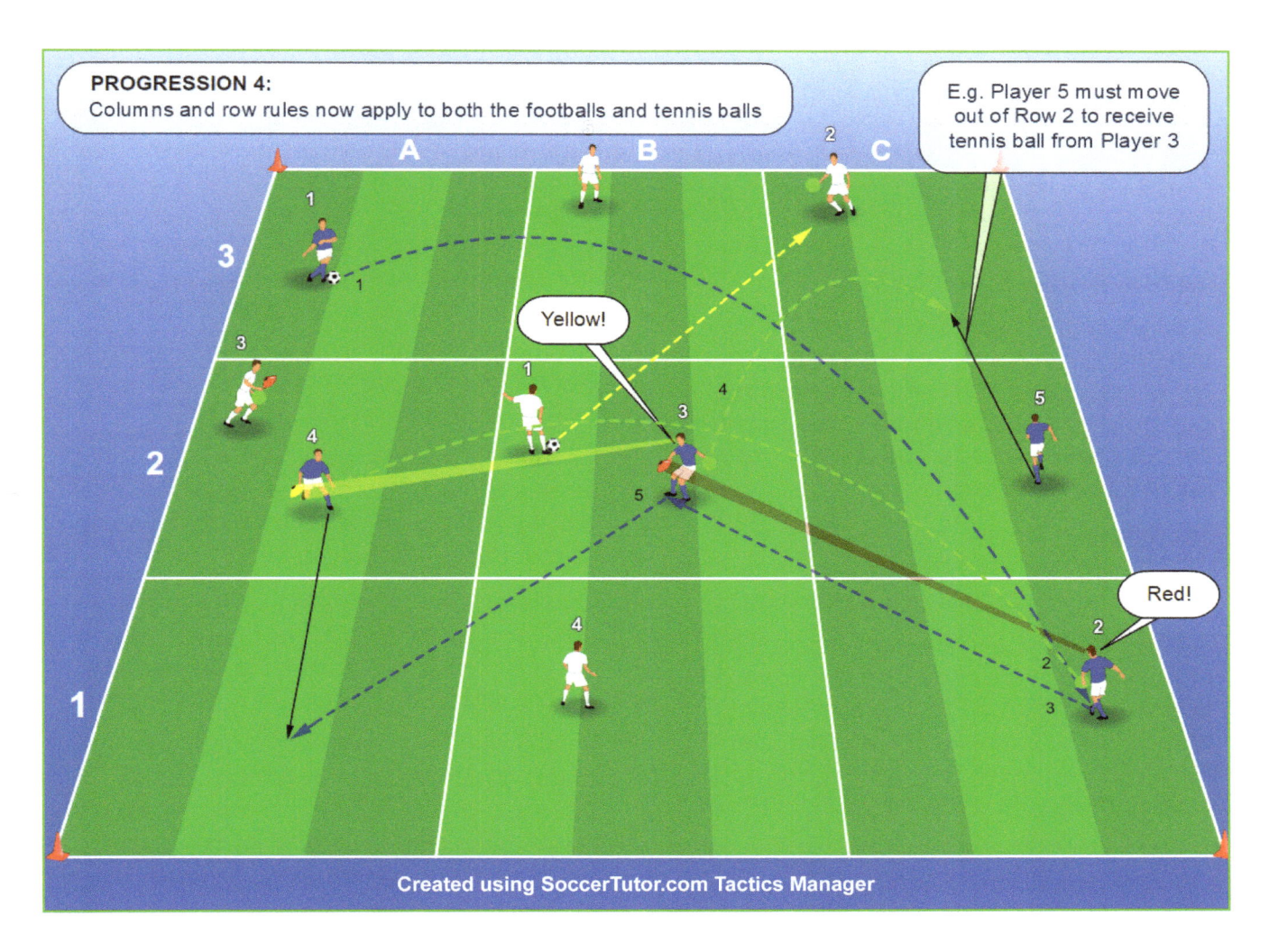

PROGRESSION 4:
Columns and row rules now apply to both the footballs and tennis balls

E.g. Player 5 must move out of Row 2 to receive tennis ball from Player 3

Yellow!

Red!

Created using SoccerTutor.com Tactics Manager

Objective: Awareness of positional relationships with teammates and incorporating off-the-ball support movements into specific areas.

Practice Description

- To progress this practice further, the columns and rows constraints now apply to both the footballs and the tennis balls.

- The players still have to have a general awareness of 4 players, but now they also have to achieve good positional relationships throughout to provide effective support to their teammates.

- The same rules and the same sequences remain from the previous practice.

- **How does it work?** When Player 2 is receiving the ball from Player 1, he must spot and call out the colour held up by Player 3 **AND** throw the tennis ball to Player 4 (who is in a different row) all before his first touch.

- You can see Player 4 move into a different row (2 → 1) to receive the football from Player 3. Player 5 also moves into a different row to receive the tennis ball from Player 3 (when 3 is receiving the football from Player 2).

Soccer eyeQ with SoccerTutor.com　　　　SCANNING - How to Train it

Game Awareness Level 2 - Realization: Reading the Game Situation

- As Player 2 passes the football to Player 3, Player 3 must spot and call out the colour held up by Player 4 and throw the tennis ball to Player 5. Remember, the football is on its way to Player 3 whilst he is doing both of these tasks!

- The practice will continue with Player 3 passing the football to Player 4, and you can see Player 1 already moving in position to receive the tennis ball from Player 4.

Practice Analysis for Coach

- Applying the columns and rows constraints to both the footballs and the tennis balls means there is **almost no opportunity to stand still – this practice forces the players to constantly move, adjust and readjust**.

- More importantly, the environment means **every move the players make has a purpose and a thought behind it**.

- As we found when we introduced the columns and rows rule for the football, you will see that a lot of players fail to concentrate sufficiently and frequently find themselves in the same column or row as their teammate throwing them the tennis ball.

- Once again, this slip in their positioning demonstrates their loss of focus and lack of awareness of their relationship with the growing number of key players around them. It may have been the briefest of moments they switched off, but it is those split-second moments that could be punished in a game.

- So far, everything we have done is about the players being aware of their relationships with their teammates.

- Another key relationship in the game is the one with the opponents and the players need to develop awareness of where they are and where the space is. Can this be done in an unopposed environment?

- **HOW DO WE PROGRESS?**
The next progression shows how we can progress to develop a basic awareness of the player-opponent-space relationship in an unopposed practice.

Coaching Points

A. Active Scanning – Know where the teammate who is passing you the tennis ball is, so you can take an appropriate supporting position. Know where the teammate who is passing you the football is for the same reason. Know where the teammates you are passing the football to and the tennis ball to are before you receive the football.

B. Body Position – Open to the player you are receiving the football from and the player you are passing it to next (in the correct area of the pitch).

C. Confirm - Check again! Look after the pass and before your first touch to spot and call out the colour held up by your teammate.

D. Decision - There are basic decision making elements in all practices but because this practice is unopposed, it is not considered as part of the game decision making process.

E. Execution – Throw the tennis ball to your teammate (so he can catch it) after the pass is played and before your first touch. Pass the football into the space just in front of the player's open body shape, and towards their back foot.

F. Follow-on – After passing the football, quickly re-engage in scanning so you can position yourself to support the player you receive the tennis ball from.

Game Awareness Level 2 - Realization: Reading the Game Situation

PROGRESSION 5: Positioning, Support, and Maintain Space from Opponents

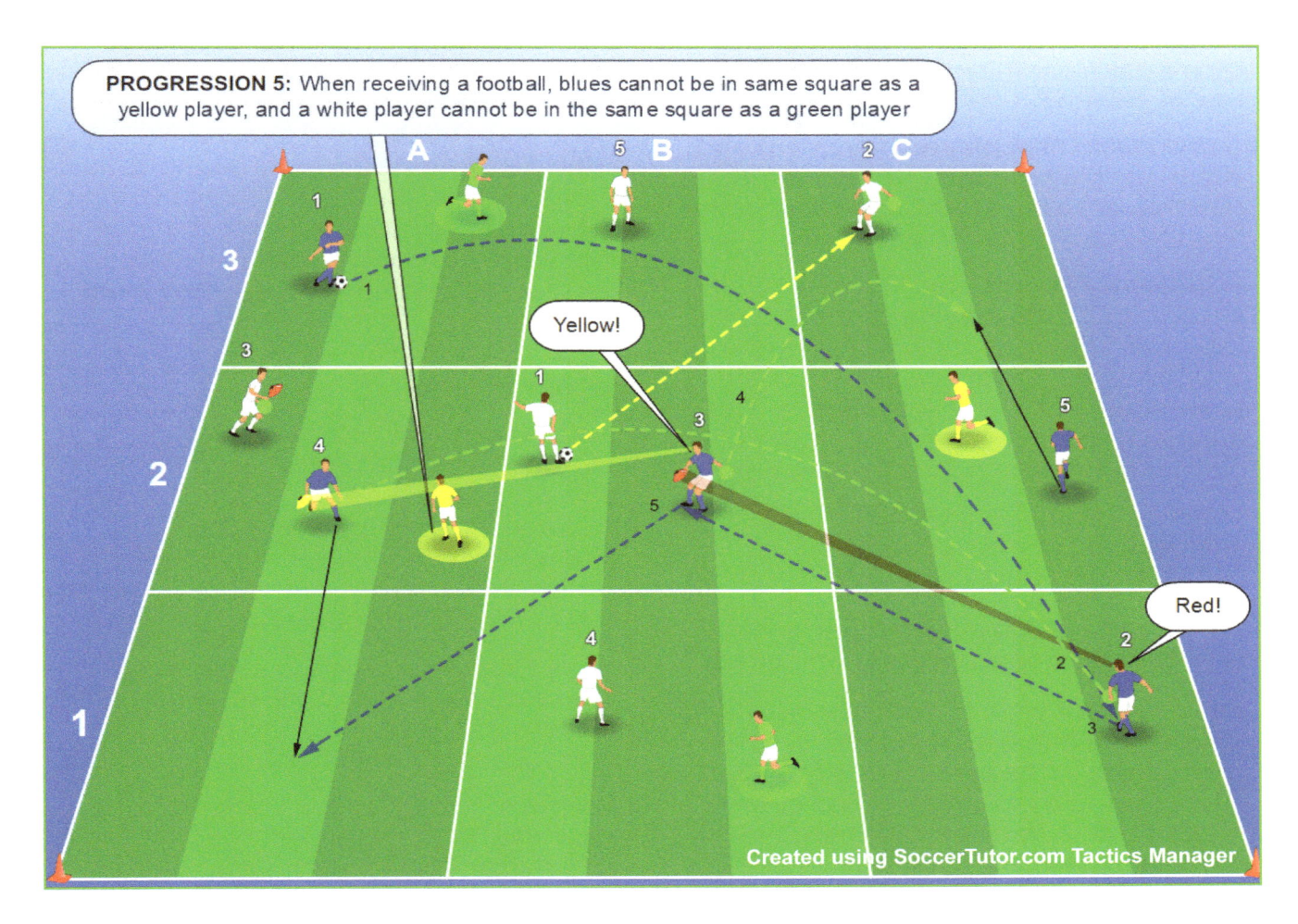

PROGRESSION 5: When receiving a football, blues cannot be in same square as a yellow player, and a white player cannot be in the same square as a green player

Objective: Develop awareness of positional relationships with teammates, specific off-the-ball support movements, and maintaining space from "opponents."

Practice Description

- All the **previous rules from the previous progressions apply but now we add 4 floating players (2 green and 2 yellow)**, who move freely around the playing area.
- When receiving a football, a blue player cannot be in the same square as a yellow floating player and the white players cannot be in the same square as a green floating player.

- The players cannot only think about the teammates they are passing or receiving from (footballs and tennis balls), they must also maintain appropriate space away from the floaters (opponents).
- This increases the general awareness demands from 4 to 6 players – who you get the football from, who you pass it to, who you get the tennis ball from and who you pass it to, and the 2 floaters that you cannot be in the same square as when receiving the football.

Soccer eyeQ with SoccerTutor.com

SCANNING - How to Train it

Game Awareness Level 2 - Realization: Reading the Game Situation

Practice Analysis for Coach

- In the diagram, you can see that Player 4 moves boxes to be away from the yellow player when receiving the football from Player 3. Player 5 also has to move rows (2 → 3) to be in position to receive the tennis ball from Player 3 - not in same row as Player 3.

- These **rules force player movement and when one player moves, it causes a chain reaction of complementary movements** from the rest of the players.

- **Additional Progression:** When receiving a tennis ball, blue players cannot be in the same square as the green players and the white players cannot be in the same square as the yellow players. This means the players have to be aware of 8 players during the flow of the session.

- Think of the challenges the players now face to their awareness and concentration skills...

- **This is what a blue player experiences with the additional progression added**:
  » Be aware of where the player who is passing him the tennis ball is, so he can be in the correct position (column/row) to catch it. And at the same time - be aware of where the green players are as he cannot be in the same square as them when receiving a tennis ball.
  » Be aware of where the player who is passing him the football is, so he can be in the correct position (column/row) to receive the football. And at the same time - be aware of where the yellow players are as he cannot be in the same square as either of them when receiving the football.
  » Be aware of where the player is that he is passing the football to, so he can spot and call out the colour of the visual cue.
  » Be aware of where the player is that he is passing the tennis ball to, so he can accurately throw the tennis ball while the football is on the way to him.

- Whilst these do not all happen at exactly the same time, they happen in very quick succession, so **tremendous concentration and mental speed is required to understand and act upon each element effectively**.

- Players are being **challenged to divide their attention and be aware of an increasing number of players that influence their position throughout**. Just like in a game, the players must position themselves appropriately for that game moment - **good supporting positions for teammates and in space away from "opponents."**

Coaching Points

A. Active Scanning – Know where the teammate passing you the tennis ball is and where the "opponents" are to take an appropriate supporting position. Know where the teammates you are passing the football to and the tennis ball to are before receiving the football.

B. Body Position – Open to player you are receiving the football from and the player you are passing it to next (in the correct area of the pitch).

C. Confirm - Check again! Look after the pass and before your first touch to spot and call out the colour held up by your teammate.

D. Decision - There are basic decision making elements in all practices but because this practice is unopposed, it is not considered as part of the game decision making process.

E. Execution – Throw the tennis ball to your teammate (so he can catch it) after the pass and before your first touch. Pass the football into the space just in front of the player's open body shape, and towards their back foot.

F. Follow-on – After passing the football, quickly re-engage in scanning so you can position yourself to support the player you receive the tennis ball from.

Game Awareness Level 2 - Realization: Reading the Game Situation

PROGRESSION 6: Maintain Space from Opponents + Outside Visual Cues

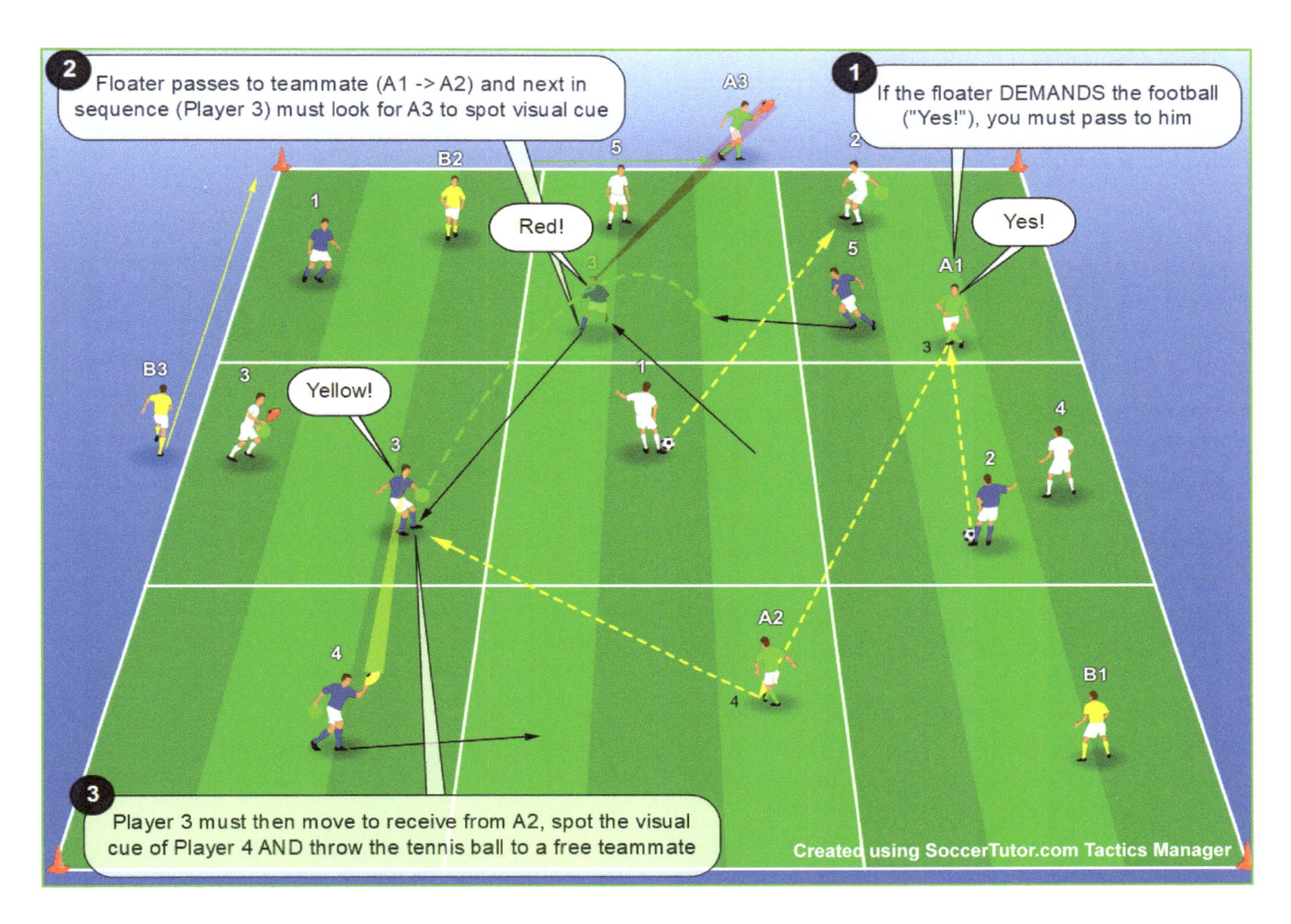

2 Floater passes to teammate (A1 -> A2) and next in sequence (Player 3) must look for A3 to spot visual cue

1 If the floater DEMANDS the football ("Yes!"), you must pass to him

Red!

Yes!

Yellow!

3 Player 3 must then move to receive from A2, spot the visual cue of Player 4 AND throw the tennis ball to a free teammate

Objective: Develop awareness of positional relationships with teammates, specific off-the-ball support movements, and maintaining space from "opponents."

Practice Description

- In this final progression, **all the rules from the previous progressions still apply, and we now add 2 colour-coded flashers (1 green and 1 yellow)** on the outsides of the playing area - **A3** and **B3**.

- The **floating players move freely around and interrupt the sequence of the passing by demanding the football**. The green floaters demand the ball from the blue players and the yellow floaters demand from the whites players. The columns and rows constraints do not apply to the floaters when receiving.

- **When a floater demands the ball, the player in possession must pass it to him (Player 2 → A1 in diagram)** instead of the next player in the sequence.

- The floater will then pass to his teammate (A1 → A2). After the pass is played and before A2's first touch, the next player in the sequence (e.g. Player 3) must call out the visual cue held up by the colour-coded outside flasher (A3).

- The sequence player (Player 3) must then move to receive from the floater

Game Awareness Level 2 - Realization: Reading the Game Situation

(A2), and must spot and call out the visual cue held up by the next player in the sequence (Player 4) **AND** throw the tennis ball as normal.

- In the diagram, Player 3 calls out the visual cue held up by Player 4 ("Yellow") and throws the tennis ball to Player 5.

Practice Analysis for Coach

- This sequence passing practice has now become **very complex and demands intense concentration throughout**, requiring lots of quick shifts of attention between an increased number of players and objects.

- The first challenge the players will face is when they need to pass to the floater instead of following the routine to pass to the next teammate in the sequence. **If the floater demands the ball, you must pass it to him**. However, you will probably notice a number of players will pass to the next player in the sequence despite the fact the floater is screaming for the ball. Whilst passing the ball to a different player who is calling for it seems like it should be quite an easy task, it actually presents a significant problem to the player for a number of overlapping reasons...

- Firstly, **bringing in the floaters as an extra passing outlet means we challenge the automatic nature of the sequence passing practice**...

- Whilst the players have had to engage in scanning, to be aware of visual cues and their positioning in relation to the other players, they have always been passing the football to the same player – the next one in the sequence. This means that most players will go on autopilot with this particular game action, and this next action in the sequence will have been reinforced by the fact they have just looked at this player to call out the visual cue they are holding up.

- However, the automatic nature of this standard performance routine is now being interrupted by the floater demanding the ball, which means the player must **inhibit (deny) his regular motor response** (pass the ball to the next player in the sequence) and **perform an adapted motor response instead** (pass the ball to the floater).

- Another challenge to the players is a phenomenon that researchers call **inattentional (perceptual) blindness**, which means may actually be completely **unaware of the floating player at that moment in time** – even though he is clearly in plain sight and calling for the ball.

- This is caused by the fact that the players are already dividing their attention between a large number of other stimuli (other players, visual cues, tennis balls and footballs) that they simply fail, or don't have the capacity to recognise this unexpected stimulus (the floating player).

- There is also the **challenge of where to be when receiving the ball back from the floater**, as the columns and rows constraints apply when receiving the ball from a floating player. You **cannot be in the same square as a floater of a specific colour (e.g. Blues can't be with yellows)**.

- In the diagram example, you can see that Player 3 has to change column to receive the ball from Floater A2 after already having changed his position once in anticipation of receiving the ball from his teammate.

- However, Player 3 cannot be in the same square as a yellow player, so he can't simply change column by moving to his right because B2 is in that square, and is forced to change both columns and rows to be in a position to receive the football.

Game Awareness Level 2 - Realization: Reading the Game Situation

- Remember that Player 3 has had to scan for A3, so he can spot and call out that visual cue when A1 is passing to A2. He also has to scan for Player 4 and 5, so it is not an easy task to be aware of the other floaters too.

- As you can see, these positional changes for Player 3 could then have an effect on Player 5 (to receive the tennis ball) and Player 4 (to receive the football).

- **Possible Progression:** We can progress this further by allowing either team of floating players (green and yellow) to demand the ball from either of the sequence passing teams (blue and white). This simple rule change has a significant impact on the challenge the players face:

  » The player receiving the football has to be aware enough to react to a call from any of the 4 floating players.

  » The player who will be receiving the football from the floater has to scan for and spot the correct colour-coded floater (2 possible points of reference) on the outside when floater 1 passes to floater 2.

  » The player who will be receiving the football from the floater cannot be in the same square as a floating player in the opposite colour of the one he is receiving the football from. If receiving from a green floater, you cannot be in the same square as a yellow floater.

  » The player receiving the tennis ball cannot be in the same square as a floating player of the same colour his teammate is receiving a football from. If his teammate is receiving from a green floater, then he cannot be in the same square as a green floater.

- Whilst some of these rules may seem simple, the highly dynamic nature of the practice and the late positional changes that may be required means the players require high levels of concentration and lightning quick thinking to adapt and re-adapt correctly to the changing game situations.

Coaching Points

A. Active Scanning – Know where the teammate passing you the tennis ball is and where the "opponents" are and take an appropriate supporting position. Know where the teammate you are passing the football to and the tennis ball to are before you receive the football. If the ball is passed to a floater, know where the second floater is (so you can position yourself to receive the football) and where the colour-coded flasher is on the outside (so you can spot the visual cue when floater 1 is passing to floater 2).

B. Body Position – Open to player you are receiving the football from and the player you are passing it to next (in the correct area of the pitch).

C. Confirm - Check again! Look after the pass and before your first touch to spot and call out the colour held up your teammate.

D. Decision - Whilst the passing of the football and tennis ball is largely predetermined, the players must identify space and make good decisions on where to position themselves to receive.

E. Execution – Throw the tennis ball to your teammate (so he can catch it) after the pass and before your first touch. Pass the football into the space just in front of the player's open body shape, and towards their back foot.

F. Follow-on – After passing the football, quickly re-engage in scanning so you can position yourself to support the player you receive the tennis ball from.

Game Awareness Level 2 - Realization: Reading the Game Situation

PRACTICE EXAMPLE 2: Pass to Opposite Colour with Team Flashers

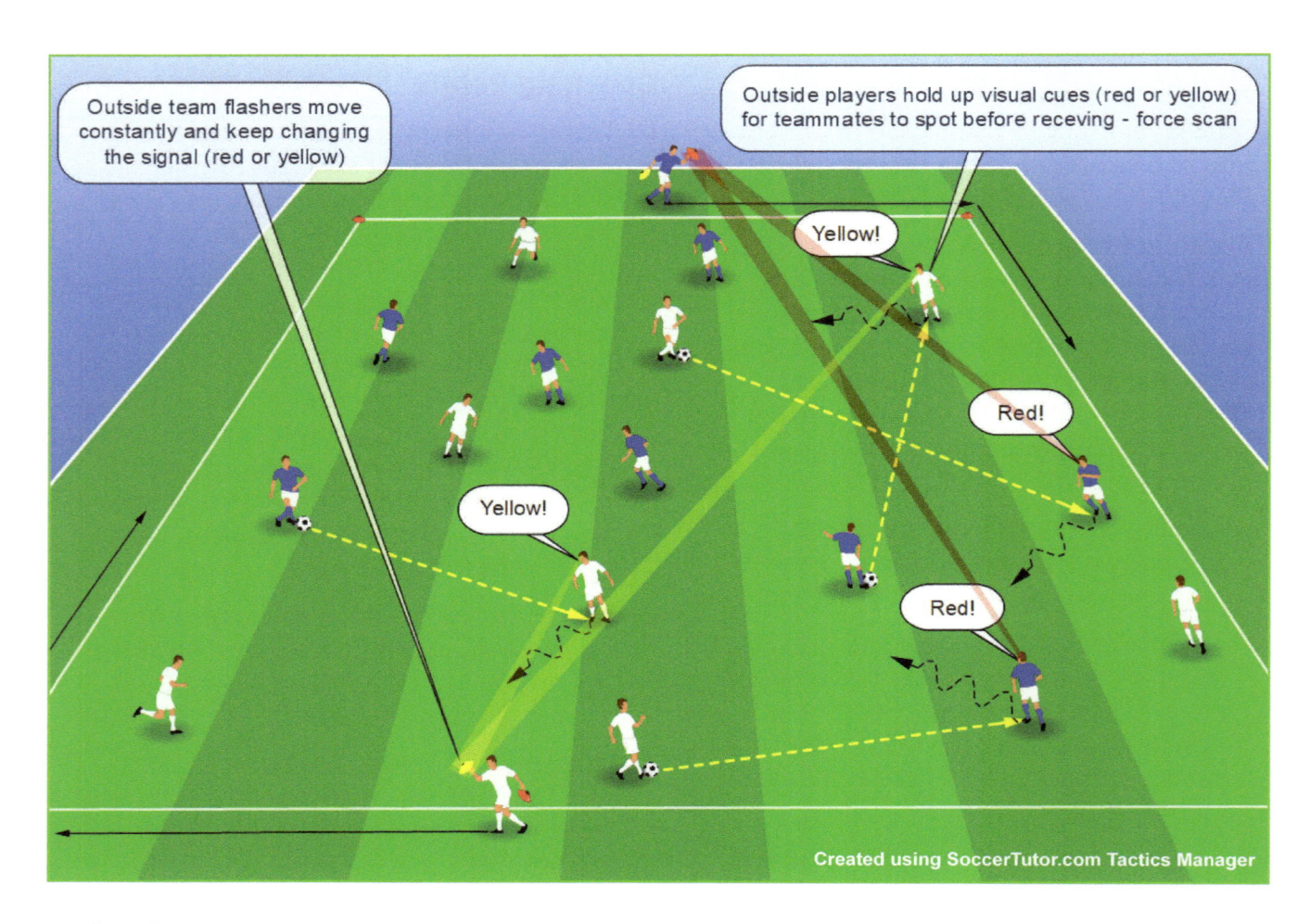

Objective: To develop awareness of specific teammates and maintaining space from "opponents."

Practice Description

- Let us have a look at how we can progress one of the practices from Level 1 **(please see pages 115-123)** to incorporate these elements.

- We will look at the **"Pass to an Opposite Colour"** practice and start from where the players had to spot the team flashers on the outside of the playing area.

- Players continue to pass to a player of the opposite colour – they do not pass to the team flasher.

- In this practice, the player receiving a pass must spot and call out the colour held up by their teammate on the outside.

- When the blue player is receiving a pass from a white player, the blue player spots and calls out the colour held up by the blue player on the outside.

- Remember, the players must spot and call out the colour of the visual cue after the ball has been passed to them and before they have taken their first touch.

- Please see the 2 progressions on the following pages where we have included Level 2 Realization aspects...

Game Awareness Level 2 - Realization: Reading the Game Situation

PROGRESSION 1: Team Flashers + Avoid Being Tagged by the Jokers

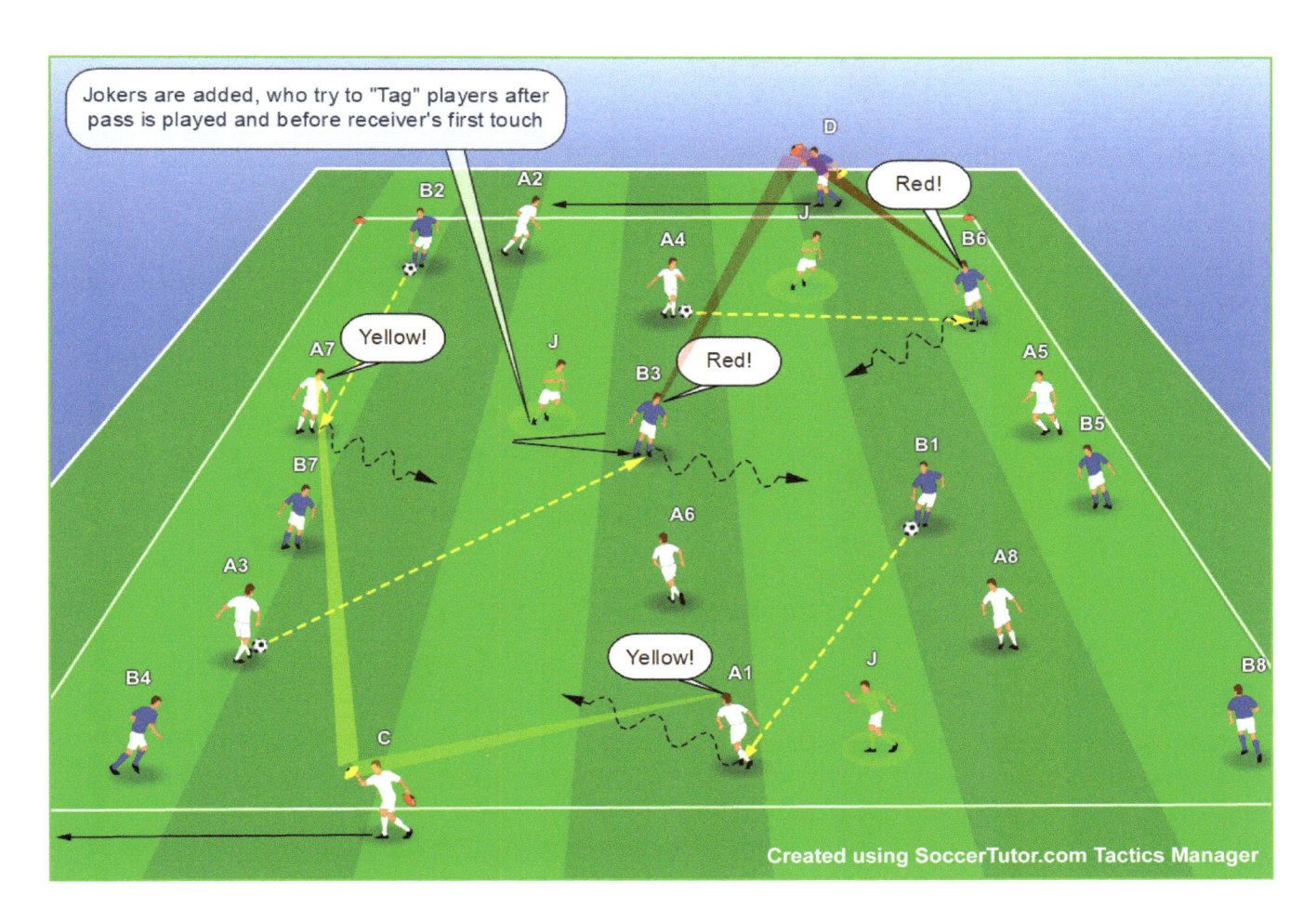

Jokers are added, who try to "Tag" players after pass is played and before receiver's first touch

Practice Description

- To progress the practice and force the players to also think about their positioning in relation to "opposition," 3 jokers are added, who move freely around the area and attempt to tag players receiving a pass.

- The **Jokers can only tag the player after the pass is played and before the receiver takes his first touch**, so as the ball is travelling.

- **Diagram Example:** A3 passes the ball to B3, who must spot and call out the visual cue held up by his team flasher (D). The nearest Joker is trying to tag B3 before he takes his first touch.

- Any player who is successfully tagged must complete a forfeit such as one push-up or a burpee.

- I like to make it competitive by playing 90-second rounds and set the Jokers a target (e.g. 6 tags). If the Jokers hit the target then all the players are given a forfeit. If the Jokers do not hit the target, then they must do the forfeit.

- You may have to monitor that the players are still passing the ball around as some players will soon realise that if you don't pass the ball, then you can't concede points! If I see this happening, I limit the players to 4-5 seconds on the ball and if they do not release it, then the

Soccer eyeQ with SoccerTutor.com

SCANNING - How to Train it

Game Awareness Level 2 - Realization: Reading the Game Situation

Jokers score a point. Swap the Jokers and Team Flashers after every round.

Practice Analysis for Coach

- Although we are still playing an unopposed practice, the introduction of the Jokers gives the players more to be actively aware of (increasing engagement in scanning) and now means we have an element of adaptive positioning.

- **Whilst the players should still be regularly scanning for their team flasher on the outside, they must also be aware of the movement of the Jokers.** The players will now have to continually adapt their positioning to maintain as much distance as possible from the Jokers, whilst also maintaining a good body shape relative to the passer and the team flasher on the outside. This is so they are in the best possible position to receive a pass. This can be quite a challenge and you will quickly see the players who are unable to split their attention and keep track of multiple players in the area.

- Furthermore, the **players with the ball must now pay more attention about who they choose to pass to**. Where they could previously pass to any of the players in an opposite colour, they now **should only pass to a player who is in enough space to receive the ball securely**.

- **Can they identify the players in space before they even receive the ball?**

- Even if they have done everything right, the receiver may suddenly find themselves being quickly closed down by one of the Jokers as the ball is on its way.

- **Can they still manage to spot and call out the colour, and get their first touch on the ball, before they are tagged?** You will find some players stay stuck in position instead of moving towards the ball and scanning (to spot the colour) at the same time.

- **KEY POINT:** At some point, the players will find themselves in a situation where they are receiving a pass and being closed down so quickly that they are likely to be successfully tagged by a Joker. In those situations, the highest priority for the player is to get their first touch on the ball before getting tagged, even if that means they do not spot and call out the colour. Maintaining quality possession is the most important thing and, in the game, if you keep the ball, you can always recycle it and build an attack somewhere else.

Coaching Points

A. Active Scanning – Know where your team flasher is before you receive the ball. Know where the Jokers are so you can take an appropriate supporting position. Know where your passing options are before you receive the ball.

B. Body Position – Open to the player you are receiving the ball from, to your team flasher on the outside, and to where you are going next with the ball. All of this should be done while maintaining maximum space from the Jokers.

C. Confirm - Check again! Look after the pass and before your first touch to spot and call out the colour held up by the team flasher.

D. Decision - Pass to a player in the maximum amount of space (free from potential pressure from a Joker).

E. Execution – Pass to the appropriate side of the player (to his "back foot" or "open" side).

F. Follow-on – As soon as the player has played his pass to an opposite colour, he should re-engage in scanning to know where his team flasher is.

Game Awareness Level 2 - Realization: Reading the Game Situation

PROGRESSION 2: Third Man Support Play with Tennis Ball Throwing

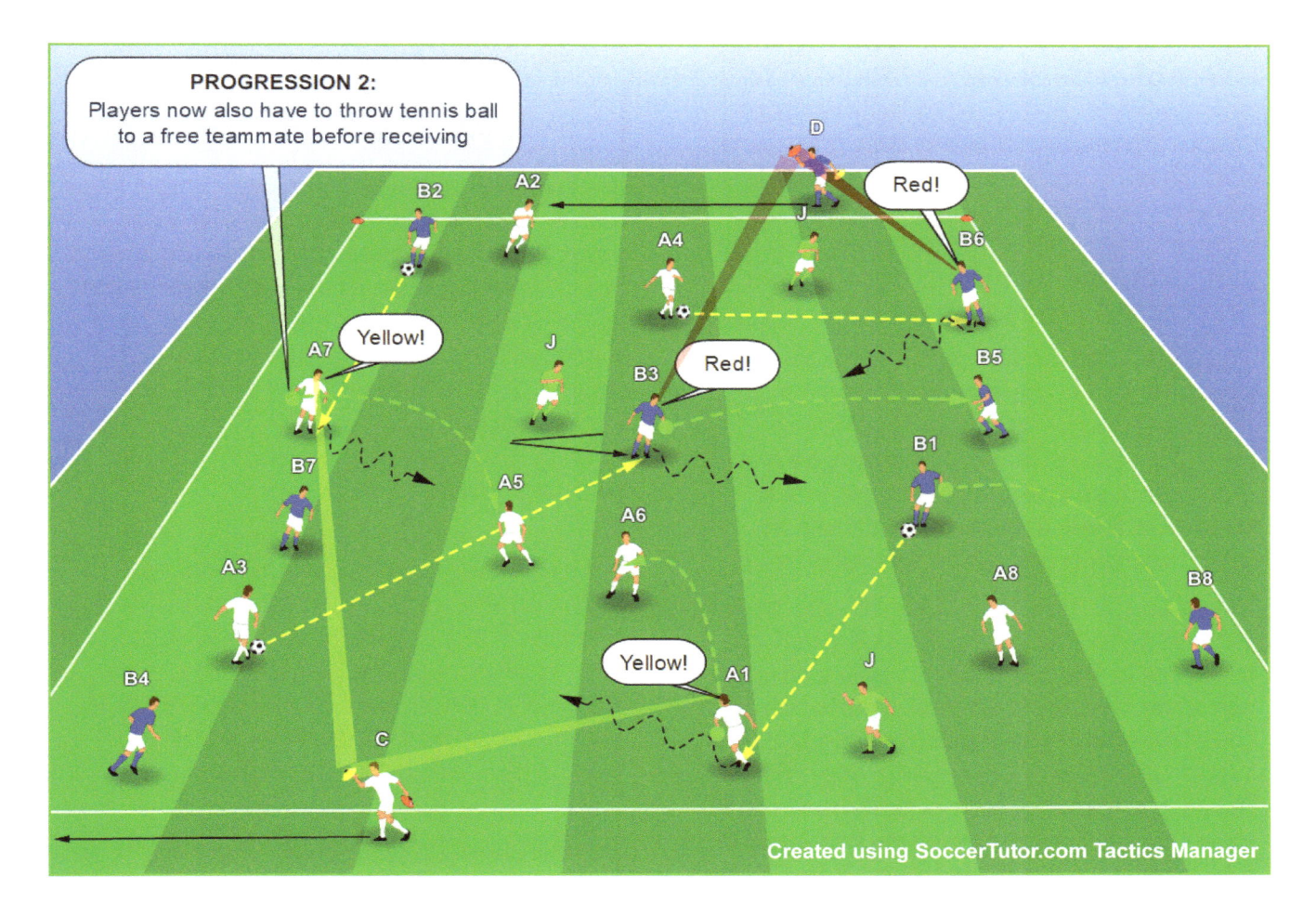

PROGRESSION 2: Players now also have to throw tennis ball to a free teammate before receiving

Objective: To develop awareness of specific teammates and maintaining space from "opponents," while incorporating off-the-ball support movement.

Practice Description

- To progress the practice further, and to force the players to be aware of more teammates, we introduce 3 tennis balls for each team.
- The players still pass the footballs to an opposite colour, but that player must be holding a tennis ball.
- The players throw the tennis balls to a free teammate of the same colour (who doesn't have a tennis ball).
- **But** the players only throw the tennis ball when the football is on the way to them.
- The receiver still calls out the colour held up by the team flasher. He must now also throw the tennis ball to a free teammate (same colour) after the pass is played and before their first touch.
- Also, they cannot be tagged by a Joker before they take their first touch.
- **Diagram Example:** When B3 is receiving from A3, he spots and calls out the colour held up by the team flasher (D) **AND** throws the tennis ball to his free teammate B5. This is all before his first touch **AND** he must not let a Joker tag him before his first touch.

Soccer eyeQ with SocccerTutor.com — SCANNING - How to Train it

Game Awareness Level 2 - Realization: Reading the Game Situation

- B3 continues with the ball and passes to a white player who has a tennis ball.

Practice Analysis for Coach

- The **introduction of the tennis balls once again forces the players to be actively aware of more players**. In addition to being aware of the team flasher (spot colour), the Joker (avoid being tagged), and passing options to opposite colour players, they must also be aware of where their free teammates are, so they can throw the tennis ball before their first touch of the football.

- They can also no longer just be aware of players in an opposite colour to pass the football to – the receiver has to be holding a tennis ball. **Demands are increased, so the players must learn to divide their attention and take in information from quick snapshots**.

- Using tennis balls not only affects the players who are receiving the football, it now also **forces those players who are not directly involved with the football to think about their positioning** too. Instead of taking up a general position, **players without a tennis ball must now look to position themselves to support a teammate who does have a tennis ball** (as they need someone to throw to).

- **KEY MOMENT: When a player has just passed the football, how quickly do they support a teammate with a tennis ball?** Some players will switch off thinking that their job is done because they have successfully passed the football to the next person. This is an example of the follow-on in the continuum and, instead of this break in performance, the players should be immediately engaging in their next action (moving to support a teammate with a tennis ball).

- **Possible Progression:** Once the players have a good understanding, allow the Jokers to also tag players who are receiving a tennis ball. This forces those players to not just think about positioning to support the player with the tennis ball, but to also maximise the space from the Jokers (not get tagged).

- So, as you can see, all of the players are forced to concentrate throughout the practice (on and off-the-ball), and they must continually adjust their adaptive positioning whether they are receiving the football or the tennis ball. This means that, once again, the **players must further increase their engagement in scanning and be in an almost constant state of awareness (of where everyone is around them)** - and - importantly, be positioned in the best way possible at every moment.

Coaching Points

A. **Active Scanning** – Know where your team flasher is before receiving and where the jokers are so you can take a supporting position. Know where free teammates are so you can throw them the tennis ball. Know where your passing options (opposite colour with tennis ball) are before receiving.

B. **Body Position** – Open to the player you are receiving the ball from, to your team flasher on the outside, and to where you are going next with the ball. All of this should be done while maintaining maximum space from the Jokers.

C. **Confirm** - Check again! Look after the pass and before your first touch to spot and call out the colour held up by the team flasher.

D. **Decision** - Pass to a player in the maximum amount of space.

E. **Execution** – Pass to the appropriate side of the player (to his "back foot" or "open" side).

F. **Follow-on** – As soon as the player has played his pass to an opposite colour, he should re-engage in scanning to know where his team flasher is.

REALIZATION PRACTICES - SUMMARY

KEY POINT: You will not be able to progress through all the stages of these practices in one session!

What we have just looked at would be built up over a number of sessions and could take some players and teams weeks or months to perform consistently well.

========================

In this section, we have looked at Level 2 Realization and shown how we can develop this level of game awareness through the environment and the use of overloads.

Remember, the body and mind will only adapt if we force it to.

Both of the practices I used started simple and easy to set-up before evolving into incredibly complex and challenging environments for the players.

Essential habits have been reinforced **(scanning)**, and new behaviours and skills developed **(adaptive positioning)**, through the implementation of overloads and constraints that are specifically designed to force the players to work on and develop those habits and behaviours. And we still haven't even introduced real opposition into the practices!

Passing Sequence Practices

Let's think about where we started with the sequence passing session, and what it asked the players to think about:

1. Who they get the ball from
2. Who they pass it to

That's it, two simple demands. As I mentioned, not all players will bother to know where the next player in the sequence is, even though that is exactly what they should know.

Think about where we are now with this practice, and the increased number of challenges the players face. Let's consider what a player experiences during this practice... They need to be aware of where the player throwing them the tennis ball or passing them the football is, where the floater players are, where the flashers are, and the rules concerning the columns, rows, and squares.

Whilst these do not all happen at exactly the same time; they do occur in very quick succession during the practice. The **demands on the players' awareness and concentration skills is intense and their speed of mind (cognitive transition) must be lightning fast**.

Game Awareness Level 2 - Realization: Reading the Game Situation

The players must make **quick observations of where the other players are and quickly process the information** to know what it means to them. They must then make **rapid-fire decisions** on how it affects their positioning in the grid and where they need to be – and be there!

Opposite Colour Practices

Similarly, with the pass to an opposite colour practices, the progressions we have implemented (team flashers, jokers, and tennis balls) have increased the awareness demands from a basic level to something that now r**equires constant engagement in scanning and purposeful adaptive positioning throughout the practice**.

As I mentioned at the beginning of this section, in the context of the game, Realization (Level 2) is not just about understanding what is going on but also demonstrating the utility of that understanding through adaptive positioning.

Achieving effective adaptive positioning continuously throughout the game requires high levels of awareness and intense concentration from the players.

Therefore, just as we would increase load to develop physical traits, we must use sessions that stress the players' capacities for attention and concentration if we want them to develop improved cognitive traits.

Hopefully, you can see from the practices in this section how we have affected these aspects and are forcing the players to work on essential behaviours in these increasingly complex environments.

How Do We Progress From Here?

In the next section **(Game Awareness Level 3 - Anticipation: Predicting How Play Will Develop)**, we will see how we can challenge the players with overloads whilst up against active opponents, and how these help the players further build their game awareness and develop **ANTICIPATION**.

LEVEL 3 - ANTICIPATION: Predicting How Play Will Develop

Game Awareness

Anticipation

Level 3

ANTICIPATION PRACTICES:
Predicting How Play Will Develop

We will now look at the development of **Level 3 Anticipation and this can only truly be done in an opposed environment**.

Of course, as you will have seen, there is an element of Anticipation required in the Observation and Realization practices. However, **it is the impact of opposition intervention where the players are really tested in their ability to predict how the play will develop**.

You will see from the practices that, even in opposed practices, **we still work through the familiar stages of Observation and Realization**. This is important because **without the fundamentals of these two levels of awareness, the players will be inconsistent in performance at Level 3**. Simply put, if the players don't look around (and if they don't position themselves properly) then their ability to anticipate the play will obviously be severely limited.

Also, I like to show that it is not necessary that you start from unopposed and work through to opposed practices to develop awareness skills. If you only want to use opposed practices with your players that's great, we can still carefully layer in the different constraints to ensure we do not miss building any of the essential foundations that are required.

One of the biggest differences from the unopposed sessions is the players are now trying to do things whilst under pressure from opposition. This means **the players will make mistakes and lose possession whilst learning the essential skills of game awareness, so you must be patient and supportive during this process**.

However, **we can manipulate the time and space component for our players by varying the size of the playing area or number of opponents to allow them opportunities for success**.

You will see from the practices that I have overloaded them in favour of the team being coached but as the players progress, it is i**mportant to increase the number of opponents and change the size of the playing area to continually challenge the players** (in the speed and efficiency that they can do things).

Once again, by introducing the simple constraints I use in these practices, you will be surprised how quickly you will see a change in the behaviours of the players. They will do the following:

1. Engage in more scanning (Observation - Level 1).

2. Optimise their body position in relation to the ball, their teammates, AND opponents (Realization - Level 2).

3. They will have to do all of this whilst still executing effective decisions with the ball.

4. And they will have to learn to read the play and anticipate the intentions of teammates and opponents from increasingly briefer glimpses of the play around them.

Game Awareness Level 3 - Anticipation: Predicting How Play Will Develop

"You play football with your head and your legs are there to help you.

If you don't use your head, using your feet won't be sufficient..."

Johan Cruyff

Game Awareness Level 3 - Anticipation: Predicting How Play Will Develop

PRACTICE EXAMPLE 1: Opposed 6v3 (+4) Vision and Awareness Practice

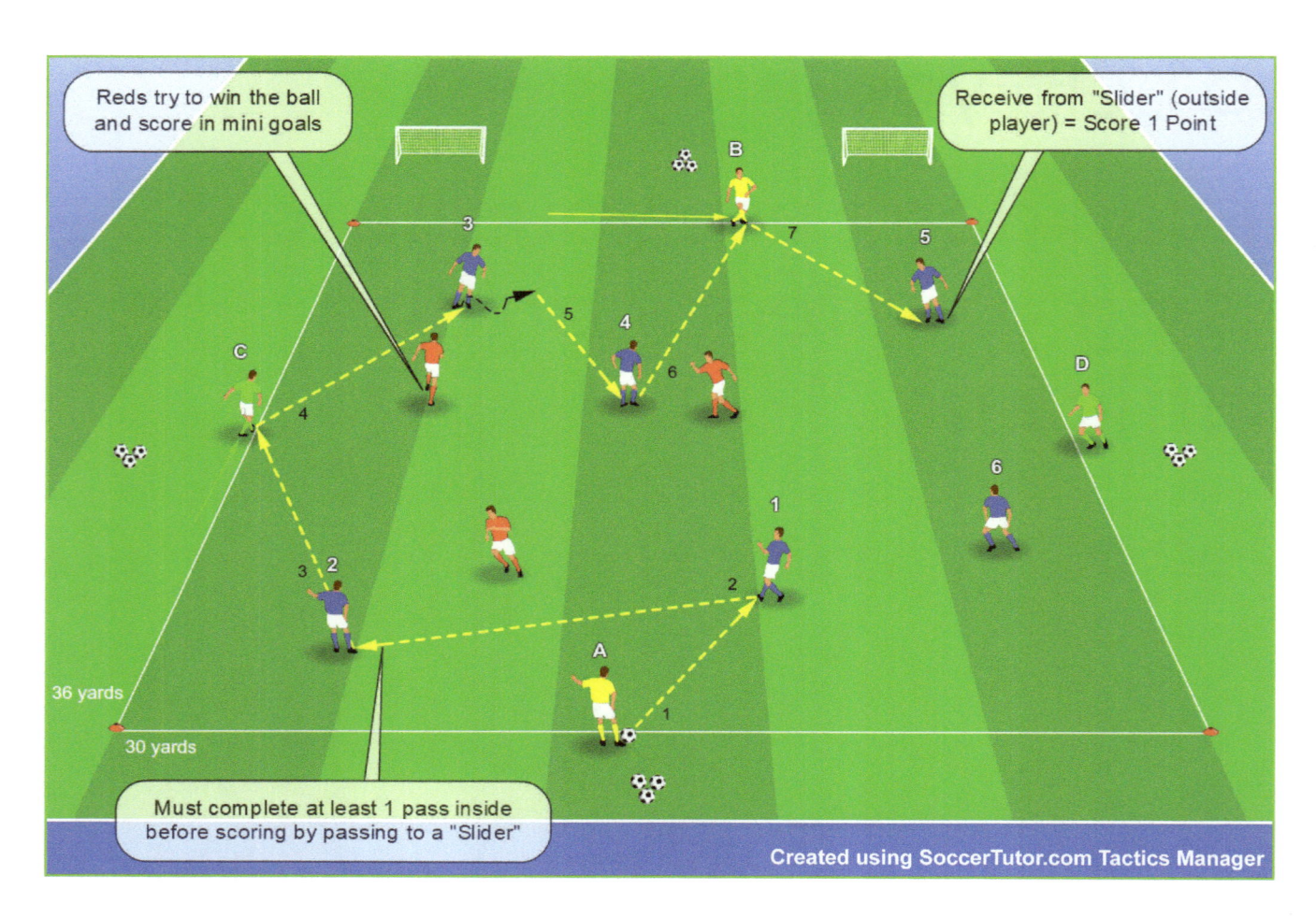

Reds try to win the ball and score in mini goals

Receive from "Slider" (outside player) = Score 1 Point

Must complete at least 1 pass inside before scoring by passing to a "Slider"

36 yards / 30 yards

Objective: To develop increased levels of concentration and awareness in an opposed practice.

Practice Description

- Use a 30 x 36 yard area (depending on the age, level, and number of players). In this example, we play with 6 attackers (blue) vs 3 defenders (red).

- There are **4 "Sliders" on the outside of the playing area**. The 2 yellow sliders are opposite each other, as are the greens. They move along their side to offer maximum support to the blue team.

- The blue team score by passing to a slider and receiving the ball back again.

- They must complete at least 1 pass inside the area before scoring again.

- If the reds win the ball, they try to score in either of the 2 mini goals.

Practice Analysis for Coach

- Here we have a simple 6v3 + 4 outside support players, which is a basic multi-directional possession practice that most of you will be familiar with.

- You can also have goals in opposite corners or have up to 4 goals for the reds to score into. The point is to **give the reds an objective if they win the ball and give the blues a purpose when they lose it**.

Soccer eyeQ with SoccerTutor.com — SCANNING - How to Train it

Game Awareness Level 3 - Anticipation: Predicting How Play Will Develop

- Usually in these types of practices, the team score by passing to a support player or completing a specific number of consecutive passes. However, I like it to be when the player is receiving the ball back inside the area, as it gives an extra emphasis to those particular moments when players have pressure from their opponents to consider.

- The blue team cannot score again until they have completed at least 1 pass inside the area, but the support players can be used anytime to retain and recycle possession. However, they are restricted to 1 touch play if there hasn't been at least 1 pass inside the area. This rule prevents the blues from just bouncing it around the outside to score easy points but still allows them to use the support players when under a lot of pressure.

- The **1 touch limitations have the added benefit of forcing the sliders to purposefully engage with the play**. In these kind of practices, the outside players tend to switch off completely if they are not directly involved in the play – particularly when the ball is towards the other side of the area.

- The support players are then prone to just kicking it back into any player in the area, and usually to the first player they see instead of passing to the player who has the right amount of time and space. This is because they fail to adequately prepare during their off-the-ball moments, with a common habit being to watch the ball instead of using this time to scan the playing area to see where everyone is.

- Using the 1 touch rule forces the sliders to concentrate on the flow of the game, so they know when they must play with 1 touch and when they have more touches available. This and the scoring element of **the practice encourages the outside players to scan more continuously** during the play, so they are constantly **aware of who their best passing option and best action** is at any given time.

- You may be asking why I don't just restrict the support players to 1 touch all the time. Well, like most coaches, I do use the 1 touch rule in a variety of ways, and it is a common constraint that I think has many benefits. However, I like the support players in this exercise to be able to act as **"playmakers"** by controlling the tempo of the play.

- By not restricting them, these playmakers can not only keep the ball moving quickly but can also choose to slow the play down when appropriate. This can offer the attackers a moment to regroup as well as being useful for inviting pressure from the opposition, which can open up space and an even better passing (or scoring) opportunity somewhere else.

- As you can see, there is a **strong focus in this initial set-up of coaching the support players (sliders) on the outside**. I think these players are often "forgotten" in practices like these, as the coaching tends to be focused on the players inside the area.

- However, it's important to take the time to help them understand how they can be as effective as possible when playing that role – the quality they can deliver will directly impact the performance of everyone.

- When you work with your players in this practice, you will probably notice that some of the players on the inside regularly have a poor body shape when receiving a pass from a sliders. They will often come to receive the ball in a "square-on" position, which severely limits their options and how efficient and effective they can be with the ball throughout the practice.

Game Awareness Level 3 - Anticipation: Predicting How Play Will Develop

- Instead of receiving the ball in a closed position, **the player's body should be open to as much of the playing area as possible**.

- You may also see that most players don't scan the playing area as much as they should, which again severely limits the options they will have with the ball...

- Instead, **we would like the players to "look" (up field especially) to see what options they have** and identify where they can hurt the opposition most.

- As coaches, we understand how scanning and an open body shape can help the player. It allows greater awareness and increases the number of possible options available to them.

- **HOW DO WE PROGRESS?**

  Simply telling players to open their body shape and look up will not necessarily work. Therefore, in the first progression on the next page we look at how we can progress this practice by using a simple constraint to help the players inside the area further develop these important behaviours.

Coaching Points

A. Active Scanning – The sliders need to know where their teammates are before they receive the ball.

B. Body Position – Open to the player you are receiving from and the player you are passing to next. Inside players should be open to as much of the playing area as possible.

C. Confirm - In this original practice setup, scanning is often limited, and players rarely make the last scan as the ball is on its way (because they don't HAVE to).

D. Decision - Which teammate has the most time and space?

E. Execution – Pass the ball to the appropriate side of your teammate.

F. Follow-on – Support the ball and scan for passing options.

Game Awareness Level 3 - Anticipation: Predicting How Play Will Develop

PROGRESSION 1: Opposed 6v3 (+4) Practice with Scanning and Positioning

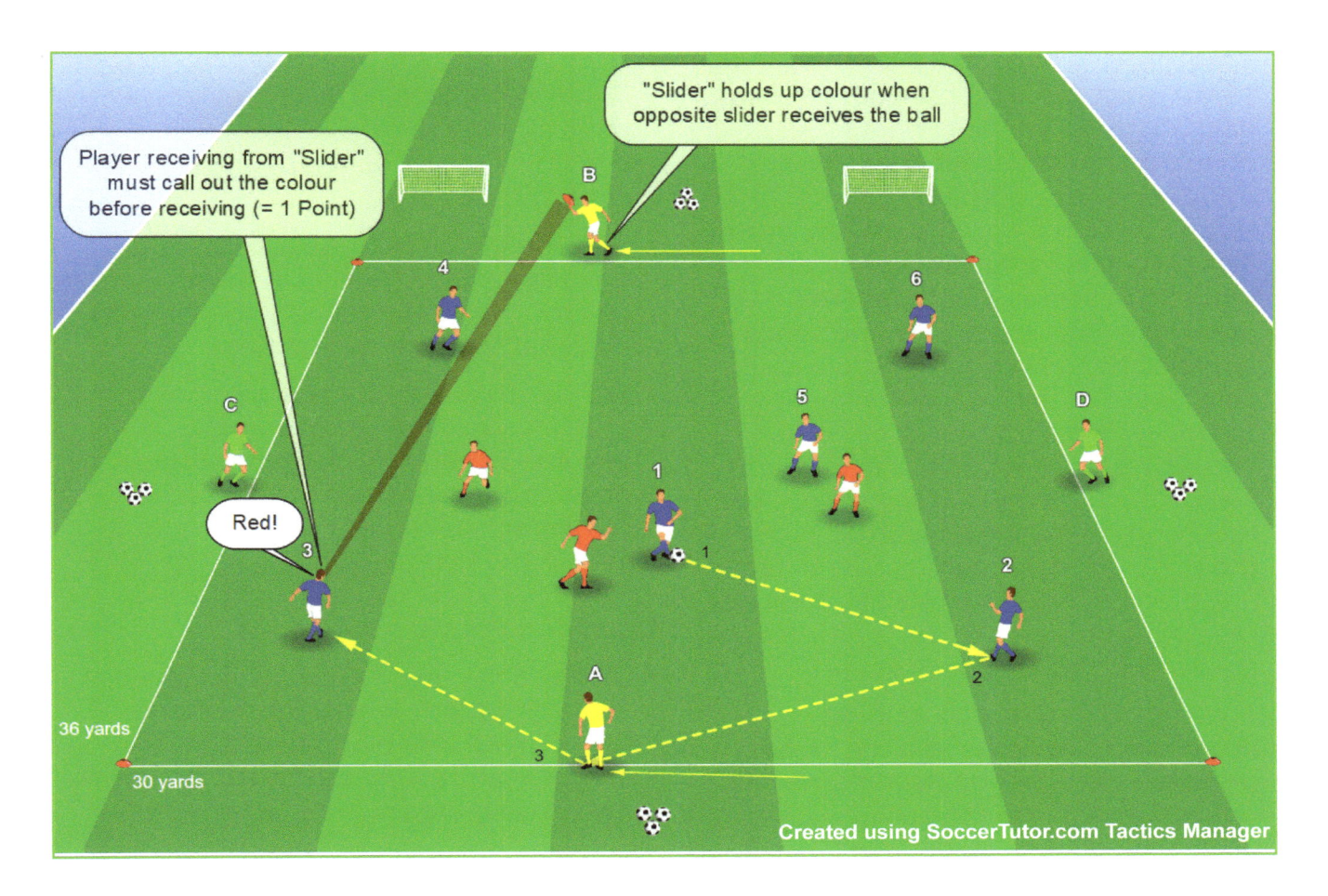

Player receiving from "Slider" must call out the colour before receiving (= 1 Point)

"Slider" holds up colour when opposite slider receives the ball

Objective: To improve body shape and develop scanning in an opposed practice.

Practice Description

- To progress and force the player receiving from the slider to engage in scanning and promote better body shape, we modify the scoring method.
- Now, when the ball is played to a slider, the opposite slider holds up a visual cue. To score, the player receiving from the slider must spot and call out the colour the opposite player is holding up (after the pass and before his first touch).
- For example, when the ball is played to Slider A, Slider B holds up a visual cue (red or yellow).

- **Diagram Example:** As the ball is being passed from Slider A to Player 3, he must spot and call out the colour held up by Slider B.
- If Player 3 does not do this after the pass and before his first touch, then the goal does not count, and the team continue to play and try to score somewhere else.

Practice Analysis for Coach

- Introducing this simple constraint has an instant impact on player behaviour. Almost immediately you will see some of the **players starting to have a quick look "up the pitch" and likely see a better body position** from the receiving player.

Soccer eyeQ with SoccerTutor.com

SCANNING - How to Train it

Game Awareness Level 3 - Anticipation: Predicting How Play Will Develop

- He will more likely open up his body shape to the flasher (opposite slider) and be open to the full field of play.

- All of this will start to happen naturally because we have now given the players a reason. However, whilst the receiving player must spot and call out the colour held up (to score), he cannot focus solely on the opposite flasher. As there are opponents who will be pressuring and trying to win the ball, the **players must also take quick snapshots of where the opposition are, as their positioning will determine how much time and space is available**. Having the most up-to-date "map" of the opposition means the player will know which direction to take his first touch, or maybe even just protect the ball. On top of this, the receiving player should also be aware of the position of his teammates so he can maybe pass first-time to a teammate or create a passing opportunity that moves the ball well away from pressure.

- Through all of this, **maintaining possession should remain the highest priority** – we score goals when we can, but we cannot lose the ball.

- While doing all of the above seems simple enough, and it is what players should do, it quickly becomes very obvious who lacks proficiency in all of these aspects. You will see some players start to mis-control the ball because they are unable to correctly assess from a limited snapshot and/or they cannot efficiently scan away from the ball and back to the ball again quickly enough.

- You will see players lose the ball under pressure from opponents because they fail to properly assess the time and space available and turn straight into opponents because they are unaware of where their opponents are.

- All of these are signs indicating that the player has a limited capacity to divide his attention between multiple things, take in key information from around them, and still perform effectively. Quite simply, they are not very good (yet!) at being aware of the ball, looking for teammates, and knowing where their opponents are.

- This is because they have previously been allowed to only look at the ball and never really trained their attention capacities.

- Fortunately, all of these aspects can be improved by training in these environments and skilfully coaching the player at the appropriate time.

- Although we are now using opposed practices, **be aware that some players we may still be at the stage of developing their basic "Observation" (scanning) skills** – just getting them to look in the first place!

Coaching Points

A. Active Scanning – Know where the ball is coming from, where the flasher is positioned on the opposite side, and where teammates/opponents are inside the playing area.

B. Body Position – Open to slider you are receiving the football from and the flasher on the opposite side.

C. Confirm - Check again! Look after the pass and before your first touch to spot and call out the colour held up by the flasher on the opposite side.

D. Decision - Pass first time or take a controlling touch?

E. Execution – Is the decision executed well? What is the line and weight of pass?

F. Follow-on – After passing the football, quickly re-engage in scanning and positioning in relation to the ball, your teammates, and opponents.

Game Awareness Level 3 - Anticipation: Predicting How Play Will Develop

PROGRESSION 2: Increased Scanning and Positioning + Tennis Ball Throwing

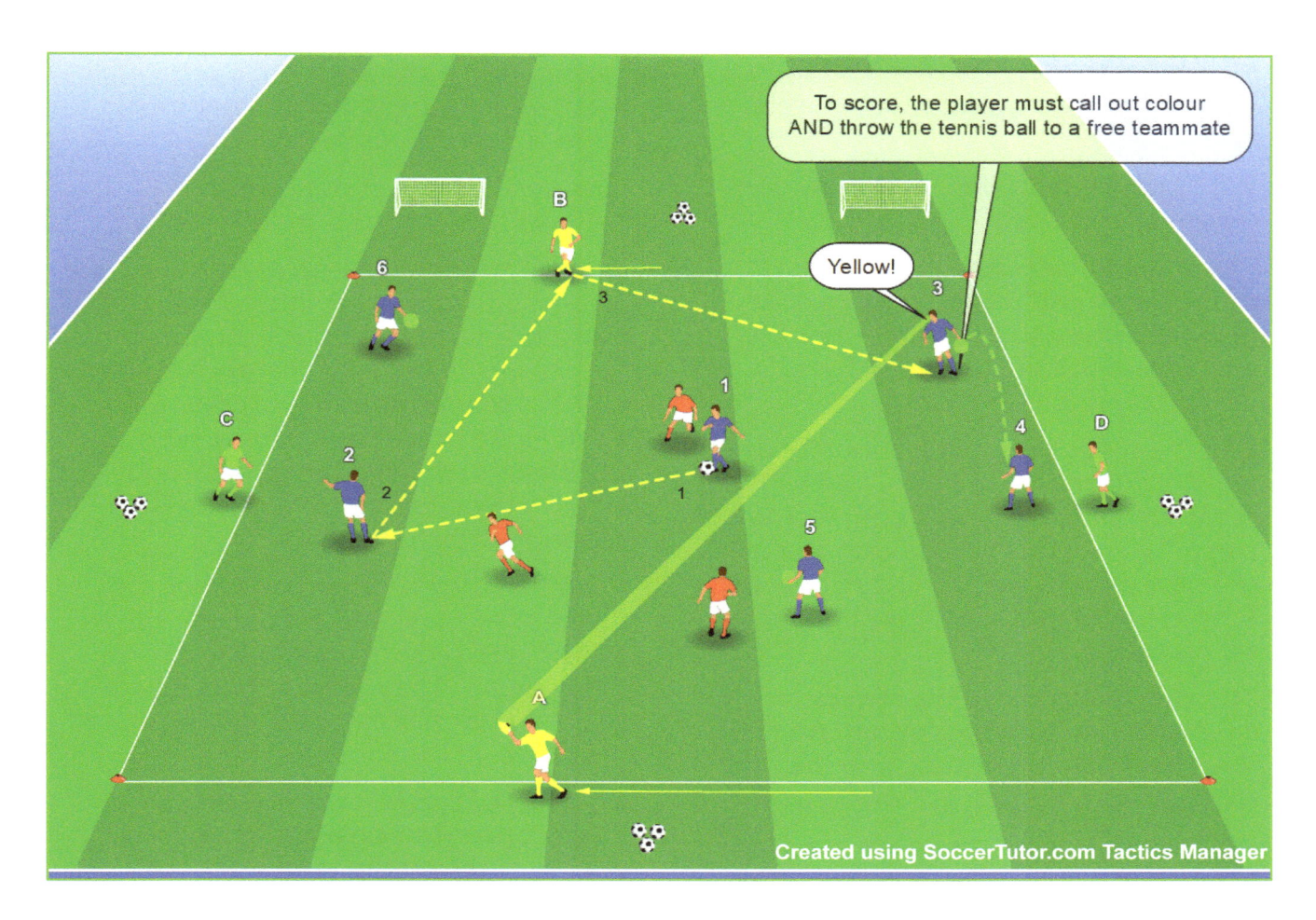

To score, the player must call out colour AND throw the tennis ball to a free teammate

Yellow!

Practice Description

- To progress the practice further, we add 3 tennis balls for the blue team and modify the scoring method again.
- To score, the player receiving the pass from the slider must be holding a tennis ball.
- The receiving player must spot and call out the colour the opposite slider is holding up and throw the tennis ball to a free teammate who does not have a tennis ball.
- All of this must be done after the slider's pass and before the receiver's first touch.

- **Diagram Example:** As the ball is being passed from Slider B to Player 3, he must spot and call out the colour held up by Slider A + throw the tennis ball to a free teammate (Player 4 in diagram).
- If Player 3 does not do both aspects after the pass and before his first touch, then the goal does not count, and the team continue to play and try to score somewhere else.
- Trying to score is the only time the players must throw the tennis ball and they do not have to throw the tennis ball when simply retaining possession, which can be done through the sliders or with teammates inside the playing area.

SCANNING - How to Train it

Game Awareness Level 3 - Anticipation: Predicting How Play Will Develop

- **VARIATION:** The blue team can score 1 point without throwing the tennis ball, and score 3 points when they do.

Practice Analysis for Coach

- Why add the tennis balls?
- How is this developing anything relevant to the game?
- We'll look at the sliders first, how does this challenge them?
- The **sliders must engage in the flow of the game and concentrate to a far greater degree** to accurately identify which passes can potentially hurt the defending team the most.
- Can the slider continually monitor where players are and identify the one with the most time and space? Of course, they can retain possession through any of the blue players, but goals can only be scored by targeting a player holding a tennis ball.
- This **practice teaches the sliders to constantly assess the play and find out their best passing option**, and the one that can hurt the opposition the most.
- What challenges is the receiving player now facing?
- The receiving player now needs to clearly identify more players in the playing area as he must spot the flasher (to call the colour), be aware of his passing options for the football AND know where the free teammates he can throw the tennis ball to are.
- The **receiving player needs to "map" where all these teammates are, and he must also know about his opponents positioning** as they will be actively applying pressure to reduce his time and space, limiting his options with the football.
- All of this forces the receiving player to take quick snapshots and use incredible speed of thought to process everything AND still be effective with the ball.
- Is helping players increase their capacity for awareness under pressure useful?
- Is helping the player learn to take the information he needs from increasingly shorter looks and think quicker in opposed situations useful?
- Finally, let's think about how the receiver's teammates are affected...
- In order to score, the receiver must have at least one player without a tennis ball available in a good supporting position to receive. This means that **those players without tennis balls should constantly be thinking how they can best support the players with the tennis balls** and adjust their position for a potential scoring opportunity.
- However, they cannot focus solely on this as they must also make themselves available to recycle possession during general play. They must also be aware of what their passing options are should they receive the football.
- Doing all of this effectively takes a lot of concentration and this dual role (supporting the tennis ball and supporting the football) means the players have to **constantly monitor (scanning) and manage their off-the-ball relationships** with teammates and opponents (adaptive positioning).

Conclusion

So, as you can see, it's not really about using tennis balls or doing something with your hands. It's about the **behaviours and habits we are trying to promote**:

- » Increased scanning.
- » Better awareness of teammates and opponents.
- » Improved positioning both on and off the ball.
- » Greater levels of concentration.
- » Every player is now constantly engaged in the practice and there is little opportunity to switch off.

Coaching Points

A. Active Scanning – Know where the ball is coming from, where the flasher is positioned on the opposite side, where supporting free players (without tennis ball) are, and where teammates/opponents are inside the playing area.

B. Body Position – Open to slider you are receiving the football from, the flasher on the opposite side, and the free player to throw the tennis ball to.

C. Confirm - Check again! Look after the pass and before your first touch to spot and call out the colour held up by the flasher on the opposite side.

D. Decision - Is there enough time to spot the visual cue and throw the tennis ball? Score or retain possession? Pass first time or take a controlling touch?

E. Execution – Is the decision executed well?

F. Follow-on – After passing the football, quickly re-engage in scanning and positioning in relation to the ball, your teammates, and opponents. Quickly support the football **AND** tennis balls if possible.

Game Awareness Level 3 - Anticipation: Predicting How Play Will Develop

PROGRESSION 3: Scan, Position, Third Man Support, and Player Rotation

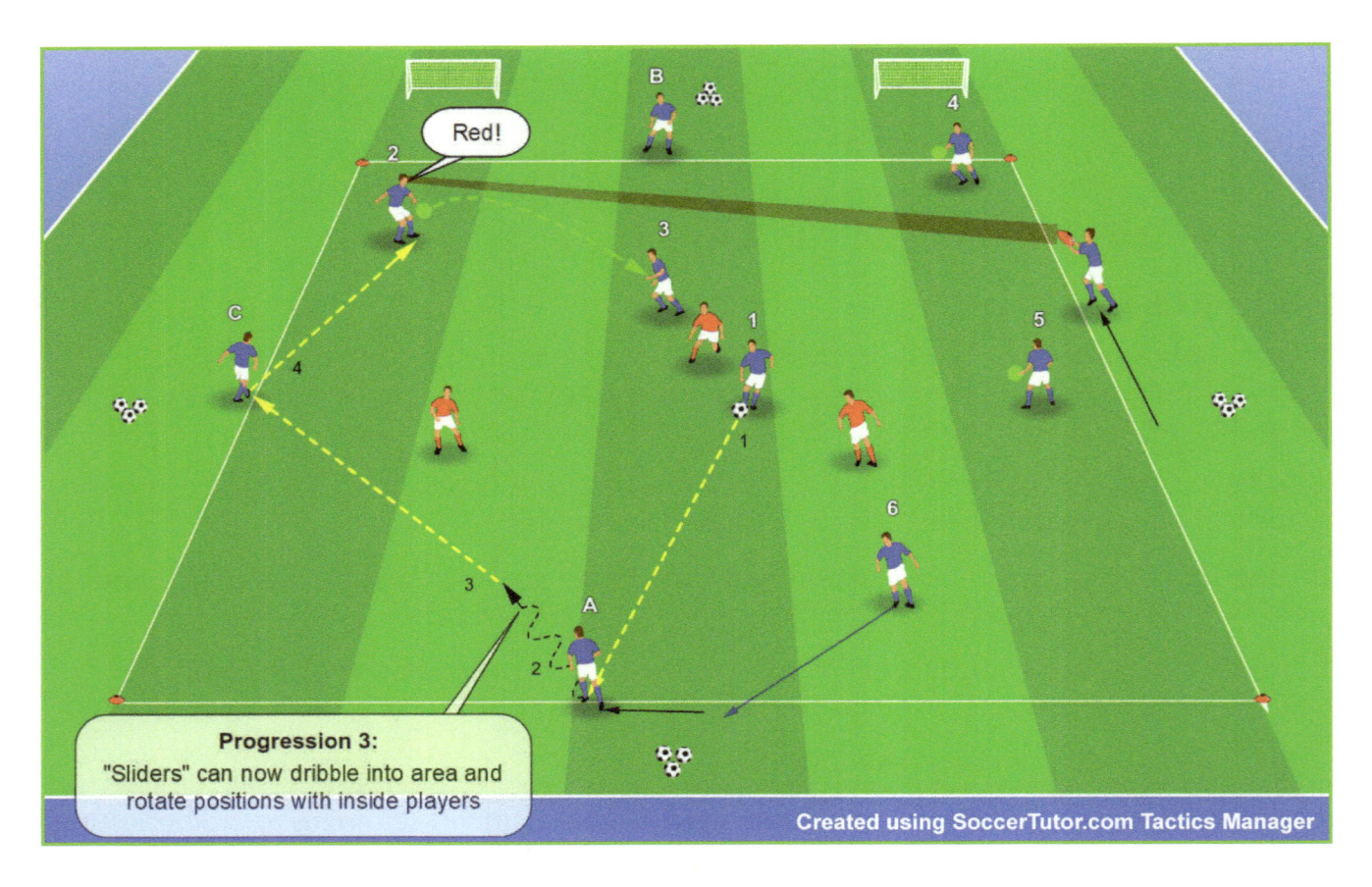

Progression 3: "Sliders" can now dribble into area and rotate positions with inside players

Objective: To develop increased levels of awareness in an opposed practice.

Practice Description

- To further progress the practice, we can incorporate some player rotations involving the sliders (4 outside players).

- Instead of the sliders being different colours, they are now all in the same colour as the blue team. However, the same rule of the opposite slider flashing a visual cue to spot is still in place.

- The sliders can now decide to dribble into the area when they receive. If they dribble (drive) into the area and successfully pass to one of the other sliders, this can then set-up a direct scoring opportunity for the blue team.

- When a slider enters the area with the football, the nearest inside player must rotate out to fill the gap (swap positions). If this player has a tennis ball, then he simply throws it to one of his teammates without one.

- **Diagram Example:** Player 1 passes to Slider A, who dribbles into the area and passes to Slider C (Player 6 rotates out). Slider C can now pass to an inside player.

- To score, Player 2 must spot the colour held up by the opposite Slider (D) **AND** throw the tennis ball to a free teammate (Player 3).

- Spotting the colour and throwing the tennis ball must be done after the pass from Slider C is played and before Player 2's first touch.

Game Awareness Level 3 - Anticipation: Predicting How Play Will Develop

Practice Analysis for Coach

- This progression enables the sliders to play a more interactive part, becoming increasingly important playmakers in the creation of scoring opportunities. It allows them to drive into space as they could do in a game, where they can find a pass to one of the other key players (sliders).

- We are now asking the sliders to **not only concentrate and continually assess where the best passing opportunities are; they should also read the play and anticipate when space is opening up that they themselves can exploit** to full effect.

- Can the inside players recognise the flow of play and anticipate these moments when the slider can drive in, and move to position themselves effectively so the team can achieve the maximum advantage?

- Both the **players with tennis balls and those without tennis balls are involved in the scoring process**. All of the attacking players should be acting and reacting off the movement of the key teammates around them, so they can offer appropriate support at any given moment.

- Can the tennis ball players be in a position to receive from a slider and spot the opposite player to score?

- Does he know where his supporting players without a tennis ball are available?

- Can the free players (without a tennis ball) be in a position to support the tennis ball player?

- Can players also be ready and in position to offer support to the ball carrier?

- Can they retain and recycle possession if required?

- Through all of this there is also the opposition to consider, as their positioning will affect how and where the players should offer support.

- Can the players continuously map and manage these positional relationships too?

- As you can see, there is a great deal for the players to think about and much more so than the "normal" game because of the demands of the visual cue and tennis ball tasks.

- The **players are in an almost constant state of focus and concentration, whilst learning to take in key information more quickly** and from increasingly shorter glimpses around the playing area.

HOW DO WE PROGRESS?

The nature of the practice set-up tells the player where to look. The game is not always necessarily like this.

The game is constantly in motion and the positioning of players can be extremely fluid, which means the players will often have to engage in scanning to locate teammates or opponents who have moved to a new position.

In the following practices, we look at how we can structure our training to help the players develop this.

Game Awareness Level 3 - Anticipation: Predicting How Play Will Develop

Coaching Points

A. Active Scanning – Know where the ball is coming from, where the flasher is positioned on the opposite side, where supporting free players (without tennis ball) are, and where teammates/opponents are inside the playing area. Can the slider identify the space to dribble (drive) into?

B. Body Position – Open to slider you are receiving the football from, the flasher on the opposite side, and the free player to throw the tennis ball to. Can the players position themselves effectively if the slider drives in?

C. Confirm - Check again! Look after the pass and before your first touch to spot and call out the colour held up by the flasher on the opposite side.

D. Decision - Is there enough time to spot the visual cue and throw the tennis ball? Score or retain possession? Pass first time or take a controlling touch? Does the slider identify the correct moment to drive in?

E. Execution – Is the decision executed well?

F. Follow-on – After passing the football, quickly re-engage in scanning and positioning in relation to the ball, your teammates, and opponents. Quickly support the football **AND** tennis balls if possible.

Game Awareness Level 3 - Anticipation: Predicting How Play Will Develop

PRACTICE EXAMPLE 2: Awareness Game (6v3) with 4 Cone Gates

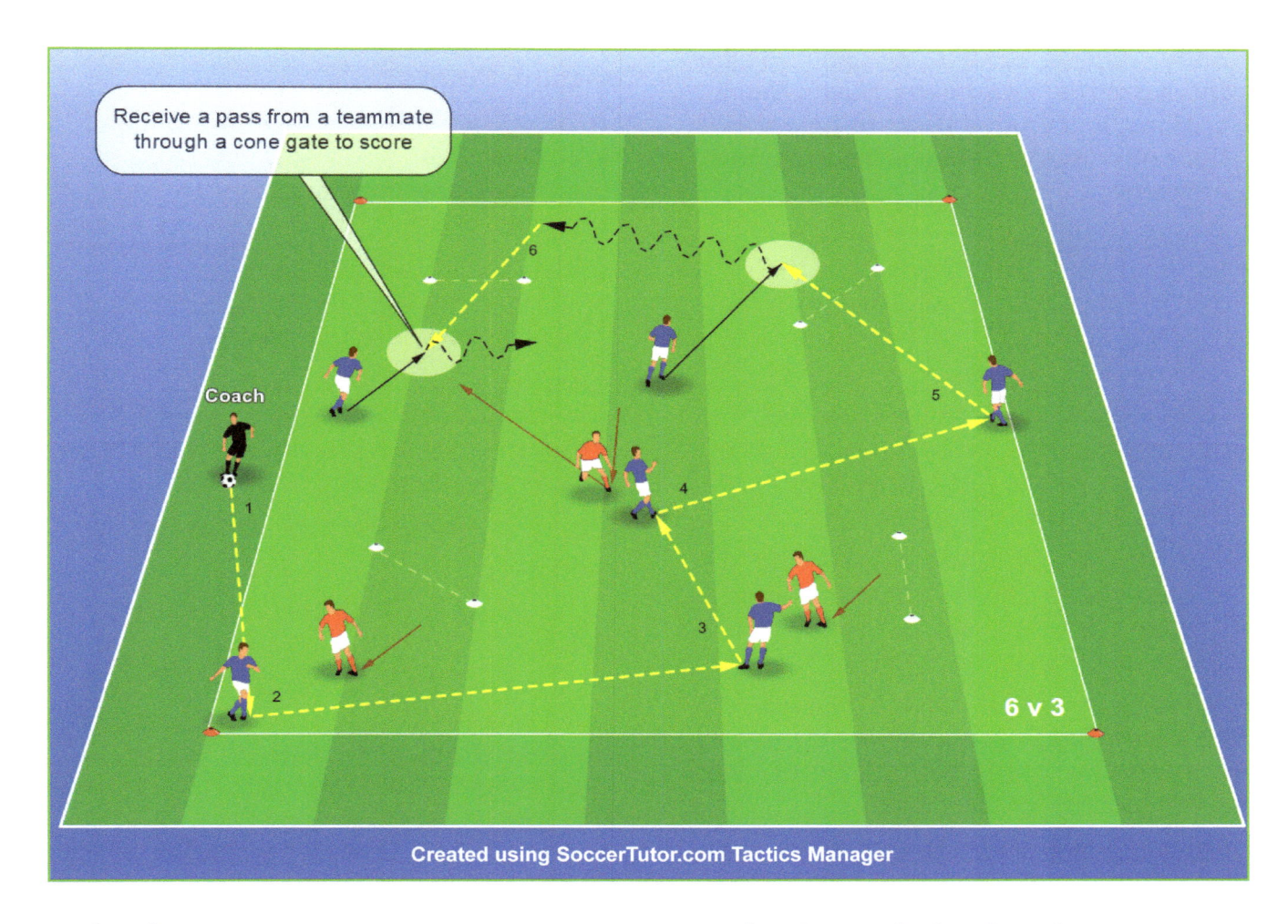

Objective: To develop increased levels of awareness in an opposed practice.

Practice Description

- There are 4 gates positioned inside the playing area and we play with 6 blue attackers vs 3 red defenders.
- The blue team score by passing to a teammate through one of the gates (the blues are shown scoring twice in the diagram example).
- The red team try to win the ball and can score by dribbling the ball out of the area - they can do this individually or combine with teammates.

Practice Analysis for Coach

- This is another simple set-up that you are probably familiar with, although the number of players or gates may vary.
- This practice is often used to encourage players to identify when and where to quickly switch the ball, in order to exploit the free space and score for their team.
- However, it is very common to see players adopt a relatively poor body shape when they come to receive the ball through one of the gates.

Game Awareness Level 3 - Anticipation: Predicting How Play Will Develop

- You will see players come to receive the ball "square-on" instead of being open to as much of the playing area as possible.

- We want the players to have an **open body shape as often as possible to allow them greater awareness, create more options, and enable them to perform their next game-action with maximum efficiency**.

- However, the players can become so focused on scoring a goal that they don't think about or prepare for what they will do next.

- You may also find that scanning is somewhat limited. As I mentioned, the players do not put much thought into what they will do next when they receive the ball through the gates.

- Of course there will be players who are at least aware of where the opponent is so they can take their first touch into the space, but was it the maximum space?

- There will be other players who are aware of teammates who are close by so they can lay off the ball quickly, but was it the most effective option?

- Most players rarely scan the full area to map their teammates, opponents, and the available space. They certainly don't get their heads up properly and "look" to see opportunities that are further away, as they would need to do in a game.

- In football, it is obviously important to know what is on around the ball. However, it is also **important to build a picture of what is away from the ball** – and position yourself appropriately to take advantage of those opportunities when you can.

- The players who can build a picture of what is away from the ball well are not only **effective at moving the ball quickly away from pressure to retain possession** - they are also **adept at launching quick attacks by spotting imbalances in the opposition and getting the ball to teammates in dangerous spaces** in advanced areas.

Coaching Points

A. Active Scanning – Know where the ball is coming from and know where your teammates and opponents are inside the playing area.

B. Body Position – Open to the player you are receiving the football from and where you want to go next.

C. Confirm - In this original practice setup, scanning is often limited, and players rarely make the last scan as the ball is on its way (because they don't HAVE to).

D. Decision - Pass first time or take a first touch?

E. Execution – Is the decision executed well?

F. Follow-on – After passing the football, quickly re-engage in scanning and positioning in relation to the ball, your teammates, and opponents.

Game Awareness Level 3 - Anticipation: Predicting How Play Will Develop

PROGRESSION 1: Visual Cues and Colour-Coded Cone Gates

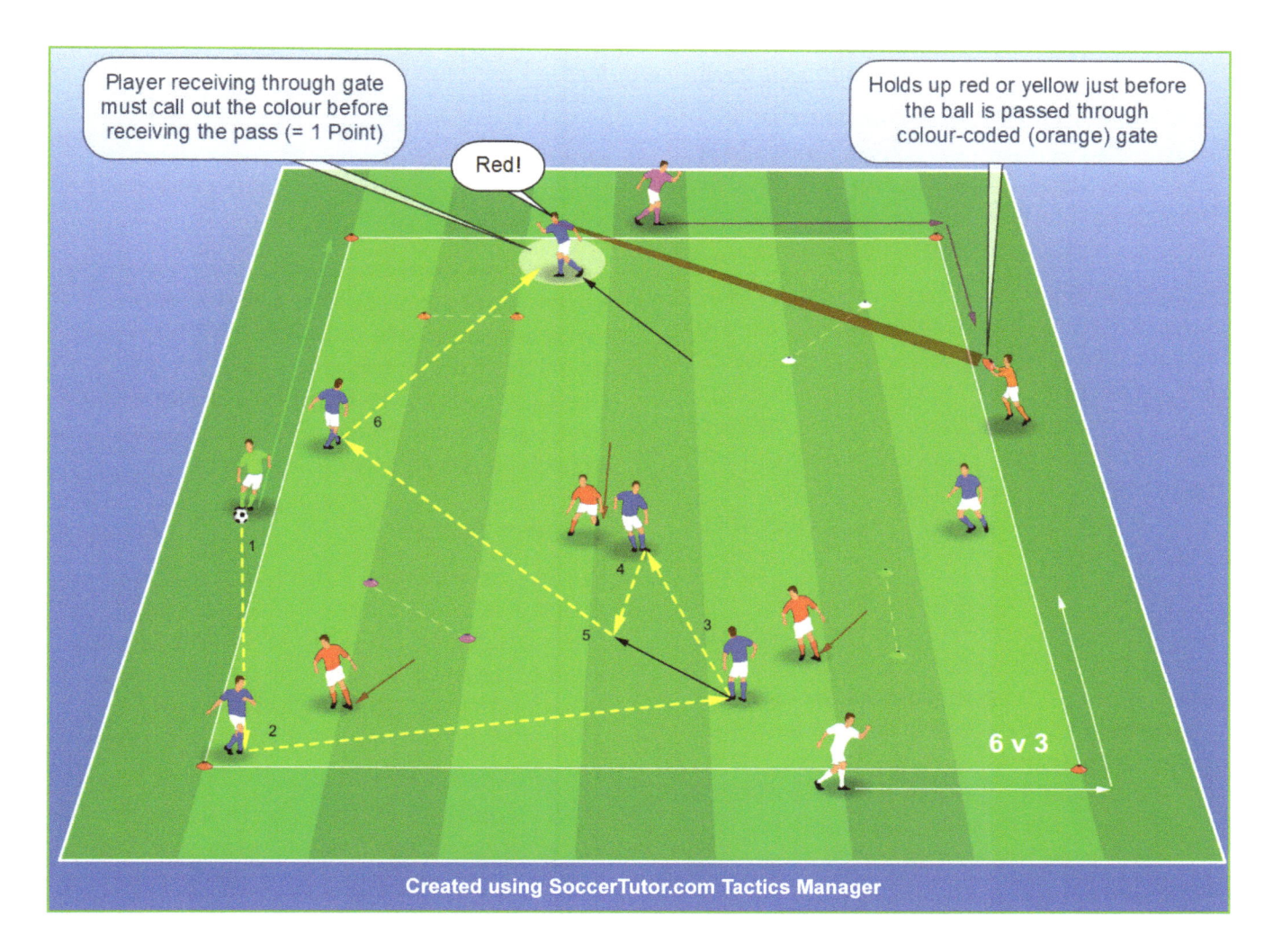

Player receiving through gate must call out the colour before receiving the pass (= 1 Point)

Red!

Holds up red or yellow just before the ball is passed through colour-coded (orange) gate

6 v 3

Objective: To develop increased levels of awareness in an opposed practice.

Practice Description

- To progress the practice, each gate is now a different colour and there are 4 colour-coded flashers on the outsides.
- The outside flashers constantly move around the outside of the entire area (360°) and hold up a visual cue as a pass is about to be played through their colour-coded gate.
- The blue team still score by passing to a teammate through one of the gates.
- The receiving player must spot and call out the visual cue held up by the flasher that matches the gate. This should be done after the pass and before the receiver's first touch.
- **Diagram Example:** The ball is being passed through the orange gate, so it is the orange flasher who must hold up a visual cue for the receiver to spot.
- The red team still try to win the ball, but now they score by passing to any of the flashers on the outside. The flasher then always passes to a blue player to continue the practice.

Soccer eyeQ with SoccerTutor.com — SCANNING - How to Train it

Game Awareness Level 3 - Anticipation: Predicting How Play Will Develop

- **VARIATION 1:** Reds keep possession after winning the ball. They score a point each time they pass to a flasher until the blue team win the ball back.

Practice Analysis for Coach

- Once again, adding in the flashers with the **visual cues will have an almost immediate impact on player behaviour**. They will **start scanning more frequently, searching for the colour-coded flasher** they need to spot in order to score.

- However, you may find most players only start looking for the flasher as their teammate is about to pass them the ball through the gate. This is too late! The players should know where the flasher is well before the pass is played. In fact, they should know his position as play is building up towards that part of the playing area.

- As play is developing, and as the player is moving out towards a gate to support play (and score), he should be taking **quick preparatory glances (pre-scanning) to locate the flasher and see what their movement is**. This way, the player can get his body shape correct so he knows exactly where to have his final look (to spot the colour).

- This is **just like a player in a game scanning further away for a specific teammate, or to see who may be in a specific area of the pitch**, who he is going to play his next pass to. Of course, just like in a game, the player cannot solely concentrate on this as he has opposition who will be applying pressure and trying to win the ball – so he **must learn to divide his attention appropriately**.

- In this practice, the aim is to pass to a teammate (through a gate) within the area, so the players must know where their teammates are to know what their options are.

- **VARIATION 2:** Bonus point if the receiver can play to the flasher using only 2 touches (1 touch to control, and 1 touch to pass).

- Whilst the player may only be playing shorter passes to teammates, he is now also developing the valuable skill of scanning further away (down the field) whilst under pressure. More importantly, he is learning to do this AND still being effective with the ball.

- The **player who can learn to consistently know where pressure is coming from, where immediate support is AND where good options are further away from the ball (and away from opposition pressure) is an invaluable asset and effective playmaker** in any team.

Coaching Points

A. Active Scanning – Know where the flasher is positioned! Pre-scan to locate the correct colour-coded flasher as the play is developing. Know where the ball is coming from and know where teammates and opponents are inside the playing area.

B. Body Position – Open to where you are receiving the football from and to the correct colour-coded flasher.

C. Confirm - Check again! Look after the pass and before your first touch to spot and call out the colour held up by the colour-coded flasher.

D. Decision - Pass first time or take a touch?

E. Execution – Is the decision executed well?

F. Follow-on – After passing the football, quickly re-engage in scanning and positioning in relation to the ball, your teammates, and opponents.

Game Awareness Level 3 - Anticipation: Predicting How Play Will Develop

PROGRESSION 2: Scan, Position, and Support Play + Throwing Tennis Balls

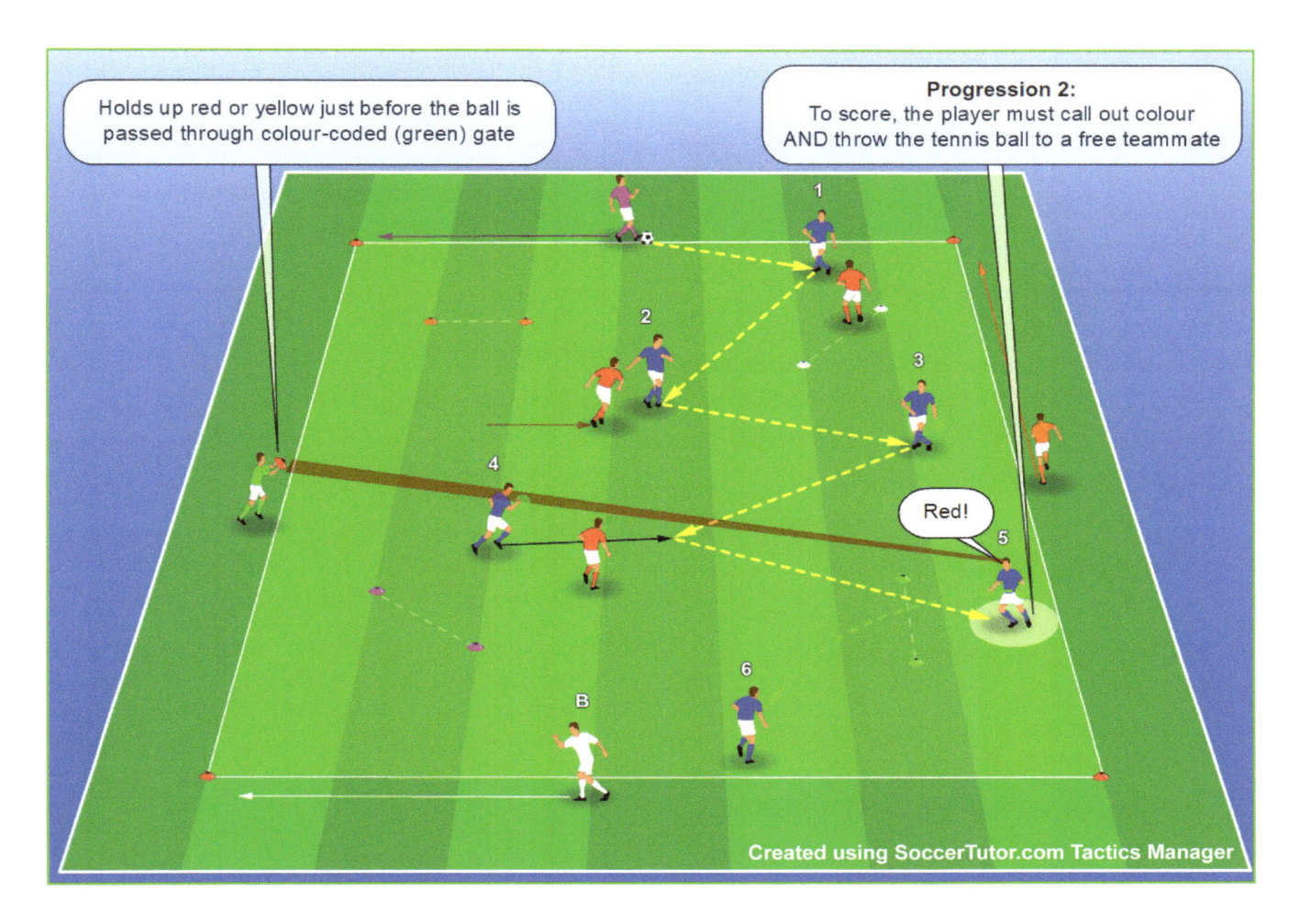

Holds up red or yellow just before the ball is passed through colour-coded (green) gate

Progression 2:
To score, the player must call out colour AND throw the tennis ball to a free teammate

Red!

Objective: To develop increased levels of awareness in an opposed practice.

Practice Description

- To progress the practice further, we add 3 tennis balls for the blue team and modify the scoring.
- To score, the player receiving the pass through the gate must be holding a tennis ball.
- He must also spot and call out the visual cue that the correct colour-coded flasher is holding up and throw the tennis ball to a free teammate who does not have a tennis ball.

- This should all be done after the pass is played and before his first touch.
- **Diagram Example:** As the ball is being passed from Player 4 to Player 5 (through the Green Gate), Player 5 must spot and call out the colour held up by the Green Flasher + throw the tennis ball to a teammate without a tennis ball (Player 6 in diagram).
- If Player 5 does not do all of this after the pass is played and before his first touch, then the goal does not count, and the team continue to play and try to score somewhere else.

Game Awareness Level 3 - Anticipation: Predicting How Play Will Develop

- As with the tennis ball progression in the previous practice, trying to score is the only time the players must throw the tennis ball and they do not have to throw the tennis ball when simply retaining possession. Scoring remains the same for the reds – pass to flasher on outside.

- **VARIATION:** The blue team can score 1 point without throwing the tennis ball, and score 3 points when they do.

Practice Analysis for Coach

- As we saw in the previous opposed practice example, **adding the tennis balls forces the receiving player to increase the number of players he is aware of**.

- **The receiver must now know**:
  » Who he is getting the ball from
  » Where the correct flasher is
  » How to position himself
  » Where his free teammates without a tennis ball are
  » Where his supporting teammates are to pass the football to
  » Where the opposition are applying pressure from

- Again, **the tennis balls force the free players (without a tennis ball) to think about their positional relationships with the tennis ball players**, so they can support them to score.

- However, they cannot focus only on that as they may be needed to help retain possession. This means they also **need to be aware of where the football is, where supporting teammates are, and where pressuring opponents are** just in case they are passed the football.

- As you can see, the **levels of concentration and awareness demanded from the players off-the-ball is incredibly intense and far greater than any "normal" training session**.

- There really is no time to switch off at all in this practice now...

- The players need to be constantly aware of where their teammates and opponents are in the area, and must think about their positional relationships with these players. In addition, they need to be **flexible enough to be able to quickly adapt to what their fluctuating role may be at any given moment** – support the tennis ball, support the football (to retain possession), position yourself to score, etc.

Coaching Points

A. Active Scanning – Pre-scan to locate the correct colour-coded flasher as the play is developing. Know where your free teammates (without tennis ball) are. Know where the ball is coming from and know where your teammates and opponents are inside the playing area.

B. Body Position – Open to where you are receiving the football from, the correct colour-coded flasher AND your free teammates who are without tennis balls.

C. Confirm - Check again! Look after the pass and before your first touch to spot and call out the colour held up by the colour-coded flasher.

D. Decision - Is there enough time to spot the visual cue and throw the tennis ball? Score or retain possession? Pass first time or take a touch?

E. Execution – Is the decision executed well?

F. Follow-on – After passing the football, quickly re-engage in scanning and positioning in relation to the ball, your teammates, and opponents. Quickly support the football AND tennis balls if possible.

Game Awareness Level 3 - Anticipation: Predicting How Play Will Develop

PRACTICE EXAMPLE 3: 6(+2) v 3 Pass to Floating Players Game

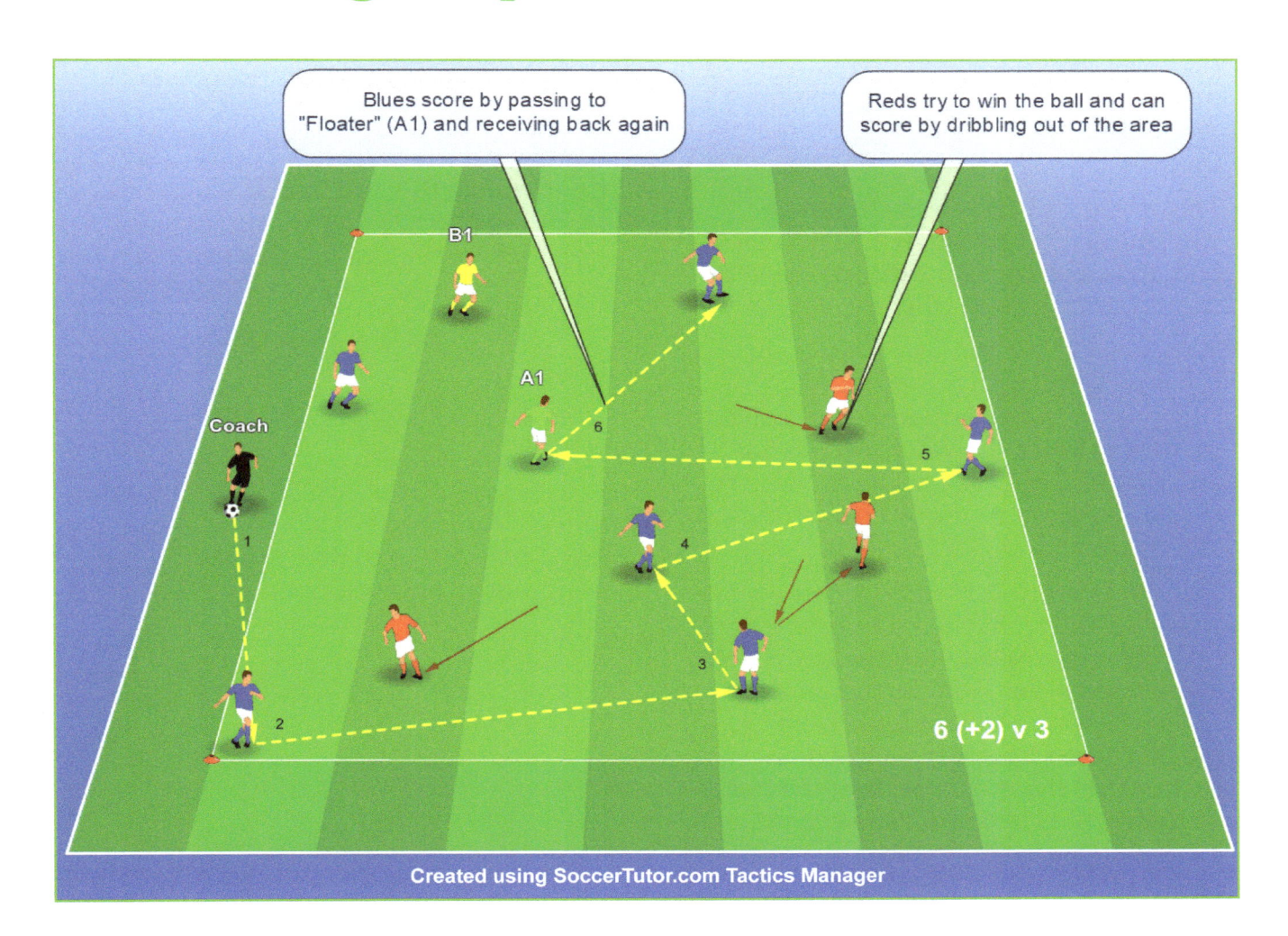

Blues score by passing to "Floater" (A1) and receiving back again

Reds try to win the ball and can score by dribbling out of the area

6 (+2) v 3

Objective: To develop increased levels of awareness in an opposed practice.

Practice Description

- We have 6 blue attackers vs 3 red defenders + 2 floaters inside the area – 1 green (A1) and 1 yellow (B1).

- The blue team score by passing to one of the floaters and receiving it back again (it does not have to be back to the same player who passed to the floater).

- The red team try to win the ball and can score by dribbling the ball out of the area – they can do this individually or combine with teammates.

Practice Analysis for Coach

- This is another very simple set-up, with the aim to keep possession and score by playing through the 2 playmakers.

- The blue team should **always be working with the aim to quickly bounce the ball off one of the floaters**. They have to move the ball quickly to get around the red players and learn to play quick passes into the floaters when the brief opportunities present themselves.

- **NOTE:** If the red players just man-mark the floaters and don't engage the blues, then also make 10 passes = score point.

SCANNING - How to Train it

Game Awareness Level 3 - Anticipation: Predicting How Play Will Develop

- The **floaters have to work hard to find space and opportunity to receive and have to use 1 touch play frequently** to simply bounce it back to another blue player.

- However, there will also be many opportunities for them to turn and switch the ball into a different area of the grid...

- This means, the **floaters should be continuously scanning whilst off-the-ball, to see what their options could be** should they receive the ball.

- In football, it is obviously important to know what is on around the ball. However, it is also **important to build a picture of what is away from the ball** – and position yourself appropriately to take advantage of those opportunities when you can.

- The players who can build a picture of what is away from the ball well are not only **effective at moving the ball quickly away from pressure to retain possession** - they are also **adept at launching quick attacks by spotting imbalances in the opposition and getting the ball to teammates in dangerous spaces** in advanced areas.

Coaching Points

A. Active Scanning – Know where the ball is coming from, and where your teammates and opponents are inside the playing area.

B. Body Position – Open to the player you are receiving the football from and where you want to go next.

C. Confirm - In this original practice setup, scanning is often limited and players rarely make the last scan as the ball is on its way (because they don't HAVE to).

D. Decision - Pass first time or take a touch?

E. Execution – Is the decision executed well?

F. Follow-on – After passing the football, quickly re-engage in scanning and positioning in relation to the ball, your teammates, and opponents.

Game Awareness Level 3 - Anticipation: Predicting How Play Will Develop

PROGRESSION 1: Visual Cues to Promote Scanning and Positioning

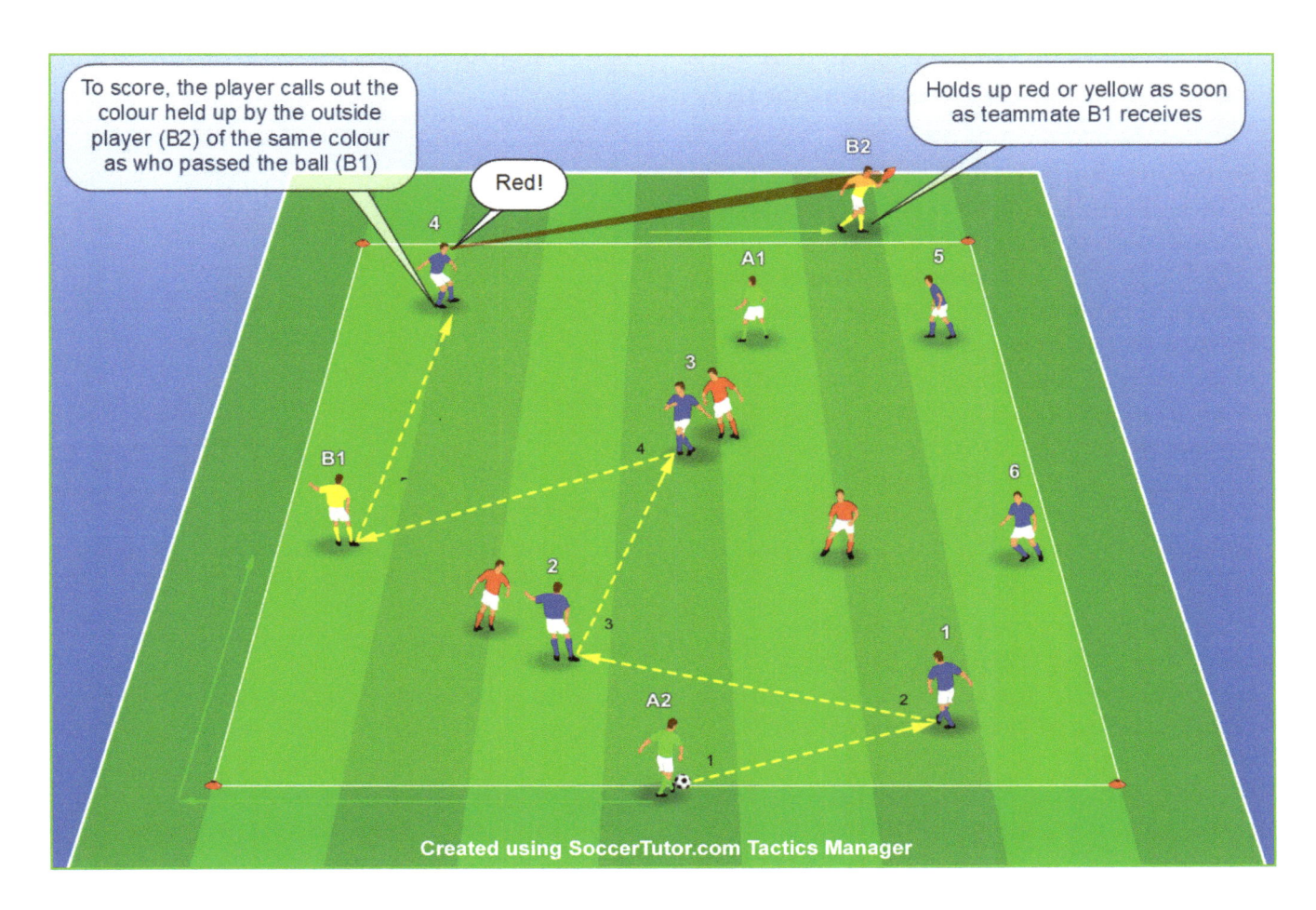

Diagram annotations:
- To score, the player calls out the colour held up by the outside player (B2) of the same colour as who passed the ball (B1)
- Holds up red or yellow as soon as teammate B1 receives
- Red!

Practice Description

- To progress, 2 outside flashers are added – 1 green (A2) and 1 yellow (B2). The flashers constantly move around the entire area and hold up a visual cue whenever the same colour-coded floater receives a pass. If the **Green Floater (A1)** receives, then the **Green Flasher (A2)** holds up a visual cue.

- The blues still score by passing the ball to a floater and receiving it back again. However, the receiving player must now spot and call out the visual cue held up by the flasher of the same colour as the floater who passes the ball to him.

- **Diagram Example:** Player 4 receives the ball from the **Yellow Floater (B1)**, so he must spot and call out the colour held up by the **Yellow Flasher (B2)** on the outside. As usual, spotting and calling out the colour should be done after the pass and before the receiver's (Player 4) first touch.

- If the red team win the ball, they score by passing to either of the 2 outside flashers (they can combine with the floaters to achieve this). The flasher always passes back to the blue team.

- **VARIATION 1:** The reds keep possession after winning the ball. They combine with the floaters and flashers and score a point each time they pass to a flasher until the blue team win the ball back.

Game Awareness Level 3 - Anticipation: Predicting How Play Will Develop

Practice Analysis for Coach

- As we have seen in the previous practices, adding the flashers with visual cues will have an almost immediate impact on player behaviour. They will start **scanning more frequently and search for the colour-coded flasher they need to spot** in order to score.

- However, you may find some players still only look for the flasher as the floater is about to pass them the ball. As always, this is too late! The **players should know where this teammate (flasher) is well before the pass is played**. In fact, they should know his position before the ball is even passed to the floater. The players must learn to start recognising when a teammate has the chance to pass to the floater and use this moment as a trigger to confirm the location of the correct flasher on the outside.

- There are also times when a player is further **away from play but can benefit from quick scans and locating the positions of the flashers** - this is whenever the ball is travelling between 2 blue teammates. Of course, he may first need to quickly assess that the team have comfortable possession, but this is a great moment of the game for a player to engage in off-the-ball scanning to great effect.

- Whenever the ball moves, **the picture changes and too many players spend these moments ball-watching, instead of using it as an opportunity to look around** and reorientate their positioning with teammates and opponents.

- **VARIATION 2:** The blues score a bonus point if they manage to pass to the flasher within 2-3 touches of receiving the ball from a floater.

- Adding this extra scoring mechanism gives even greater context to the scanning required to locate this player - not only do the players have to spot and call out a colour, but now they use this player as an active outlet for the ball too.

- **NOTE:** If the red players start to man-mark the floaters and don't engage the blues, we can adapt the practice slightly:
  » Ask each pair of flasher and floater to cooperate and interchange positions.
  » Allow the inside floater to drop out of the area and the outside flasher to move inside the area.
  » For example, if the green floater (A1) feels he is being marked too tightly, he can drag his marker away and then step out of the area to allow the green flasher (A2) to move into the area unmarked.
  » Can the blue team quickly adapt to this new situation to take advantage of the space A2 now has?

Coaching Points

A. Active Scanning – Know where the flasher is positioned! Pre-scan to locate the correct flasher as the play is developing. Know where the ball is coming from, and where teammates and opponents are inside the area.

B. Body Position – Open to where you are receiving the football from and the correct flasher.

C. Confirm - Check again! Look after the pass and before your first touch to spot and call out the colour held up by the flasher.

D. Decision - Pass first time or take a touch?

E. Execution – Is the decision executed well?

F. Follow-on – After passing the football, quickly re-engage in scanning and positioning in relation to the ball, your teammates, and opponents.

Game Awareness Level 3 - Anticipation: Predicting How Play Will Develop

PROGRESSION 2: Scan, Position, and Support Play + Throwing Tennis Balls

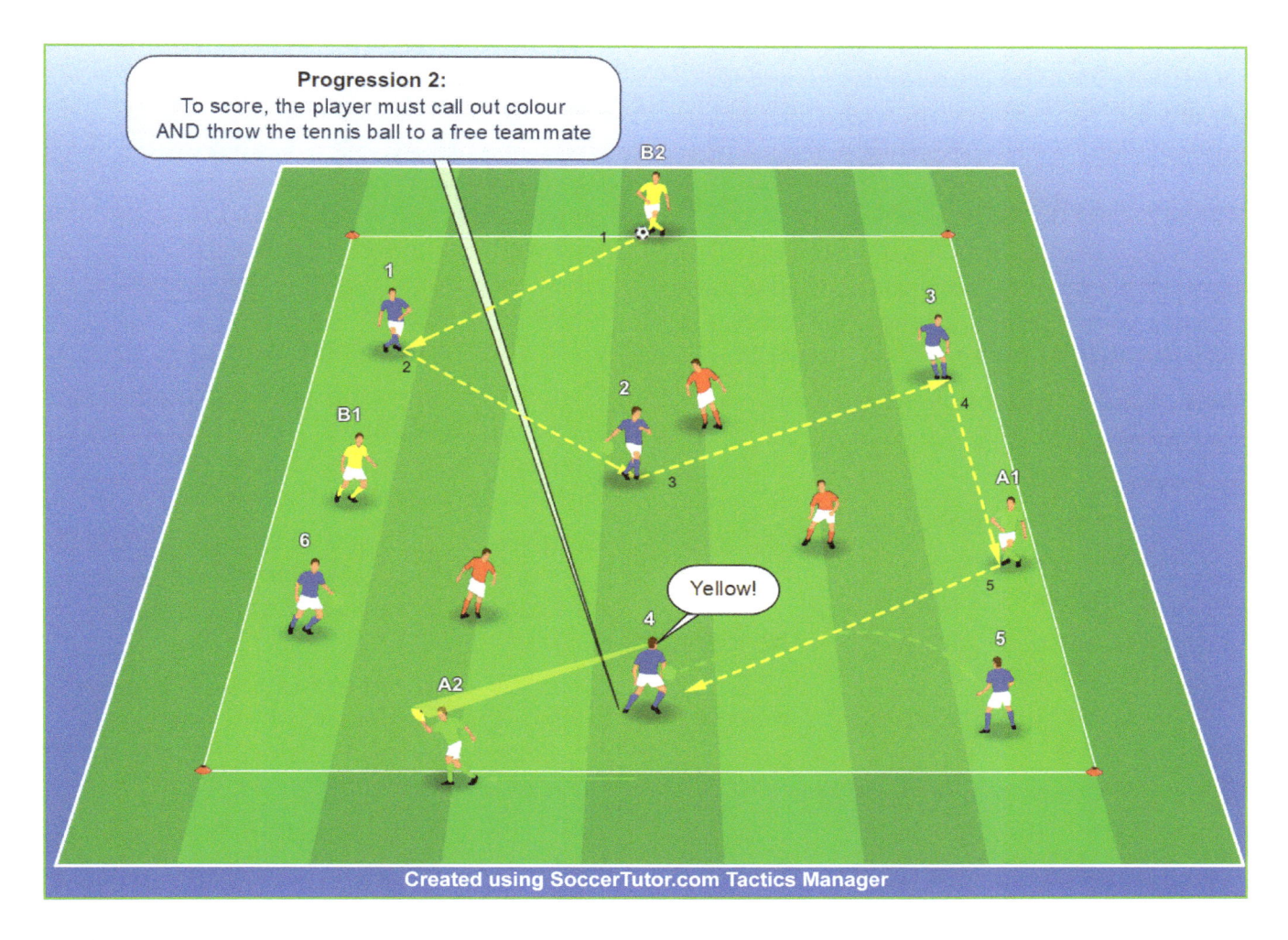

Progression 2:
To score, the player must call out colour AND throw the tennis ball to a free teammate

Objective: To develop increased levels of awareness in an opposed practice.

Practice Description

- To progress the practice further, we add 3 tennis balls for the blue team and modify the scoring.

- To score, the player receiving the pass from the floater must be holding a tennis ball.

- He must also spot and call out the visual cue that the correct colour-coded flasher is holding up and throw the tennis ball to a free teammate who does not have a tennis ball.

- This should all be done after the pass is played and before his first touch.

- **Diagram Example:** As the ball is being passed from Green Floater (A1) to Player 4, Player 4 must spot and call out the colour held up by the Green Flasher (A2) + pass the tennis ball to a free teammate (Player 5 in diagram).

- If he does not do all of this after the pass and before his first touch, then the goal does not count, and the team continue to play and try to score somewhere else.

- As with the tennis ball progression in the previous practices, trying to score is

Soccer eyeQ with SoccerTutor.com   181   SCANNING - How to Train it

Game Awareness Level 3 - Anticipation: Predicting How Play Will Develop

the only time the players must throw the tennis ball - they don't have to throw the tennis ball when retaining possession.

- Scoring remains the same for the reds – pass to any flasher on the outside.
- **VARIATION:** The blue team can score 1 point without throwing the tennis ball, and score 3 points when they do.

Practice Analysis for Coach

- As we saw in the previous opposed practice example, **adding the tennis balls forces the receiving player to increase the number of players he is aware of**.
- <u>**The receiver must now know**</u>:
    » Which floater he is getting the ball from
    » Where the correct flasher is on the outside
    » How to position himself
    » Where his free teammates without a tennis ball are
    » Where his supporting teammates are to pass the football to
    » Where the opposition are applying pressure from
- Once again, the tennis balls force the free players (without a tennis ball) to think about their positional relationships with the tennis ball players so they can support them to score.
- However, they cannot focus only on that as they may be needed to help retain possession. This means they also need to be aware of where the football is, where supporting teammates are, and where pressuring opponents are.
- Once again, you can see that the **levels of concentration and awareness demanded even when a player is off-the-ball is incredibly intense**.
- The players **should not switch off at any point and should be constantly**

updating their map of where teammates and opponents are. This is so they can adapt and offer appropriate support in any given moment – support the tennis ball, support the football (to retain possession), position to score, etc.

Coaching Points

A. Active Scanning – Pre-scan to locate the correct flasher as the play is developing. Know where free teammates (without tennis ball) are, where the ball is coming from, and know where teammates and opponents are inside the playing area.

B. Body Position – Open to where you are receiving the football from, the correct flasher AND the free teammates without tennis balls if possible.

C. Confirm - Check again! Look after the pass and before your first touch to spot and call out the colour held up by the flasher.

D. Decision - Is there enough time to spot a visual cue and throw the tennis ball? Score or retain possession? Pass first time or take a touch?

E. Execution – Is the decision executed well?

F. Follow-on – After passing the football, quickly re-engage in scanning and positioning in relation to the ball, your teammates, and opponents. Quickly support the football AND tennis balls if possible.

ANTICIPATION PRACTICES - SUMMARY

We have looked at 3 different formats of opposed practice and shown how we can layer in the different constraints (visual cues and tennis balls) to promote scanning, and develop greater awareness, all whilst under pressure from active opponents.

Although one of the primary ways we are helping to build awareness is by developing the habits required to engage in scanning to locate the flashers on the outside, the players cannot solely focus their attention on this task. They still have to work with each other to maintain possession inside the grid. This means **each player must also be constantly aware of his relationships with the ball, teammates, and opponents, and continually optimise his positioning** in order to have the greatest effect.

Once again, the players must learn to divide their attention effectively and prioritise the most important elements. For example, **does the player have time to spot the colour or does he forego the opportunity to score and simply retain possession?** The players will encounter decision-making moments like these numerous times and for a variety of reasons - opposition pressure, speed of the pass, etc.

Although there is an extra emphasis when the players are receiving a pass, you can see that **the levels of concentration and awareness demanded from the players when they are off-the-ball is incredibly intense and far greater than any "normal" training session**. There really is no time to switch off now. The players need to be constantly aware of where teammates and opponents are in the area, and thinking about their **positional relationships** with these players, whilst being **flexible enough to be able to quickly adapt to what their changing role may be** at any given moment – support the tennis ball, support the football (to retain possession), position to score, etc.

Practices like those in this section will **develop and sharpen the essential tools players need** (such as scanning, positioning, and concentration) in order to **quickly recognise the signals, situations, and scenarios in the game**.

Furthermore, **these practices will sharpen these tools to such an extent that the players will be able to read the game, and predict how the play will develop, much quicker than ever before**.

SECTION 3

Adding the Soccer eyeQ Method to Existing Practices

SECTION 3: Adding the Soccer eyeQ Method to Existing Practices

PRACTICE DIAGRAM KEY

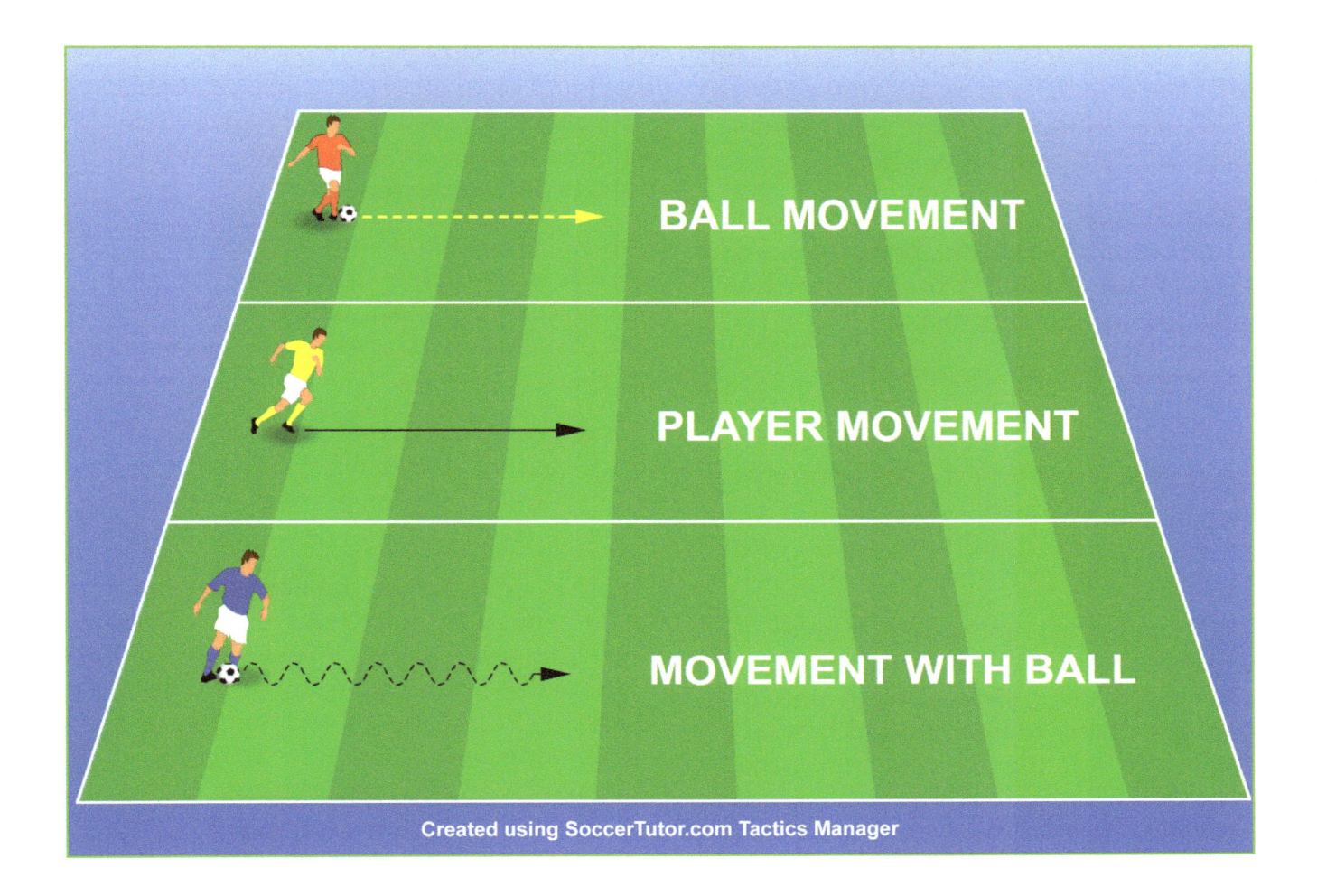

- BALL MOVEMENT
- PLAYER MOVEMENT
- MOVEMENT WITH BALL

Created using SoccerTutor.com Tactics Manager

PRACTICE FORMAT

- First the original practice is displayed, including the source.

- This is followed by Kevin McGreskin adding the Soccer eyeQ game awareness training methodology to the same practice.

- The aim is to add scanning and game awareness training into any existing practice, so the players are always training this key skill. The method can be input into almost any training practice that you want to use.

- The original practice includes a full description. The Soccer eyeQ practice descriptions answer the following questions: What have we added? Why have we added it? How does it improve game awareness in this practice? What benefit will the players get?

SECTION 3: Adding the Soccer eyeQ Method to Existing Practices

SOCCER EYEQ: Coaches can Add Game Awareness Skills to Any Practice

It is very important to understand that you (the coach) can apply these Soccer eyeQ scanning and game awareness methods to almost any practice.

By adding these methods to existing practices and sessions, the players can improve and develop these essential skills and create a habit.

Too many coaches assume players are always looking around, but I believe we need to really coach it. Scanning is an essential foundation for good awareness and effective decision-making. And it is one of the key elements which can vastly improve player performance.

The **Soccer eyeQ methodology helps players develop this essential habit of scanning by using simple constraints that force the player to look around far more frequently** than they need to in "normal" sessions.

All of these **ideas can be easily implemented into your training sessions** to increase active scanning and improve game awareness.

As you will have seen from Section 2, the practices in this book are similar to ones that many coaches are using. As I mentioned before, this is very much on purpose, as I like to show that **you don't need to drastically change what you are already doing to get results**.

My intention is not to change, but to ADD layers into the practices that put an extra emphasis on scanning, forcing the players to look around more often and be more aware of everything that is going on around them.

By always having game awareness elements in your practice, you will **help your players develop and enhance their abilities to scan and take in information quickly during the game**.

This will **give the players the tools they need to make better decisions** and really unlock their potential, which will improve individual player development and overall team performance.

This section shows some common practices in which I have added the Soccer eyeQ game awareness methods to increase training of the habit of scanning.

The first example (on the next page) is a Rondo which Jürgen Klopp used with his Liverpool team during pre-season training at Melwood Training Ground, Liverpool, 20th July 2021. How to add the Soccer eyeQ game awareness method to it is displayed with a full description.

NOTE: We don't show any progressions with tennis balls in this section, so please refer to the Realization and Anticipation practices in Section 2 to see how the tennis balls are incorporated. You can easily add them to the practices in this section.

SECTION 3: Adding the Soccer eyeQ Method to Existing Practices

RONDO EXAMPLE:
Liverpool Rondo with "Magic Player"

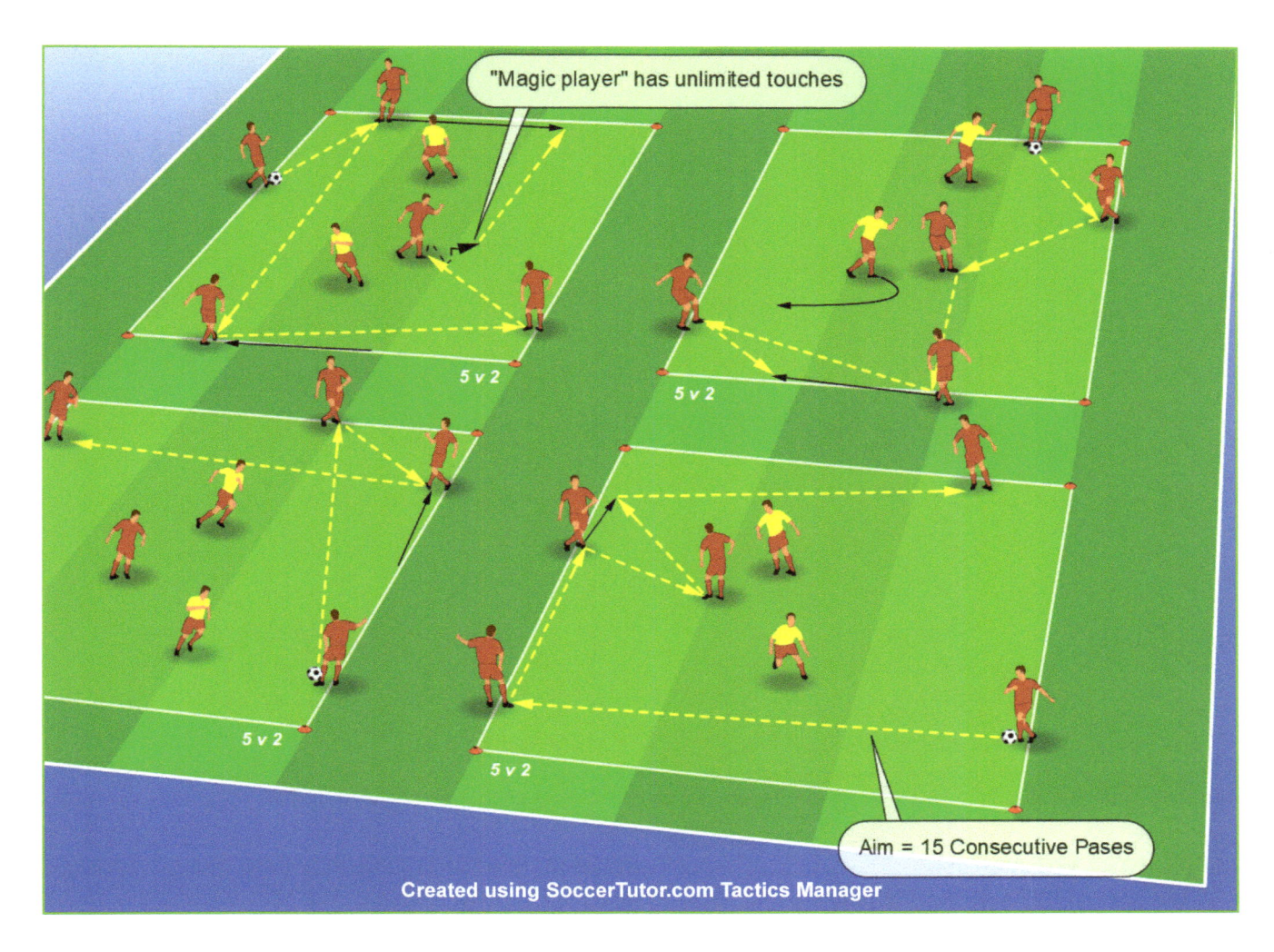

"Magic player" has unlimited touches

5 v 2

Aim = 15 Consecutive Passes

Created using SoccerTutor.com Tactics Manager

Practice Description

- The players work in groups of 7 in a 10 yard square area. It is a 5v2 rondo.
- For the possession team (reds), there are 4 players who operate on the outside, and are limited to 2 touches.
- The reds also have one "magic player" who can move freely (inside and outsides of square) and has unlimited touches.
- The 5 red players aim to keep possession of the ball.
- The aim is to complete 15 consecutive passes to score a point and avoid switching roles with the defenders.
- The 2 defending players (yellow bibs) work together to try and close the angles and win the ball.
- If a player loses the ball (before 15 passes), they switch roles with the player that wins the ball.

SOURCE: Jürgen Klopp's Liverpool FC training session at Melwood Training Ground, Liverpool - 20th July 2021

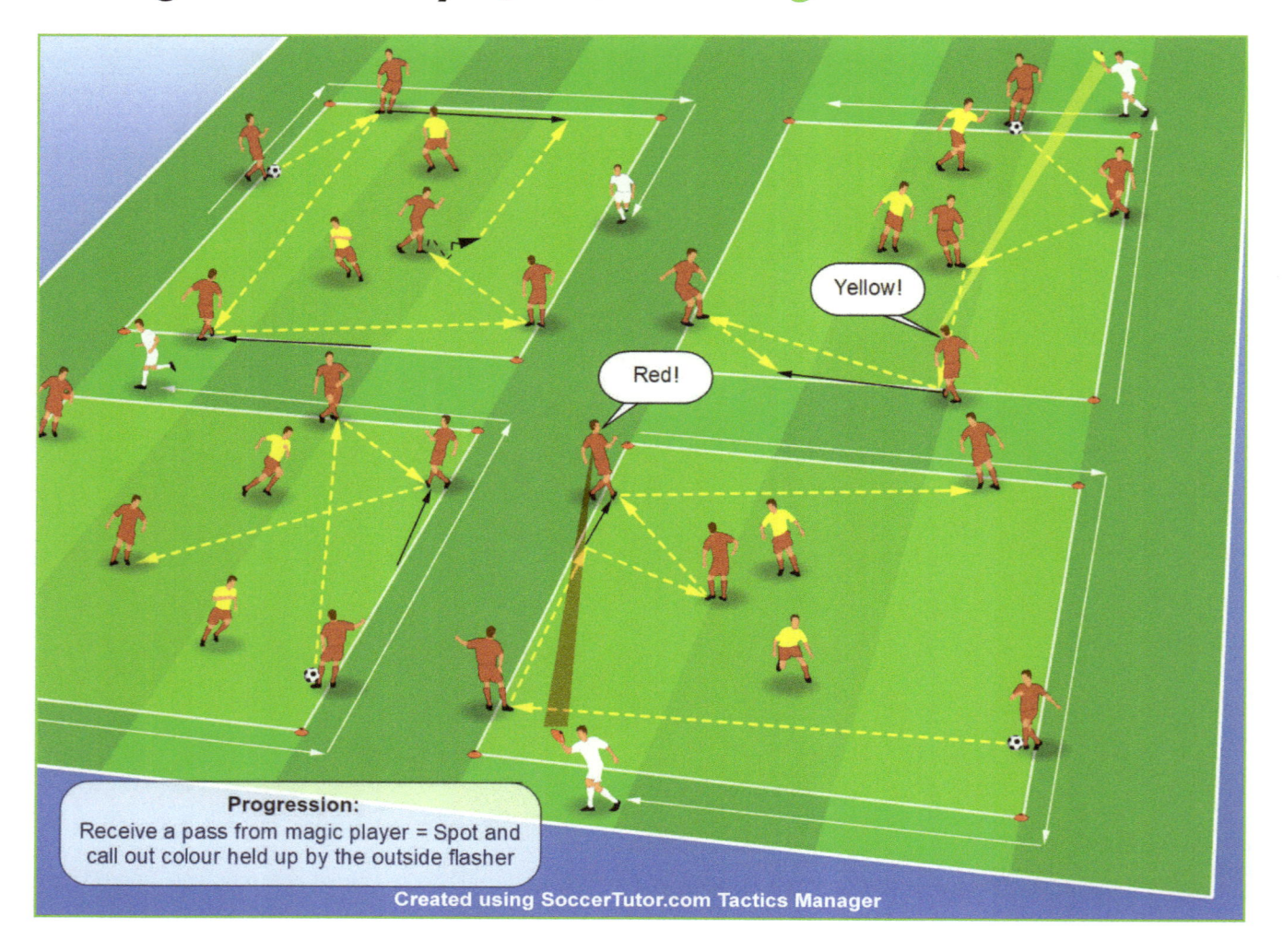

SECTION 3: Adding the Soccer eyeQ Method to Existing Practices

Adding the Soccer eyeQ Method - Progression

Progression:
Receive a pass from magic player = Spot and call out colour held up by the outside flasher

Created using SoccerTutor.com Tactics Manager

What have we added?

- We add an outside flasher, who moves around the outside of the whole square.
- Whoever receives a pass from the "magic player" must spot and call out the colour held up by the flasher on the outside (bonus point).
- If the 2 defending players (yellow bibs) win the ball, they score by passing to the outside flasher.

Why have we added it?

- In the basic rondo, players focus on the inside of the grid and tend to rely on peripheral vision.
- The addition of the flasher promotes more scanning.

How does it improve game awareness?

- The flasher means that the players must lift their heads to scan and look at the "Bigger Picture."

What benefit will the players get?

- The players develop the habit of scanning away from the ball throughout the Rondo.
- Learn to divide their attention.
- Take in quick snapshots of the positioning of teammates.
- Increase confidence and competence.

SECTION 3: Adding the Soccer eyeQ Method to Existing Practices

PASSING DRILL EXAMPLE 1:
Passing "Y" Drill

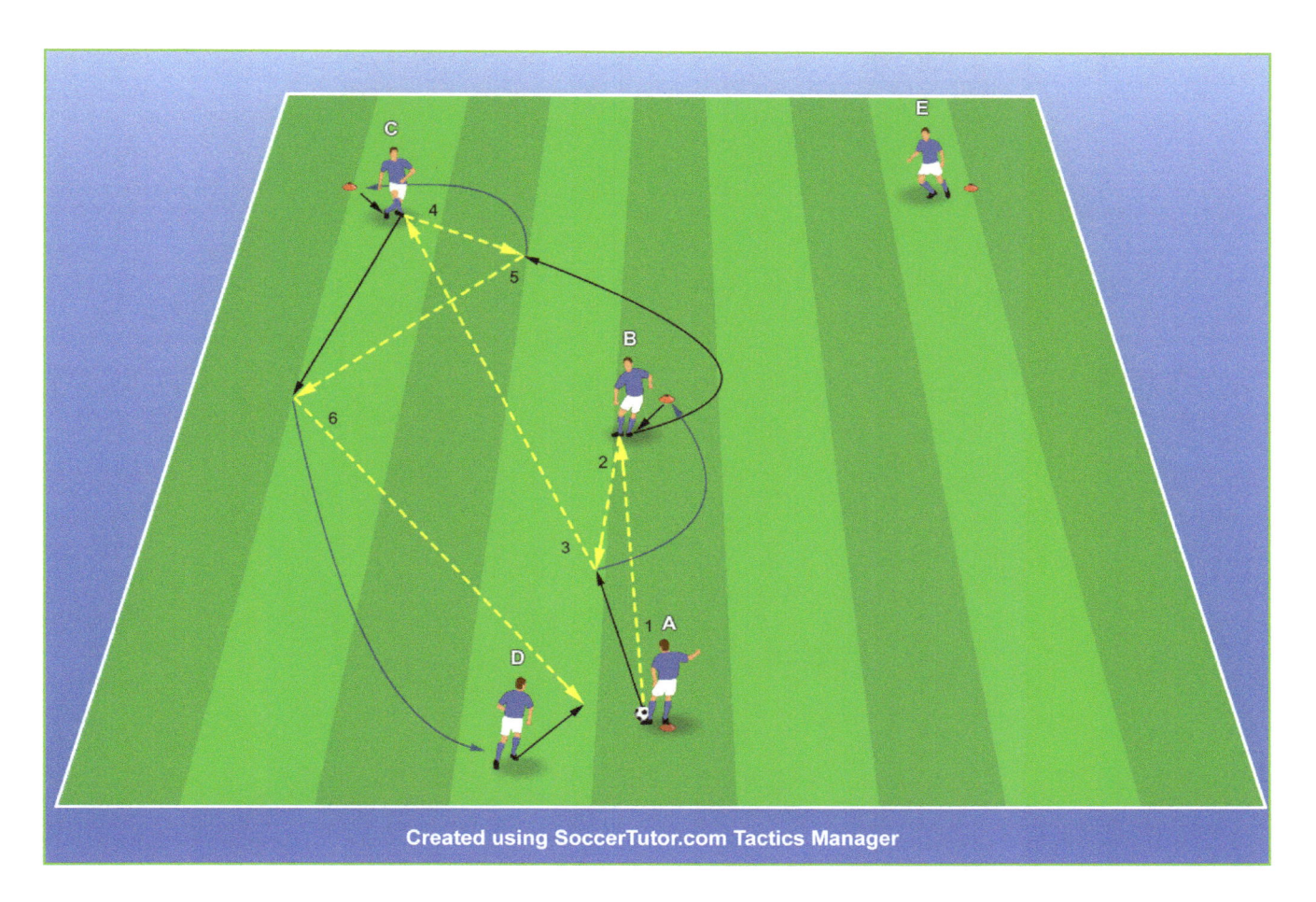

Practice Description

There are 5 players (A → E) set out in a "Y" shape as shown, and they play a predetermined passing pattern. The blue curved lines show their movement after their pass (to the next position).

1. Player A passes to Player B.
2. Player B passes back for Player A to move forward onto.
3. Player A passes diagonally to Player C.
4. Player C plays a short pass timed for the movement of Player B.
5. Player B then passes in the opposite direction for C to run forward onto.
6. Player C passes to the next player waiting (D). The same passing sequence is then repeated on the right side involving Player E.

Coaching Points

1. The second pass (lay-off) needs to be weighted well for Player 1 to receive the ball on the move, who should time their run for the pass.
2. Make sure players pass and receive with both feet.
3. Progress the practice by limiting the players to 1 touch.
4. Make sure the players communicate with their teammates and heads are up.

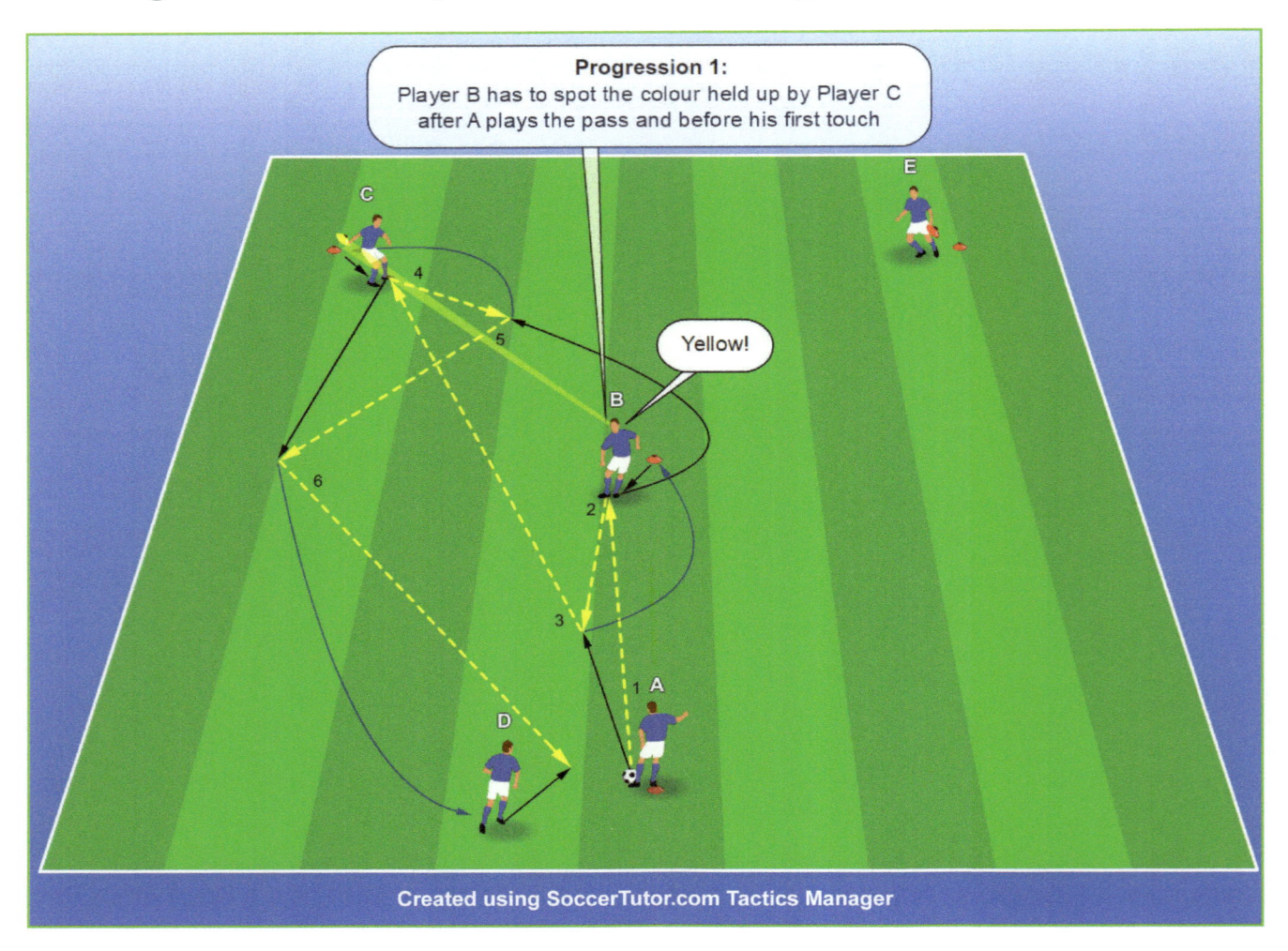

SECTION 3: Adding the Soccer eyeQ Method to Existing Practices

Adding the Soccer eyeQ Method - Progression 1

Progression 1:
Player B has to spot the colour held up by Player C after A plays the pass and before his first touch

Yellow!

What have we added?
- A visual cue is flashed by the end player (Player C in diagram) when the middle player (B) is looking to receive.

Why have we added it?
- Force the middle player (B) to scan and locate the player flashing the visual cue.
- Force scanning as the ball is travelling, so Player B can spot and call out the colour (visual cue) before taking a first touch.

How does it improve game awareness?
- Player B has to look away from the ball to know the positioning of the key player.
- Player B's body shape improves, as he must be open to see Player C's position.
- Players cannot solely focus on the ball, as they must spot the visual cues at the correct time to locate the positioning of their teammate, and then spot the colour held up as the ball is travelling towards you.

What benefit will the players get?
- They develop the habit of scanning away from the ball at key moments.
- Learn to divide their attention.
- Take in quick snapshots of the positioning of teammates.
- Increase confidence and competence.

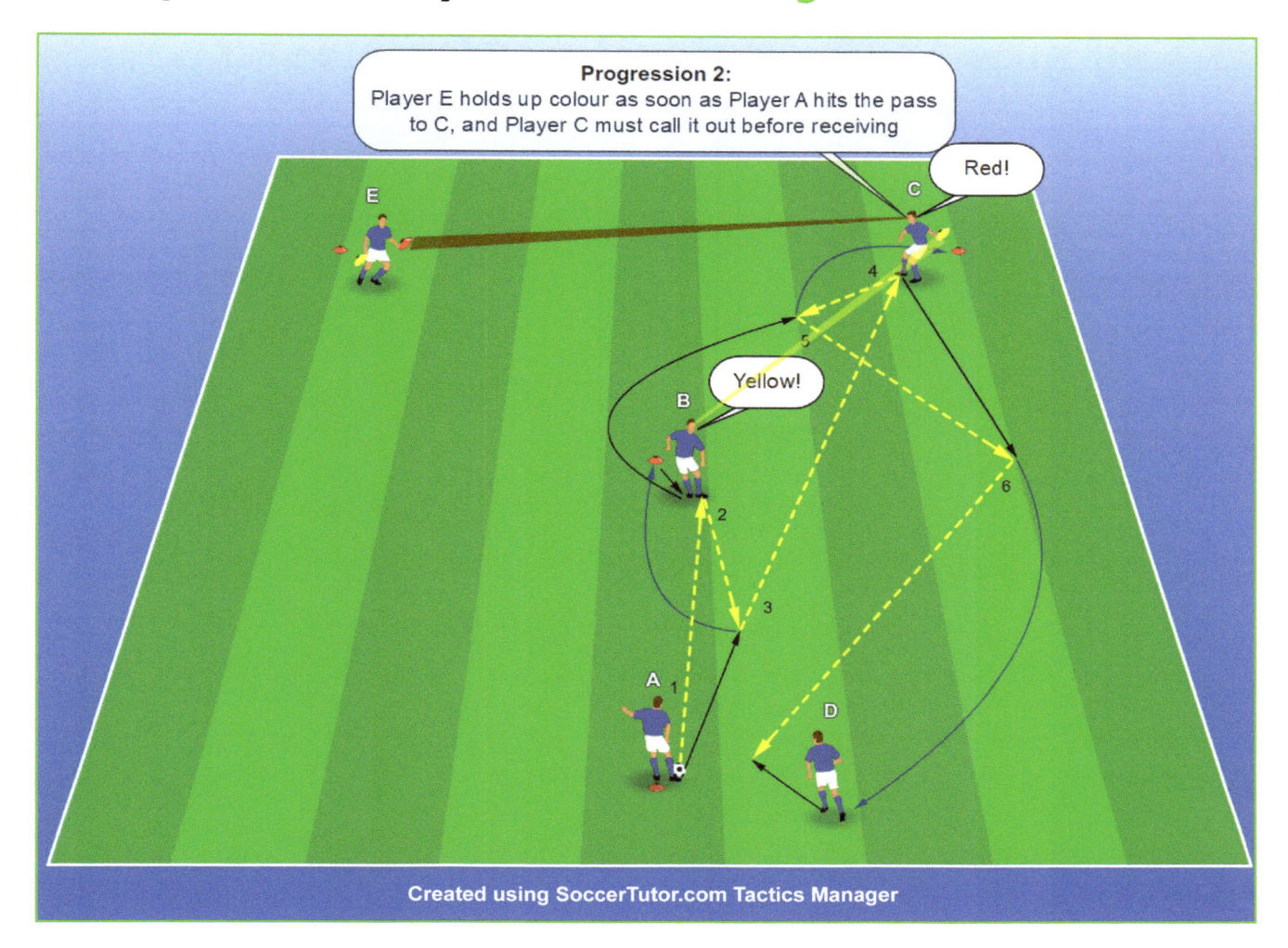

SECTION 3: Adding the Soccer eyeQ Method to Existing Practices

Adding the Soccer eyeQ Method - Progression 2

Progression 2:
Player E holds up colour as soon as Player A hits the pass to C, and Player C must call it out before receiving

Created using SoccerTutor.com Tactics Manager

What have we added?

- **NOTE**: All components of Progression 1 on the previous page remain.
- The extra component added for Progression 2 is that the end player (Player C in diagram) must spot the visual cue held up by the other end player (E) before receiving.

Why have we added it?

- We are now forcing two players within this passing drill to scan and locate a teammate flashing a visual cue.
- We also again force scanning as the ball is travelling towards them, so they can spot and call out the colour (visual cue) before taking a first touch.

How does it improve game awareness?

- Now we have two players who must look away from the ball, and who have improved body shape to get a full picture of all the players' positioning.
- In addition, the player not previously involved in the pattern (Player E) now has a role and must stay concentrated to lift the visual cue at the correct time.

What benefit will the players get?

- The benefits are exactly the same as Progression 1 (see previous page), except now all players are involved throughout the practice - and must demonstrate good awareness.

Soccer eyeQ with SoccerTutor.com   191   SCANNING - How to Train it

SECTION 3: Adding the Soccer eyeQ Method to Existing Practices

PASSING DRILL EXAMPLE 2:
Short and Long Passing Circuit

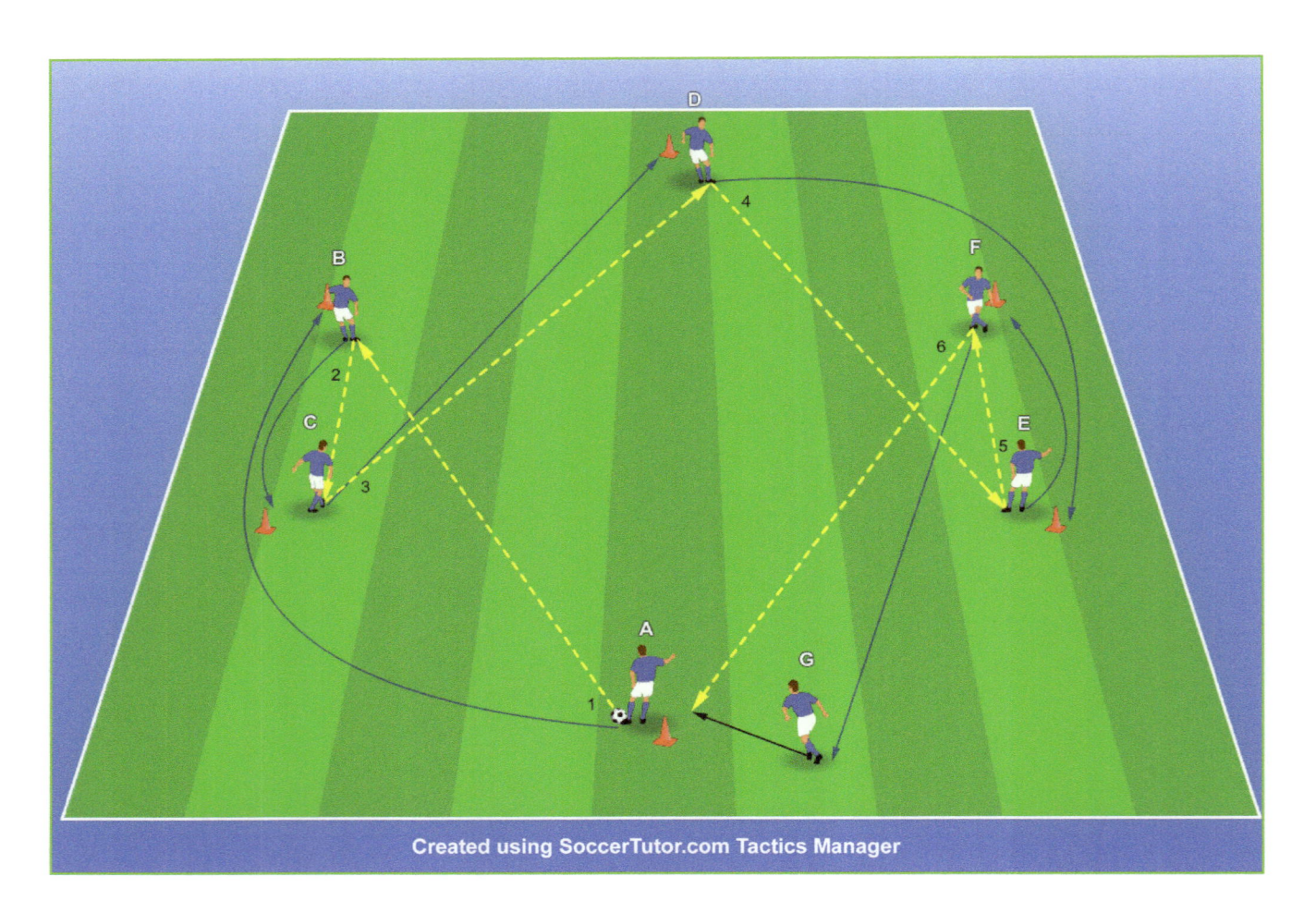

Practice Description

There are 7 players (A → G) set out in the starting positions shown, and they play a mix of shot and long passes.

The blue curved lines show the players' movement after their pass (to the next position).

1. Player A passes diagonally to Player B.
2. Player B plays a lay-off pass to Player C.
3. Player C passes diagonally to Player D.
4. Player D passes diagonally to Player E.
5. Player E plays a lay-off pass to Player F.
6. Player C passes to the next player waiting (G). The passing sequence continues with all players having moved to the next position.

Coaching Points

1. Players should use the inside of the foot for the short passes as it is the most controlled and accurate way.
2. For this passing sequence to be quick, players should check away before moving to receive the pass, which creates space and makes it easier for the players to play with 1 touch.

Soccer eyeQ with SoccerTutor.com

192

SCANNING - How to Train it

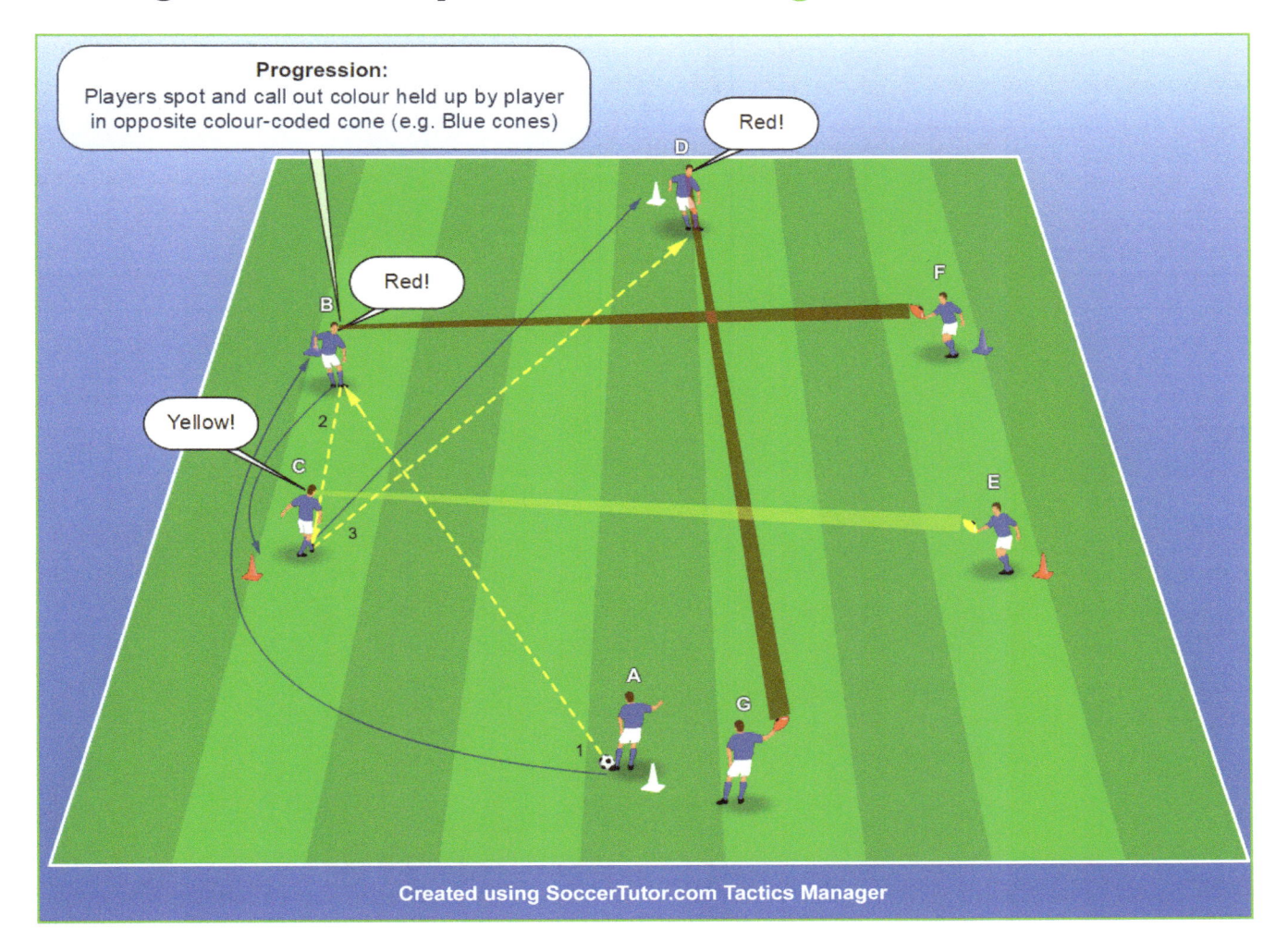

SECTION 3: Adding the Soccer eyeQ Method to Existing Practices

Adding the Soccer eyeQ Method - Progression

Progression:
Players spot and call out colour held up by player in opposite colour-coded cone (e.g. Blue cones)

Created using SoccerTutor.com Tactics Manager

What have we added?

- Visual cues are flashed by players when their teammate positioned on the same colour-coded (opposite) cone is receiving a pass.
- In the diagram example, all 3 examples are shown with the opposite blue, red, and white cones.

Why have we added it?

- To force the players to take their eyes off the ball and scan other areas of the playing area.
- Force scanning as the ball is travelling, so the player receiving the pass must spot and call out the colour before taking a first touch.

How does it improve game awareness?

- The player receiving the pass must take one last look away from the ball just before receiving a pass.
- In addition, a player not previously involved in the pattern at that moment now has a role and must stay concentrated.

What benefit will the players get?

- They develop the habit of scanning away from the ball at key moments.
- Learn to divide their attention.
- Take in quick snapshots of the positioning of teammates.
- Increase confidence and competence.

Soccer eyeQ with SocccerTutor.com   SCANNING - How to Train it

SECTION 3: Adding the Soccer eyeQ Method to Existing Practices

PASSING DRILL EXAMPLE 3:
Dynamic Passing Double Square

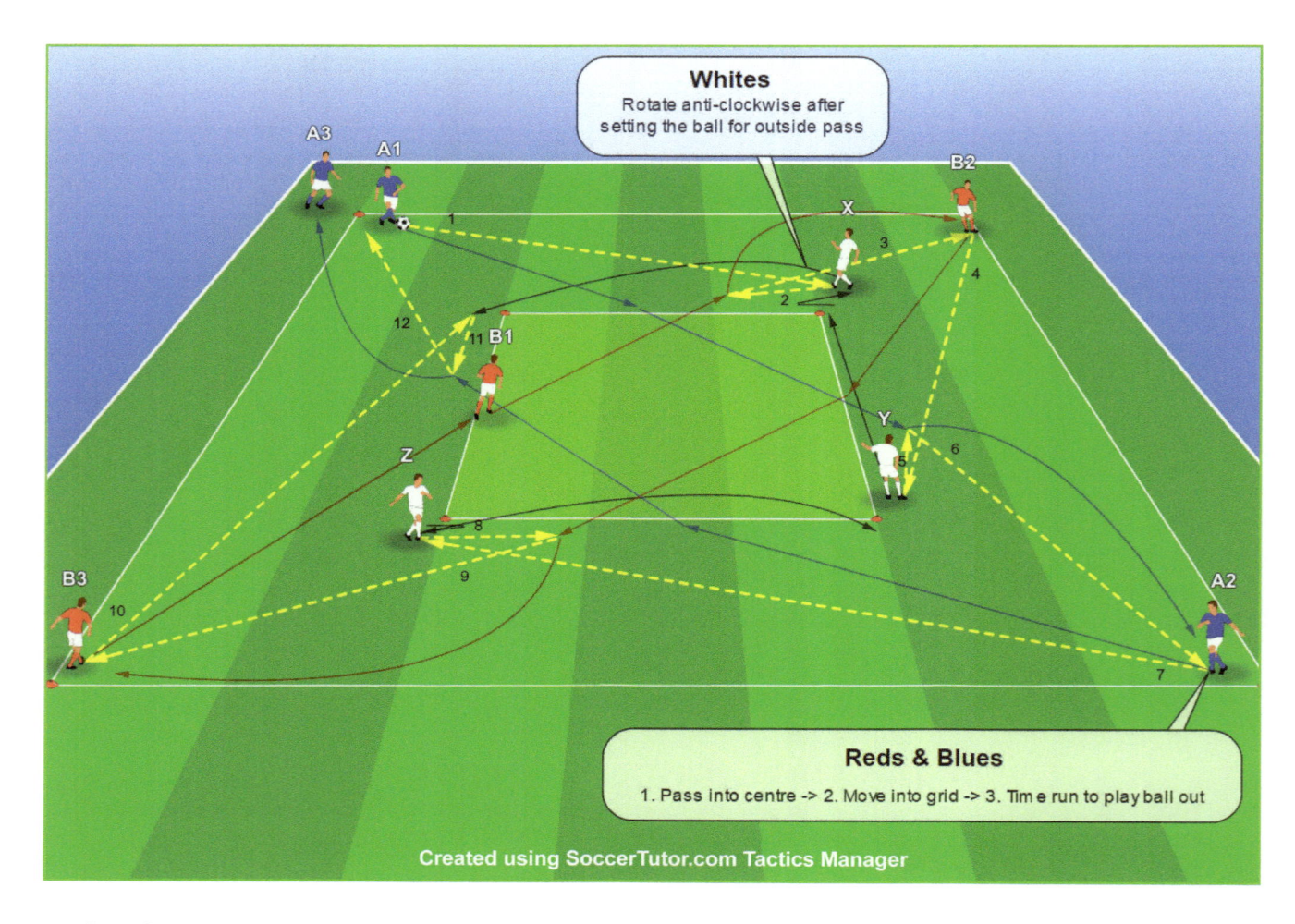

Whites
Rotate anti-clockwise after setting the ball for outside pass

Reds & Blues
1. Pass into centre -> 2. Move into grid -> 3. Time run to play ball out

Created using SoccerTutor.com Tactics Manager

Objective: To improve one-touch passing, combination play, and timing of movements needed to provide support.

Practice Description

- In a 25 yard square area, mark out a smaller square in the middle as shown. There are 6 players who start on the outside and 3 inside players.

- An outside player starts (A1), and the rhythm is to pass into the centre, move into the centre grid, and then time your run to receive and play the ball out.

- In the diagram, A1 passes to X, who lays the ball back for the run of B1.

- B1 then plays the ball out to B2.

- The same process is repeated with B2's pass to Y and then Y's lay-off for A1 to run onto and play the ball out to A2.

- The practice is continuous in a clockwise direction as shown.

- The red and blue outside players follow their pass and the white inside players rotate anti-clockwise.

- Rotate the practice so the blue and red players work in an anti-clockwise direction (practice with both feet).

- Change the inside player roles often.

Soccer eyeQ with SoccerTutor.com   SCANNING - How to Train it

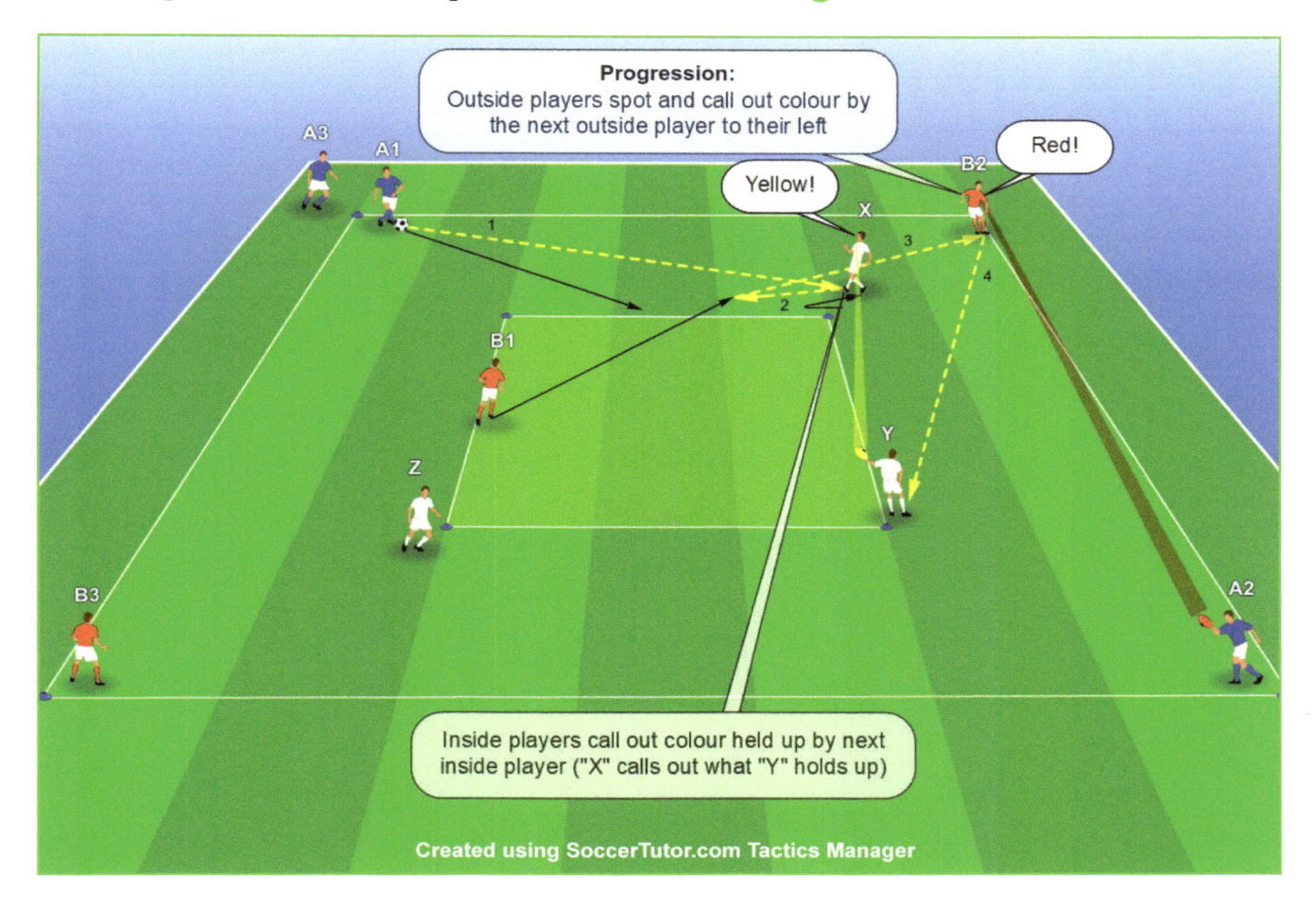

SECTION 3: Adding the Soccer eyeQ Method to Existing Practices

Adding the Soccer eyeQ Method - Progression

Progression:
Outside players spot and call out colour by the next outside player to their left

"Yellow!" "Red!"

Inside players call out colour held up by next inside player ("X" calls out what "Y" holds up)

Created using SoccerTutor.com Tactics Manager

What have we added?

- Visual cues are flashed by players at key moments when specific players are receiving the ball.
- The outside players spot and call out the colour held up by the next outside player to their left e.g. B2 calls out A2's colour in the diagram example.
- The inside players spot and call out the colour held up by the next inside player.

Why have we added it?

- To force the players to take their eyes off the ball and scan other areas of the playing area.
- Force scanning as the ball is travelling, so the player receiving the pass must spot and call out the colour before taking a first touch.

How does it improve game awareness?

- The player receiving the pass must take one last look away from the ball when they are receiving a pass.
- In addition, a player not previously involved in the pattern at that moment now has a role and must stay concentrated.

What benefit will the players get?

- They develop the habit of scanning away from the ball at key moments.
- Learn to divide their attention.
- Take in quick snapshots of the positioning of teammates.
- Increase confidence and competence.

SECTION 3: Adding the Soccer eyeQ Method to Existing Practices

POSSESSION GAME EXAMPLE 1:
Pocket Box Possession Game

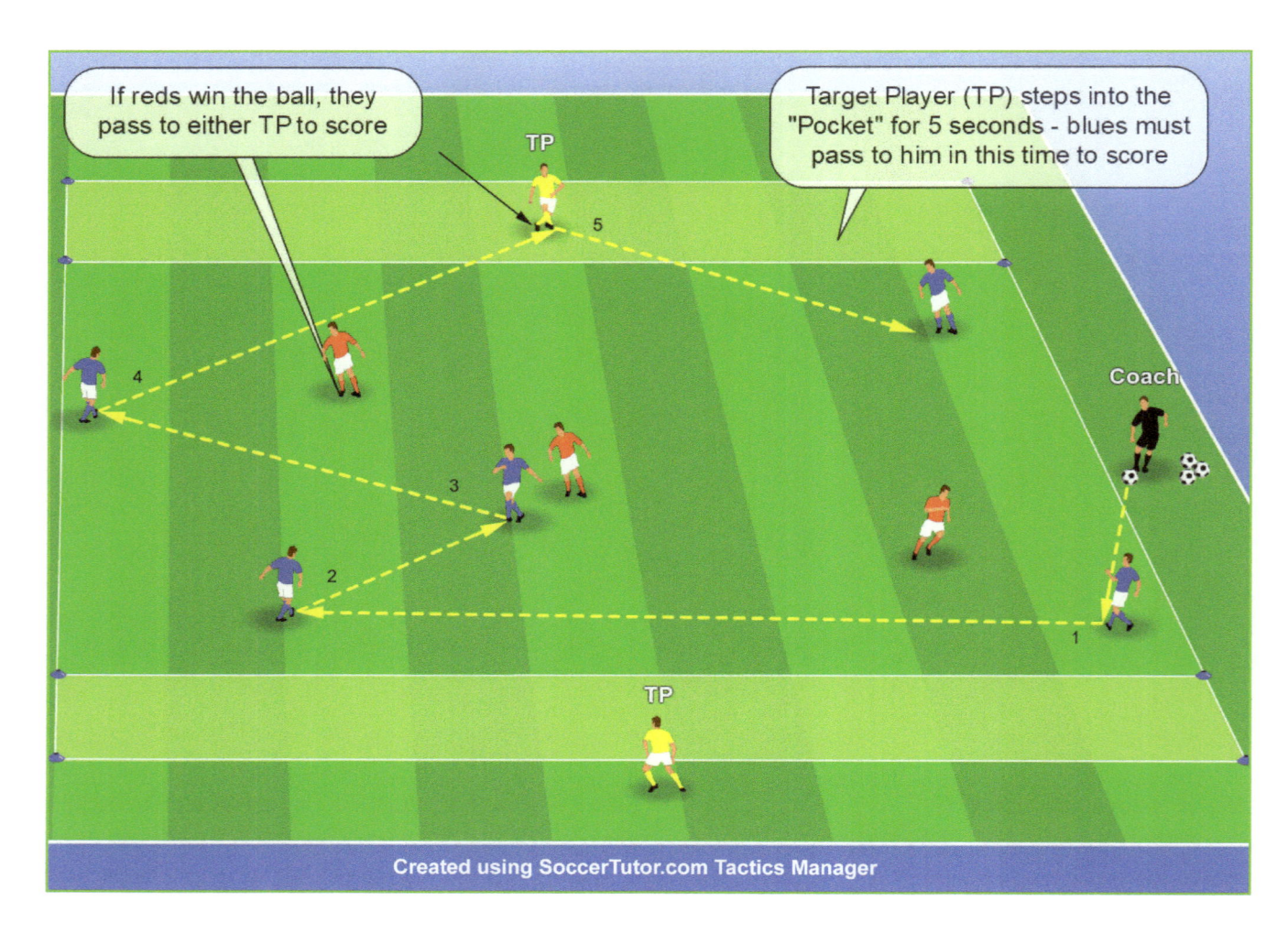

Diagram callouts:
- If reds win the ball, they pass to either TP to score
- Target Player (TP) steps into the "Pocket" for 5 seconds - blues must pass to him in this time to score

Practice Description

- Use an area size appropriate for the age/level of the players and mark out 2 end zones, as shown in the diagram. We play 6v3 + 2 Target Players (TP).

- The practice starts with the Coach and the blue team try to maintain possession. The target players start outside of the area.

- The blue players must stay aware of the positioning of the 2 target players.

- If a target player moves into one of the end zones, the blue team must pass to that player within 5 seconds to score.

- The red team work together (pressing) to close off the angles and try to win the ball.

- If the reds win the ball, they pass to either target player to score.

Soccer eyeQ with SoccerTutor.com — SCANNING - How to Train it

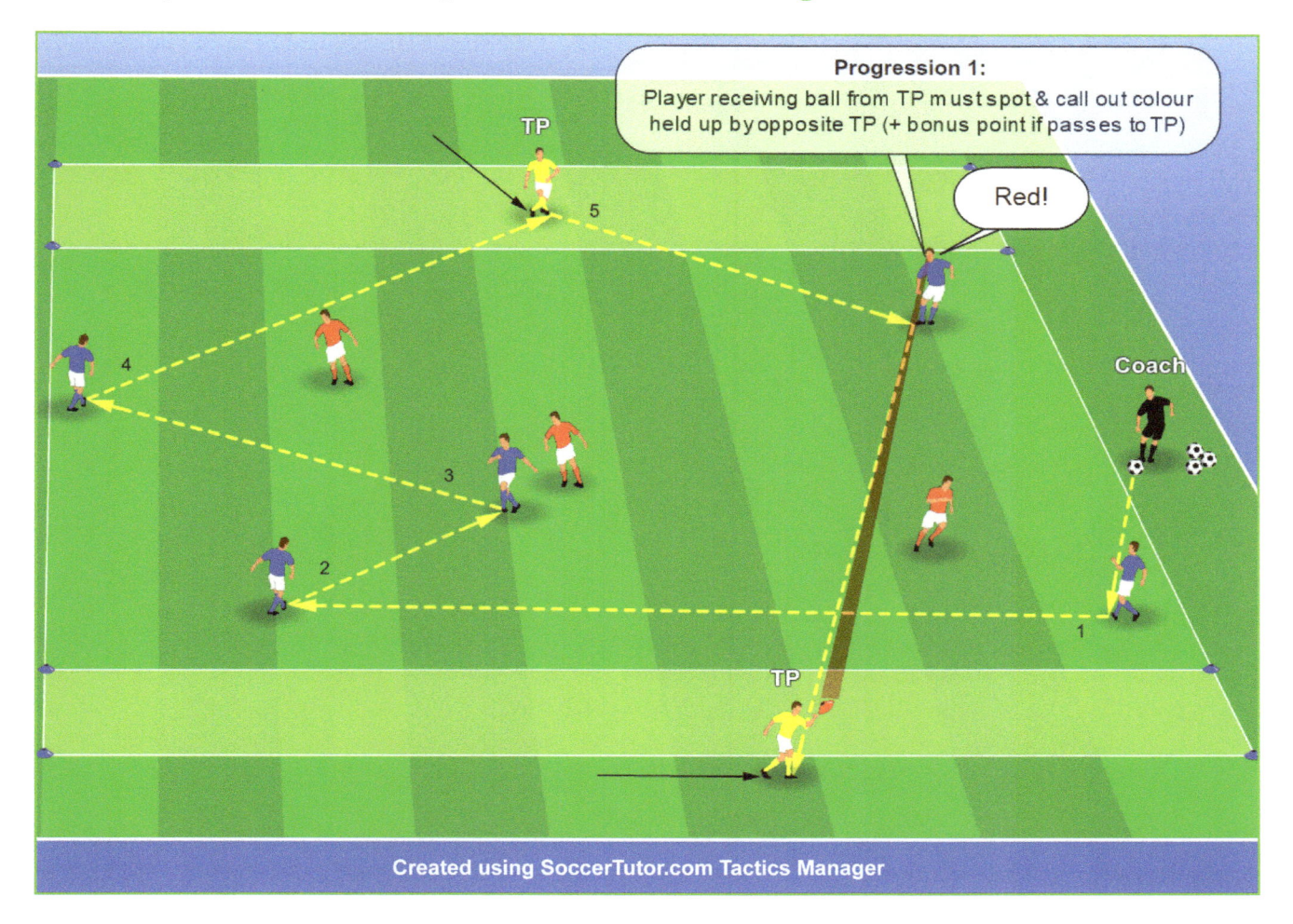

SECTION 3: Adding the Soccer eyeQ Method to Existing Practices

Adding the Soccer eyeQ Method - Progression 1

Progression 1: Player receiving ball from TP must spot & call out colour held up by opposite TP (+ bonus point if passes to TP)

"Red!"

Created using SoccerTutor.com Tactics Manager

What have we added?

- Visual cues are flashed by the target player when the opposite target player receives. The blue player receiving must spot and call out colour held up.
- There is a bonus point available if the blue player is then able to pass to the TP.

Why have we added it?

- To force players to take their eyes off the ball and scan "up the pitch" to locate the position of the target player (TP).
- Scanning "up the pitch" encourages an open body position to maximise the player's field of view (entire area).
- The player receiving from the TP must take a final look to spot the colour held up before their first touch.

How does it improve game awareness?

- As the ball is travelling into a TP, players will begin to have early looks to locate the position of the opposite target player.
- Players will adopt an open body position when receiving the ball from a TP + take one last look away from the ball.
- Player cannot only focus on the position of the opposite target player (to spot the visual cue) - they must also assess the positioning of their opponents.

What benefit will the players get?

- Habit of scanning away from the ball at key moments + learn to divide attention.
- Take in quick snapshots, positioning of teammates and opponents.

SECTION 3: Adding the Soccer eyeQ Method to Existing Practices

Adding the Soccer eyeQ Method - Progression 2

Progression 2: Target Players (TP) are now on the blue team and rotate into the area after receiving

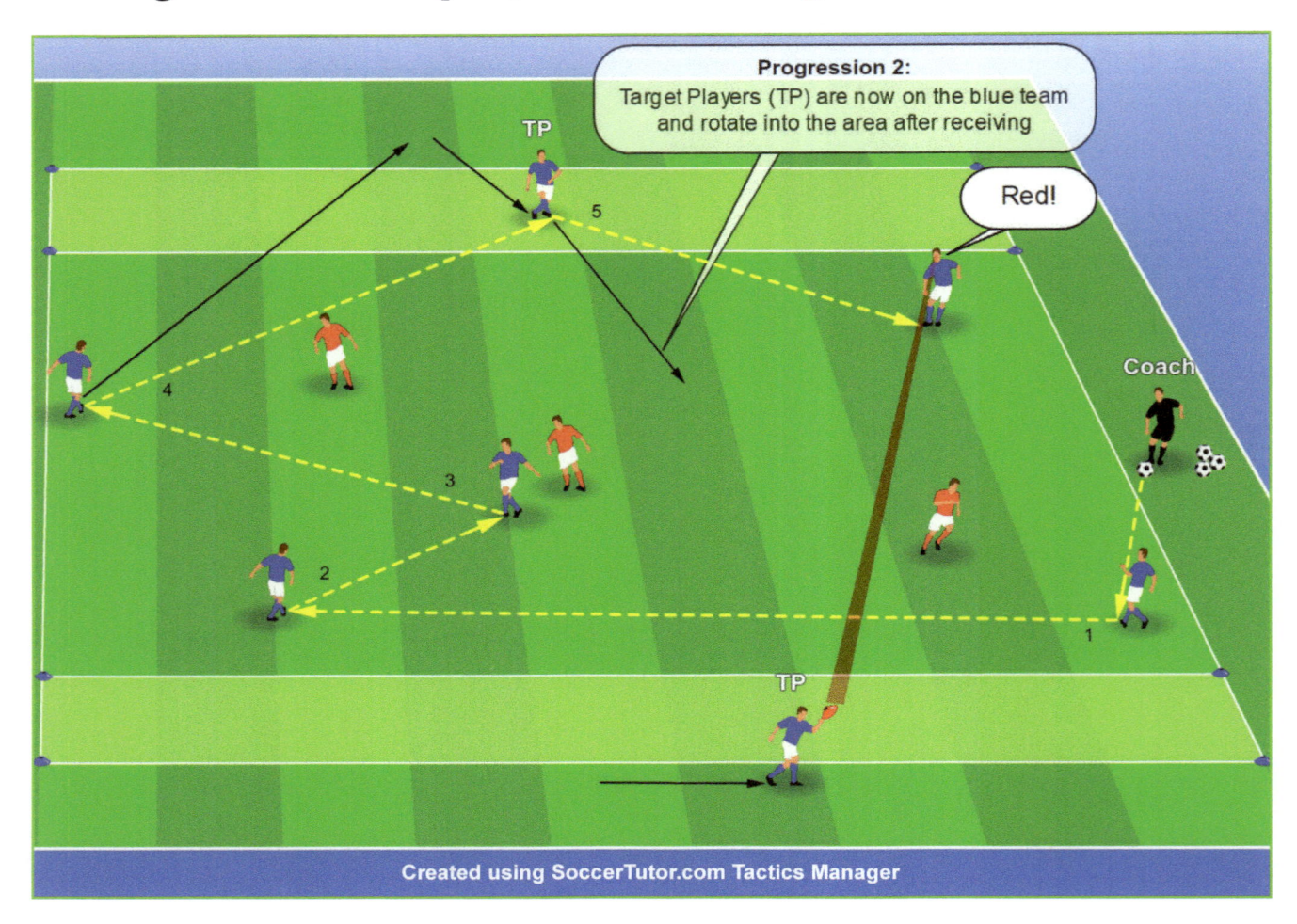

Red!

What have we added?
- **NOTE**: All components of Progression 1 on the previous page remain.
- All major points remain the same, but now we add the rotation of the players with the role of the target players, as shown in the diagram example.

Why have we added it?
- Players must adapt their positioning based on the players moving in and out of the playing area.

How does it improve game awareness?
- Players must learn to adjust their adaptive positioning based on the players rotating in and out of the playing area.

- Adaptive positioning is all about using what you see to be in the best position in relation to teammates and opponents.

What benefit will the players get?
- Same as previous Progression 1.
- + Increased demands on adaptive positioning due to the players rotating in and out of the playing area.

Soccer eyeQ with SoccerTutor.com | 198 | SCANNING - How to Train it

SECTION 3: Adding the Soccer eyeQ Method to Existing Practices

POSSESSION GAME EXAMPLE 2:
End to End 3 Zone Possession Game

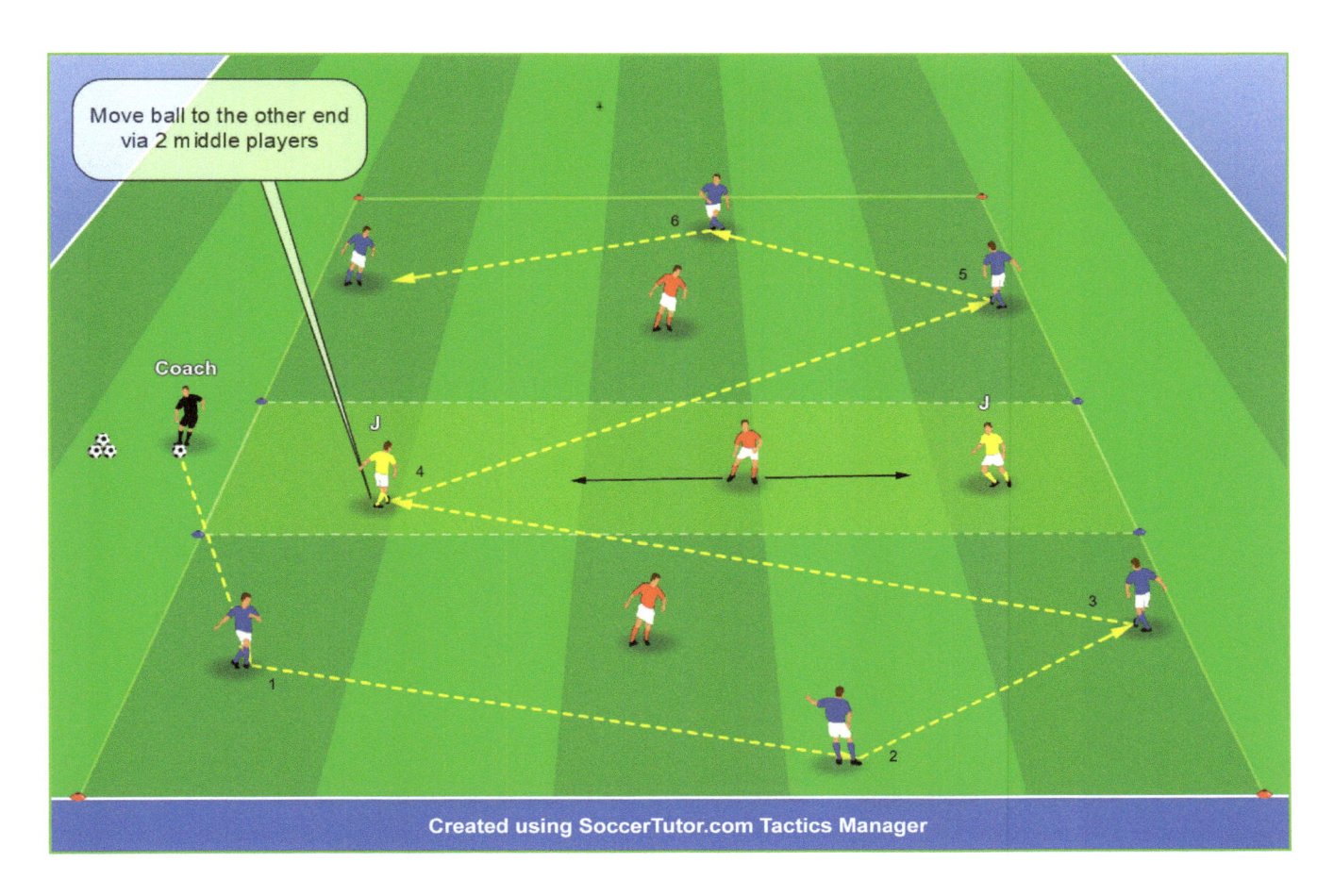

Move ball to the other end via 2 middle players

Practice Description

- Use an area size appropriate for the age/level of the players.

- Mark out 2 larger end zones and a smaller middle zone, as shown in the diagram. We play 6 (+2 Jokers) v 3.

- The practice starts with the Coach's pass to a blue player and there is a 3v1 situation in one of the end zones.

- The aim for the 3 blue players is to pass to one of the 2 middle Jokers, who then plays to a blue player in the opposite end zone.

- The red player in that zone tries to win the ball and dribble over the end-line to score (middle red player can join in).

- The red player in the middle zone tries to block and intercept any passes towards the Jokers in the middle zone.

- Change the 3 defending players (reds) roles often.

Soccer eyeQ with SoccerTutor.com SCANNING - How to Train it

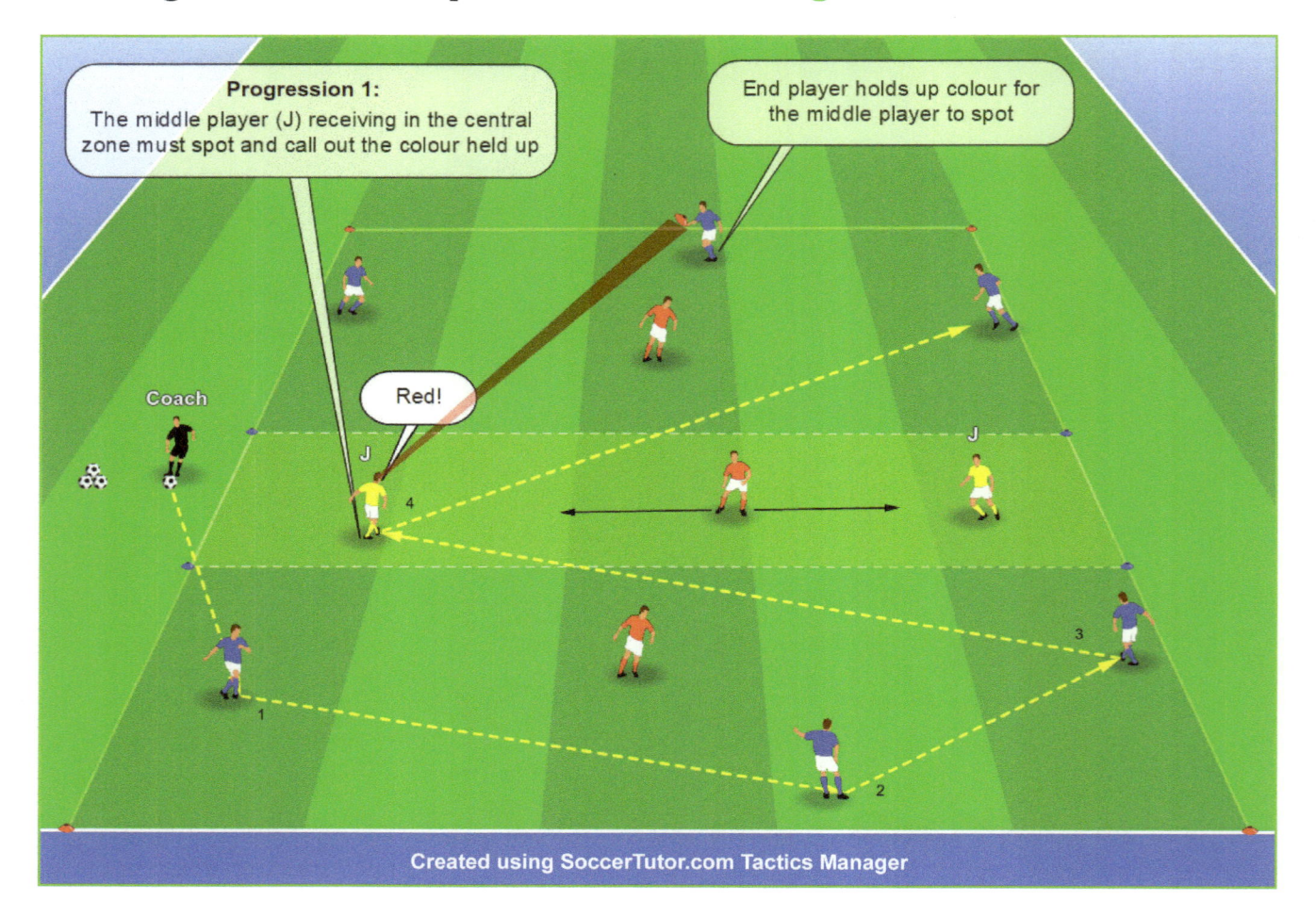

SECTION 3: Adding the Soccer eyeQ Method to Existing Practices

Adding the Soccer eyeQ Method - Progression 1

Progression 1: The middle player (J) receiving in the central zone must spot and call out the colour held up

End player holds up colour for the middle player to spot

Red!

Coach

Created using SoccerTutor.com Tactics Manager

What have we added?
- Visual cues are flashed by a player at the opposite end when one of the middle Jokers is receiving a pass - Joker must spot and call out the colour held up.

Why have we added it?
- To force players to take their eyes off the ball and scan "up the pitch" to locate the position of the target player.
- Scanning "up the pitch" encourages an open body position to maximise the player's field of view (entire playing area).
- The receiving player must take a final look to spot the colour being held up before their first touch.

How does it improve game awareness?
- Jokers will begin to take early looks to locate the opposite end players when the ball is circulating between the 3 players.

- The middle Jokers will adopt an open body position as this makes it easier to spot the visual cue, as well as making it easier to transfer the ball between zones.
- The player receiving the pass cannot only focus on the ball as it is coming and must take one last look away from the ball when they are receiving a pass.
- The player receiving the pass cannot focus only on the position of the opposite end player (to spot the visual cue), as they must also assess the positioning of their opponents who apply pressure.

What benefit will the players get?
- Habit of scanning away from the ball at key moments + learn to divide attention.
- Take in quick snapshots, positioning of teammates and opponents.

Soccer eyeQ with SoccerTutor.com   SCANNING - How to Train it

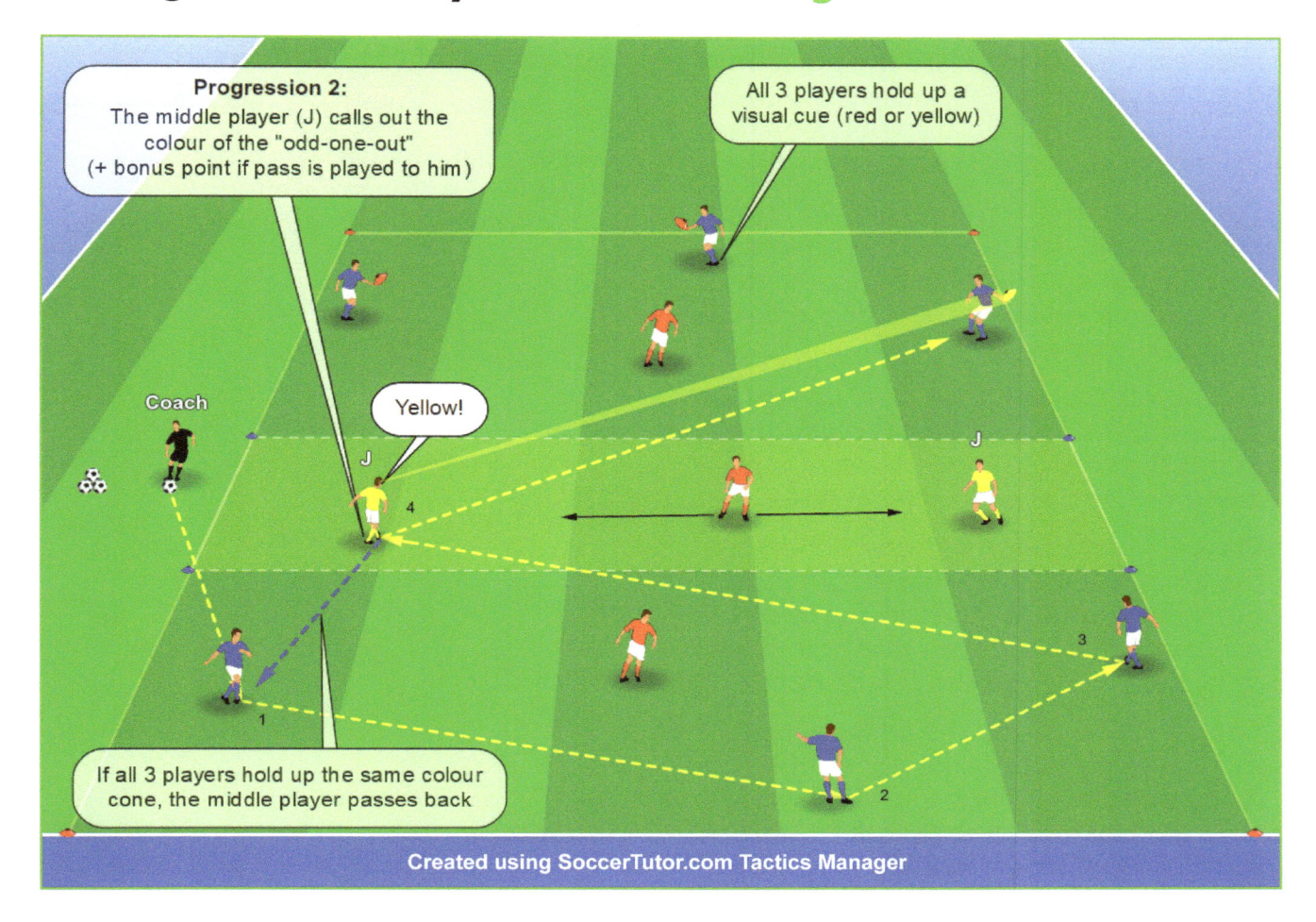

SECTION 3: Adding the Soccer eyeQ Method to Existing Practices

Adding the Soccer eyeQ Method - Progression 2

Diagram callouts:
- **Progression 2:** The middle player (J) calls out the colour of the "odd-one-out" (+ bonus point if pass is played to him)
- All 3 players hold up a visual cue (red or yellow)
- Yellow!
- If all 3 players hold up the same colour cone, the middle player passes back

What have we added?

- **NOTE:** Some of the same components of Progression 1 (previous page) remain.
- Now all 3 players in the opposite zone flash a visual cue when one of the middle Jokers is receiving a pass.
- When receiving the ball, the Jokers must spot and call out the colour of the "odd-one-out" of the 3 colours being held up by the 3 players in the opposite zone.
- The Joker can play to any of the three players but scores a bonus point if he passes to the odd one out.
- If all 3 are colour signals are the same colour e.g. All 3 are red like in the diagram example, then the Joker must pass back into the first zone.

Why have we added it?

- Force players to take their eyes off the ball and scan "up the pitch" to assess the position of all 3 players in the opposite end zone.
- Force scanning as the ball is travelling, so the player receiving must take a final look to spot and call out the correct colour before taking a first touch.
- Needing to scan "up the pitch" when receiving a pass encourages the player to adopt an open body position, which will maximise their field of view of the entire playing area.
- A quick adjustment is required if all 3 colours are the same and the player has to play the ball back into the first zone.

How does it improve game awareness?

- The middle Joker players will begin to have early looks to locate the position of the 3 players in the opposite zone when the ball is being circulated between the 3 blue players in the first zone.

- The player receiving the pass will adopt an open body position as this makes it easier to spot the visual cues, as well as making it easier to transfer the ball between zones.

- The player receiving the pass cannot focus only on the ball as it is coming and must take one last look away from the ball when they are receiving a pass.

- Players must respond appropriately to the visual cues – if there is an odd one out, he can transfer the ball to the new zone; but if all 3 are the same colour, he must pass back into the first zone.

- The player receiving the pass cannot focus only on the position of the players in the opposite zone (to spot the visual cue), as they must also assess the positioning of their opponents who apply pressure.

What benefit will the players get?

- They develop the habit of scanning away from the ball at key moments.

- Learn to divide their attention.

- Take in quick snapshots of the positioning of teammates and opponents.

SECTION 3: Adding the Soccer eyeQ Method to Existing Practices

POSSESSION GAME EXAMPLE 3:
6v4 +6 Outside Support Players

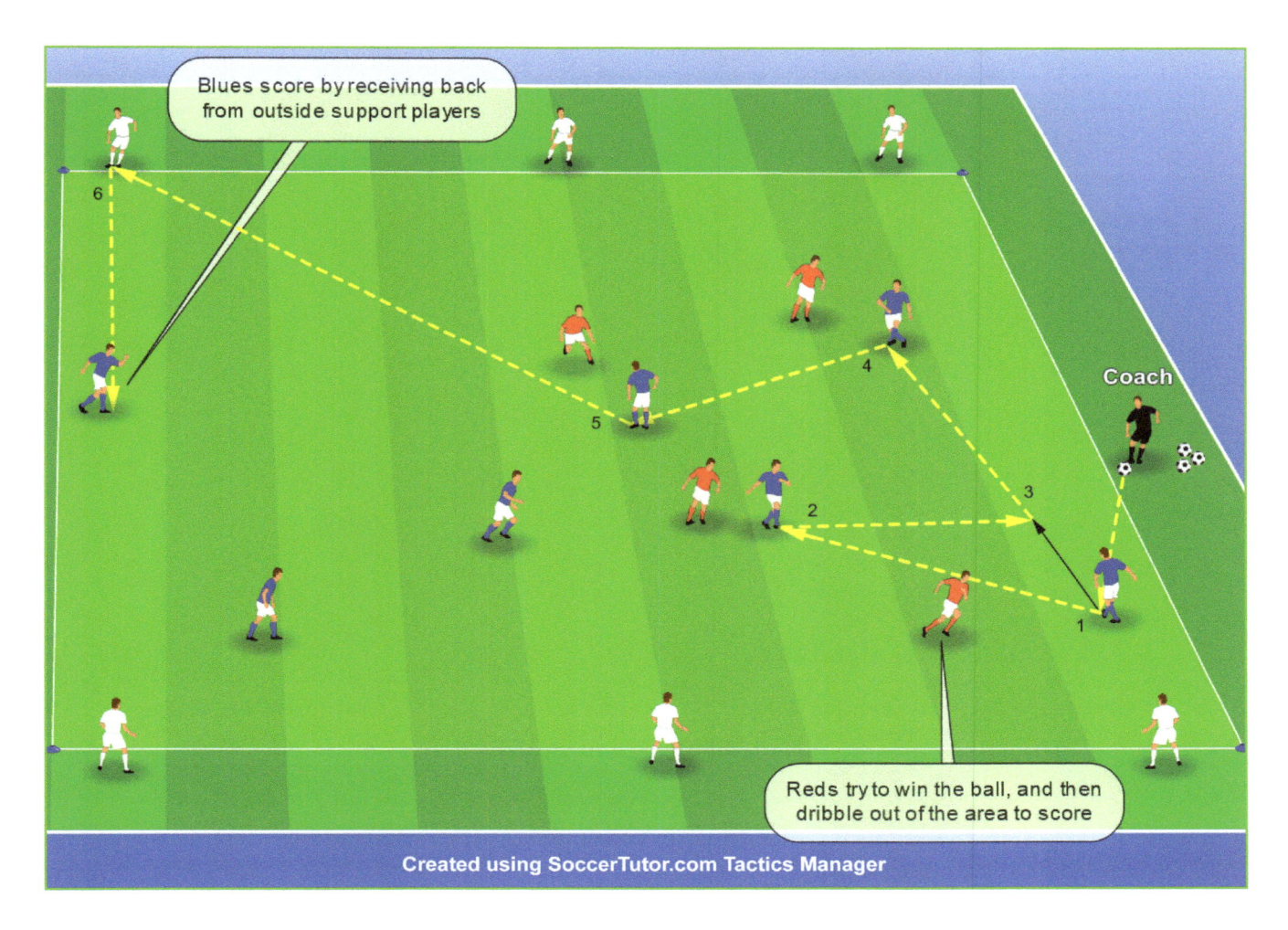

Blues score by receiving back from outside support players

Reds try to win the ball, and then dribble out of the area to score

Created using SoccerTutor.com Tactics Manager

Practice Description

- Use an area size appropriate for the age/level of the players.

- We have a 6v4 situation inside the area + 6 outside players in the positions shown, who provide support for the team in possession (blues).

- The practice starts with the Coach's pass to a blue player and the blue team try to maintain possession.

- To score, the blue team must pass to an outside white player and then successfully receive a pass back, as shown in the diagram example.

- The red team work together (pressing) to close off the angles and try to win the ball.

- If the reds win the ball, they simply dribble the ball out of the area to score. Alternatively, you can position 2-4 mini goals around the area for the reds to score into.

Soccer eyeQ with SoccerTutor.com | 203 | SCANNING - How to Train it

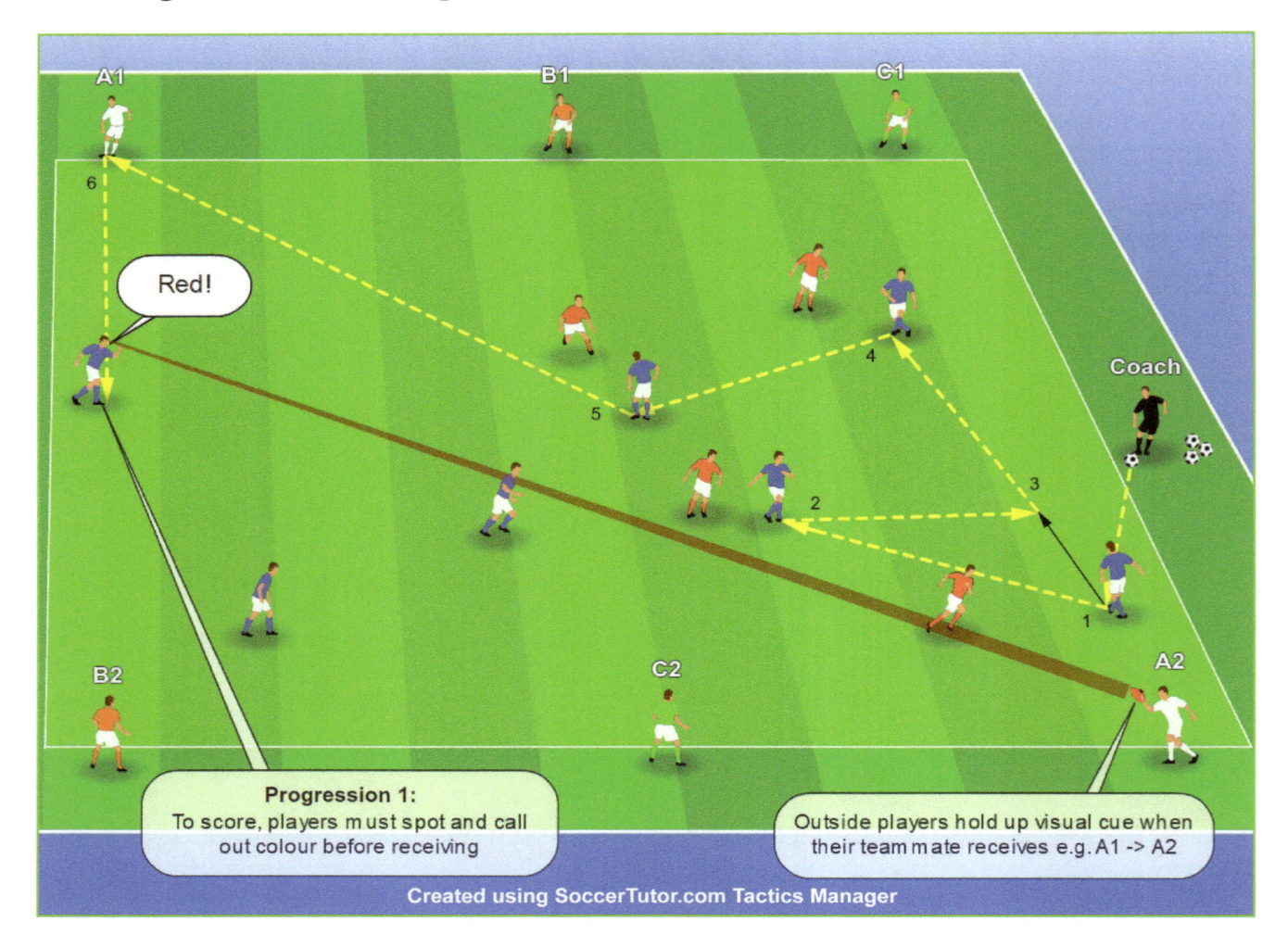

SECTION 3: Adding the Soccer eyeQ Method to Existing Practices

Adding the Soccer eyeQ Method - Progression 1

Progression 1:
To score, players must spot and call out colour before receiving

Outside players hold up visual cue when their teammate receives e.g. A1 -> A2

What have we added?

- We have colour-coded the support players. When a support player receives, his opposite teammate of the same colour must flash a visual cue.
- The player receiving from the support player must spot and call out the colour being held up on the opposite side.

Why have we added it?

- To force players to take their eyes off the ball and scan "up the pitch" to locate the position of the correct support player.
- Scanning "up the pitch" encourages an open body position to maximise the player's field of view (entire playing area).
- The receiving player must take a final look to spot the colour being held up before their first touch.

How does it improve game awareness?

- Players will begin to have early looks to locate the position of the flasher on the opposite side when the ball is being passed out to a support player.
- The player receiving cannot only focus on the ball as it is coming and must take one last look away when receiving a pass. He also cannot only focus on the position of the flasher on the opposite side (to spot the visual cue), as they must also assess the positioning of their opponents.

What benefit will the players get?

- They develop the habit of scanning away from the ball at key moments.
- Learn to divide their attention.
- Take in quick snapshots of the positioning of teammates and opponents.

Soccer eyeQ with SoccerTutor.com

SCANNING - How to Train it

SECTION 3: Adding the Soccer eyeQ Method to Existing Practices

Adding the Soccer eyeQ Method - Progression 2

Progression 2: After a pass is played, 2 outside players must switch positions

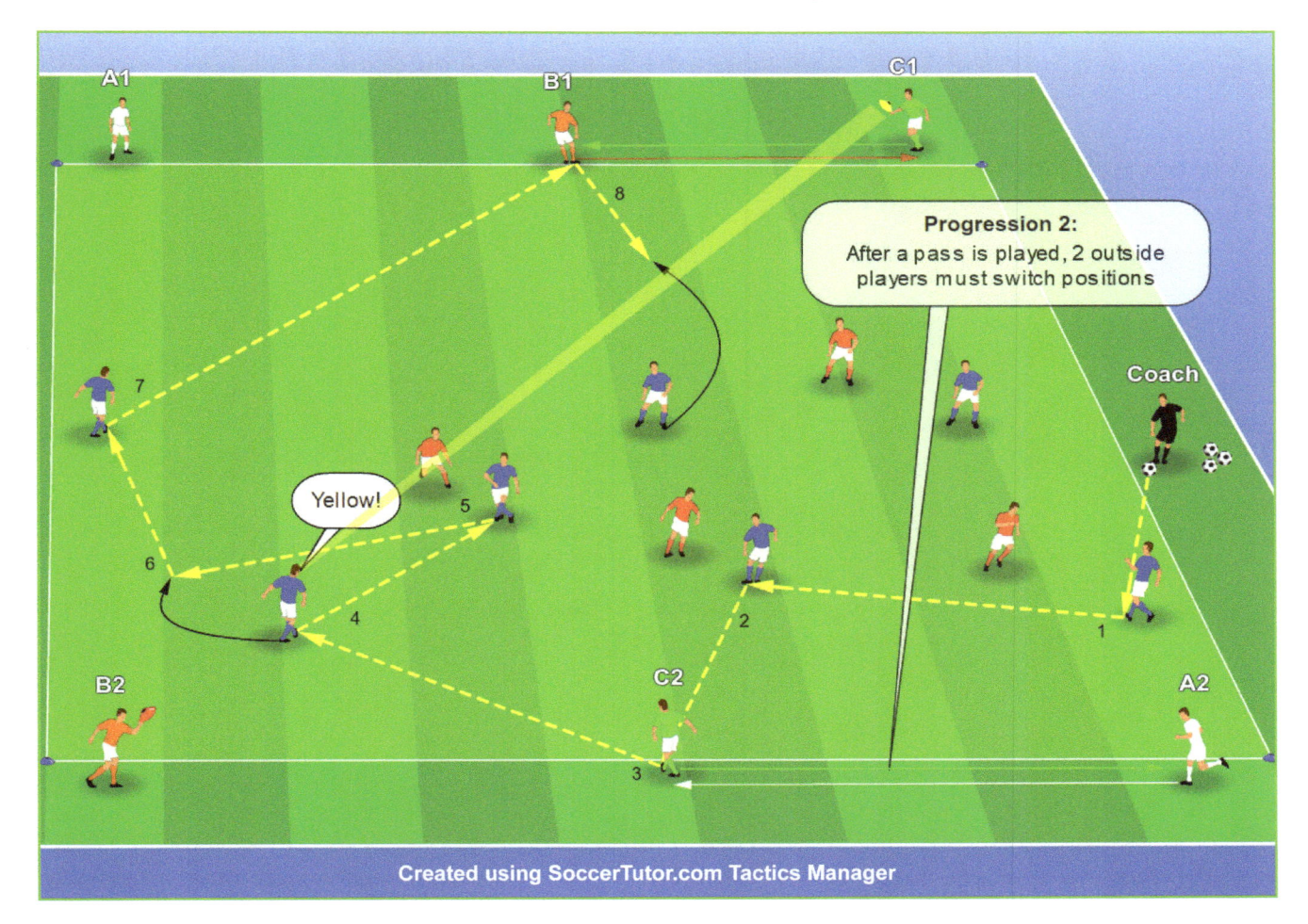

What have we added?

- **NOTE**: All components of Progression 1 on the previous page remain.
- After a support player has passed the ball back into the area, he must switch positions with one of the other support players next to him.
- The wide outside players switch with the middle player, and the middle player can switch with either player.

Why have we added it?

- This will mix up where the support players and flashers are, which forces the players to engage more extensively in scanning to locate the position of the correct flasher, as he could now be in any of the 3 support positions.

How does it improve game awareness?

- The players no longer know which of the 3 positions the flasher on the opposite side will be in, so they cannot simply memorise this at the start. They must now engage in scanning to search for the correct flasher and assess where he is positioned on the opposite side.

What benefit will the players get?

- Same as the previous **Progression 1**.

SECTION 3: Adding the Soccer eyeQ Method to Existing Practices

SMALL SIDED GAME EXAMPLE 1:
Scan to Play Forward Bounce Game

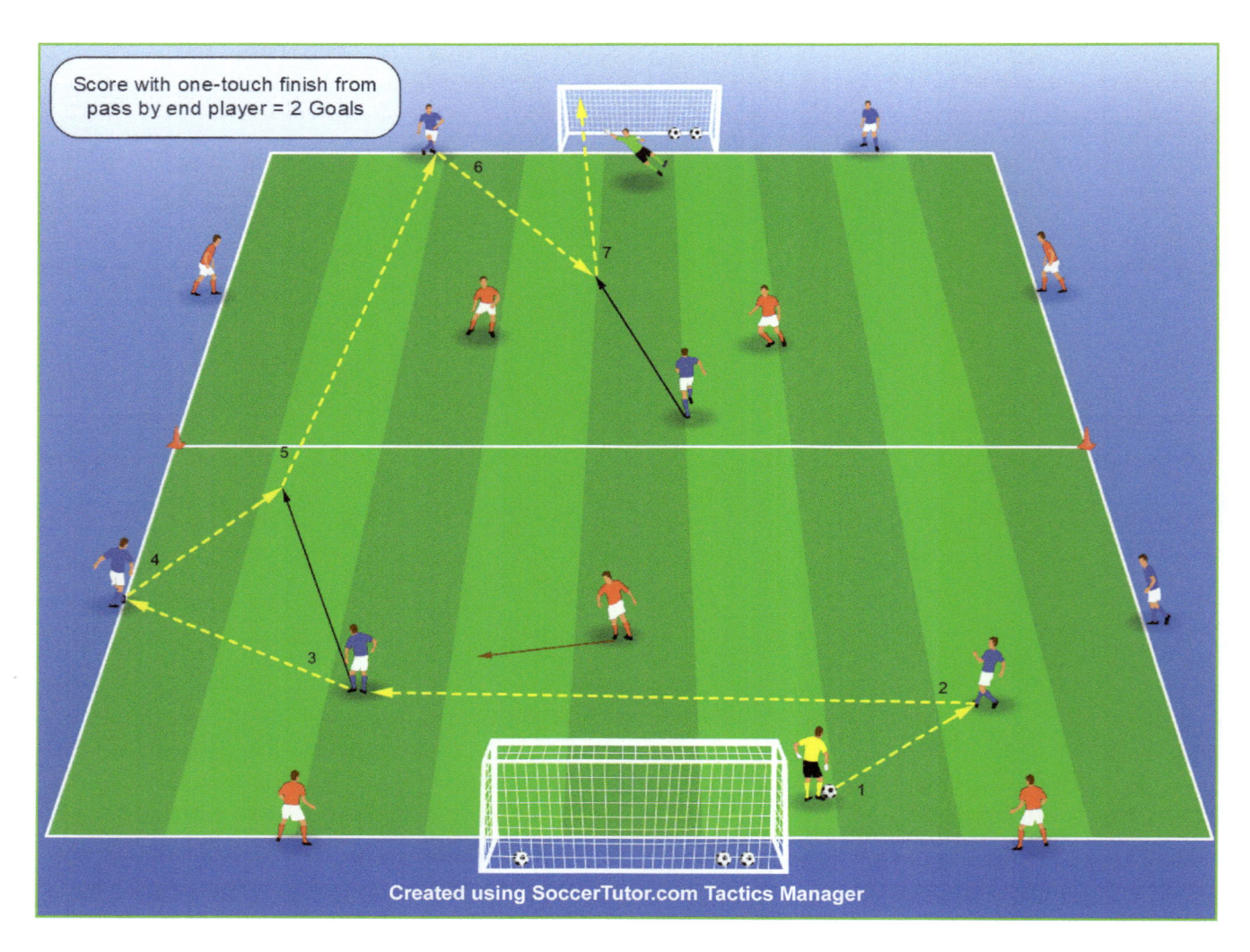

Score with one-touch finish from pass by end player = 2 Goals

Practice Description

- Use an area size appropriate for the age/level of the players for this game. There is a 3v3 situation inside the area (+2 GKs) and each team has 4 outside players.

- The practice starts from a GK and both teams try to score by utilising their bounce players.

- Both teams have 1 bounce player on each side in their own half, who help the team maintain possession, recycle the ball, and build up play.

- The 2 bounce players on either side of the goal in the attacking half help set up goal scoring opportunities.

- If you can score with a one-touch finish after a pass from an end bounce player, the goal is worth double.

Coaching Point

- Can the team play forward early when it is on and quickly join the attack to provide support?

Soccer eyeQ with SoccerTutor.com   206   SCANNING - How to Train it

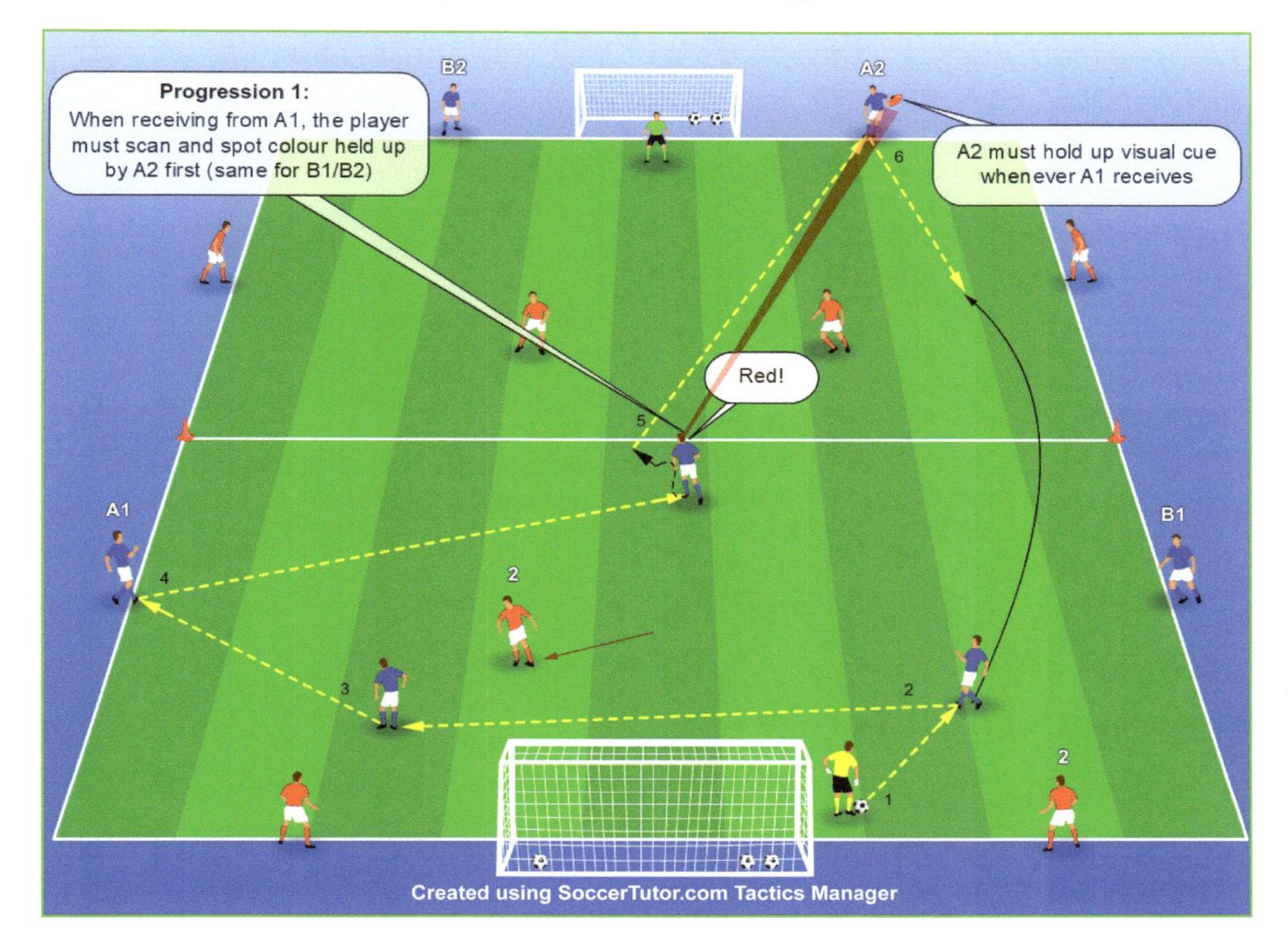

SECTION 3: Adding the Soccer eyeQ Method to Existing Practices

Adding the Soccer eyeQ Method - Progression 1

Progression 1:
When receiving from A1, the player must scan and spot colour held up by A2 first (same for B1/B2)

A2 must hold up visual cue whenever A1 receives

Red!

What have we added?

- When a support player (A1 in diagram example) on one side receives the ball, the bounce player (A2) on the opposite side of the goal must flash a visual cue.

- The player receiving the ball from the support player must spot and call out the colour being held up by the correct flasher (A2).

Why have we added it?

- To force the players to take their eyes off the ball and scan "up the pitch" to locate the position of the correct flasher.

- Force scanning as the ball is travelling, so the receiving player must take a final look before taking a first touch.

- Needing to scan "up the pitch" when receiving the pass from a support player encourages the player to adopt an open body position "facing forward," which will maximise their field of view of the entire playing area.

- Players who are away from the ball must maintain concentration in order to hold up a visual cue at the correct time.

Soccer eyeQ with SoccerTutor.com

207

SCANNING - How to Train it

SECTION 3: Adding the Soccer eyeQ Method to Existing Practices

How does it improve game awareness?

- Players will begin to have early looks to locate the position of the flasher on the opposite side when the ball is being passed out to a support player.
- Players will adopt an open body position "facing forward," as this makes it easier to spot the visual cue being flashed by the bounce player on the opposite side of the goal.
- The player receiving the pass cannot only focus on the ball as it is coming and must take one last look away from the ball when they are receiving a pass.
- The player receiving the pass cannot only focus on the position of the flasher on the opposite side of the goal (to spot the visual cue), as they must also assess the positioning of their opponents applying pressure.

What benefit will the players get?

- They develop the habit of scanning away from the ball at key moments.
- Learn to divide their attention.
- Take in quick snapshots of the positioning of teammates and opponents.

Rule Variations

1. Spot the visual cue before your first touch, otherwise possession changes (restart with the opposing GK).
2. Spot the visual cue before your first touch + players are limited to 1 or 2 touches.
3. Spot the visual cue before your first touch + the receiving player has unlimited touches.
4. Spot the visual cue before your first touch + if the receiving player can pass to the flasher within 2 touches, then a bonus goal is scored (see diagram example).

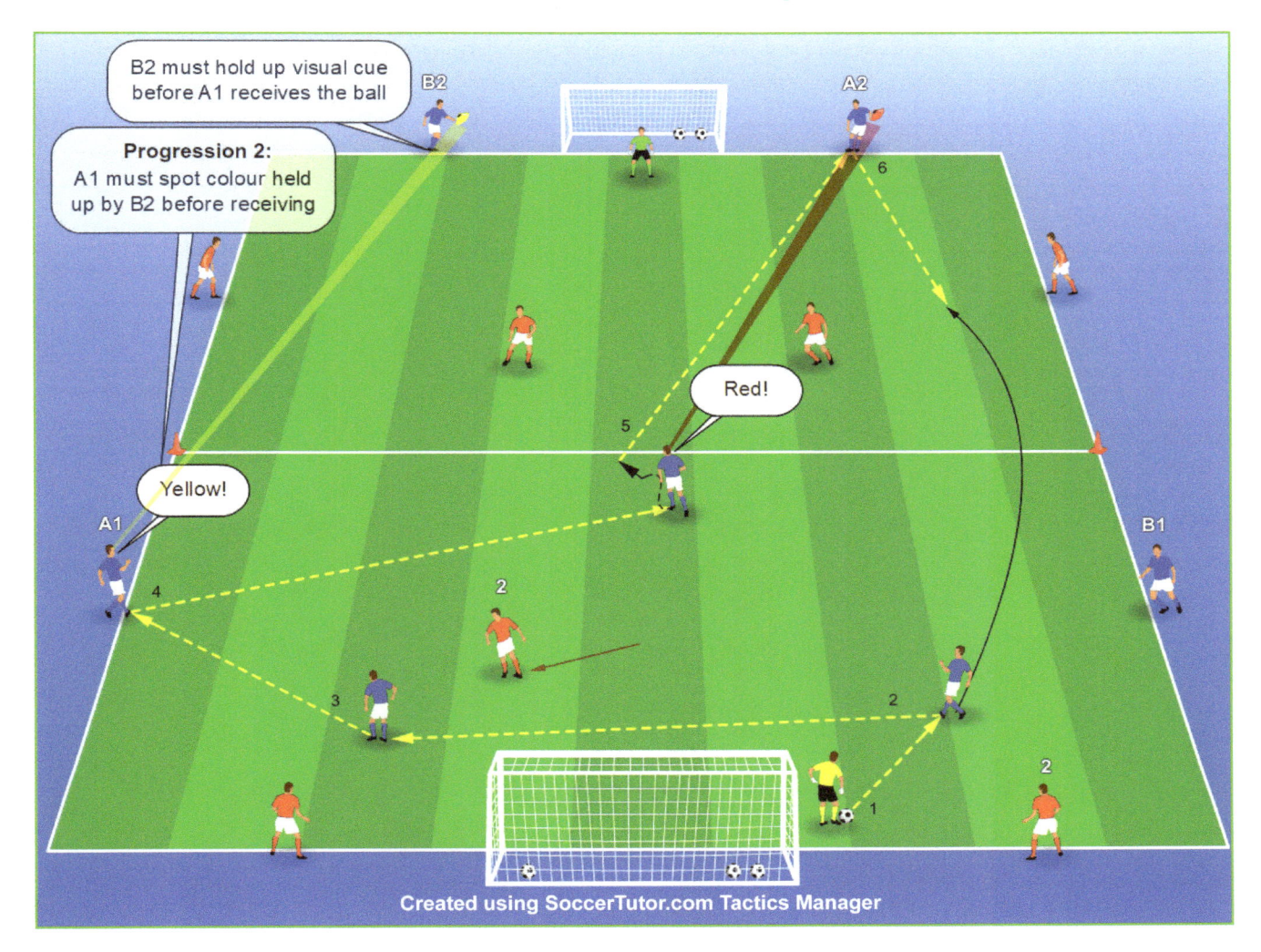

SECTION 3: Adding the Soccer eyeQ Method to Existing Practices

Adding the Soccer eyeQ Method - Progression 2

Diagram annotations:
- B2 must hold up visual cue before A1 receives the ball
- Progression 2: A1 must spot colour held up by B2 before receiving
- Yellow!
- Red!

What have we added?

- **NOTE**: All components of Progression 1 on the previous page remain.
- When a support player receives the ball (A1 in diagram example), the outside support bounce player on the same side of the goal (B2) must flash a visual cue. The bounce player receiving must spot and call out the colour flashed before taking his first touch.

Why have we added it?

- Now the bounce players must also take their eyes of the ball when receiving a pass. They scan "up the pitch" to spot and call out the colour of the visual cue being held up.

How does it improve game awareness?

- The bounce player will have to practice their scanning and learn to look "up the pitch" whenever they receive the ball.
- The bounce player cannot only focus on the ball as it is coming and must take one last look away from the ball when they are receiving a pass. He also cannot only focus on the position of the flasher on the same side of the goal (visual cue), as they must also see the positioning of their teammates and opponents to quickly assess the best passing option back into the playing area.

What benefit will the players get?

- Same as the previous Progression 1.

SCANNING - How to Train it

SECTION 3: Adding the Soccer eyeQ Method to Existing Practices

SMALL SIDED GAME EXAMPLE 2:
Play to Advanced Wide Players Game

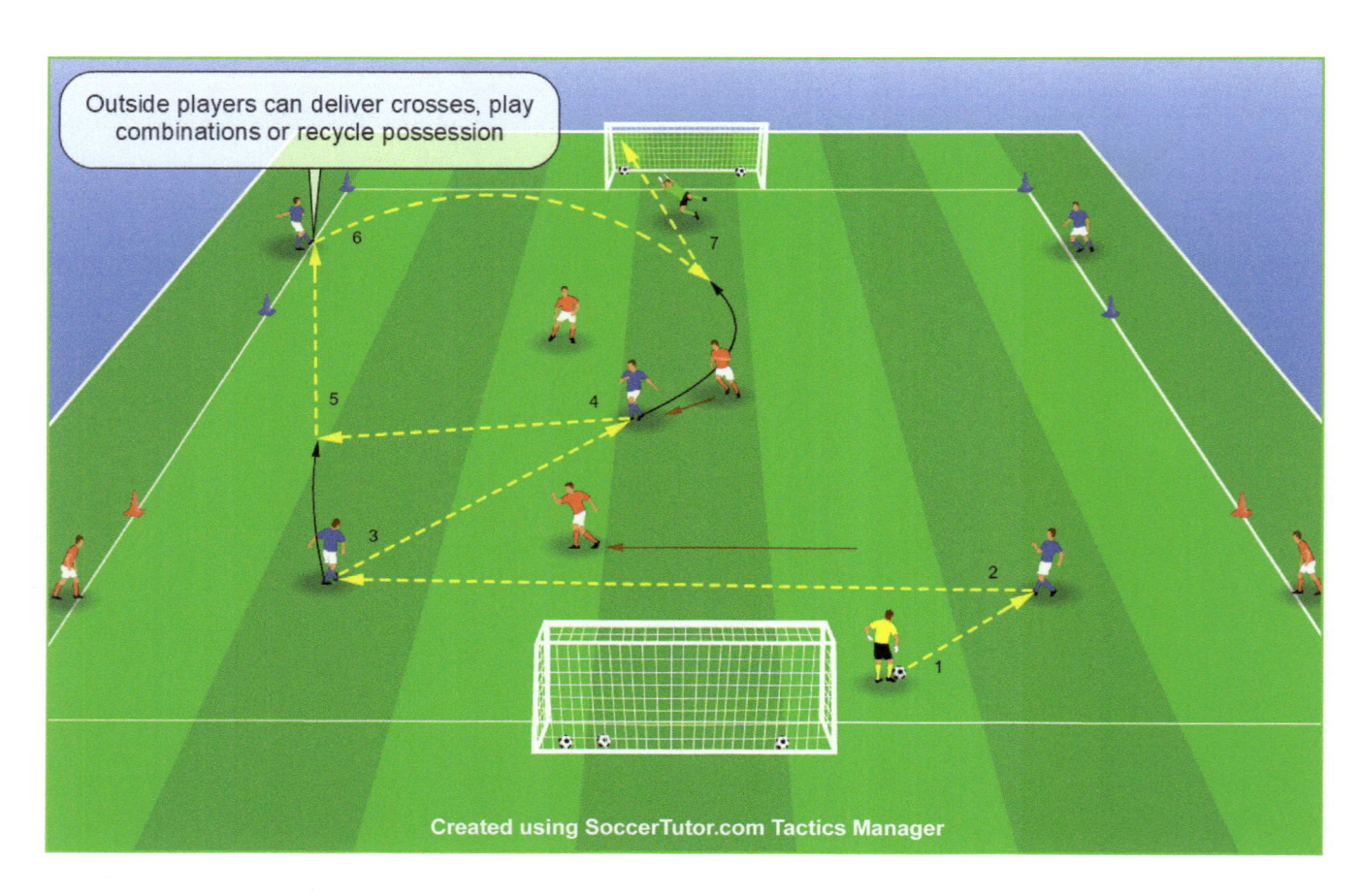

Outside players can deliver crosses, play combinations or recycle possession

Practice Description

- Use an area size appropriate for the age/level of the players for this game.

- There is a 3v3 situation inside the area (+2 GKs) and each team has 2 outside players.

- The outside players are limited to the space high up and wide, marked by the cones as shown.

- The main aim for these outside players is to deliver crosses, but they can also combine and recycle possession depending on the situation.

- The practice starts from a GK and both teams are trying to score.

- The team in possession (blues in the diagram example) should look to get the ball wide to utilise their outside players and make fast supporting runs to score from crosses.

- If it's not possible to try and create a goal scoring opportunity, the players should look to simply maintain possession instead.

Soccer eyeQ with SoccerTutor.com

SCANNING - How to Train it

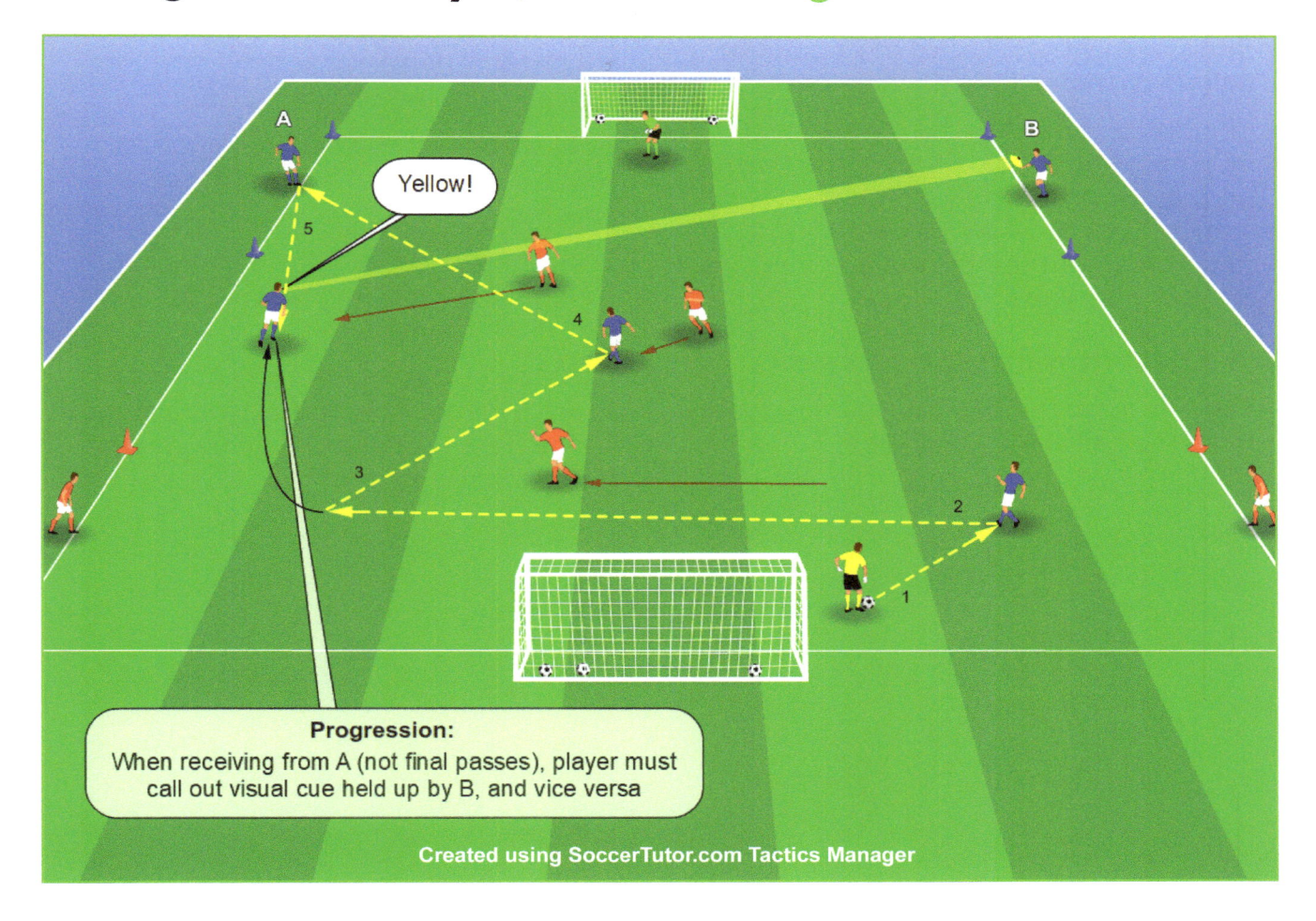

SECTION 3: Adding the Soccer eyeQ Method to Existing Practices

Adding the Soccer eyeQ Method - Progression

Progression:
When receiving from A (not final passes), player must call out visual cue held up by B, and vice versa

What have we added?

- When an outside support player (A in diagram example) receives the ball, the outside player on the opposite side (B) must hold up a visual cue.

- If a player receives the ball from the outside player back into the playing area, he must spot and call out the colour being held up by the flasher on the opposite side (B).

Why have we added it?

- To force players to take their eyes off the ball and scan across the pitch to locate the position of the flasher on the opposite side.

- Force scanning as the ball is travelling, so the player receiving the pass must take a final look before their first touch.

- Needing to scan across the pitch when receiving the pass from a support player encourages the player to adopt an open body position, which will maximise their field of view of the entire playing area.

- Players who are away from the ball must maintain concentration in order to hold up a visual cue at the correct time.

How does it improve game awareness?

- Players will begin to have early looks to locate the position of the flasher on the opposite side when the ball is being passed out to an outside support player.

- Players will adopt an open body position as this makes it easier to spot the visual cue being flashed by the outside player on the opposite side.

SECTION 3: Adding the Soccer eyeQ Method to Existing Practices

- The player receiving the pass cannot only focus on the ball as it is coming and must take one last look away from the ball when they are receiving a pass.
- The player receiving the pass cannot only focus on the position of the flasher on the opposite side (to spot the visual cue), as they must also assess the positioning of their opponents who are applying pressure.

What benefit will the players get?

- They develop the habit of scanning away from the ball at key moments.
- Learn to divide their attention.
- Take in quick snapshots of the positioning of teammates and opponents.

Rule Variations

1. Spot the visual cue before your first touch, otherwise possession changes (restart with the opposing GK).
2. Spot the visual cue before your first touch + players are limited to 1 or 2 touches.
3. Spot the visual cue before your first touch + the receiving player has unlimited touches.
4. Spot the visual cue before your first touch + if the receiving player can pass to the flasher within 2 touches, then a bonus goal is scored.

ADDING THE SOCCER EYEQ METHOD TO EXISTING PRACTICES - SUMMARY

As we discussed earlier in the book, a study of elite level training in the Netherlands revealed that the players scanned significantly less in the various types of practices they experienced in training than they needed to in competitive matches **(see page 80 for full details)**.

This means that the vast majority of practices we use are not developing scanning to the level the players need and we are actually encouraging the habit of constantly looking at the ball.

We can easily see this in the **passing and receiving drills, where the players eyes follow the ball around the pattern** and then, when it's their turn to receive the ball, they watch it all the way from the passer's foot into their own first touch.

There is **very little scanning by the players during these types of practices**. This is largely because they have no real reason to look around the playing area - they know where they are getting the ball from and they always know where the next player is that they are passing to.

However, whilst passing and receiving drills may have these limitations, it is the rondos that recorded the least amount of scanning.

Does this mean that we should not use passing and receiving drills or rondos?

Of course not, all of these practices have their place in a coach's toolkit. I am **only suggesting that we should look at ways of promoting extra scanning in these practices** by layering in additional constraints, which will force the players to take their eyes off the ball and more closely replicate the amount of scanning required in the game.

Throughout this book, I have used examples of various types of practices (passing drills, unopposed practices, possession games, and small-sided games) and have shown you how simple constraints can be added in to promote far more scanning during the course of the practice.

My aim has not been to give you 101 practices you can copy and paste. Instead, I have tried to give you the why and the how of the Soccer eyeQ game awareness methodology. This way, you will be able to incorporate the ideas and concepts into your favourite sessions that you already use.

I hope you and your players enjoy the challenges of these new ideas.

Soccer eyeQ Videos

SOCCER TUTOR.COM
Football Coaching Specialists Since 2001

Developing Vision & Awareness Volume 1
Soccer eyeQ
see more | think quicker | play better

Developing Vision & Awareness Volume 2
Soccer eyeQ
see more | think quicker | play better

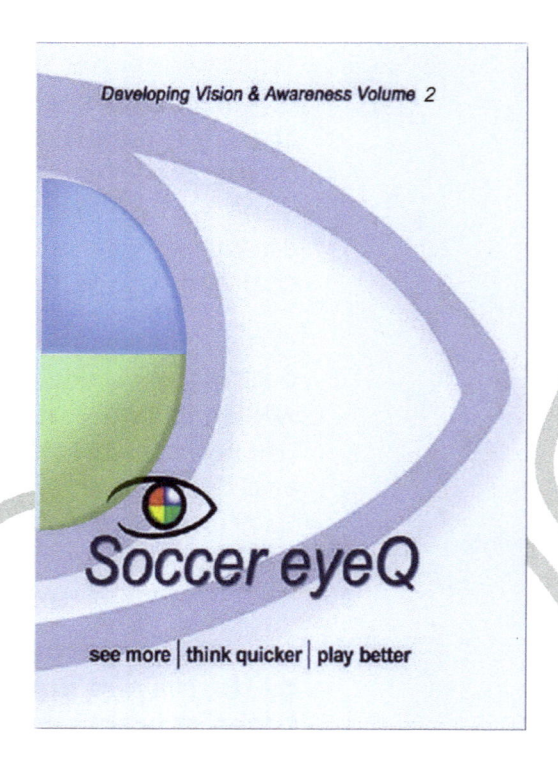

Coaching Videos Available via Coach Viewer Apps
PC | Mac | iPhone | iPad | Android Phone / Tablet | Kindle Fire

FREE COACH VIEWER APP

www.SoccerTutor.com

SoccerTutor.com

Football Coaching Specialists Since 2001

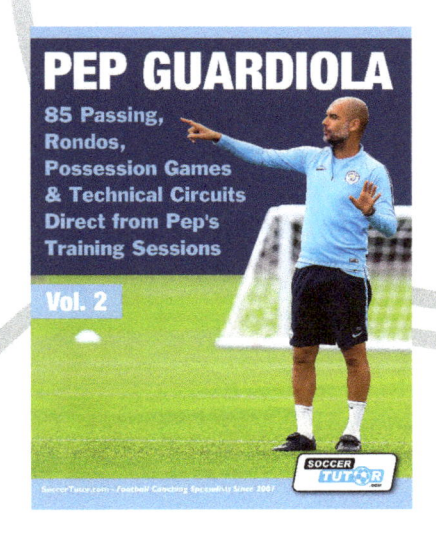

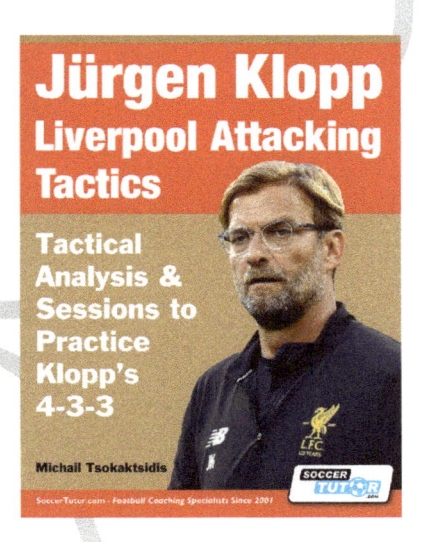

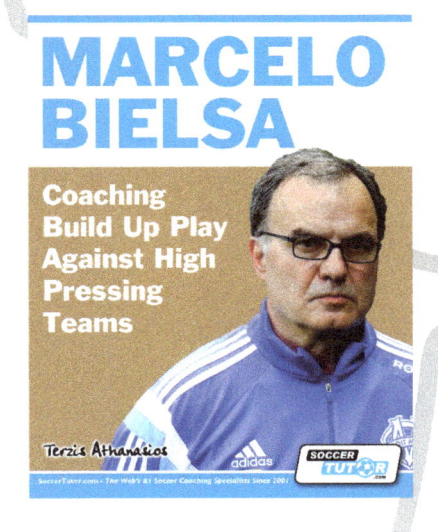

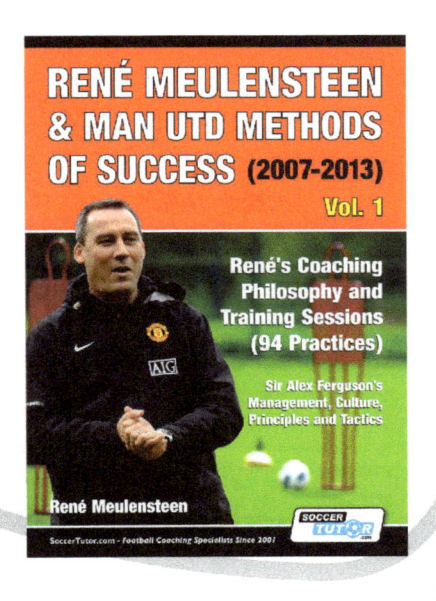

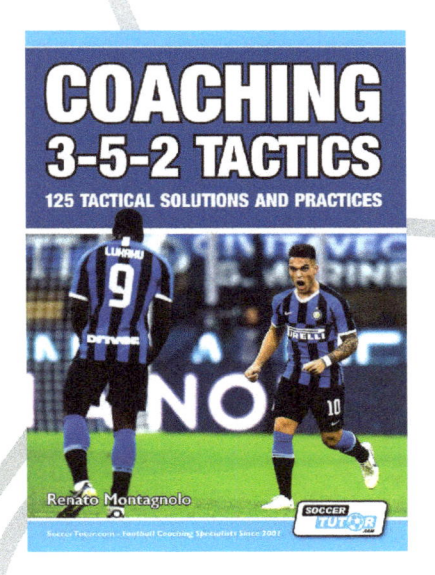

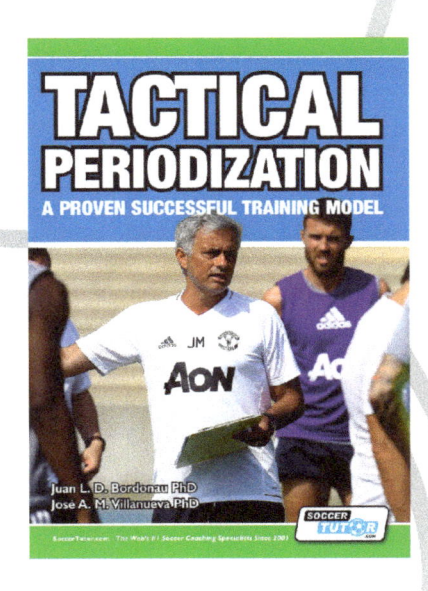

PEP GUARDIOLA
85 Passing, Rondos, Possession Games & Technical Circuits Direct from Pep's Training Sessions
Vol. 2

Jürgen Klopp
Liverpool Attacking Tactics
Tactical Analysis & Sessions to Practice Klopp's 4-3-3
Michail Tsokaktsidis

MARCELO BIELSA
Coaching Build Up Play Against High Pressing Teams
Terzis Athanasios

RENÉ MEULENSTEEN & MAN UTD METHODS OF SUCCESS (2007-2013) Vol. 1
René's Coaching Philosophy and Training Sessions (94 Practices)
Sir Alex Ferguson's Management, Culture, Principles and Tactics
René Meulensteen

COACHING 3-5-2 TACTICS
125 TACTICAL SOLUTIONS AND PRACTICES
Renato Montagnolo

TACTICAL PERIODIZATION
A PROVEN SUCCESSFUL TRAINING MODEL
Juan L. D. Bordonau PhD
José A. M. Villanueva PhD

Coaching Books Available in Full Colour Print and eBook!
PC | Mac | iPhone | iPad | Android Phone / Tablet | Kindle Fire

FREE COACH VIEWER APP

www.SoccerTutor.com